LINCOLN CHRISTIAN COLLEGE AND

Imagining the Sacred

FAITH MEETS FAITH
An Orbis Series in Interreligious Dialogue
Paul F. Knitter, General Editor

Editorial Advisors
Julia Ching
Diana Eck
Karl-Josef Kuschel
Lamin Sanneh
George E. Tinker
Felix Wilfred

In the contemporary world, the many religions and spiritualities stand in need of greater communication and cooperation. More than ever before, they must speak to, learn from, and work with each other in order both to maintain their vital identities and to contribute to fashioning a better world.

FAITH MEETS FAITH seeks to promote interreligious dialogue by providing an open forum for exchanges among followers of different religious paths. While the series wants to encourage creative and bold responses to questions arising from contemporary appreciations of religious plurality, it also recognizes the multiplicity of basic perspectives concerning the methods and content of interreligious dialogue.

Although rooted in a Christian and Maryknoll theological perspective, the series does not endorse any single school of thought or approach. By making available to both the scholarly community and the general public works that represent a variety of religious and methodological viewpoints, FAITH MEETS FAITH seeks to foster an encounter among followers of the religions of the world on matters of common concern.

FAITH MEETS FAITH SERIES

Imagining the Sacred

Soundings in World Religions

Vernon Ruland, S.J.

ORBIS BOOKS

Maryknoll, New York 10545

The Catholic Foreign Mission Society of America (Maryknoll) recruits and trains people for overseas missionary service. Through Orbis Books, Maryknoll aims to foster the international dialogue that is essential to mission. The books published, however, reflect the opinions of their authors and are not meant to represent the official position of the society.

Copyright © 1998 by Vernon Ruland

Published by Orbis Books, Maryknoll, New York, U.S.A.

All rights reserved. No part of this publication may be reproduced or transmitted in any form or by any means, electronic or mechanical, including photocopying, recording, or any information storage or retrieval system, without prior permission in writing from Orbis Books, P.O. Box 308, Maryknoll, NY 10545-0308, U.S.A.

Manufactured in the United States of America

Library of Congress Cataloging-in-Publication Data

Ruland, Vernon.
    Imaging the sacred : soundings in world religions / Vernon Ruland.
      p. cm. – (Faith meets faith series)
    Includes bibliographical references and index.
    ISBN 1-57075-209-5 (pbk.)
    1. Religions.   I. Title.   II. Series: Faith meets faith.
  BL80.2.R86   1998
  291–dc21   98-28478

Cover Design: outline of pavement labyrinth, probably a symbol for Christ's harrowing of hell. Nave of Chartres Cathedral, France. In initiations worldwide, passage through a maze may be centrifugal or centripetal — the Sacred broached as a liberating horizon outside borders, or a mystery treasure at the center.

Contents

98626

Acknowledgments

We must love them both —
Those whose opinions we share,
Those whose opinions we don't share.
They've both labored in the search for Truth
and have both helped us in finding it.
— Thomas Aquinas

The first benefit of travel to foreign lands, even to lost continents of the soul, begins the moment your own homeland suddenly looks foreign. The second benefit comes with the recognition that what seems just a solo trek is actually propped up by a vast anonymous network of helping hands at every phase of the journey.

I am indebted to Fr. Paul Bernadicou, S.J., associate professor of religious studies at the University of San Francisco, and Dr. Paul Knitter, professor of religious studies at Xavier University, Cincinnati, for encouragement and feedback on earlier drafts of this book. For help in proofreading I thank my cousin Dr. Richard Ruland, professor of English at Washington University, St. Louis, and Fr. Alden Stevenson, S.J., Editor of *Western Jesuit Magazine.* Patrick Steacy, University of San Francisco media production manager, photographed the illustrations, mostly a set of variations on the mandala motif, from my own collection of folk carvings and tourist art.

I pay renewed tribute as well to the numberless faces hovering as unnamed resources behind this book and its predecessors — foremost, all my students and counselees from different nations and religious backgrounds. Then too, my friends and family, Jesuit colleagues, the many homes hosting and guiding my forays through Southeast Asia and elsewhere, cordial librarians and computer technicians, and a providential line of teachers and counselors and spiritual directors, whose wisdom and example have helped shape my own spirituality.

Tattooed mask of Ah Ping, Tree of Life, the cosmic axis — personified umbilical root connecting sacred forces of sky and netherworld. Chief nature spirit for the nomadic Punan Dyak people in Indonesian Borneo. Hand-carving on eight-inch teak shield, stained reddish brown.

Prologue

Two young disciples, grumbling at their new Zaddik's Way,
unlike the only Way they'd learned before, drew this rebuke:
"A God to be served in just one Way, what sort of God is that?"
— HASIDIC TALE

The aim of this book is to expand the imagination, to experience at close range what it means to live and wonder and pray from within a religious tradition other than one's own. As the snug neighborhood anywhere broadens into a global village, its skyline will be dotted with a richer montage of church spires, mosques, synagogues, and temples. I yearn for the moment when a religious stranger no longer surfaces as the feared and hated *other,* but someone to befriend on a common pilgrimage.

From each of the major extant religious traditions I have chosen a few central personalities, rites, and motifs, and tracked down their widening spiritual implications. What do Passover and David Ben-Gurion mean to a Jew, for example, the Quran and Mecca to a Muslim, Marx and the human rights movement to a Humanist? You can watch our best literary critics single out a pivotal image or scene in a text and enlarge this circle of significance until it reaches out to encompass the whole work, then the implied vision pervading an artist's corpus, and finally the trends of an entire era. Not in encyclopedic detail but with this sort of judicious selectivity, I want to explore the principal world spiritualities.

The common thread in all religious experience is the human imagination, with its resourceful but limited ways of groping toward the sacred mystery. Only a gifted imagination can excel at empathy, which means literally the capacity to feel into, or feel inside, another situation. Few know better what this process implies than the great lyric poets. G. M. Hopkins talks of inscape, Rilke of *einsehen,* and Keats of annihilating his very self and entering into the natural world around him. Bold novelists like Dostoyevsky or Faulkner strain your imagination to its limits, helping you train a third ear to detect an extraordinary inner life even in the brutal criminal. What at first seems so repelling about fictional characters like Raskolnikov or Joe Christmas soon discloses itself as bewildered pain, the compulsion and fear that might drive almost anyone to violence.

Through empathy, entering the lives of others, you begin to experience, believe, and value as they do. To prompt this immersion, Coleridge urges an attitude of poetic faith, the "willing suspension of disbelief" — more accurately, a temporary soft-pedaling of your own religious worldview. Such a frame of mind does not mean sheer identification or projection. It implies a balanced participant observation — sharing in the identity of another, yet still retaining your own. The excessive observer is remote and impersonal, unable to savor life from the inside. The excessive participant, however, is immersed mind and heart in some situation, but often enmeshed in it, too, and thus stripped of the outsider's knack to challenge premises so ingrained that few insiders ever think to question them.

Cross-cultural explorations in world religions, I am convinced, depend mostly on the habit of disciplined empathy. One illustration to be developed in chapter 4 will clarify what I mean. The Vietnamese Buddhist monk Thich Nhat Hanh commends a meditation exercise for developing compassion toward someone you instinctively dislike. Picture in detail the lips, ears, hair, and hands belonging to this repulsive figure. Dwell for some time on the features that upset you most. Then try to discover what is distinctive about the feeling, humor, and style of reasoning behind this face. Conjecture what causes worry there. Then imagine in detail the ways such a person is most likely misunderstood and victimized by others. You are urged to repeat this meditation on the same individual until you begin to feel empathy.

While teaching a course in Asian religious traditions I once met a forty-year-old American Vietnam War veteran numb to these imaginative sources of empathy. Wearing a massive cross around his neck as a badge of born-again faith, he proved at first an enthusiastic student. Yet he disappeared one day and only showed up months later to explain his reasons for dropping the course. Triggered by class discussions and films, some painful war memories had emerged from his past. For years the man had excelled in combat, killing again and again, solaced by an image of Christ fighting at his side against a godless enemy. Yet his faceless victims were now beginning to demand he acknowledge their concrete religious identity — Buddhists, Taoists, or worse, Asian fellow Christians, all perhaps no less religious than he. He was not ready to face up to his shocking self-deception.

I am convinced that to understand and appreciate the religious outsider, your imagination must be trained with the rigor Nhat Hanh describes. Your lens has to focus, of course, not on group abstractions — such as everyone poor, feminine, old, Buddhist, or handicapable, all to be loved or hated in a global hazy prejudgment — but on one distinct person at a time. Then someday beneath the rigid ayatollah, the bouncing saffron-clad neophyte, the witch doctor twitching in a wild trance-dance, you might uncover a saga of human dreams and misery not unlike your own. Mere tolerance must not satisfy you. Absorbed in befriending someone from a differing religious tradition, you may at times catch yourself trying on and trying out the perspective and values of this person. Suddenly it should strike you how much your own spiritual identity depends on happenstance or providence. Stir the mix of chromosomes or skin pigment, and you might have ended up a different person. Born elsewhere, within some other family and culture, you might have been shaped by a different church, ashram, mosque, or no identifiable religious group at all.

During rehearsals the veteran Balinese dancer, whose performance will be analyzed in chapter 1 on Primal traditions, can be observed touching prayerfully a row of sacred traditional masks. Communing with each mask and its implied story, one after another, until actor and role become almost identical reflections, the actor's body registers a change in tension, tempo, and breathing to mark each distinct role. In a similar way, when I spend hours with a Muslim friend, for instance, this actual person at moments may activate a virtual Muslim among the many spiritual possibilities within me. Here begins an honest phase of warming up to someone, learning to respect the other as other, not just as a clone of oneself. I am fascinated by the imagination as it initiates the process of self-enlargement or self-transcendence. This is the crucial teaching moment. Though beliefs and values in each religious tradition, of course, must submit to an eventual test of coherence, veracity, and practicality, I yearn as a teacher and theologian to prolong this more basic exploratory moment, both in myself and in others.

In addition to the participant-observer dialectic I have just exemplified, another crucial balance follows as a corollary. I agree with Gandhi that each person has a unique spirituality, and there exist as many spiritualities as individuals. Yet like overlapping Venn circles, all these perspectives touch along shared margins and often overreach accustomed boundaries. Among anthropologists and cross-cultural theologians, for each lopsided particularist, you can always locate a corresponding lopsided universalist. The exaggerated particularist theologian, nearsighted and alert to the fine print in each religion, tends to view differing traditions like distinct computer software programs, each with its unique virtual world, no tradition able to interact or be compared with another. At the other extreme, a farsighted universalist inflates the thinnest parallels of theme and structure between religions. I know one affable ecumenist, his memory and hearing impaired, prone to treat everyone the same because he confuses their names and faces. Like some of my less capable students taking an exam in world religions, the universalist is tempted to trim unique features, confuse one Way with another, and conflate all religions into one vague simplistic path to the Sacred. Both universalist and particularist excesses must be avoided.

In Raymond Carver's story of exacting understatement, "Cathedral," a blind visitor of eager imagination is left alone to communicate with the narrator, someone insensitive even if physically able to see. In a haze of alcohol, weed, and sleep deprivation, both men make various attempts at conversation, caught up at last in a documentary about Gothic cathedrals flickering on the late night TV screen. Never having seen a cathedral, Robert urges his laconic host to describe this phenomenon. At a loss, the narrator can only say they're really big, or that people in those days built high to be close to God, for God then seemed to matter. He admits that he himself, like most people today, is in no way religious. As the exchange warms up, both men draw near each other on the carpet. The narrator attempts to sketch a cathedral in ball-point on a shopping bag, with the blind man's hand riding over the artist's uncertain fingers. While Robert feels the excitement of tracing a cathedral outline for the first time, the narrator closes his eyes and discovers the wonder behind cathedrals, or more accurately, behind anything visual. "It's really something!" he observes. Assisted by the imagination of a blind prophet, the allegedly religionless narrator learns how to build his own cathedral, reaching for one instant beyond his ordinary boundaries.

Ready to identify with both characters in this story, I am first the dull, bumbling narrator, prodded to raise a cathedral of my own, observing but not grasping in depth. As one proverb claims, in the country of blind citizens, the lone one-eyed is king. A decade ago I wrote my first book on world religions, *Eight Sacred Horizons: The Religious Imagination East and West* (Macmillan, 1985). There my own subjectivity stands concealed behind the voice of an invisible detached author. Am I now the same person who wrote those pages? Revisiting some of the same motifs and personalities today, after years of fresh experience and research, I scarcely recognize the old terrain, once mapped into tidy manageable categories. The more it advances and deepens, life becomes harder to simplify. In a more recent work, *Sacred Lies and Silences: A Psychology of Religious Disguise* (Liturgical Press, 1994), I began to reinstate the complexity and subjectivity missing from that earlier perspective. The inner life, once charted so clearly, now reveals itself as more and also less religious than it first appears. For the loftiest religious ideals can be lived in reverent silence, and also betrayed by selective inattention or the parody of inflexible pursuit.

I recognize myself not just in Carver's narrator but also in Robert the blind guide of this story, the wounded healer. Though an outsider to most languages, cultures, and spiritualities featured in the present book, I hope to compensate for my relative blindness by developing a prophetic second sight, a second naïveté. I long to bring insight not only to the religiously estranged but also to the religiously self-assured. Yet what is my claim to vision, daring to write about religious traditions I have never lived? For twenty-five years now at the University of San Francisco I have taught college courses in world religions and served as priest and counselor in international student residence halls. I have learned from long exposure to a wide range of ethnic dialects, dress, music, and aromas from portable hot plates. Mistakes in my class lectures have been set right again and again by devout students from various religious traditions, including a Kashmir Shiavite who seldom ceased mumbling his prayer beads, Chinese Buddhists with tales of ghosts and miraculous divination, and a feisty group of Saudi Muslims whose devout Friday *salat* prayers I attended an entire semester in their campus mosque.

Dialogue does not occur between textbook abstractions like Hinduism and Christianity but between this individual Hindu and this individual Christian. The most plausible basis for opening oneself to the faith of another individual is affection first for the person and then readiness to hear out and respect the most cherished convictions of this person. In my own counseling or teaching, for instance, I have often stalled before some apparent fallacy or incoherence, say, in the Taoist or Muslim worldview. But then a practical litmus test comes to mind: How would devout, informed friends like Linlee or Zahid have lived out this paradox and made sense of it?

This book is a reflective theological essay, mostly experiential and personal in style. It will play up the sort of vital personal experiences just mentioned, especially when they have clarified stock misunderstandings or steered me toward a particular choice of material. Cross-cultural and interdisciplinary in scope, this work pauses now to examine a biography of Ataturk or Gandhi, now a Maori myth, now the pavement labyrinth in Chartres Cathedral. Its perspective ranges across a wide spectrum, from spiritual classics like the Bhagavad Gita or Tao Te Ching, to a contemporary film, short story, or personal anecdote.

My intended audience is, first, the literate, college-educated public and, second, the questioning, intelligent undergraduate or graduate student, to all of whom I have been teaching earlier drafts of this book for years. Though using inclusive language throughout, the text will at times preserve the original patriarchal flavor of scriptural quotes. The Asian chapters favor those accepted transliterations with fewest subscripts and diacritical marks. Notes are located after the text, so that readers can investigate a preferred subject further, check the accuracy of my sources, or verify if a controversial interpretation is based on a wider consensus or just my own idiosyncratic viewpoint.

The eight chapters in this work can be grouped into four sets, treated more or less in historical sequence — 1, 2-3-4, 5-6-7, and 8. The six middle chapters balance between two religious families, the Wisdom legacy and the Prophetic legacy.

Chapter 1 on Primal Ways introduces the root ingredients common to every religious tradition. Chapter 2 interweaves Confucian, Taoist, and Shinto Ways into a single Tao cluster of religions. Whereas the paradise sought in Primal Ways is located in primordial time, the Golden Age of these later Ways is projected as either beyond or long before the Axial Era associated with figures like Confucius and Lao Tzu. Then, as the climax to this Asian Wisdom legacy, chapters 3 and 4 study two Indian traditions, the Hindu and Buddhist Ways. Besides Gandhi, the Hindu chapter centers first on Vedanta founders Vivekananda and Ramakrishna, then on Krishna Consciousness founder Prabhupada and his remote prototype Caitanya. Major Buddhist figures include such activists as U Nu, U Thant, Aung San Suu Kyi, and spiritual teachers Buddhadasa, Thich Nhat Hanh, and the Dalai Lama.

Chapters 5, 6, and 7 comprise the Abrahamic Prophetic heritage, or the Jewish, Christian, and Muslim Ways. Major activists in search of a liberated society include Jews like Golda Meir and David Ben-Gurion, Christians Konrad Adenauer and Kenneth Kaunda, and Muslims Kemal Ataturk and Ayatollah Ruhollah Khomeini. Prophetic teachers in these traditions are represented by such theologians as Martin Buber, Abraham Heschel, Karl Rahner, Reinhold Niebuhr, and Muhammad Iqbal. Chapter 8 will sketch the Humanist tradition, centered on an ideal humanity interconnected with the evolving cosmos, a spirituality interpreted as a secular alternative to the previous religious Ways. As a culminating summary, too, this final chapter will piece together an implied dialogue with Humanists unfolding in the previous seven traditions.

Cross-religious understanding might broaden through friendships beyond religious and cultural boundaries, and through library research, world travel, or a few exotic liturgies, but all these together cannot suffice. It is rare to find people so caught up in formulating and living a public tradition that they can be said to represent that religion with authority. Fewer have the skill or even the impulse to interpret with empathic accuracy a tradition other than their own. For some of my traditionalist colleagues, too, just the decision to treat spiritual alternatives with equity — with the same respect and balanced scrutiny shown your own religion — might seem to endanger the privileged claims of your tradition, and thus disqualify you to speak for it. However, no matter how clumsy, hazardous, and fallible this sort of cultural and religious translation may turn out, I am convinced it must always be attempted.

The sun mandala, a widespread Primal symbol of the cosmic Center. Canvas and bead medallion in orange and blue on white background. Pine Ridge Sioux Reservation, South Dakota.

1

Primal Ways

Maps that trace the distribution of major world religions leave huge patches of the earth unlabeled. This emptiness stands mostly for the differing self-contained civilizations of indigenous peoples scattered through Central Africa, the Amazon basin, northern Australia, Melanesia, Siberia, the Arctic, and the reservations of North America. As a child I used to enjoy exploring a large globe mounted on a swivel stand in our living room. On its surface I would spend hours tracking down random specks and creases and annexing them as secret kingdoms of the imagination, now a Jules Verne island fortress, now a Conrad jungle labyrinth. Years later, attending seminars of Mircea Eliade at the University of Chicago or watching TV interviews with Joseph Campbell, I found their accounts of rite and myth were more compelling in proportion to the distance separating these great teachers from their concrete historical sources. For remoteness in time and place can invite a more unhampered range of conjecture and poetry.

Today these indigenous blank spaces have taken on more recognizable identities, like the emergent image on a developing photo negative. During a single evening, TV documentaries or photo magazines, such as those produced by National Geographic, transport their audiences into the presence of the Macchu Picchu ruins, the elongated stone heads of Easter Island, handprints and animal sketches on Aborigine cave walls, or a monkey hunt by dart pipe along the Congo or Amazon. The critical viewer, however, must put up with a recurring bias in the presentation of this material. First, in nature and travel films especially, film editors tend to downplay, delete, or allot slipshod research time to the explicit religious dimension in a culture — perhaps to sidestep controversy or complexity. The camera fixates instead on pageants, exotic fashions, cuisine, the enticing details of everyday work and love. Second, these documentaries are prone to trim down all indigenous cultures to a single model for sermonizing — a nostalgic utopia, picked clean of modern urban crime, environmental pollution, taxes, and moral hang-ups.

Joanne Greenberg's story "Supremacy of the Hunza" is a tart commentary on this romantic excess. Margolin, the hard-nosed anthropologist, confronts Westercamp, the mushy environmentalist, two unexpected allies trying to mobilize their suburban neighborhood against a power-tower incursion on the landscape. For Westercamp, human beings should learn from the Mexican Chontal Indians, as once depicted by a parachute journalist: "He never saw an adult strike a child. Crime and insanity don't exist there. He never saw violence. The people live on their land simply and in peace. He saw women of seventy and eighty carrying water in huge jugs for miles without tiring." To this rhapsodic account, Margolin offers a quick rebuttal: "I'll lay you odds that the women of seventy were thirty and looked seventy. Employment means staying alive till tomorrow. The absence of crime is the absence of an idea of private ownership. The harmony is chronic malnutrition, the tranquillity is coca-leaf."[1]

As disputes about the Chontal, Hunza, or any other indigenous people suggest, each premise underlying an exploration into their religious life must be brought under scrutiny. Because one can never separate the interpreted data from the mind interpreting it, no observer should risk getting locked within the perspective of a single anthropologist or philosopher of religion. I stumbled upon this unconscious trap some years ago on a research visit to a remote Pacific island. In my notebook I scribbled information from articulate local guides, as we toured major shrines and burial sites. It seemed heartening to hear the platitudes I had picked up from elementary textbooks now confirmed by the lips of actual people who lived that religion. However, a shock awaited me. Introduced a few days later to the revered chief mentor of these guides, I discovered he was a fellow American Catholic priest. After he invited me to peruse his few books and modest lecture notes, I met most of my familiar manuals again, marred by the inaccuracies I could still identify. Ignorant of their own heritage, local guides had pressed this foreigner to help give their religious customs a respectable Eurocentric veneer for tourists. I glanced again at the ironic recycling of a few banal insights, transformed from dated textbooks to the excited fresh discoveries recorded in my notebook.

Though cautioning a dose of skepticism during any safari, I want at the same time to encourage more positive attitudes of wonder and empathy that distinguish the best anthropologists. In other words, the hermeneutic of suspicion must never undermine a prevailing hermeneutic of second naïveté. Margaret Mead, for example, trained herself to perceive a house in other cultures, or even in her hometown, as a fresh impression. She tried to feel surprise that houses exist at all; that they are square or oval, have walls, let in sun, or keep out wind or rain; and that people happen to eat or work in the same space where they dwell. Otherwise, if you take things like this for granted, you might treat what is new and distinctive merely as a variant of something already known. "Seeing a house as bigger or smaller," she says, "grander or meaner, more or less watertight than some other kind of house one already knows about, cuts me off from discovering what this house is in the minds of those who live in it."[2] Here she describes the habit of empathy or surprised openness, highlighted in my prologue, a mind-set indispensable for understanding a spirituality, culture, or temperament different from your own.

Granted the astounding number and diversity of indigenous cultures and the limited ethnographic data accessible, most explorers hanker for some common underlying patterns. In any conflict among religious anthropologists, it is helpful to respect the dialectic mentioned in my prologue. Though attentive to the farsighted universalist tracing similarities of theme and structure between cultures, you must also listen to the nearsighted particularist, focused on the fine print in each idiosyncratic culture. My intent in this chapter is to reach a balance between these two polarities — to recognize, even celebrate, each unique religious or cultural difference, but at the same time to spot any insightful parallel that transcends the differences.

ENTRANCE TO THE PRIMAL

If privileged to witness a regional Sioux powwow, Aborigine corroboree, or Haitian Voodoo gathering, you recognize an indigenous creed is not so much to be formulated and preached as to be lived and danced out. Siding with this preference for lived experience, I shall sketch some concrete encounters of my own with indigenous religions, and only then distill a few definitions.

On my dorm room shelf is a shrine of fragments that three other professors and I collected three decades ago, each of us with pretensions of the amateur anthropologist, digging in rubbish dumps near the ruins of La Venta, Palenque, and Chichen-Itza along the Gulf of Mexico. Whenever I touch these potsherds with their design and color still visible, or the old knife blades of black and gray obsidian, I feel a secret bond with Mayan or even the earlier Olmec civilizations. I imagine the religion of these people as not a separate noun but an adjective permeating all of ordinary life.

A few years ago in a similar context I took a meditative early morning walk through temple ruins at the Honaunau Refuge near Kona on the large island of Hawaii. This was once a Primal sanctuary, where noncombatants and defeated warriors fled, or taboo breakers came to be absolved by the ancient Hawaiian priest, before resuming their lives elsewhere. Surrounded by black volcanic sand and the ocean on one side and by colossal stone walls on the other, no one in this sacred space was permitted to suffer harm. Housing the bones of at least two dozen chiefs, the temple mausoleum spread its spiritual power throughout the refuge to guarantee even further protection.

As a further illustration, I recall visiting some of my former students near Bangkok — at their homes and also at such family businesses as a jewelry store, cloth-spinning factory, or farm. Almost every shop and home in this district had erected its separate platform nearby to display an eerie doll-house temple or palace, lacquered mostly gold and white, with characteristic pointed Thai roofs. Because my friends took such spirit presences for granted, I too opened my imagination to the original Primal guardians of the place, displaced by the arrival of Buddhist missionaries and modern construction crews. All these Buddhist families thought it a wise insurance policy to appease the spirits and court them back as friendly household Gods.

My fourth scenario introduces a sharp-witted army veteran living a few blocks from me in San Francisco, a middle-aged Apache rooted in the Mescalero and White Mountain clans of the Southwest. You can anticipate his militant veto whenever the University of San Francisco cuts down a tree on campus or tampers with the neighborhood skyline by adding one more building. Proud of his spiritual kinship with the powers behind thunder and sunset, he calls them Brother, Grandfather, and Mother Earth. He has tried repeatedly to make his people's own territorial burial sites accessible for pilgrims from neighboring clans who also hold these locations sacred. Employed by his tribe as a full-time real estate agent, he invests their assets in shrewd land purchases throughout California. His most outspoken complaints center on shortsighted tribal elders anywhere, greedy to rent their sacred land to Mafia-types for casinos or to the U.S. government for nuclear waste dumps.

Of these four contacts with indigenous traditions, my Bangkok and San Francisco experiences describe a spiritual interaction today, whereas the Mexican and Hawaiian examples suggest the bookish antiquarian past. I cannot imagine a case study more

alive than my Apache friend, intractable to the us-explaining-them sort of anthropology, bristling whenever he catches someone projecting a glib archetype on his inner
silences. The man has grown up among a people caught in huge cultural and political
upheavals, with most of them zealous to become the sole authoritative interpreters of
their own religious tradition.

On reflection, however, I can defend my Mexican and Hawaiian illustrations as
less archaic and academic than they first appear. For Mayan religious life, flourishing
at present in rural Mexico, Guatemala, and Belize, has evolved far beyond a mere
fossilized religion. And you should not overlook the random Hawaiian flower leis
and food offerings placed today alongside lava fissures in Kiluea Volcano Park, as
votive gifts for the Goddess Pele. In fact, Primal rites and magic now surface with
increasing regularity, borrowed and reinterpreted by New Age spirituality. During
the past decade, for example, British police have continued to boot out thousands of
present-day Druids and New Age travelers camping near the celebrated Stonehenge
ruins, especially at the rites of summer solstice. Thus, indigenous Ways should never
be underrated as freeze-dried memories left from what Darwin or Freud called a pre-
historic Primal horde. Many of them are vital spiritualities, adjusting constantly to
outside influences through their long histories.

To name something is to pass judgment on it and thus to affect its destiny. As a
counselor, for instance, I have watched how the labels of sin or craziness or illness,
pasted on someone by parents or friends, trigger symptoms in the client and pre-
determine diagnosis. Suppose I decide to sum up whole cultures as undeveloped or
underdeveloped or as preliterate or illiterate. Such names would endorse the doubtful superiority of technological expertise or the written word. Similar distortions are
fostered by terms like tribal, local, ethnic, folk, and especially primitive. A weasel
word favored by armchair anthropologists of the last few centuries, "primitive"
means barbarism to Hobbes, infantile regression to Freud, and unspoiled simplicity
to Rousseau.

I shall apply the term "Primal" to all indigenous religions for three reasons. The
name directs attention to a basic dimension in all religious traditions. It suggests continuity but not simplistic identification with the supposed rituals of earliest Paleolithic
hunting cultures. And the label at present seems least obnoxious to the persons described. Also, by describing a culture as a *religious Way,* I mean its characteristic
behavior and values and language show apparent signs of awe, commitment, ecstasy,
and moral seriousness. Thus, the ideal religious society or person is one living, more
or less, a religiously integrated existence. A religious quality could be expected to
permeate that life, as the center from which everything else derives its meaning, or
without which all else would be meaningless. This center of ultimate coherence —
whether person or force, imaged or imageless, named or unnameable — will be called
the Sacred.[3]

Like the Tao, to be discussed in the next chapter on China and Japan, the Primal outlook presumes a cosmos vibrant with magic, its spiritual and human and
physical realms all interwoven. Just to survive, such a culture must learn an agile
intercommunion with natural forces which its members lack the technology or incli-
nation to dominate. Rather than compile sacred scriptures, most Primal Ways prefer
to hand down legend and rite orally from teacher to disciple. After all, who knows
better than the spiritual guide at what moment each individual disciple is mature and

spiritual enough to receive the revelation? Also, the secret word might be endangered or profaned by capturing it in print, even if a written language happens to exist.

Living in small-scale communities cemented by kinship and locale, a Primal society is now deprived, now enhanced, by its marginal encounter with urban values. I cannot forget the repeated disappointment voiced by lawyer, counselor, and teacher friends who have worked for years on various Native American reservations. Too many fine reservation athletes or students, having left their settlements for a hopeful new career, end up retreating home for a destiny of terminal unemployment, after their first setback or homesickness outside. The strength of a Primal Way, its rootedness in the specific clan or sacred neighborhood, may turn into a major weakness. It does not readily survive export or family dispersal. Most important, enticed by the mind-set of urban secularity, followers of a Primal Way may venture to discard or tamper with the Primal center of meaning, only to risk wiping out an entire culture interwoven tightly around this religious pivot.

Many outsider anthropologists of religion, once quick to spot fetish cults and polytheism in almost any unfamiliar ritual, today favor the so-called African Triangle premise in interpreting a Primal Way. Here the Sacred is divided first into a Godhead source at the apex, a mystery so unapproachable that it is often left unnamed. Radiating down from this source, then, are two legs of the triangle, ancestral spirits and nature spirits, accessible to popular devotion.

Such a theory can open an observer's mind to the possibility of a subtle and diffusive monotheism, but it also projects an implicit monotheism where it may not exist. I prefer an approach alert to the comprehensive way individual persons do not just explain their faith but implicitly live it out. I want to measure the interplay between their religious self-understanding and the horizons shaped by their language, political institutions, and social psychology. For example, given the graded levels of social behavior and custom among the African Nuer people, anthropologist Evans-Pritchard shows no surprise at their concept of sacred power, refracted into a complex hierarchy of separate spirits. Or consistent with the Aztecs' dual language patterns, "water" and "hill" stand for a town, "shirt" and "blouse" for an attractive woman. Thus the anthropologist Leon-Portilla questions if the Sacred within this linguistic perspective could be anything but dualistic or polytheistic.[4]

Whenever a Primal religion faces a more aggressive world religion, a few outcomes are possible. The two competing traditions may accede to a relaxed juxtaposition of both religious identities. On the one hand, a successful accommodation occurs, for instance, in the exuberant indigenous Bon imagery and ritual that distinguish Tibetan Buddhists from their Buddhist neighbors, and in the unique funeral rites shared by Toraja Christians in Indonesia with their Toraja indigenous Ancestors. On the other hand, the conquering religion may demand fierce loyalty that obliterates every trace of a rival. Even after conquest by a more self-confident tradition, however, the Primal dimension may yet survive as a stubborn residue.

The celebrated Black Elk, for instance, dictated his youthful shamanic experiences to John Neihardt because he wanted his people to preserve and appreciate their dying Oglala Sioux tradition. Once his first book appeared, however, the elderly Sioux was pressured by his current Jesuit pastor to issue a retraction in Sioux and English. Notarized before witnesses on the Sioux reservation, a church document reaffirmed Black Elk's Catholic faith throughout the last forty uninterrupted years since his conversion.

The readers of this document are directed not to mistake the influential elder Catholic catechist for what he himself calls the "Pagan medicine man" of his youth. Yet despite the parish priest's scruples about single-minded loyalty, I am convinced Black Elk's conscience had no trouble integrating his later vocation as Catholic teacher and mystic with his earlier vocation as Primal healer and visionary.

A far different Sioux voice, the feisty saboteur against all enforced acculturation, surfaces in the book *Lame Deer: Seeker of Visions.* Informed of plans to build a huge tepee-shaped Catholic chapel on his reservation, with a peace pipe hanging next to a cross above the altar, elderly shaman John Lame Deer voices this complaint: "It is dishonest.... There will always be a difference, as long as one Indian is left alive. Our beliefs are rooted deep in our earth, no matter what you have done to it and how much of it you have paved over. And if you leave all that concrete unwatched for a year or two, our plants, the native Indian plants, will pierce that concrete and push up through it."[5]

A similar resistance to assimilation underlies the Nigerian story "Dead Men's Path" by Chinua Achebe. Impatient with the timid concessions urged by his colleagues, a young Ibo Christian headmaster introduces rapid reforms into his mission school. Proud of the school's modern educational standards, Mr. Obi especially admires the gardens and hedges beautifying his Eurocentric compound, circled by a barbed wire fence that happens to obstruct a path between the traditional Ibo village shrine and the village cemetery. This path marks the alleged spirit road that dead relatives travel to depart from this life and that babies travel as they emerge from childbirth. To block it, then, is to insult the Primal spirits and cut off the Ibo life source. To the village shaman's complaints against this fence, Obi replies with scorn that school grounds cannot be a thoroughfare, nor would the Ancestors object to a little detour. "Dead men do not require footpaths," he says. "Our duty is to teach your children to laugh at such ideas." As the tragic result of this collision, all of Obi's greenery is uprooted in retaliation, one of the school buildings demolished, and the modernizing headmaster himself fired in disgrace.[6]

The above montage of Mayan, Polynesian, Nuer, Aztec, Sioux, and Ibo Ways may at first seem bewildering and blur crucial landmarks and boundaries. But any serious student of the Primal must face such a montage. After all, the Sacred discloses itself in a unique way not just to each Primal tradition, and to each of 550 distinct registered peoples swept under the generic Native American label, but also to each individual within all these traditions. For this reason, it seems wise to focus on a paradigm from a single indigenous people, or better yet, from a central religious myth and rite in a particular culture. Then from this basis it may be possible to spot parallels elsewhere.

My choice is the Huichol Indians, a people from the rugged coastal Sierra Madre area of west-central Mexico. One reason for selecting them is the depth of scholarly, varied, and recent anthropological materials about them. Monographs by Mexican scholars and other specialists on Huichol religion, economy, medicine, and family structure abound. I have visited extensive displays of Huichol culture and yarn paintings at the anthropological museum in Mexico City and especially at the famous 1979 Huichol exhibit at the De Young Museum in San Francisco. Accessible films on the Huichole include at least one hour-long ethnographic documentary of the entire peyote hunt. The hunt portrayed in the present chapter refers to a specific pilgrim group and hunt leader — Ramon Medina Silva — who invited anthropologists Barbara Myerhoff and Peter Furst to join the pilgrimage under his leadership.[7]

It is urgent to recognize that these data on the Huichole have been filtered through the fallible worldview of various anthropologists, theologians, artists, and museum curators. Even the museum itself is a cultural and historical creation, with its own limitations. Depending on the shifting fashions of political correctness in the United States, for instance, Native American peoples have been packaged as the noble savage, the vanishing Indian, the stone-faced frontier Indian, the urban guerrilla Indian — a lineage culminating today in the New Age Indian, exemplary artist and visionary and gentle environmentalist. For the last century, collections of their baskets, pots, and masks have moved from natural history museums to ethnographic museums and more recently to museums of fine art. Once viewed simply as part of the natural landscape, next as remnants of a culture sentenced to extinction, Primal artifacts tend to surface today as works of individual creativity, often valued by standards at variance with the aesthetic of the artists' own cultures. For the curator may decide arbitrarily to arrange a pastiche of ahistorical motifs, or trace historical interactions between Primal and Eurocentric styles, or sift out a usable past in order to spark an artistic renewal.[8]

From an analysis of the annual Huichol peyote hunt, I shall extract four motifs essential to an appreciation of almost every Primal religion: the hunt, the shaman, the gift, and the mask. These four combined themes will act in turn as a grid transparency working to highlight realms of the Primal hunt in Huichol data which might otherwise seem random and incoherent.

THE HUNT FOR GENESIS

Once a year small Huichol bands set out from their homes in the Sierra Madre of west-central Mexico and travel three hundred miles northeast down through Jalisco and Zacatecas to the Chihuahuan deserts of San Luis Potosi. Their aim is to gather peyote in a place their legends call Wirikuta, a vast desert without roads at the base of two sacred mountains. Since the cactus used throughout the year in religious ceremonies would be just a cheap purchase at local markets, it is clear the journey itself and the particular Wirikuta cactus have symbolic importance. Huichol myths identify Wirikuta as the Middle World where Gods and human beings once dwelt together at the beginning of time. Pilgrimage there is a ritual passage back to human origins, a recovery of continuity between human flatlands and the sacred upper world, or between human beings and the magic energy of plants and animals.

The exact ethnic and geographical origins of the Huichole are disputed, but anthropologists agree about the relative insulation of these people from Aztec and Spanish influence. Subjected to an entire century of ethnographic study, they show evidence of a clear self-identity and of stubborn fidelity to every detail of their peyote pilgrimage. The Huichole do claim Wirikuta as site of their actual historical beginnings and have given Huichol names to clumps of trees, water holes, and rocks along the route northeast to Wirikuta. On that road their ancestors are believed to have traveled during some massive primordial exodus.

The Wirikuta journey can be distinguished from pilgrimages in most other world religions by its emphasis on rites of the sacred hunt. Though dependent today mostly on maize farming, the Huichole still linger in imagination on their recent past as a hunting society. In many cultures the hunt is a significant rite of passage, cutting its participants away from the protective and the orderly, bracing them to wander into the perilous natural world and return in mastery. Some rituals prepare a hunter for separation from society; others produce medicines, spells, and prayers to outwit the adversary. And still further rituals purify the returning hunter from dangerous contact with the prey's magic powers.[9] Huichol myths center on the exploits of Kauyumari, the Sacred Deer figure, their ancestral trickster hero. An animal guide in human form, intermediary between Gods and the pilgrimage leader, he animates each group of hunters with his presence. And thus, his tail and antlers are carried as banners throughout the journey.

As the martial arts teach in Taoist and Buddhist traditions, a familiar and complex relationship develops between hunter and hunted. The target proves to be the hunter's own shadow or double, a sacred presence — now courted, now appeased, before it freely sacrifices its life. The transcendent moment in this relationship is portrayed superbly by "The Bear" and other tales of the hunting initiation rite in William Faulkner's *Go Down, Moses:* "Suddenly the buck was there, smoke-colored out of nothing, magnificent with speed," as twelve-year-old Ike McCasslin squeezes the trigger. Then he hears the cry of Sam Fathers, his elderly Indian guide, "Olé...Chief, Grandfather." These words confirm that Sam and the prey carry the same Indian blood in their veins. Sam smears the boy's face with blood from the slain deer. Humble and trembling at this baptism, Ike promises the animal, "I slew you. My bearing must not shame your quitting life. My conduct forever onward must become your death."[10]

It is preferable to make the Wirikuta pilgrimage on foot, chanting prayers and songs the whole rigorous month, fasting, offering sacrifices at daily wayside shrines marked by Huichol names and legendary associations. Today most people cover the distance in cars, open trucks, or busses, scores of pilgrims zipping by the shrines, tossing impetuous offerings at them. Yet by whatever transportation the travelers reach Wirikuta, they must cross the last few miles on foot.

Soon they begin the extraordinary ritual of a combined deer and peyote hunt. The pilgrims have long prepared for this moment by a series of traditional hunting purification rites — a bath before beginning, then during the trip an abstention from sexual relations, from bathing and most sleep, and from most food and drink. Their families at home share vicariously in the pilgrimage by adhering to most of these proscriptions. In a similar gesture of solidarity, Muslims worldwide celebrate the annual Id al-Adha festival to mark the actual day of animal sacrifices witnessed by pilgrims at Mecca. In a less solemn situation, I once found myself invited to dinner with a Michigan family, just as the older men completed intricate rites of packing their fishing gear. During the hours of the fishing expedition, those at home were urged to pray and adhere to some rigid taboos, including not mentioning the word "fish."

At Wirikuta itself, the hunters pray for many hours, even more intensely than before, blowing a horn and slapping the hunting bow to soothe the deer at its impending death. They crouch to seek animal tracks, in imitation of their ancestral Ancient Ones, stalking the prey. Once the first peyote plant is spotted, their leader, the *maraakame,* takes aim with his bow, sinking one arrow after another around the cactus, and finally cuts it off at the base. "Look there, how sacred and beautiful, the five-pointed deer," he says, apologizing and grieving for this death, honoring the deer-cactus with gifts. "Take them, Elder Brother, and give us our life."

The climax of this sacred hunt is a communion ritual. Here the Huichole draw on the sacred meal symbolism common to many world religions. Broken segments of the first cactus in the hunt are given a significant name, "Elder Brother's flesh." These are placed in a votive gourd and passed around to all the communicants, beginning with veterans from previous pilgrimages. Now the maraakame touches a peyote bud to each person's forehead, eyes, throat, and heart. Then he places it on the tongue, urging each pilgrim, "Chew it well; chew it well. For thus you will see your life."

At this point the Wirikuta half of this sacred hunt concludes. Later, carrying baskets of peyote, if not intercepted by a venturesome Mexican narcotics agent, the pilgrims will return home to prepare within five days for an actual deer hunt. A bowl containing some of the first Wirikuta plants will then be carried like a compass to guide them to their new quarry. The Sacred Deer must be trapped without arrows or bullets and led gently from the snare back to the sacrificial altar. The victim is honored with its favorite food and encouraged to surrender its life generously. Slices of its heart and blood are sprinkled over the seed corn, for without this medicine of fertility, there could be no maize, rain, or life.

Rites of Pilgrimage

N. Scott Momaday's *The Way to Rainy Mountain* tells of his trip from the Yellowstone Mountains eastward to the Black Hills and down through the plains of Oklahoma to visit his Kiowa grandmother's grave in the shadow of Rainy Mountain. Like the Huichol Wirikuta, this desolate mountain in the Wichita Range is revered by Momaday and his people as the center from which earth originated. His own trip home, a personal rite of passage, reenacts the seventeenth-century migration of the Kiowa nation in their descent southward, adapting gradually to use of the horse, to the Plains rituals of worship and warfare, and to the status of a mature self-confident people. Each two-page unit in the book contains first a Kiowa legend, followed by a paragraph of linguistic or ethical commentary, then a brief epiphany drawn from the author's memory of his own individual life. A journey like Momaday's must be made, he says, "with the whole memory, the experience of the mind which is legendary as well as historical, personal as well as cultural.... There are on the way to Rainy Mountain many landmarks, many journeys in the one."[11]

These overlapping dimensions of the Rainy Mountain experience all come into play in the Huichol passage to Wirikuta. Each pilgrim and also the entire Huichol community hope to recover their Sacred Center and historical identity. As a pilgrimage, the hunt shows all the familiar marks of what Victor Turner calls *limen* and *communitas*.[12] The first term refers to the idealized threshold toward which pilgrims climb, a moment in and out of time. Here pilgrims experience the Sacred, by means of either a miraculous cure or an inward spiritual transformation. The second term points to the intense comradeship gradually developed along the way, a fellowship of the hunt. Huichol pilgrims pray, eat, and sleep many days together, especially if they travel the entire journey by foot. They experience a sense of closeness, stripped of antecedent status, long remembered afterward by those suffering together through boot camp or any other critical ordeal.

The Huichol pilgrims' mutual confessions around the campfire will be treated later. The various rituals of purification equalize everyone and establish a bond of shared secrets. Ramon the Maraakame tells about an earlier pilgrimage, when he and the group refused to tolerate a young woman's reluctance to confess and feared for the group's ritual pollution until she could be persuaded to change her mind. Ramon further mentions the special vulnerability of any maraakame during pilgrimage, awake all night to guard the others. Without shared faith and the trust extended by all his companions, Ramon would feel deprived of power, unable to use his gifts. A few impressive rites reinforce this motif of solidarity. Huichol families assemble special pilgrim costumes for use exclusively during the Wirikuta journey. The insignia of tobacco gourd and squirrel tail are worn by veterans as a badge of rebirth long after their return. The maraakame invests everyone with a new sacred name before setting out, and years later fellow pilgrims still greet each other by these pilgrim names. At the commencement and finish of the journey, pilgrims celebrate a special banquet at home, witnessed by their backers, who share spiritually in the journey.

In addition to the climax of peyote communion described above, the ritual of the sacred cord also confirms this pilgrim fellowship. Before the pilgrims depart from home, they gather in a circle and pass around a cactus fiber cord; the cord is then scorched in the fire and saved for a more solemn repetition later. After two more such rituals at Wirikuta, the maraakame prays silently and calls each pilgrim to his side one-by-one. He ties a knot to represent each kneeling person. Describing this umbilical cord and chain as a bond "knotting us into unity," he says, "Now we are all of one faith, one affection, one heart." The knots will be undone carefully after the return home. Ramon tells of one fervent pilgrim band that retained the knotted cord and vowed to return on four successive pilgrimages together.

A student friend of mine, a counselor representing the California Service League, visits the San Francisco county jail each week to hold group therapy sessions with the prisoners. Seated in a circle, people recount their life stories, often in graphic confessional detail, and offer insight and encouragement to one another. Drawing upon his Chiricahua Apache and Hispanic background, at times this young counselor shares some tribal wisdom with them. What has proved most effective in his presentation, he thinks, is the Native American notion of an intimate sacred circle binding all the participants. He asks the prisoners to pledge respect for everyone in the therapy circle — listening with reverence, and especially, protecting the confidentiality of anything they hear.

A letter from one of my Michigan students tells of a local Potawatomi sweat lodge ceremony he attended as a climax to a weekend retreat of male bonding and spiritual renewal. Made of saplings and tarpaulin, the ceremonial lodge enclosed a pit filled with hot rocks. Nude or in swimming trunks, the men all prayed or chanted there together and were encouraged, but not forced, to confess and unburden themselves. As each sweated out his impurities, he directed his gaze only toward the unseen Presence within the fire and scooped-out pit and did not address or interrupt anyone else. All took an oath of mutual secrecy. Their Potawatomi elders reminded them, "Bring your troubles to the lodge and leave them here." From the lodge my friend said he took away memories of ordeal and relief, spiritual purification, and a sense of real community.

These situations illustrate the ardent fellowship of shared spiritual ordeals, common to pilgrims in all religious traditions. I have met eager Hindu pilgrims traveling huge distances to bathe in the Ganges at Benares, Muslims on hajj for Mecca, and Catholics headed for Rome, Jerusalem, or the popular scattered Marian shrines at Lourdes, Fatima, or Guadalupe. They report almost identical trials of fasting and sleeplessness, hospitality from strangers, the solidarity of immense rallies, astounding miracles of healing and conversion. Maybe the profane counterpart to this self-described religious pilgrim is not the mere tourist but the authentic secular pilgrim. I know many American families who on an annual trip to distant national parks or camping grounds or Disneyland search for emotional and spiritual renewal, a deeper family bonding, and even a restored patriotism about their land and its history. Like all other pilgrims, Huichol travelers each have their own particular motives for the ritual journey. They go to fulfill a vow, to repent sins, to gain merit or power, to heal disease or beg some other favor, to show respect for familial or ethnic traditions, to feel closer to the Sacred. Each Huichol aspirant must be screened to qualify for pilgrimage, and like the Muslim hajji leaving Mecca, each will return with a new indelible status, expected now to give evidence of a converted life.

When you hunt and eat the sacred peyote at Wirikuta, then you intensify a number of crucial relationships in the spiritual life. You expand your ordinary consciousness and feel an intense communion first with this immediate group of pilgrims. Then you identify, too, with the First Ancestors in their primordial hunting culture, with the totem deer Kauyumari himself in his kinship with the animal and natural universe, with the life-force of Sacred Sun and Fire that pulses through the maize and deer blood.

THE WOUNDED SHAMAN

The Huichol maraakame shows many features of the classical shaman, notably as described in the works of Mircea Eliade. The shaman is a figure prominent in inner Asia and is recognizable with some modifications throughout most Primal societies. Possessing the gift of controlled ecstatic trance, a shaman's soul can leave his body to visit the domain of clan and nature spirits. This realm could be the sky, underworld, or metaphysical center, depending on the spatial myths assigned by a particular worldview to the dead and the Sacred.

What is the goal of this trance journey? Shamans are supposed to guide the recent dead through dangerous roadblocks to their rest. They try to retrieve a soul drifting loose from its diseased body or to appease a long troublesome hungry ghost. Again, they might search out clairvoyant spirits for knowledge about the future or for magic remedies. Shamans can be identified by standard trademarks worldwide: a costume of bird feathers or reindeer or horse skin for ecstatic flight; psychodrama and leaping dances to pantomime hazardous adventures of the trip; and trance enhancements like music and rhythmical chants and often drugs. Usually the shamanic vocation comes just to those privileged with some unique visionary call in their lives.

A near encounter with death will perhaps familiarize them with borderlands to the other world.[13]

Ramon the Maraakame once explained to his anthropologist friends that the shamanic faith healer must integrate all of a modern Eurocentric society's fragmented specialties of physician, psychotherapist, priest, poet, and philosopher. From his sixth year, Ramon had recurrent dreams that the sun God had elected him a disciple. Then at eight he was bitten by a poisonous snake. When his grandfather, a maraakame, was summoned to cure him, the elder prophesied about the boy's vocation, and after six months of paralysis and meditation, Ramon was set apart for prolonged spiritual apprenticeship. Under a senior maraakame, Ramon had to learn "how one cures, how one goes to Wirikuta,...those stories of ours which are our history. How one makes the sacred offerings." Besides intelligence, spiritual sensitivity, and judgment, a maraakame should have the talent of singing, storytelling, creating beautiful works of art as offerings, and proficiency in the ways of practical Mexican society in order to protect and counsel his people. Ramon's wife, Lupe, trained in Huichol lore and values, assists her husband in all his rituals, especially guarding him in moments of vulnerability when his energy is drained and his animal-spirit helpers are busy elsewhere. Ramon has admitted that each successive pilgrimage proves more taxing to his stamina, for he takes on "more of the weight of his people."

Ramon's powers bind him closely to his community yet keep him at a mysterious distance from it. The followers' private dreams and peyote experiences are meant for individual enjoyment and meditation, but the leader's dreams are public revelations of the Sacred to the whole community. The mediation of Ramon is needed especially as the pilgrims cross through the Gateway of Clashing Clouds, the critical boundary between everyday life and Wirikuta sacred space. He blindfolds all first-time pilgrims, more vulnerable than the others to sacred glare and whirlwinds barring access. "This walk will be very hard," he warns. "It is a great penance, this journey to Wirikuta, and you will cry very much." These words might be taken at face value, or perhaps mean the opposite, a moment of great joy. For at this special time everyone uses ritual reversal language, which will be discussed later. Praying and singing, addressing unseen guiding spirits, sprinkling the pilgrims with holy water, rhythmically beating his bow to accompany their march, Ramon leads the group in single file. They move through a mythical aperture that their Sacred Deer guardian pries open, before the gates slam shut.

Healer and Psychotherapist

Frontiersman and mediator between worlds, Ramon is also an accomplished healer. A barren woman from his group prays at various wayside shrines on the journey to conceive a child. The shaman joins his prayer to hers, blows tobacco smoke over her body, and makes sucking and spitting sounds to extract obstructions from the vagina. He strokes her womb with holy water, a peyote bud, and his magic feather wand to bring fertility.

A more spectacular purification rite for everyone occurs at an earlier stage of the pilgrimage. In a penitential service around the campfire, as indicated above, all pilgrims, including the maraakame, are asked to confess publicly every sexual misdeed in their lives. A transgression unconsciously omitted is eagerly brought to memory by one's spouse or neighbors, for a deliberate omission can endanger the ritual purity of every pilgrim present. Departing from the confession rituals in most other religious traditions, in this ceremony only sexual transgressions are cited, apparently more to symbolize the violated taboo than to elicit regret for moral sinfulness. For the mood of pilgrim auditors is one of laughter, prowess, and teasing rivalry, characteristic of veteran macho hunting companions. As an additional gesture, Ramon ties knots in a sacred cord for each act listed. Then, after the others draw as near as possible to the scorching heat of the Fire God, some even touching or leaping over the flames, he rolls the cord into a spiral and throws it into the fire. "Now you see that you are new. The Fire God has burned it all away.... Now we can cross over there. The maraakame has the power to do and undo."

Shamans in most Primal societies function in the same pattern as the Huichol maraakame — the inaugural vision, magic cure, and rites to bridge the mystical divide between human beings and the Sacred. Confession by one patient or an entire clan, for example, is often demanded as the precondition for a holistic cure. A shaman must often enlist telepathic powers to sort through these sins and ferret out the breach of taboo causing individual illness or a community plague, as in the stricken land of Sophocles' *Oedipus Rex*. Other traditional explanations given for the origin of sickness include an intrusion by some object or hostile spirit, a soul drifting astray, unrecognized leaks of magic energy, or attacks by an evil sorcerer. Nigerian and Ethiopian friends in San Francisco have told me repeatedly of unsolved poisonings and of alleged curses placed on them by some former neighbor envious of their chance to study abroad. As a Catholic priest I was once invited to the home of a young Ibo couple in San Francisco, impatient for a blessing to cure them of infertility. Distrustful of Eurocentric medicine, fearing unreasonable fees, neither the husband nor wife would consider approaching a gynecologist or fertility clinic. The husband could interpret this misfortune only as a curse, the black magic of his enemies, envious of his successful trip abroad.

Depending on the particular mythical rationale for disease, shamans see their healing as a concoction of the right sacred potion, a search for wandering souls, or a combat often aided by guardian animal spirits against alien magic. The ecstatic trance seems indispensable to their healing arts. Some cultures sanction the use of hallucinogens to achieve trance, whereas others restrict themselves to similar mind-altering chemicals triggered in the body by fasting, sleeplessness, intense meditation, and hypnotic rhythms. Most Primal peoples treat the shaman as an unbounded spiritual factotum, whereas a few cultures sharply limit and differentiate this role. Members of some African traditions often consult the *nganga* or medicine man for help to pass a driver's test, select a wife or husband, recover lost property, and detect or even prevent a crime. This inclusive figure can be a priest, lawyer, policeman, physician, and magician. Yet in Achebe's reconstruction of Ibo village life in his novel *Arrow of God,* the aging priest Ezeulu and his herbalist brother Okeke quarrel because their father split his more comprehensive powers between them. When Ezeulu's family needs medicine, he shows contempt for the profession by sending for some worthless herbalist whose doctoring cannot even support the man with three meals a day.

Some cultures interpret the shaman's role according to popular Hindu beliefs about the karma-determined fate of each migratory soul. Thus, they often consult the shaman not as protector of the dead or as warrior against alien spirits but as medium and seer to locate new reincarnations. The Primal Sinkyo tradition in Korea sets up an interesting distinction between male and female shamans. The men are *pansoo* exorcists, playing drums and brasses, shouting mantras to summon or banish spirits, whereas *mutang* women mediums dance and entertain the spirits, communicating with them in an ecstasy.[14] A Korean friend of mine recently attended his father's nine-hour funeral rites in Seoul, conducted by a group of shaman women. During her intense dancing and trance, one medium addressed him in his father's voice, lamenting that this son had not yet married nor succeeded in business. Two shamans dressed themselves like infants, representing his brother and sister, dead shortly after birth, whom he had never heard about before. Grains of rice dumped at random on a tray were construed as a butterfly. Assisted by the shamans, my friend interpreted this design as an indication his father would return in his next life as a butterfly, a free spirit whose unbridled youth had been repressed during his previous incarnation for the sake of family duty.

Shamans within these traditions, of course, can abuse their powers and are commonly warned by prophets in their midst against religious distortion. The Navajo story "Coyote Holds a Full House in His Hand" by Leslie Silko gives a bawdy critique of the adulation and perks that too many shamans take for granted. In this story, all the Hopi men have withdrawn to kiva caves to prepare for the annual Bean Dance, leaving the women vulnerable, especially to a laid-back Laguna drifter visiting the reservation. Introducing himself to a house of self-assured women as a reluctant medicine man, the drifter, named after the trickster folk-hero Coyote, offers to cure a sick woman elder only if all her clanswomen will participate in the ceremony. He plays on their gullibility — the cure is free; the shaman is handsome; and all the participants must do is lift their skirts to have him rub wood ash on their thighs. No one doubts his healing power during the solemn ritual. Once the line of eager patients ends, they overwhelm him with gifts of pastries. Calculated to outrage the protective macho Hopi warriors, the final trophy Coyote carries with him in his escape back to Laguna territory is a snapshot of all these ash-streaked devotees surrounding their favorite shaman.[15]

It is customary in many Native American societies for a young male to undergo an initiatory vision quest as an introduction to his lifelong spiritual journey. He endures a long fast and vigil in some isolated hole or hut, praying to be given this crucial vision. In some cultures shamans are selected precisely because of their predisposition to enter and control trance states. They have the capacity to empathize, sometimes even replicating the patient's illness by induced hysterical symptoms. I shall never forget a scene of impassioned Christian faith healing in Daniel Petrie's 1980 film *Resurrection.* Cameras close in on the sensitive hands and face of the extraordinary actress Ellen Burstyn. Touching her elderly patient gently, gesture by gesture she takes on symptoms of this contorted arthritic victim, who in turn marvels at her own gradually rejuvenated body. Similarly, among Tenino Indians near the Columbia River in Oregon, the shaman tries to suck an alien spirit out of the patient's body, stiffens, falls into convulsions, and loses consciousness. Then, propped up by two assistants, he spits this captive spirit into his cupped hands and sets it in flight, back to its suitable place in nature.

Astounding empathy, psychodrama and mime, hypnosis, the placebo-authority and charism of the healer's costume and repute — all these shamanic techniques of cure have their recognizable parallels in psychoanalysis and the best current styles of psychotherapy. Over the patient's body the shaman utters an incantation, derived from a social myth believed deeply by the sick woman and her community. The anthropologist Lévi-Strauss offers a persuasive interpretation of this cure. Most shamans relive again and again in all its original pain the earlier crisis from which their own neurosis stemmed, before it had been overcome. They abreact or reenact this sacred moment of their visionary experience and introduce it as an explanatory myth into the patient's consciousness. Inserted by pantomime and magic into the patient's inner life, the healer takes the place of her injured ego and tries to connect her pain with the guardian or malevolent spirits in which she has never ceased to believe.[16]

Although most contemporary psychotherapies depend more on listening than on oratory and incantation, I am convinced their cures bank on a secure atmosphere surrounding the myths of transformation implied in each therapy. The psychologist Rollo May, for example, has described the almost magical reassuring effect of psychological labels, such as primal scene, resistance, or transference. He believes the task of psychotherapy is to give the unconscious a name, not as a substitute for transformed behavior but as an aid to it. Names are symbols of the attitudes adopted toward a person's disturbance. The image you have of yourself can change by adopting new names and a new myth.[17] Jung tells how he would often reach for an old alchemy book from his office shelf to portray a frightened patient's mad fantasy, expressed in a slightly more creative form centuries before. One therapeutic effect of such an approach is to welcome back into the mainstream of human history an isolated schizophrenic, for instance, now promised solidarity with great poets and religious visionaries. Out of the terrifying psychotic break, like the shaman's inaugural vision and initiatory journey into the unconscious, it is possible to gain the power to heal others. For "only the wounded physician heals."

MAGIC OF THE GIFT

After two years working in a reservation legal aid office, a close friend of mine told about the breakup with his girlfriend, a young Navajo woman, and about his search for new work in a law firm. As a parting gift to my friend, a man of Asian-American and Christian background, the woman treated him to a prayer meeting with her shaman, so the couple could each find strength, healing, and foresight into job prospects. The young lawyer described that windy December evening when they were both ushered into a reservation hogan built just for storage and religious purposes. Dressed in jeans, boots, and a cowboy hat, the old shaman whom she addressed as Grandfather sat facing east, cross-legged on a blanket. He opened a case brought with him — arrowheads, eagle feathers, peyote buttons, a prayer staff. Each item would make its appearance at the correct ritual moment.

At the center of the dirt floor was a fire, with patterns of live coals from which the shaman proceeded to decipher sacred forecasts. Singing and praying, the shaman also wandered outside for ten-minute intervals to blow a thin bone whistle for attracting the spirits. The evening culminated in a blessing with his eagle feather, catching up smoke twirls to anoint my friend's body. As the old man later packed up his case to leave, he mentioned feeling wiped out after these sessions. He felt that any shaman worthy of the name must at times turn down pleas for help because the ritual takes too much out of him.

Most people agree that the perfect gift represents what both the giver and recipient commonly value most. Weighing the implications of this Navajo woman's farewell gift, you feel certain of her spiritual values, and also probably of her departing lover's. The human and sacred implications of any gift exchange first occurred to me during a museum tour of the celebrated Hideyuki Oka packaging and gift-wrapping collection from traditional Japan. In a range of samples from lacquered chests of candy to giant bamboo-lined buckets, materials of wood, straw, and paper were crafted in the most daring and brilliant ways to present a few rice dumplings or pickled eggs handed from one Japanese to another. It is certain that ritual presentation and exchange prove more important than the things exchanged.

Roland Barthes has a stunning snapshot of two Japanese women in kimonos bowing low before each other, arms and knees resting in a decreed position, with a gift situated halfway between their faces. This is not an encounter between two ego domains, but a flowing ceremonial network of forms, a gift suspended between two vanishing shadows. In the act of giving I empty myself, transcending the mere hunger to give and accept, to love and be loved.[18]

In practice, however, gifts are touched by your own mortality. They betray the unconscious values, needs, and expectations of the giver, and most of all, the image the giver has formed of the recipient. You might map out a young girl's career by the gift of a recipe book or nurse's uniform, or confirm your possessive claim over her by childish gifts that arrest her maturity. The Huichol woman described earlier in this chapter, the one Ramon attempted to cure of infertility, shapes a remarkably touching gift to offer the Gods of Wirikuta. It is a small votive gourd, decorated on the inner surface with an angular stick figure of beeswax imprinted with colored beads and bright wool yarn — the image of a baby. Few things could seem of greater value to her at that time. Perhaps the Gods resemble her enough to smile at the sight of a small baby. And besides, busy in governing the universe, they need a memento of her petition.

In a comparable illustration from the Chickasaw Native American story "Making Do" by Linda Hogan, a young mother endures the tragic deaths of one baby after another and a series of shiftless lovers. Yet like her mother and grandmother, Roberta has always learned to "make do" — turning Coke bottle-caps, for instance, or empty bleach containers into works of art. Far from the reservation, working in a Colorado mountain town grocery store, she manages to get on with life. There she fills the store windows with wooden birds she has whittled as gifts to delight the spirits of her dead children. Now and then Roberta sends some of her carved toys back to be placed on their graves at the Chickasaw reservation.[19]

The religious rationale and feelings behind a sacred offering seldom differ from one's habitual gift-giving attitudes toward other human beings. For instance, inspired by feelings of solidarity as described before, the pilgrims are swept into a heartfelt gift exchange during their hours at the sacred Wirikuta threshold. Picking cactus to fill their buckets, many address a plant in terms of endearment and lay aside what seems the largest, juiciest, or most symmetrical specimen. They chew peyote constantly as they work, eager to bring the finest peyote gifts back to families left behind. Pilgrims wander from one person to another, handing over their most cherished buds and receiving some in return, blessing a person and placing a piece on the tongue. Every communal peyote-eating ceremony during the rest of the pilgrimage emphasizes this ritual exchange.

For the Huichol and most other Primal religions, the community cannot be separated from its Sacred Center. Illustrating the African Triangle premise, the Huichole address almost all their prayers to an active realm of ancestral and nature spirits — imagined as the Ancient Ones who made the first pilgrimage, for example, or Tatewari the Fire God, or Deer-Peyote, the totem guardian spirit. At every Huichol meal, showers of tortilla bits, egg, and melon are scattered up and down and in four directions to feed the Gods before people begin eating. At shrines stationed along the pilgrimage route, pilgrims leave coins and lighted votive candles to accompany their prayers. The sacred water holes of San Luis Potosi are the choice location to open packages of handmade gifts, bless them with holy water, and display them carefully "for our Mothers to see." Some of the arrows, yarn designs, food, or gourds are then placed in the water holes, offered with prayers for rain, fertility, and a successful harvest. And from these maternal cavities, life-giving water is bottled and taken home to sprinkle the maize.

Later Ramon piles up the remaining gifts at Wirikuta near holes left by the uprooted peyote. There he chants for a while and sets the gifts ablaze. Then with his feather wand he fans the smoke or gift essence toward the sacred mountains of Deer-Peyote. Tatewari the Fire God is often the focus of these offerings. The families left behind feed a sacred fire throughout pilgrimage time with a wood supply selected earlier by each pilgrim. Pilgrims at every meal during the journey set aside portions, which they offer to Tatewari's flames once they return home. The fire will also include whatever tobacco and sacred Wirikuta cactus spines still remain in their pouches. Just as the Huichole must befriend and propitiate the slain deer, or the cut maize, so they must somehow reciprocate toward Deer-Peyote for the cactus taken from Wirikuta and toward the fire for its generous warmth. Collect more cactus than needed, neglect to leave gifts, and Deer-Peyote on the next pilgrimage might adopt your very attitudes, measure for measure. Perhaps he will hide the sacred cactus or withhold other crucial gifts from his people.

Primal religions have seemed more aware than most other religions about our immersion in debt to invisible spirits, the dead Ancestors and tradition, the forces of nature. The world is a "Thou," alive with spiritual power flowing back and forth, and the most worthwhile achievements depend on access to the source of this power. Never to be regarded as an unconditional possession, power must be balanced and replenished for individuals and the community by the regular performance of ritual. All that exists is already a gift. To keep things in balance, we must give to one another and, by offerings, give to the spirits, so that power will continue circulating from the invisible to the visible world.[20]

Prophets in many religious traditions tend to dismiss magic as phony science or as manipulative religion. Yet for Primal societies magic implies a sense of kinship and empathy among human beings, animals, plants, and the world of spirits. In Wagner's *Ring of the Nibelungs,* Siegfried tastes a drop of dragon blood after slaying Fafnir and realizes he can now understand the language of birds and the natural world. The religious offering and sacrifice — a peyote banquet, for example, or the holocaust of a prized deer to release its gift-essence skyward — are a prayer of request not only to approach the Sacred Center but to share in the vision and life-giving magic of the Gods.

Potlatch and Its Counterfeits

It is tempting to magnify this Huichol utopia of gift-giving into a scenario of Primal everyday life. Dealings within a Primal community, of course, are seldom mere economic transactions. The anthropologist Marcel Mauss calls them a total social fact. Such exchanges imply reciprocal giving for the sake of friendship, magic power, security, status, social and moral influence. The same range of attitudes for gift-exchange within the community, even the attempt to bribe and bargain, will influence the mood of each person's ritual offerings to the Gods.

On trips to many cultures older and more homogeneous than my own, I am often stunned by their unsparing hospitality. At the same time, the ruinous expenses of their festivals to celebrate birth, initiations, marriage, death, and other social rites look outrageous. For example, at a random compliment of mine about their artistic taste, a young Saudi neighbor once made a prompt surrender of his expensive prayer rug, and a poor widow in Madras tried to force on me the single valued picture on her wall. Yet I never intended my compliments to be taken so literally, and I worried that by receiving such presents I might incur some insane new obligation. In another instance, a Chinese friend throughout our meals together likes to select with chopsticks the best morsels from her plate and transfer them onto my own. At the risk of provoking a cross-cultural misunderstanding, I recycle a few of my own best morsels back to her plate, but she refuses to take them.

Just as gifts unsuitably cheap may humiliate some people, so gifts too valuable may impose a crushing obligation. After the Second World War, for example, the Marshall Plan built important friendships for the United States. Yet I can imagine why it produced some resentful satellites. Handed enormous grants, a nation might fret that the price exacted had to be endless gratitude and an endorsement of unilateral American foreign policy decisions.

The Sun Dance giveaway rite of Canadian Northern Blackfoot Indians fascinated the psychologist Abraham Maslow as a model for a humane socialist economics. Civilizations handle their wealth by either funneling or siphoning. Wealth funneled toward the rich makes them richer at the poor's expense. Yet wealth siphoned off the top by philanthropy or a graduated income tax can enrich the whole society. During the Sun Dance giveaway ritual the entire Blackfoot community gathers in a circle around piles of blankets, food, clothes, and cases of Pepsi-Cola, which their leader, White-Headed Chief, has gathered for years. Then standing up to boast of his family's legendary glory, in a lordly gesture he surrenders all this wealth to widows, orphans, and the disabled. Stripped of all material wealth but the clothes he stands in, he has proved his generosity and thus a profound inner wealth. In this community, the citizen listed as possessing the most cattle and horses is not even acknowledged as wealthy by the group. For, they complain, "he keeps it." If this neighbor won a lottery, others would envy or loathe his winning. On the contrary, if White-Headed Chief won, almost everyone would enjoy it.

There is no human value so exalted that it cannot be twisted to undermine the very self-conversion such a value demands. "Potlatch" is the Chinook Indian generic name

given to the ceremony just described, prevalent with some variations among indigenous people of Alaska and the Vancouver region, Melanesia, and Polynesia. Potlatch
is a ritual gift-feast, expressing the host's rank and prodigality. It may occasionally
aspire to magnanimity, which means a forthright generosity that does not humiliate
others. Often its goals have turned out more pedestrian: to announce a group claim
to some title or privilege, to celebrate a family change of status, or to return with
interest those gifts received at a previous potlatch. At times behind the hospitality,
Lévi-Strauss and other anthropologists find a thinly concealed agenda — "to surpass
rivals in generosity, to crush them if possible under future obligations which it is
hoped they cannot meet, thus taking from them privileges, titles, rank, authority, and
prestige."[21]

Masters of the fine art of one-upmanship, coastal Haida Indians used to stage
face-saving potlatches to blot out some specified affront to the host's dignity, and
vengeance potlatches where two clans would line up in mad competition. By shred-
ding blankets and pouring out expensive oil, sometimes with nasty joviality, they
seemed to work out their aggression by reciprocal destruction of property. Perhaps
an ironic parallel in the recent past might be the American-Soviet nuclear missile
build-up, each vying for years to outspend the other, until one at last caves in to
bankruptcy.

Haida family members of a successful potlatch host could expect afterward to occupy privileged seats at feasts, speak first at public meetings, be quick to threaten
a new vengeance potlatch at any infringement of their recently vindicated status. A
poor person would be impotent to confront a richer opponent, who in turn might
destroy more property than the poor could amass. In this parody of the exalted
reciprocity principle, you chance upon a Primal-society scenario of conspicuous con-
sumption, the conscience-money philanthropy of robber barons, or those proud lapel
buttons that say "I gave."

MASKS AND THE SHADOW SIDE

The distinctive style of headgear and garb worn for the Huichol pilgrimage has
already been emphasized. This consists of feather caps, cloaks of skin from the slain
totem animal, amulets, rattles, bells, the maraakame's magic feather wand, and a
ritual drumhead fashioned from the scrotum of a Sacred Deer. Special vestments establish a new identity for the shaman, who in many Primal societies will heighten
this alteration by the use of body paint and facial or full-body masks. To convey hazards encountered or wisdom retrieved in trance, the shaman paints, composes poetry,
dances, sings, and dramatizes journey details.

The Paleolithic cave drawings at Lascaux, and most recently at Grotte Chauvet,
are often cited as the earliest shamanic art. Perhaps the history of drama also began
in the shaman's visionary pantomime. For once the sacred animal guide takes over,
shamans will howl or snort and imitate graphic animal movements. They sing to keep
up their courage during the descent to the underworld, leap or pant at arduous climbs,
balance on imaginary tightropes, shade their eyes when confronted by radiant spirits.

The shaman's incantations and frenzied gestures during a cure may at first look
like tricky showmanship. However, besides the obvious intent to dazzle and com-

pel belief, this performance often mimes the legendary travels of an ancient tribal hero. Or as mentioned before, it reenacts the exact prayers and dance that occasioned the inaugural vision in this particular shaman's earlier life. According to the Joycean monomyth pattern of most hero legends, a hero separates from ordinary life, journeying into a realm of sacred wonder, encounters dangers, wins a victory, and returns home with magic power and wisdom to share with the community. By dramatizing this visionary quest again, the shaman hopes to entice a sick soul into the dynamics of the myth and to recover the right healing magic.

More egalitarian than most other shamanic adventures, the Huichol pilgrimage plunges both maraakame and the other travelers into a single monomythic quest. Before they leave home, each is assigned by Ramon a God's name and a specified offering at Wirikuta to express affinity with that God. At the Wirikuta campfire, Ramon lets the peyote grip him completely, and as he stares at the fire and enjoys intimacy with the Fire God, ribbons of flame spell out to him new pilgrim names to be borne by each person until all reach home. First-time pilgrims are blindfolded because of their special vulnerability. Confined now and then to an abbreviated diet of baby food, they are reminded of their need for an initiatory rebirth. All the pilgrims are invited to discard their old identity and, especially by receiving peyote communion, to assume the Sacred Deer-Peyote identity that now flows through their bloodstream. Throughout their pilgrimage, Ramon becomes the Fire God, and his followers become the deified Ancient Ones who followed Tatewari in the primordial exodus.

Comprehensive mask traditions in Primal cultures include not only the carved face mask but full African and Polynesian costumes of cloth and raffia and leaves, ornamentation in the form of tattoos and body mutilation, paint and cosmetics, stilts or any other device to alter one's ordinary identity. I have often studied the imaginative African masks in glass cases at the De Young Museum in San Francisco. Though it looks lifeless, a mask is usually a long-established script to be interpreted by the dancer in a trancelike performance before an audience chanting and clapping to music. A mask may protect its wearer from the evil eye and predatory spirits, enhance the warrior's image of invincibility, change a shaman into the uncanny totem animal, bold and unpredictable. Eyeholes are sometimes omitted intentionally to enclose the wearer's field of vision within an inner cell of contemplation.

Although explanations vary, the ancestral spirit or God is believed to be present somehow within each sacred mask. Thus mask carvers do not so much dominate their materials as search meditatively for a presence there and bring it to new life. Aspirana Taylor's "The Carving" is a subtle Maori tale about an artist straining to find his own sacred identity. By daytime Willy feels diminished by nine hours of digging fence-post holes or by pressure from his wife to repair the bathroom tiling. By night he works at his true love, the gradual carving of a great, muscular Paleolithic ancestor, with an erect penis. Like the sacred mask already described, his emerging statue represents the heroic ancestral spirit that Willy would like to embody. Yet at no stage in the creative process does he feel either his own life or his carving has achieved this reincarnation. After he watches thousands of his own Maori people on television in a protest march over the loss of their land, he realizes this huge statue is just a lie. So in anger he dismembers the figure, from its assertive masculinity to the tattooed massive arms and legs.[22]

In many Primal traditions, when the sacred power in a deteriorated mask needs new embodiment, the old mask remnants must be interred with reverence. A Shinto temple in Tokyo, for instance, annually cremates old dolls and Bunraku puppets at a special liturgy. Most Primal masks not in present use are concealed and guarded, encircled by severe taboos. To destroy the dramatic illusion by peeking at performers behind their masks violates taboo and threatens to dispel the sacred power concentrated there. Achebe's novel *Things Fall Apart* pictures the desecration of an Ibo masked ancestral spirit by the militant Christian convert Enoch. Enoch has already tested the impotent taboos of his former religion by killing and eating a sacred python revered by the entire village. During the annual Earth-Goddess ceremony, with bands of masked spirits abroad, women and all the uninitiated are forbidden to gaze on them. When some wandering spirits begin to cane Enoch for his earlier violation of the snake taboo, he catches one of them and rips off his mask. The others immediately surround their exposed companion to shield him from the profane glance of women and children. All pledge to revenge the Ancestor's murder by burning down the local Christian chapel.

Role Reversal and Possession

The Huichole have devised a unique dramatic rite to signal their entrance into the final sacred vicinity of Wirikuta. With playful ingenuity they begin to refer to each action and object by its antonym. Directions to the right mean left; complaints of cold mean heat; women are addressed as men; joy can be expressed only by sadness. Antonyms offered spontaneously as jokes become confusing obligatory game rules from then on. "We shall now begin to pick flowers," one pilgrim remarks, "under a full moon in Mexico City."

Is there some hidden religious significance to the reversals? "We change the names of things," Ramon explains simply, "because when we cross over there into Wirikuta, things are so sacred that all is reversed." Clearly one effect of a ritual reversal is to diminish the sense of conventional time and space and the habitual patterns of identity. A recurrent theme in most mystical traditions is the metaphorical eclipse or annihilation of the ego, a topic that will be developed in later chapters. "In the depths of this darkness," says Van Ruysbroeck, a medieval Christian mystic, "where the loving spirit has died to itself, the revelation of God and eternal life begins." Utopia and paradise, the almost impossible dream, can also be represented effectively by a world upside-down, by paradoxes of negation and reversal. The imagination behind Thomas More's *Utopia,* for example, thrives on privative nouns and name inversions, which deprive the reader of what they pretend to describe. Utopia in Greek means nowhere, the Achoreans are people without a place, Anydus a river without water, Ademus a leader with no people to lead.

In Primal religions, and also in any tradition permeated and at times besieged by an active spirit world, a person's repressed hostility and hidden shadow often show up in experiences of possession by spirits or demons. Haitian Voodoo, for instance, offers disciples a range of conventional trance-roles, each with its distinctive biography. If you are mounted by the snake-spirit, your tongue flickers and you writhe on the ground. If mounted by the feminine sea-spirit, you prance about seductively. Yet in many other trance traditions, the spirits may be more elusive and anonymous.[23]

Possession is a sanctioned religious situation, where people have the chance, with partial or complete loss of consciousness, to articulate and act out the urges usually repressed. During the annual Singapore Thaipusan rites, for instance, I once observed and even interviewed a number of young Hindu Tamils gradually fading into trance. I backed away in frightened disbelief as a skinny young clerk, who seemed quite shy in our interview before, began thumping his chest in trance, bellowing like Tarzan. And a svelte, mannerly woman now gorged herself in animal frenzy. In those societies that view possession as diabolical, a trance condition is expected to plunge you into the forbidden underside of social conventions and also of your own unconscious life. Exorcism seems a plausible corollary, then, to restore self-mastery.

A showcase in modern secular life for observing the impact of reversals is the Carnival rite. This celebration is generally accepted as a safety valve for society's repressed deviants, whose classical prototypes are the clown and transsexual exhibitionist. The reversals turn conventional expectations inside out and expose their arbitrariness. However, the grotesque false face may also trigger a sadistic orgy for robbers and Halloween pranksters. In my own teaching experience, I have been shocked to see an otherwise reticent college student changed into a boisterous extrovert by performing in a Meeting of Minds classroom psychodrama. A mask usually releases you from the ordinary repertoire of defenses, from the everyday face you hide behind. If you are now no longer your conventional self, maybe you can risk testing out other potential selves. The director Peter Brook, for example, often asks his cast to perform wearing plain white masks. Liberated for a time from their subjectivity, actors often approach a role with new insight, and by withdrawing attention from the face, they gain heightened awareness of their whole body.[24]

The actor par excellence for Brook is the disciplined Balinese he observed during rehearsals, touching prayerfully a series of sacred traditional masks. In my prologue, I described this dancer's habit of communing with each mask in succession, until actor and role became almost identical reflections of each other. A definite tension and tempo in the body, a change in breathing, can be discerned for each specific role, even before the actor dons a single mask. Balinese usually dip a frangipani petal in holy water and sprinkle it on the mask, and then on their own face. Actors have been known to take a mask home to study its traits and story and pray before the mask, now propped on the family altar. They may even sleep next to it, hoping to evoke dreams associated with its image. The role or mask might contain forces within itself greater than the forces at an actor's conscious disposal, and sometimes almost by magic may transform the good actor into a truly inspired one.

The interpretation of spirit-possession, trance, and any other type of temporary breakdown or breakthrough depends on differing cultural expectations. During trance participants might passively observe their own estranged performance, might feel some voluntary control of events, or might lose consciousness and have no recollection later. In his virtuoso analysis of children riding wooden horses on a carousel, the sociologist Erving Goffman has observed younger children terrified or mesmerized by the role of heroic rider. Yet older children develop sophisticated ploys to mock or tamper with a role they can no longer take seriously. You develop techniques to play a role or play at it, to get into a role and be taken in by it or get beyond it.[25]

The Huichol pilgrim is invested with the name and identity of a God. The Kono dancer in various West African traditions receives instructions on how to serve the spirit dwelling within a sacred mask. In both situations, each individual responds with attitudes that range from ecstatic immersion to partial or even ironic detachment. For the committed believer, the ritual of donning the mask is a sacrament. The believer prays for self-abandonment, for openness toward the mask's magic power, for the rapt experience of possession by the Sacred. Only the shallow actor playing a saint's role night after night can remain untouched by the perspective and values shaped through this new identity. The goal for a Huichol pilgrim, as for the follower of any spiritual tradition, is to live out the Wirikuta experience of worship and sacred fellowship after return home from the pilgrimage.

In summary, by a religious Way I mean whatever explicit or partially conscious drive, credo, or value system lies at the root of behavior marked by awe, commitment, ecstasy, and moral seriousness. If you probe underneath daily behavior and values and language to find that which ultimately underlies the life of a people or an individual, you will find a source that you can label religious. This center of ultimate coherence — whether person or force, imaged or imageless, named or unnameable — I have called the Sacred.[26]

Granted the random diversity of indigenous Ways, the Primal religious factor cannot be located readily without a rudimentary map. I have introduced a grid transparency of four motifs — rites of the hunt and pilgrimage, shamanic guidance, gift-giving, and mask-transformation. Such a grid highlights the underlying religious patterns in Primal and most other Ways, notably in the Huichol peyote pilgrimage.

Small Huichol groups each year set out on pilgrimage to Wirikuta. By the time they return home, they have completed a ritual passage back to their historical origins as a people — reestablishing a bridge now between human flatlands and the sacred upper world, or between ordinary human needs and the magic energy of plants and animals. They have been led by a shaman with the power to heal body and mind, forgive sins, and induce a sacred trance during which he receives visions of import for his people. The small community deepens in solidarity by repeated group rites of confession, purification, peyote communion, animal sacrifice, and meaningful gift-offerings to one another, to the ancestral spirits, and to the forces of nature. To be initiated into the realm of Wirikuta means to adopt a new godlike mask of identity, speak and dress and see in a new symbolic way, and undergo an inner transformation.

Most Huichol rites, sacred stories, and attitudes call to mind immediate parallels from other major religious traditions. Such comparisons have been suggested throughout this introductory chapter and will become more evident as the book unfolds. Stunning as these parallels appear, our ability to grasp them fully is limited, because the human imagination, after all, is finite. The mind runs up not only against a limited number of narrative-blueprints in plotting a novel but against a limited set of archetypal patterns to structure experience.

Drawing near to the various religious traditions, you will hear people of spiritual sensitivity recounting comparable experiences marked by metaphors of flight, combat, courtship, or homecoming. Their common religious destination is often a city ruled by ideal justice, a communion banquet with the Gods, a garden reuniting nature and all living beings, or a definitive new birth. In all these Ways, too, you meet a few recurring polarities — the dialectic between an original group charism and its historical embodiment in institutions, for instance, or between traditionalists and progressives responding to the challenge of contemporary secularity.

Sketch of the yin-yang process — two forces complementary but not contradictory, each needing the other for completeness. From this dialectic eight trigrams evolve, which then combine to form the sixty-four hexagram chapter headings of I Ching, the Book of Changes.

2

Chinese-Japanese Ways

The survey questionnaire in a magazine reads, "Do you practice or belong to a religion?" Most people I know from Chinese and Japanese family backgrounds greet this question with a quick flustered no. A Japanese student attending the University of San Francisco, for instance, first introduced herself to me as someone of no *shukyo,* no religion. She attends no church, says no formal bedtime or table prayers, and avoids the religion section in bookstores. Yet after more patient listening, I realized she has long been developing a self-critical conscience. She follows a disciplined life of study. She even meditates along the ocean beach. Though identified with no institutional religion, she at present owns up to *shukyo shin,* a true religious heart and feeling.

In a parallel situation, two friends of Hong Kong origin, reluctant to identify themselves with any religion, abruptly decided to marry, offering reasons which at first sounded bizarre, if not oppressive. Her grandfather had been warned by a fortune-teller of his own impending death, so he determined to have at least one immediate great-grandchild before he died. How soon could his eldest grandchild get married? She and her parents did not hesitate to obey his wishes. However, her wedding had to occur in the remaining few months of that year, not the next year, when the groom's sister planned to marry. For the planets do not permit two family marriages within the same year. Before setting the date, both their families next sorted through lists of those restaurants large enough to hold many guests and found every place nearby booked for months except for one weekend, left universally untaken. This date turned out to be a time that local astrologers thought unlucky for everyone. The couple's wedding announcement could be printed only on red paper, an auspicious color, and had to include the yin-yang complementary sketches of a phoenix and dragon. Foods chosen for the banquet had to maintain a yin-yang balance of ingredients and possess names avoiding any echo of the Mandarin or Cantonese terms for catastrophe.

THE TAO PROFILE

The ordinary way to identify your own individual religion is to piece together a statement of your ultimate beliefs. However, your closest friends could discern your religious identity also by watching your most important values reveal themselves in characteristic behavior or in patterns of worship and meditation. The Primal Ways, as described in the first chapter, are intended more to be danced than to be preached or theologized. Their most highly developed features are not a creed, but rituals, taboos, and stories. In a comparable way, when the young Chinese groom mentioned above insists he is in no way religious, he refers mostly to creed. Yet alert to a minefield of taboos, both husband and wife have in fact been shaped by a tacit Way that reaches into every area of their lives. Though a Confucian creed may not be fathomed by the average follower, the Confucian Way is a highly sophisticated tradition of moral attitudes and ceremony. No doubt its authoritative model is Confucius himself, no mere Humanist ethician, but in many specific ways an overtly religious man. In the Analects, the most widely quoted Confucian classic, you can observe him performing rites toward ancestral spirits faithfully, offering sacrifices to exorcise illness or purify an army before military expeditions, and directing his daily prayers to what he calls Heaven or the Will of Heaven.

For insight into the Chinese-Japanese Ways, it is vital to retain a few other premises that surfaced while exploring the Primal Ways in chapter 1. I can think of at least four. First, the religious factor permeates every dimension of life, as the center without which nothing else has meaning. Religion can be spotted readily in shrine attendance, consulting a sacred text, chanting a formal prayer. But it is no less present when a person kowtows in respect to an elder, tries to balance bodily forces through acupuncture or herbal medicine, or arranges flowers and food ingredients just so. It is crucial to search for the religious factor in everyday situations, not just in an extraordinary crisis, healing, or epiphany.

Second, many Primal traditions have shown an identity flexible enough to retain essentials even while merging into a more aggressive religion. Similarly, Chinese spirituality often includes a harmonious blend of Confucian, Taoist, Buddhist, and Primal ingredients. To the first three, Japanese spirituality may add a further Shinto factor. With true religious integrity, perhaps you live by a Confucian ethic and a Taoist aesthetic, get married at a Shinto wedding, and are buried at a Buddhist funeral.

To appreciate a third similarity between the Primal Way and the Tao, it is helpful to remember the African Triangle premise, with its diagram of a sacred source at the top, often left unnamed. Emanating from this God or Godhead are two triangle legs, the ancestral and nature spirits, who are the focus of everyday Primal worship. Almost all prayers cited in the Huichol Wirikuta pilgrimage, for instance, are addressed to ancestral spirits, the so-called Ancient Ones, and to two nature spirits — Tatewari the Fire God and the totem guardian spirit Deer-Peyote. In a parallel situation, I seldom hear my non-Christian Chinese and Japanese students speak of a Creator God at all. Instead they represent the Sacred by ancestral spirits or impersonal cosmic forces for good and evil. Prayer and healing occur only in this dramatic setting. Such ancestral spirits bear the authority and function that the Judeo-Christian-Muslim God represents in Eurocentric societies. No physical or mental suffering will be cured until the ancestors are remembered daily and treated with more respect. This attitude prevails even among Buddhists, whose theology would otherwise stress the ongoing reincarnation of dead ancestors among the living.[1]

As a final similarity, the Primal interaction of cosmic and magic forces prepares one to appreciate the Chinese-Japanese sacred cosmos. Many reflective Taoist believers, for example, will describe the Sacred not as a Supreme Being separable from everything created but as the originating process itself. It is an electromagnetic field of yin and yang, people interacting with their natural environment, physical with spiritual forces, dead ancestors with the living, microcosm with macrocosm. Hungry ghosts or cycles of stars might tamper with one's destiny. A single moral choice today could temporarily disrupt or reconfirm the evolving harmony of the universe. This ordered process and the plan regulating it are what I mean by Tao.

The term "Tao," essentially untranslatable, has been prized for its baffling flexibility. Someone once computed that the Taoist classic Tao Te Ching uses this term seventy-six times, and seldom with exactly the same connotations. The noun means path or channel; the verb means to tell or guide. Thus, the many schools contemporary with Confucius and Lao Tzu each taught their own Tao, their doctrine, code of moral guidance, or spiritual Way. Tao at a more metaphysical level means the dynamic cosmic process described in the preceding paragraph — primordial chaos emerging into a balanced yin-yang dialectic. But Taoist, Shinto, and Confucian traditions each contribute a distinctive coloration to the term.

Despite quarrels between some of their adherents, the Confucian and Taoist perspectives, for instance, can be appreciated as opposite ends on a spectrum, two polarities which, like yang and yin, are complementary, not contradictory. Each without the other is a parody of itself; each needs the other for completeness. In this chapter the terms Confucian, Taoist, and Shinto will be abstracted for a moment from their ragged evolution in time and defined along lines set out by relatively recent scholars who are adherents of these Ways. This process of definition is complex. Even the Confucian and Taoist sacred texts cannot be approached as fundamentalist scriptures giving the exact mind of the masters; rather, the texts are multilayered compilations by later schools. For instance, the name Confucius, latinized form of Kung Futze or Master Kung, will stand in this chapter for core teachings of the Confucian school.

Different from both Taoist and Shinto emphases, the Confucian Tao refers to the Will of Heaven inscribed on every human heart. Legendary sages of the golden age came closest to embodying this ideal, so their example and teachings offer a human Tao virtually replicating the heavenly Tao. Wisdom of the revered past must be scrutinized and interpreted by each individual, and this teaching should be followed only when it matches the dictates of your interior *jen-tao,* a conscience that is truly human.

"*Jen* is the distinguishing characteristic of a human being," the Book of Mencius explains. "As embodied in human conduct, it is called Tao." The Chinese ideograph for jen consists of the word for "human being" and the numeral two. Jen can be defined as human-relatedness, implying love and compassion, but in an explicitly widening social perimeter. I shall call it large-heartedness. Defining each human being as a rational animal, Aristotle highlights the marks of reason and of continuity with the animal kingdom. Confucius, on the contrary, stresses that humanity is relational at its very core. The isolated, self-sufficient ego is not a complete human being. As the developing center of relationships within a community, you are expected to live compatibly, to learn empathy and civilized compromise.

Confucian Tao emphasizes the human person, social relationships, and civil order — in other words, the yang principle. Yang is associated with the heavens, light, fire, and masculinity. In contrast, yin connotes the earth, darkness, stillness, and femininity. And by reasserting this yin polarity, Taoists aim for a better yin-yang balance than they think Confucians can appreciate. The impersonal or transpersonal yin forces in the natural world have their own shape and rhythm, too dynamic to be contained by human institutions.

Unlike the Confucian emphasis, however, Taoists treat the ultimate Tao itself as unnameable, the sacred mystery underlying all reality. All you can do is try to ponder, worship, and live it. Yet this unreachable Tao has left its distant imprint in the natural world and yourself — *te* or *chi,* an uncoiling spring of hidden energy, the only Tao about which Taoists feel competent to teach. Unlike the medley of competing spiritualities, therapies, and creeds introduced from outside, the inner *tao-te* is your own unique human nature, viewed as potentially directive. This perspective suggests a few parallels in European thought: Bergson's elan vital, or the inner natura-naturans of Spinoza, Schelling, and later Idealist philosophers.

If the Taoist tradition tries to distill the essence of Tao-ness itself, Japanese Shinto is fascinated by an expanding multitude of Taos. The visitor to Japan cannot help but notice the confidence and gusto of a grandmother raking leaves in her yard, the elevator operator saluting her customers, the airport security guards moving in unison to check one's baggage. The most commonplace duty or role can be cultivated into a genuine art, an individual's own rigorous spiritual Way. What matters here is not substance but form, style, or training. The arts of self-defense or *judo,* fencing or *kendo,* flower arrangement or *kado,* calligraphy or *shodo,* and the tea ceremony or *chado* bring to mind a line of traditional techniques and rituals. Most arts of the ordinary have the syllable *do* or *to* as a suffix, the Japanese for Tao. The Sacred lies hidden in interior attitudes of commitment, serenity, and care.

Given this overview of the Confucian, Taoist, and Shinto Ways, the implications of each Tao will now be explored at greater depth.

THE CONFUCIAN WAY

The Confucian ideal is the wise gentleman prince, with a nobility not of pedigree but of moral achievement. The crucial means by which this prince reaches inner peace, and the entire society reaches a stable outer peace, is a life of ritual propriety or *li.* History has situated Kung Futze or Confucius alongside Lao Tzu and Chuang Tzu in China, Zoroaster in Persia, Gautama Buddha and Mahavira and the Upanishad texts in India, Plato and Aristotle in Greece, and the major Hebrew prophets. They flourished during the era of remarkable spiritual and moral insight from 800 to 300 B.C.E., which philosopher Karl Jaspers has called the Axial Period. Within all five centers of civilization a protest erupted almost in unison against patterns of dying symbol and ceremony no longer integrated with the rest of life. The conscientious believer was summoned to reinterpret the old religious myths, to recover a vital balance between ritual sacrifice and ethical responsibility.

For an illustration of moral outrage against abused religious formulas, compare the prophet Jeremiah in Israel with Confucius in China: "You keep saying, 'This place is the temple of the Lord, the temple of the Lord, the temple of the Lord!' This catchword of yours is a lie," says Jeremiah. "You steal, you murder, you commit adultery and perjury. . . . Do you think that this house that bears my name is a robbers' cave?" In the Analects, Confucius complains, "They say, 'It is li, it is li.' They say,

'It is according to the rules of propriety.' Are presents of gems and silk all that is meant by li? Music, music! Does it mean no more than bells and drums?"[2]

The Chinese ideograph for li portrays a sacrificial vessel with two pieces of jade raised above it, almost elevated for worship. Connotations of this word bear the stamp of a wide history — the liturgy of wine and food offerings to ancestral spirits; then the courtly feudal codes upholding privilege and stability; then a diminishing spectrum of everyday courtesies, rites of interaction, and familial obligations. Perusing the "Records of Ritual and Practice" in the Li Chi, a manual normative for centuries before Confucius edited it, you can locate the exact times, gestures, and music required for each specific sacrifice. You can look up the hierarchical placement of carriages in a cortege, for instance, or the customary period of bereavement regulated differently for each surviving family member. This is a manual of correct dress, bows, titles, with directions even how to cut and serve a melon depending on each person's rank at table.

In other words, li means the social-moral norm, a sense of appropriateness or suitability — what the French suggest by words like *politesse, courtoisie, urbanite, les forms, savoir-vivre*. I shall call it moral suitability. All these terms suggest the image of a charted, predictable life, with the aesthetic balance and elegance of a gavotte, each detail fitting into its proper place.

Confucius during the fifth century witnessed a China in chaos. The centralized Chou dynasty had been broken up into squabbling feudal enclaves. The gentry were displaced by merchants and entrepreneurs, the wisdom tradition and every chivalric code of warfare forgotten. What remained of value from the past seemed only tatters of li — rubrics of sacrifice, gestures of courtesy, proverbs that no longer made sense, all a heritage from the Hsia, Shang, and Chou dynasties. A famous Jewish Hasidic tale recounts the progressive distancing of successive generations from their central religious ritual, a malaise familiar to prophets in almost all world traditions. A rabbi of the first generation would carry the burden of his people to God by lighting a fire and saying a prayer at a definite place in the woods. In the final era, after the erosion of detail through history, a rabbi sits in his chair and realizes he does not know the prayer, the spot in the woods, nor how to light the fire, but at least can tell the story about how it was once accomplished. Experiencing a comparable spiritual diminishment in history, Confucius remained hopeful because he could at least reconstruct his people's sacred vestiges of li. Master of pragmatic compromise, he attracted conservatives by canonizing the forgotten past. Then he gradually enlisted progressives by reshaping the legendary past as an innovative criterion against which to measure both present disorder and a repudiated immediate past.

The Confucian reform insisted first on a recovered fidelity to the rubrics of traditional state and family liturgies of sacrifice. However, the ritual deed was to be matched by a devout state of mind. "I cannot bear to see . . . ritual performed without reverence," the Analects say, and "if someone is not genuinely 'present' at the sacrifice, it is as though there were no sacrifice." A second intent of the Confucian reform was to enlarge the scope of reverence and religious seriousness — shifted from particular sacrificial ceremonies to the realm of every human activity. Confucius reminds the ruling classes, "Deal with the common people as though you were officiating at an important sacrifice. Do not do to others what you would not like done to yourself."[3] The Golden Rule of ethics is reconnected back to its vital religious roots, so that all of life becomes ceremonial and harmonious, permeated by the Sacred.

There must be no mistake about Confucius's scorn for empty ritual. Jen and li must both be present in one's life and must work together. For instance, a selfless fidelity to the rubrics of moral suitability can, according to Confucius, gradually sink into one's bones. This process can in turn lead to a conversion of attitudes, so that the inner Tao will animate all ritual. As a parallel to this style of practical ethics, the pragmatist James-Lange theory, popular in the early twentieth century, prompts you to adopt and hold fast to an expression of tears, anger, or a smile until your inner feelings begin to accompany and become one with the outward gestures. The person who makes every effort to perform the mother's role, for example, will eventually become a true mother. "Let the prince be a prince, the minister a minister, the father a father, and the son a son." This is what Confucius means by "rectifying names" in the basic husband-wife, parent-child, friend-friend, elder-younger, ruler-subject relationships. You will not find li worthy of the name until it includes the large-heartedness and humanity of an inner jen-tao.[4]

Widespread distortions of Confucian moral suitability today, and a few garbled clichés in what might be called textbook Confucianism, deserve a careful audit. Stalled before these obstacles, critics often have no chance to appreciate a mature life shaped by genuine Confucian values. You can expect to meet at least three major fallacies, which will now be examined.

Tyranny of the Elders

Much of Chinese popular religious practice is centered on befriending clan and nature spirits, tapping their secret knowledge through arts of astrology, geomancy, and augury. I cited the efforts before by my Chinese-American friends to adjust their marriage plans to every sanction of the planets. They also wanted their new home to face an auspicious compass direction. Chinese students in my classes recount how many families before purchasing a new home commonly launch inquiries to guarantee that a building's former occupants have left no legacy of suicide or hungry ghosts. Radar as sensitive as this, tracking down every possible taboo, seems heightened to a feverish intensity by Confucius's reinstatement of ancestral rites.

At least once a year, some of the more affluent traditional Chinese families I know converge across oceans to celebrate a grave-site reunion in Hong Kong or Taiwan, trying to maintain a stable emotional and religious bond with the dead. In fact, many Taoist temples I have visited in Hawaii, Hong Kong, and Taiwan are lined wall after wall with snapshots of the recent dead. It is not surprising that someone brought up to pay exceptional respect to live elders will continue to seek the mediation and advice of these lordly figures after death. Clan gatherings to invoke and feed the ancestors symbolically at grave-sites or home altars, of course, strengthen ties not only between living and dead members but also among the living clan. Many prayer experiences and family rituals of my Chinese students center on their relationship with the entire clan, many of whom now reach back from the spirit world to make contact with living relatives.

A Korean Catholic priest once told me of prolonged sadness ever since his childhood shock over the premature death of his father. This young priest thought his traditional society, still swayed by unquestioned Confucian values, had treated all children without a father as crippled, lacking a suitable Confucian teacher and model. As potential delinquents, such children must try harder than others to earn esteem. Growing up under this fatalistic cloud, he found himself in irrational prayer even today, rebuking his father's spirit for dying on him. In another example, Maxine Hong Kingston recalls in *China Men* the many desperate letters her cousin Sao in America got for years from his mother in China. The woman would complain of starvation and neglect, begging for a fraction of the cash spent on his TV set, refrigerator, and other luxuries. After her death, her ghost finally lashed Sao into a frenzied trip home, where he heaped up extravagant offerings on her grave — gifts of food, shoes, clothes, and paper money. He poured wine on the earth and exploded firecrackers, neglecting not a single Chinese funeral custom. "Rest, Mother, rest," he wept in guilt, craving to get her ghost off his back.[5]

A stock theme in Confucian fiction is the wife's universal dilemma — to retain her own integrity while showing proper respect toward a new mother-in-law. In her Singapore story "Or Else, the Lightning God," Catherine Lim centers on a young pregnant wife, boastful that she has liberated herself from the Confucian taboos and superstitions. However, the "old one," forced upon Margaret and her husband because none of the other sons will put up with her imperious style, collides with Margaret repeatedly. At last the mother-in-law, pushed from the house in a rage, lays this grisly curse on her: "Those who are cruel to their elders will never prosper. You are bearing a child, but I curse you!" The remaining narrative shows how the allegedly liberated Margaret gradually caves in to the curse's psychological effects, so that her pregnancy is threatened. In the final scene, with Margaret sobbing for forgiveness, her reluctant mother-in-law writes down a retraction of her curse. A temple shaman burns the paper, dissolves it in water, and directs the humbled Margaret to drink the potion.[6]

It seems unfair to blame the teaching of Confucius for both an excessive control by living and dead elders and any exaggerated submission to these authorities. I think Confucius would respond that young people surrender too much authority, which their elders are overeager to snatch. And both sides have forgotten yin-yang balance, the golden mean stressed in his moral teaching — a vice is a virtue carried to extremes. In fact, he does warn against too much concern for the imagined whims of ancestors. "Till you have learned to serve human beings, how can you serve ghosts? Till you know about the living, how are you to know about the dead?"[7]

Among living people, those of age and experience get obvious deference in the Confucian system. A deserving old age, however, is no mere accumulation of years. Yuan Jang, whom most commentators identify not as some young disciple but as an unmannerly old colleague, sat in a sprawling position in wait for Confucius. "The Master told him, 'In youth, not humble as a junior should be. In manhood, doing nothing worthy to be handed down. And merely to live on, getting older and older, is to be a useless pest. . . . ' With this he hit him across the shins with his stick."[8]

Tyranny of the Past

The second common charge against Confucian teaching is its endorsement of past conservative political traditions. I concede that the much-quoted Analects at times reveal a flawed Confucius, insensitive to the dogmatic bias of his own era, caste, and gender. For example, his disciple Yu upholds training in family piety as the cornerstone to render a whole people cowed and docile toward civil authority. For "no instance has ever occurred in which such people would start a revolution." Or the Master himself complains, "Women and people of low birth are very hard to deal with." Perhaps the most far-reaching blunder of Confucius was to base his family ethics on the vertical father-son relationship, instead of a balanced husband-wife partnership.[9]

Quarrels between reactionary and reformed Confucians at the end of the last Chinese dynasty in 1911 sound like many current debates among Christian theologians. How can the genuine biblical Christian Tao be disentangled from the climate of anti-Judaic militancy among early Christians and from that era's tacit acceptance of slavery and patriarchal domination? In a comparable way, both Confucian parties dredged up quotes from the Master to vindicate their side in 1911. According to leftist commentators, for example, the Confucian saints now most favored must not include obedient clods, but just those who because of their integrity had once chosen official banishment. It is true that Confucius referred to a past golden age, the exemplary reign of sage-emperors like Yao, Shun, and Yu. Yet this was not an actual historical past, but a legendary timeless situation, where Confucian moral ideals prevailed. He could readily have projected his dream into a future Marxist utopia, where only Confucian saints will be chosen to rule and citizens will treat all children and parents as their own. Widows and orphans will be fed by the community. All will have steady work and a stable home. The presence of jen and li are the constant sociomoral criterion against which every era must be measured.

In 1925, Kuo Mo Jo, close friend of Mao Tse Tung, wrote a short satirical dialogue, "Marx Visits the Ancestral Temple of Confucius." Marx arrives in a red lacquered sedan chair, at first bristling and apprehensive that Confucius and his school will reject Marx's irreligious materialism. Yet Marx's explanation of a classless society proves so idealistic that Confucius approves it with matching quotations from his own utopian dreams. However, Confucius suspects Marx has not calculated the human cost for this dream's radical implementation. Both thinkers diverge, of course, on one serious issue. Confucius is driven to tolerate inequality for the sake of public harmony, but Marx scorns any so-called peace that condones injustice.[10]

Four decades after this essay, violent Red Guards of the 1960s pounced on four "olds" as their enemies — old customs, habits, culture, and social thought. They yearned to root out every vestige of traditional China, a crusade sustained by Mao in his Criticize Confucius Campaign of the early 1970s. It was no longer an honor to be old. Many grim narratives continue to surface today that disclose the ruinous upheavals sanctioned at various stages by Mao and his followers in the name of the "new."

One illustration of the Cultural Revolution that still rivets my attention is the image of an elderly man, once the prestigious headmaster of a grammar school. His five-year-old grandson, deeply respectful of this great man, watched in terror from outside a basement window as soldiers continued to pummel his grandfather, forced to crawl on the floor in front of his jeering students. A successful San Francisco businessman today, this grown boy could barely hold back tears as he told me the implications of what happened at that window. He knew I would feel sympathy if I had to watch my own grandfather disgraced. But he wanted me to realize that from the Confucian worldview in which he had been raised, what he saw was unthinkable. It shattered his moral universe and left it empty.

In contrast, I admit that portions of Mao's critique against distorted Confucian values seem deserved — vicious family narcissism, the itching for privileged status and money, esteem for mandarin professors rather than workers and peasants, the enslavement of women. In other words, the loss of authentic large-heartedness. But I came across an old cartoon that captures the irony here. An argument between two men in Mao jackets is settled the moment one of them insists, "Mao say." The stereotyped Chinese in Charlie Chan and Fu Manchu films had always been programmed to observe, "Confucius say." In the Maoist era the same pseudo-Confucian servility or even idolatry was present, but the name of the idol had changed.

Written in mainland China during the later reaction against Maoist excesses, Chitsai Feng's story "The Mao Button" is a robust satire on this same incongruity. Exhausting every other strategy, Mr. Kong trades his Mao button collection on the black market for a gigantic button that will give him supremacy among his office colleagues. He had discovered that no matter how much status or income you had, the acid test of merit and political loyalty was just the size of your Mao button. Once this mad button-era ended, the narrator explains in his final lines, you could not find a single Mao button anywhere.[11] Reacting to this story in my class discussion, a few mainland Chinese students have confirmed that the buttons and Mao cultus did disappear for a decade until the Tiananmen Square crisis of 1989. However, today the buttons can be tracked down in antique shops as desirable collectors' items. Songs from the Cultural Revolution era have returned to popularity, at times in rock and roll parodies. And Mao's portrait now appears everywhere — on billboards, portable pagers, even on the side of many vehicles as a charm to protect true believers.

Artificiality and Artifice

The damaging connotations of words like "artifice" and "artificiality" indicate the third widespread misunderstanding about Confucius and his teaching. In my earliest encounters with Chinese and Japanese students, one phenomenon disturbed me consistently, and I think this reaction is representative enough to deserve retelling. On occasion a nearby Taiwanese-American family would invite me to their home for supper. The husband and wife showed lavish politeness in English toward their guests but would break into Mandarin at times with what seemed an indignant gesture and tone of voice, directed at each other. I wondered if she were being told to shut up or never to cook again. In a comparable situation, my Japanese and Chinese neighbors in the college residence halls have often seemed eager to tell me what they surmised I wanted to hear, not what they actually thought or felt. Sometimes their conjectures would miscarry, as when one Japanese woman, trained to venerate elders, complimented me by saying that though I claimed to be sixty, I looked a healthy seventy.

For those from a non-Asian background, the Confucian drive to preserve moral suitability at all costs, or the anxiety about gaining, keeping, and losing "face" or *mien tzu,* can promote ugly stereotypes. We conjure up the foxy diplomat, a fawning smile pasted over sinister intrigue. Perhaps a Renaissance European would have felt more kinship with the Confucian style. For instance, Baldassare Castiglione's model courtier depended mostly on the trait of *grazia* to integrate all the other courtly talents. Since ambition and the manipulation of other people backfire by calling attention to themselves, these endowments would need a surface of casual simplicity, art that conceals art. Yet Europe's later Age of Elegance, familiar by now with the smooth Castiglione style, would offer two cynical definitions of politeness. Samuel Johnson called it fictitious benevolence, and Rousseau called it a mask of dishonest irony that assumes the appearance of every virtue without the reality of any at all.

Influenced by my own era and culture, I prefer frank informal relationships. I want to get beyond the social cocoon to reach the naked person often imprisoned inside. At times I assume that the "outside" is evasive facade and that the person preoccupied with correct social surfaces probably signals distance and indifference to any warm "inside" overtures of friendship. However, I have learned to work against this instinctive bias, especially in befriending people shaped by the Confucian tradition. The attribute of jen has already been described as the capacity for human-relatedness. Prompted by jen, the true Confucian will search for ways to give others suitable respect in their assigned high or low, close or distant position. The group itself, the harmonious system of power relationships, deserves at least as much respect as the individual, if not more. This is the plausible Confucian rationale for what at times can be mistaken for artifice or artificiality.

So in the Confucian spirit, you bow in deference or dismissal, compliment your dullard son-in-law, attend an unwelcome party. By observing the forms, each person guarantees minimal conditions of security for the others. The possibility of a better relationship at least remains dormant and is never scrapped definitively. To be kind implies responding not to the prompting of subjective moods but to the "outside" situation and conjectured needs of other people. Yet the disciplined Confucian golden mean, as always, lies between extremes of an egotism wallowing in sincerity and a repression of honest feelings.[12] Fidelity to moral suitability, achieved in even one balanced human relationship, restores a broken continuity. It links the present community again with its past source of religious meaning, portrayed in the Confucian myth of wise ancestral spirits and a golden age paradise.

THE TAOIST WAY

The Taoist tradition promotes the intuitive rather than the studied mannerly deed. It implies a romanticist identification with the natural world untainted by civilization and a respect for the simplified contemplative life. I have often studied the scrolls and intricate jade carvings in the Brundage Asian Art collection at the San Francisco De Young Museum. Tiny pilgrims, hermits, and poets dot the huge boulders and mountain forests and meditate away from the crowded towns. It has been claimed that Taoist painters transformed routine mountain and river backdrops in their portraits into an independent landscape genre. The Taoist master Wang Wei once explained his theory of artistic creativity this way: "The wind rises from the green forest, and foaming water rushes in the stream. Such paintings cannot be achieved by physical movements of finger and hand, but only by the spirit entering into them."

Each time an era seems to get lost in its own abstractions, technology, and political institutions, the prophetic voices in society call for a healing return to basics and to the natural world. The term "Taoist" will be used in this chapter mostly to identify widespread countercultural movements in steady counterpoint to the Confucian establishment. Protest rallies and experimental lifestyles of the 1960s come to mind — the greening of America; the zest for yoga, handicrafts, organic foods, natural medicines; and a rebellion against the conventional verities.

Throughout history the Taoist label has been applied to an astounding variety of religious life, which ranges on the spectrum from *tao chia,* a reflective moral-aesthetic teaching, to *tao chiao,* more popular devotional and institutional forms. When I first went in search of Taoists practicing their religion, I mostly came across temple rites and myths from the latter category, too inclusive and intricate for me to get a unified impression. The African Triangle premise, applied in the previous chapter to Primal traditions, helped me sort out a few patterns — the Jade Emperor or absolute Tao at the apex, with a bewildering array of intermediary nature spirits and ancestral spirits.

I once entered a shop in Singapore that sold nothing but paper models of TV sets, refrigerators, Mercedes cars, flasks of Scotch, all designed to be burnt at Taoist funerals, so that these favorite luxuries could offer symbolic comfort to the dead spirit during its journey to the afterlife. Scenes came to mind from a film documentary of a Taiwanese Taoist funeral in which the priest-shaman burned paper money. Its smoke-essence was intended to help both shaman and the dead bribe their way past border guards into the other world. So in the huge brazier of one Hong Kong temple, for example, I was able to recognize smoldering fragments of this funeral money. In Hong Kong, Taiwan, Singapore, and Honolulu, I would wander through Taoist temples alongside reverent crowds of people who bowed with joss sticks before statues, left offerings of food and money, and from a small metal urn picked up slips of paper with an oracle or mantra inscribed.

The Taoist pantheon of Gods has room for every spirit imaginable — Gods of rain and trees, Gods that personify attributes like mercy or longevity, Gods of medicine and war, the Kitchen God whose province is family harmony, Gods that were once heroes in actual history. Heading this multitude are the most popular Gods in Chinese art and literature, the Eight Immortals, some of whom were actual Taoist sages who reached spiritual and physical perfection before their death. Each Immortal is given different attributes. The Taoist canonical scriptures of more than a thousand books, most of them accessible only to their own hereditary line of priests, continue to mystify scholars outside the tradition. Their priests are prepared to instruct you in yoga or martial arts, perform exorcisms, hold seances to communicate with ancestral spirits, or name the specific God and mantra you should approach for a particular favor.

As recently as 1994 in the People's Republic of China, all Taoists — the popular Zhengyi Movement, especially — were required to register with the government-sponsored Taoist Association and were to hold their public rites in approved shrines or temples, not in private homes. Though in these approved spots people can chant, say morning and evening prayers, and perform funeral rites, they are forbidden to dabble in geomancy, exorcism, trance-possession, or fortune-telling. "Superstitions" of this sort have been declared harmful to society and public health. However, the Taoist practices attractive to most citizens are not these occult techniques, but yoga, meditation, and the martial arts. As China opens itself further to capital investment and tourism, the socialist state continues to rebuild and modernize many classical Taoist temples and mountain shrines. It also permits a limited number of candidates to take religious vows in Taoist monasteries.[13]

A Taoist friend of mine once pointed out an eighty-year-old woman performing slow tai chi gyrations on a sandy stretch near the ocean. He saw her as the model Taoist Immortal, with a body trim and supple, her skin preternaturally smooth, as if age had overlooked it. For me, the stereotyped Taoist throughout history has been someone obsessed with finding the key to immortality through meditation, yoga, diet, and alchemy. Such a quest, of course, must be both spiritual and physical, in a yin-yang balance. But our own youth culture and consumerism today prompt many to misconstrue this search as just a cosmetic spirituality of organic foods, body-building, and mental hygiene. In an important cautionary Taoist tale, a certain wise man once claimed to have discovered the secret of immortality. Hearing of this wonder, a Taoist priest left everything to join the man's disciples. But by the time he reached the distant hermitage, this saint had died. Though discouraged, the priest began to ask himself why he had come all this way. Why should he grieve when a would-be Immortal ended his present life? In fact, maybe he had misunderstood the nature of this secret from the beginning.

Thus acquainted with popular Taoist practice, I began only much later to study the two central texts in the Taoist canon, the Tao Te Ching poems of Lao Tzu and the parables and dialogues of Chuang Tzu. Each work, of course, has its own emphases, the first addressed to the court, the second to a larger public. Each has been claimed to antedate the other, but tradition readily combines them both into one Lao-Chuang scripture. Here you can piece together the tao chia — more a spiritual Taoist attitude and style than specific doctrines and rituals of the tao chiao I had experienced earlier. In this subtle teaching, the dialectic between Taoist and Confucian Ways becomes unmistakable.

Like the Confucian golden age of Yao and Shun, the Taoist ideal society has been retrojected to a mythical utopia when the mountains had no trails, the rivers no bridges, and people and the natural world all lived at peace together. Chuang Tzu has his own version of the Fall. Once upon a time, human beings were loving and trust-worthy, unaware they were already living what would later be called the Confucian path of generosity and moral suitability. "In the simplicity of an uncarved block they attain their true nature. Then along comes the sage, huffing and puffing after benev-olence, reaching on tiptoe for righteousness, . . . snipping and stitching away at his rites. . . . Then for the first time people learned to stand on tiptoe and covet knowledge, to fight to the death over profit, and there was no stopping them."[14]

A corollary to this insight is Lao Tzu's ironic observation, "The more laws that get promulgated / The more thieves and bandits there will be." I think this argument offered by both Taoist masters takes the following direction. Excessive statutes are more likely to prove oppressive and unenforceable and thus spark contempt for even the few worthy laws. Likewise, excessive Confucian harping about moral suitabil-ity could talk the authentic Tao to death. Or it could prompt the mere appearance of large-heartedness to be mistaken for its actuality. As Chuang Tzu says, "When the Way was lost, then there was virtue. When virtue was lost, then there was benevo-lence. When benevolence was lost, then there was righteousness. When righteousness was lost, then came rites. Rites are frills of the way and forerunners of disorder."[15]

In other words, with the emergence of self-consciousness and an anxiety to preserve social appearances, the original harmony between people declines into aggressive coveting. As a Christian parallel to this Taoist teaching, Paul's Letter to the Romans offers some psychological conjectures on the origins of guilt in himself and others. Paul is convinced the Mosaic Torah piled a moral burden on people without giving them inner power to master this burden. Without the spiritual strength which Christians interpret as the gift of Christ, a person can only despair. "I should never have known what it was to covet if the Law had not said, 'Thou shalt not covet....' But when the commandment came, sin sprang to life and I died."[16]

Paradoxes of Actionless Action

Central to the Taoist frame of mind is *wu-wei,* usually translated as not-doing, effortless effort, or creative inaction. *Wei* means action, and *wu* means no-thing, an absence of perceptible features — or, with overtones of mystery and wonder, the Void. To heighten the mystery here, Taoists often use the phrase *wei-wu-wei,* indicating that such not-doing is an active stance indeed.

As explained earlier, the absolute Tao resists conceptualization, whereas tao-te, its earthly replica, can be broached dimly through analogies, such as water, valley, mother, or energy. Deprived of such analogies, we have only the Void. This latter apophatic approach or Path of Negation, to be explored more fully in chapters 3 and 4, treats the Sacred as remote from ordinary concepts and sense experience. We converge on it best by a series of negations, which gradually eliminate any possible comparison with our everyday experience — for example, the In-finite, Im-mutable, or In-comprehensible. Chuang Tzu enjoys the playful use of denials in order to back into positive assertions: "I can conceive of the existence of nonexistence, but not the nonexistence of nonexistence.... How could I ever reach such perfection?"[17]

One brief line from Lao Tzu sums up the full baffling impact of wu-wei: "No-action yet not no-action." Tao does not look active, but through Tao everything gets done. From this root insight further paradoxes evolve, axioms that permeate the spirituality of most world traditions. Die in order to live, no self-completion without self-emptying, the soft overcomes the hard and the weak the strong, glory cannot be won except by letting it go, one who knows does not speak and one who speaks does not know. Lao Tzu says the Tao is slight and almost without savor. "If one looks for Tao, there is nothing solid to see. If one listens for it, there is nothing loud enough to hear. Yet if one uses it, it is inexhaustible."[18] Some aspects of truth are so momentous or so fragile that they can be grasped only through the poetic indirection of myth and paradox.

The subtle, ironic texture of this thinking makes it ripe for conflicts in interpretation by adversaries and also by its own disciples. Commending simple lifestyles, Chuang Tzu tells of a gardener's refusal to use a labor-saving device because "where there are machine worries, there are bound to be machine hearts. With a machine heart in your breast, you've spoiled what was pure and simple."[19] Passages like this prompt some enthusiasts to disdain technology or to withdraw as confirmed mountain ascetics or just to live an austere, detached inner life while actively involved in society. I know some Taoists who in an ecstasy of spirit are almost indifferent to the threat of physical death, and others intent to prolong youth and sexual potency through ritual diet, yoga, and alchemical potions.

Nowhere do Taoist positions differ more dramatically than in their conclusions about practical politics. Does the wu-wei attitude promote a stable, responsible government or anarchy? Nations are asked to meet hard aggression by reluctant counterforce or, more often, by soft, pacifist nonresistance. Chuang Tzu devotes an entire chapter to a parable series in which various kings offer their throne to one scholar and simpleton after another, all of whom wisely turn down the offer. The author himself also refuses political office. Reluctant to give up his fishing pole, he prefers, he says, to remain a live tortoise dragging its tail in the mud than to become a sacred jeweled tortoise, mummified and venerated. A robber seems to offer the most caustic estimate of China's corrupt political order: "The petty thief is imprisoned but the big thief becomes a feudal lord."[20] All this seems grist for dissent and anarchy. Yet I think every Taoist complaint can be turned upside down to vindicate the existence of a government that is both forceful and compassionate.

Many pages of Lao Tzu and Chuang Tzu yearn for a model ruler who lives the Tao. The attitude of wu-wei, prized in common citizens, becomes precisely the best qualification for office. "Only the person who has no use for empire is fit to be entrusted with it," says Chuang Tzu, who then explains why the state of Yueh dug the uncooperative Prince Sou out of his cave and dragged him back to run the government.[21] Those too eager for power are prone to abuse their position in order to gratify compulsive inner needs. The wise permissive leader, ruling serenely without seeming to rule, must be a balanced, low-profile human king, disposed to rule others only as the leader would expect to be ruled, diffident to rank and glory.

A ruler of this sort would have to presume a citizenry of utopian maturity, of course, governed by the inner Tao and able to appreciate such leadership. This empathy and responsibility of the leader toward an entire people are exemplified in Po Chu's amazing reverence for the corpse of an executed criminal. Chuang Tzu describes this man wrapping the body in his own royal robes and crying, "The world is in dire misfortune, and you have been quicker than the rest of us to encounter it.... They pile on responsibilities and then penalize people for not being able to fulfill them." And Lao Tzu says, "Only one who takes upon oneself the evils of the country can become a king."[22]

I have developed the theme of Taoist political theory expansively to suggest a pattern for appreciating most Taoist polemics against Confucian orthodoxy. In the actual record of history, though ideological animosity and debate raged between them for centuries, both traditions drew closer in practice. For they both professed the same ethic of a golden mean. Confucius could be parodied as stilted, effete, and hypocritical. Chuang Tzu adds the mischievous touch of introducing him as a Taoist saint or a groping Taoist convert. Yet few critiques seem so explosive that they cannot be turned around to support the correctly interpreted Confucian teaching on jen and li. The Analects affirm, "What can someone without jen have to do with li?" Taoists scrutinized their own society and found only the facade of li. Confucius and the two Taoist masters agree on the centrality of jen but differ significantly in their estimate of li. Confucian li is acceptable to Lao Tzu and Chuang Tzu only insofar as it conforms to the more comprehensive natural rhythms of wu-wei.

Taoist No and Yes

A spirituality based on wu-wei implies two fundamental stages. The first I shall call an iconoclastic preliminary. Some of Chuang Tzu's most eloquent pages explain this process: "People have to understand the useless before you can talk to them about the useful.... You must fast and practice austerities, cleanse and purge your inner mind, destroy and do away with your knowledge." Another name for this discipline is listening, not with physical ears but with the spirit. For "spirit is empty and waits on things. The Tao gathers in emptiness alone. Emptiness is the fasting of the mind."[23] The debris of truly useless habit and cliché must be cleared away, and what has previously been disparaged as useless must be given a new spiritual reappraisal. In the Christian Pauline sense, those thinking themselves wise according to the standards of this passing age must become fools to gain true wisdom. We begin to respect the uselessness of a tree spared by woodcutters because of its age and rot. Neighbors pity the hunchback Shu, yet soon realize he is given the largest dole of grain and waves goodbye to others his own age forced into military service.

The iconoclastic features of this Taoist preparation have been celebrated in Plato's Socratic dialectic. Socrates cannot begin the search for knowledge until he demolishes the pretensions to knowledge, every shred of false confidence. Teacher and disciple must admit their mutual ignorance before proceeding further together to learn. Socrates' attack can be stinging, and few pages in Plato are more memorable than those regarding the plight of some unwary expert tripping over a series of self-contradictions, with the master professing ignorance, the mask of wise Socratic irony. Like disturbing Taoist paradoxes, the dialectical shock tactics of Socrates were misunderstood by literal minds, quick to bring charges against him for corrupting the young. This teacher was allegedly encouraging the young to ask irreverent questions that might threaten Greece's political and religious authority.

Chuang Tzu calls this first stage "thawing and freeing the icebound," stripping oneself down to the condition of an unconscious infant, "its body like the limb of a tree, its mind like dead ashes."[24] Readers are warned not to mistake this for the highest stage. You may recall Thoreau's exasperation at those visiting his Walden hermitage, expecting only to find a hermit and reformer forever chanting to himself, "This is the house that I built. This is the man that lives in the house that I built." Thoreau abandoned noisy Jacksonian politics, machines, cities built on ruins of older cities, taxes and institutions with their rapacious paws, professors inexperienced in the art of life, philanthropists intrusively doing good without being good. His renunciation of all these things was indeed a criticism of them in the best Taoist tradition. But more important, he intended to simplify life of all this clutter, so that "the laws of the universe will appear less complex, and solitude will not be solitude, nor poverty poverty, nor weakness weakness." In summary, "not till we have lost the world, do we begin to find ourselves." The log cabin of *Walden* or the jail of "Civil Disobedience" is a sanctuary where you retreat to penetrate facades, find real priorities, and then return to the world.[25]

The second and final stage of wu-wei is *tzu jan,* naturalness and spontaneity, the so-called Natural Way. This is not quietism, but action that is relaxed and intuitive. It is attuned to the yin-yang cyclical pattern of seasons and stars — letting the world go, letting others be. This process can be described, too, as a return to original simplicity and harmony, to the Tao that Lao Tzu calls root or silence, "the always-so." It is not surprising to meet so many fishermen, farmers, and contemplative drop-outs in Taoist literature, or to track most Taoist similes back to worlds far removed from civilized human life — silence, baby and savage, wild horses, wood and stone and water. No matter how comprehensive the Natural Way may appear, it clearly excludes attributes like artificiality and artifice and the will to manipulate, possess, or intrude.

In one famous Taoist tale, a sculptor is employed by his sovereign to carve a mulberry leaf out of precious stone. He takes three years just to shape a leaf with texture and color, delicate enough to draw compliments that it looks almost natural. Hearing of the miracle, a Taoist seer observes with irony that nature's rapid creativity cannot compete with the slow, labored perfection of human art. In a comparable story, "The Nightingale," by Hans Christian Andersen, a Chinese emperor is enraptured by a real nightingale's song, even if disappointed by the bird's drab appearance. He soon discards it for a wind-up artificial bird of silver and gems, mailed him as a gift. Far more beautiful on the outside, this bird sings almost as well, but just a single repeated song. Still, it proves more dependable than the natural bird, whose songs and concert times occur at random. After a year, however, the mechanical apparatus runs down and cannot be fully repaired. The emperor falls ill and, yearning to hear music again, turns from the artificial bird to a tune outside his window, sung unexpectedly by the real nightingale now, a voice of compassion and hope.

All the reverence that Confucius brings to moral suitability is channeled by Lao Tzu and Chuang Tzu into wu-wei, and this task demands a stunning control and sensitivity. The photographer Eliot Porter, for example, in preparing to capture a flight of birds on film, explores with care the habits of a particular bird so that he can anticipate the ideal instant for an exposure. Or he knows a grove of aspens so well that he can plan the time of day and season to capture specific variations in tone and color. His theory is to discover rather than invent — not impose a pattern on the natural world, but compose a picture that reveals a design not usually perceived because of distractions. This same receptive creativity can be observed in the sculptor who tries to carve with the grain, the poet whose meaning springs uncharted out of half-conscious wordplay, the ballerina whose body dances almost by itself.

For teachers and counselors like myself, the Taoist masters offer some unforeseen applications of the wu-wei attitude. Chuang Tzu gives a shrewd psychological sketch of the truly receptive teacher, whose approach to things is "to go along with them and be merry.... So there may be many times when, without saying a word, one can induce harmony in others. Just standing alongside others, one can cause them to change, until the proper relationship between father and son has found its way into every house." Again, the tutor of a pampered prince is advised: "If he wants to be a child, be a child with him. If he wants to follow erratic ways, follow erratic ways with him. If he wants to be reckless, be reckless with him. Understand him thoroughly, and lead him to the point where he is without fault."[26] A mature father or mother, neither controlling nor surrendering control, appreciates the risky balance a careful wu-wei attitude implies. No less does the client-centered therapist, alert to the art of interpreting without manipulating.

Despite its heavy-footed satire, Jerzy Kosinski's novelette and film *Being There* show this creative receptivity brilliantly in Chauncy the Gardener. Here is a character with obvious affinities to Forrest Gump and to a long tradition of court jesters, clowns, and holy fools. Genial, unthreatening, and mentally tuned out from the world around him, Chance wanders naively among leaders of American politics and finance. His ignorant silence is misunderstood as deep compliance with any questioner's viewpoint; his literal comments on gardening are inflated into oracular metaphors by the press. As a pliable confidant, he draws the worst but more often the best out of those befriending him.

The spontaneous rhythms of wu-wei are best symbolized in the sacred dance of tai chi. Early morning in many public parks and on beaches, groups of Asian people gather to engage in these slow-flowing gestures. Tai chi allegedly originated in the experience of a thirteenth-century monk, Chang San Feng, who once noticed a shrike and snake in combat. The bird would swoop down and attack, while the snake in casual sinuous movements managed to escape the line of attack and turn the hunter's force back upon itself. The shrike eventually collided against a rock and broke its neck.[27]

According to one legend, when this monk traveled through the snow, he would not leave footprints but puddles of melted ice. For his inner force or chi generated intense heat. He could also catch hawks in his bare hands or speeding arrows in his teeth. These fantasies almost turn into fact when performers like the astonishing Shanghai Acrobatic Troupe put on a show, with bodies hurtling and flipping, one weightless configuration after another. The same magical feats have become stock endowments today for the heroes and heroines of Kung Fu cinema — they zap their opponents with a sudden expulsion of chi, shatter a threatening sword, or kick flying through the sky. What lies behind myths of such miraculous agility is no doubt the popular Taoist fascination with spiritual and physical immortality. In the Boxer Rebellion in China in 1899, for instance, many Taoist priests and Buddhist monks, drawn from "Boxer" martial arts societies, rushed into battle convinced of their own invulnerability. According to a senior American diplomat's report to Washington at the time, these people trusted rashly that if they "go through certain gymnastic movements and repeat certain incantations, they will become impervious to all weapons and nothing can harm them."[28]

The true meaning of Taoist martial arts, of course, will never be typified by warfare, brick-shattering displays, or a full-contact karate slam. Karate, Taekwando, and Aikido, for example, are not arts of fighting but of controlled aggression, finding a path around conflict. Besides physical durability, they aim at the mental and moral endowments of responsibility, confidence, and respect for your opponent. If you can control your anger and fear, you are less likely to react violently to attack and can discover the least harmful way to disarm or immobilize an aggressor. Proponents defend the moral superiority of this attitude to mere pacifist surrender, for you train yourself to protect innocent victims, yourself, and even your opponent from harm.

Many of my Asian students have been shaped in this martial arts tradition since childhood and have by now turned such training into a comprehensive spiritual Way. Chuang Tzu gives a superb image of the ideal they try to embody. A man is training a fighting cock for King Hsuan, who after every ten days asks again whether the training has been completed. The king receives different temporizing answers each time, such as, "Not yet, the cock is vain and fiery." Or "Not yet, he starts up at shadows and echoes." At last the trainer answers, "Near enough. If another cock crows, he shows no change. From a distance he looks as if he is made of wood. His power is complete. Other cocks would turn and run rather than face him."[29]

One principle behind most of the Chinese and Japanese spiritual martial arts is to sidestep the offensive momentum of your opponents and reverse it as a counterforce against them. More noticeably in tai chi than in the other martial arts, you are both hunter and quarry, the quiet watchful protagonist and, at the same time, the inner resistance to be healed and reintegrated. The graceful movements of tai chi, numbering about forty basic postures, circling and converging on the body's spinal center of gravity, alternate in a steady cosmic rhythm. By closer alignment with chi forces in the universe, you replenish your inner reserves of chi.

As the slow gyrations of tai chi unfold, now your body and mind express the gentle receptivity of yin, now the assertive creative power of yang. In microcosm this rite tries to reenact the origin of the macrocosm out of primordial chaos. You dance out expressively the pulse of the inner Tao within yourself — spirit and body, nature and the human person.

THE SHINTO WAY

In his autobiography, Soko Yamaga, one of the earliest apologists of Shinto and Bushido, recounts how books by sages such as Lao Tzu and Chuang Tzu corrected inadequacies from his own Confucian background. The Taoist masters gave him "more life and freedom. The identification of human mental activity with the mystic activity of nature produced deep insight. From that point on I followed the impulses of my own nature. All was spontaneous."[30] Drawing upon Yamaga's insight, I have tried to understand Shinto as an attempt to integrate a fierce Confucian loyalty with a sensitive Taoist affinity toward the natural world. But at times these two factors seem to undercut each other dramatically.

Two contrasting images will underline the paradoxes in Shinto. The first is a Japanese painter who once let me observe her at work with her *sumie* brush, whisking a casual track of ink over a fibrous piece of rice paper. White space combines with deft squiggles and blots to suggest a branch of plum blossoms, fragile and evanescent. Juxtaposed with this instant of Shinto beauty is a second different image, a scenario of Shinto patriotism. Imagine the bewildered face of Sergeant Shoichi Yokoi, convinced that the Second World War had never ceased. Twenty-seven years after Japan's defeat, his clothes woven from strands of tree bark, surviving on a diet of papaya, frogs, and rats, the sergeant was discovered hiding in a cave on Guam. During a summer of teaching in Guam, I was once shown the patch of dense foliage that concealed his celebrated tunnel hideout. The man had been taught that ritual seppuku, even solitary burial alive, was preferable to shameful surrender. And all military orders had to be obeyed with disciplined literalness. Interviewed upon his return to Japan, he groped to explain his mixed feelings: "I'm ashamed to have come home alive."

For one Japanese, this war never ended, and an aftermath of contrition had not yet arrived. For five decades after the Second World War, many of Japan's neighbors waited with impatience for the Japanese government to offer a state apology for atrocities that accompanied its wartime military rule. At last, in August 1995, not the Parliament, but Prime Minister Murayama, speaking in his own name, used the unambiguous word *awabi,* meaning to apologize, not just to regret. At first impression, I recalled the shameful dispute among Catholic bishops at the Second Vatican Council over whether to condemn or merely to deplore the church's centuries of anti-Semitism. Also, it seemed ironic that a people accustomed to bow in polite apology over a trivial slip-up in etiquette should take so many years to acknowledge what others, if not official Japan itself, view as a massive wrong. Yet I could also sense why many Japanese still interpret that war as a justified liberation of Europe's Asian colonies from Eurocentric subjugation or as the plot of a small military elite which victimized the entire Japanese people.

Few outsiders, however, appreciate the extent to which many Japanese, like Sergeant Yokoi, have been trained in filial loyalty. For days after the prime minister's apology, his cabinet members, one by one, were observed visiting the nearby Yasu-kuni Shrine, a place to honor Japan's dead, especially those canonized soldiers who died in battle. Promising the Ancestors Confucian homage, a traditional Japanese would never dispute the bravery and sincerity of their sacrifice. And most of all, no citizen today has the right to criticize policies of a past emperor, who throughout the era was thought to be a Shinto God.

Shinto somehow animates people as disparate as the sergeant and the sumie artist, a Confucian-Taoist dichotomy that may seem less jarring the further it is explored in this chapter. Yet I acknowledge the disquiet I still experience at the dissonant blend of militarism and aesthetics in such films as Akira Kurosawa's 1980 classic *Kage-musha, the Shadow Warrior* — the overwhelming beauty of armies on horseback in symmetrical masses, an eerie ocean of blood, silver and bluish glint of steel in the moonlight, butchered corpses, multicolored banners flapping in the wind . . .

Shin-to — the *to* or Tao of the *Kami* — is the name adopted by Japanese scholars to distinguish their indigenous faith from Buddhist imports. Kami means the Sacred, represented either as a radiating force or as personified spirit(s). Any physical object, energy, moral attribute, living person, or dead hero or heroine felt to be somehow kami or superior and *ka* or mysterious can be worshiped as Kami. The many Gods of Taoist popular religion, as introduced before, represent this same enormous range of divinized moral virtues, natural forces, and historical people. In an earlier explanation of Shinto's many Taos, I indicated that any activity pursued with intense commitment is perceived as a virtual Tao. According to the same reasoning, all reality, filtered through anyone's enlightened affectivity, is potentially sacred.

I have discovered Japanese shrines to the Kami in many unexpected places, as reminders that nothing is too ordinary to be sacred. During hikes in the Japanese countryside through a moss garden, near a waterfall, or up a mountain path, I would chance upon a tiny orange torii gate, strips of fluttering paper, or a mirror, to indicate a sacred presence at places of eye-catching beauty. Guiding me through the Tokyo Zoo, for example, a former student of mine pointed out a small, quiet cemetery with flowers and food offerings. He identified this as a shrine to the sacred spirits of dead animals, such as a monkey or lion that many visitors had befriended. I once stayed as a weekend house guest with a young Japanese couple in Toyohashi near the ocean. Waking from an austere night's sleep on tatami mats covering the cold wooden floor, I enjoyed a long walk early each morning with the entire family for miles atop a huge dike. At frequent intervals, we would come across impromptu shrines and flower offerings to Kami of the sea for a safe boat voyage or a plentiful catch of fish.

Most social commentaries on modern Japan stress the religious sinkhole that opened up for many people after the military defeat in 1945 and the loss of a deified emperor. Mere economic success could never fill this gap, of course, and about two hundred thousand new religious movements have tried, most of them derivatives of a long Shinto and Buddhist heritage. The recent Aum Shinrikyo cult, for instance, accused of the March 1995 lethal sarin gas attacks in the Tokyo subway, has claimed at least ten thousand followers in Japan alone.[31] The younger generations live in transition today, partly shaped by traditional mind-sets but also cut adrift, ready to try out new ways. I often hear Japanese student friends regretting the loss of a recognizable religious identity.

At times on televised New Year's Eve celebrations I have watched thousands of Japanese standing with candles in reverent silence at the great Tokyo Meiji Shrine, waiting for a midnight countdown. Granted that people of Tokyo and New York each have their unique ways to conceal or flaunt religious feelings, I myself feel more at home with this Japanese moment of hushed welcome, than with the routine champagne and "Auld Lang Syne" to cheer a huge cartoon apple descending in New York's Times Square.

Gathering at the Meiji park is only one instance of various journeys to shrines on national holidays that look like pilgrimages in everything but name. Accompanying some of my Japanese students and their families, who consistently describe themselves as religionless, I have traveled to a few celebrated Shinto and Buddhist sacred places in Japan. We would join large crowds of people, most of them glad to put in an annual appearance before some favorite statue, to picnic on the lawn, to wander through a flower garden or watch the brilliant colors of swimming carp, and to stand in line to have their fortunes read. I had not expected to witness each of my secular friends, eager to pass exams or get a job, purchase a small amulet memento to carry away in their pocket or purse. Recalling the distinction between shukyo and shukyo shin with which the present chapter began, I suspect most of these pilgrims would connect their lives with the religious adjective but not the religious noun.

The Code of Samurai Loyalty

My favorite embodiment of the samurai ideal is Kambei in Kurosawa's celebrated 1954 film *Seven Samurai*. A leaderless wandering samurai, Kambei has a heart for the poor and exploited. Struggling to live out his values, he feels impelled to round up a disheveled band of samurai to defend a community long pillaged by bandits. In an early scene, he shaves off his topknot, last remnant of his samurai identity, to soothe the suspicions of a thief with whom he must bargain to save a kidnapped baby. The peasants for whom he later risks his life feel reluctant to organize under his leadership. Most of them have never fought for a cause more inclusive than their individual property.

Bushido is the name given to distinctive moral values of the samurai warrior class. At the logical center of this code is the notion of *chugi*. *Chu* means human-heartedness, and *gi* stands for trustworthiness, fidelity, gratitude. Thus, chugi describes not the obedience of a dog to its master but a truly human relationship, lifelong and totally committed. Such loyalty implies the ritual subjection of vassal to lord or emperor, the fealty common to Christian knights and others in feudal eras throughout the world.

Attitudes prevalent in Japan since the earliest Shinto legends took classical shape during the seventeenth-century Tokugawa Shogunate. Indebted to both Shinto and Buddhist sources, the famous Hagakure handbook emerged half a century later. Widely distributed during the decade of ultranationalism before the Second World War, this Bushido classic spells out the four heroic vows of chugi: "Never to be outdone in the Way of the Samurai. To be of good use to the master. To be filial to my parents. Manifesting great compassion, to act for the sake of humanity."[32]

One feature distinguishes the samurai's loyalty from that of his European counterparts — citizens obedient to their king reigning by divine right, or monks obedient to their religious superior mediating God's will. Shinto adds a note of fierce tragic expendability, almost an eagerness to risk death. The following lines from the Hagakure have had the deepest impact on later centuries: "Bushido consists in dying. That is the conclusion I have reached. Never in my life have I placed my own thoughts above those of my lord and master. . . . Every morning prepare your mind to get ready to die. . . . When your mind is always set on death, your way through life will always be straight and simple." It is hard to pick up this text today without recalling the sinewy corpse of novelist Yukio Mishima, filmed at his moment of public seppuku, partly a gesture of protest over Japan's impotent disarmament. Not long before his death, he had penned the manifesto introduction to a new 1967 textual edition of the Hagakure, which passed through sixteen editions in forty days.

At its most graphic, this yearning for self-annihilation pervades the many diaries, haiku, and letters left behind by young kamikaze pilots from the final sea battles of the Second World War. Hours before soaring up like Icarus to the sun, they write as if in exalted trance. For instance, after holding a branch of cherry blossoms in his hands to pose for a last snapshot, ace flyer Yokita in a note of farewell and reassurance to his parents quotes the squad's training officer: "To die while you are pure and fresh, this is truly Bushido. . . . If in doubt whether to live or die, it is always better to die."

Not until years afterward would the Japanese public learn of the distorting group pressures often concealed behind these certainties. Saburo Sakai recounts stumbling one night upon a hidden colleague near the Iwo Jima runway, afraid to report back after surviving a suicide attack. Once when kamikaze planes had to turn back to the carrier because of poor weather conditions, pilots each had to endure a humiliating slap in the face. "Contemptible cowards!" their commander screamed, "Why couldn't you have died courageously?" Sei Watanabe will never forget his reaction to news of the war's end two days before his scheduled suicide mission. "I cried and felt hurt, for I was deprived of death."[33]

Besides fixation on self-immolation, the classical samurai code bears a second feature that would succeed in delaying the vindication of women's rights well into the present century. Bushido reinforced a longstanding attitude of virile protectiveness toward women, a code perhaps even more repressive than the courtly feudal standards of other nations. In her 1992 autobiography, the cross-cultural psychologist Lydia Minatoya analyzes this harmful legacy of feudal Japan, which suffocated her own American childhood in the 1950s. Taught a subservient responsibility toward her own toys and clothing, she felt henpecked, lost in the struggle for dominance.

She could hear imaginary shrieks from her mittens and dolls if stained or misplaced, or she would say "excuse me" when bumping against a chair. Just as her mother insisted that all women must be silent and yielding, her father tried to steer her away from scientific studies into a career as a nurse or librarian. "Daughters need duty," he would say, "not daring." Japanese-American boys were to be trained to swim upstream like carp, girls to be careful and safe. The old storybooks infuriated Minatoya, where "men are warriors, fierce and bold. But a lady never lunges to slash the throat of an assailant. Instead, she writes a poem about harsh winters, . . . then kills herself in protest."[34]

An anonymous document from the Tokugawa period lists the following endowments of a model samurai wife: "obedience to a father before marriage, to a husband when married, and to a son when widowed. . . . She should never give way to passion inconvenient to others, nor question the authority of her elders. For her no religion is necessary either, because her husband is her sole heaven, and her whole duty lies in serving him and his."[35] Today it is heartening to rediscover samurai heroines early in the present century who managed to break free of this compliance.

In 1966, for example, the Japanese government dedicated a belated memorial to Hideko Fukuda, a woman of a low-ranking samurai clan, author of perhaps the first Japanese woman's autobiography, published in 1902. Pacifist and socialist, founder of various newspapers and women's schools, reformer of prison abuse, dangerous conditions in textile mills, and injustices in the family system, she had been groomed at first for a more traditional feminine role. She writes of herself at fifteen: "I took lessons in tea ceremony, flower arrangement, sewing, and the general rules of etiquette," and in playing "string instruments like the two-string koto and the Chinese lute."

Years later, increasingly frustrated with the hypocrisy and cowardice of various reformist male colleagues, Fukuda decided that "men are easily bought off by titles of nobility and medals. In this respect women are more reliable." Selecting Joan of Arc as her model, she sums up the credo underlying her newly established Benevolent Publishing Firm: "My object was to teach women to become independent and self-sufficient so that they would cease being slaves to men, and to make it possible for us to fulfill our natural functions as women without hindrance. I also hoped to influence men so that they would cease behaving in a tyrannical and vulgar fashion."[36]

Surviving the Tokugawa and Meiji eras, and even the state Shinto militarism of the 1930s, the Bushido spirit has left many traces in contemporary Japanese culture. Martial arts and epic samurai "easterns" flourish, maybe even more popular as exports. Audiences have accustomed themselves to a parody of samurai aggressiveness in the swaggering rogues played by Toshiro Mifune or the sly antiheroic buffoonery of Zatoichi, the blind swordsman. Even the stylized chugi vocabulary has been allegedly adopted within some Japanese Mafia and right-wing political groups. The fealty and entrenched hierarchy typical of many Japanese corporations today — a disciplined esprit almost military — date clearly from the rise of the samurai class to Meiji business leadership.

Helping to inaugurate the Tokugawa period, Confucian scholars like Razan Hayashi and Soko Yamaga had labored to Confucianize manners of the seventeenth-century samurai caste. They did this by constructing bridges between the rough warrior and the Confucian scholar-prince ideal. A genuine samurai must excel in the arts of war and also of peace. "A person who is dedicated and has a mission to perform is called a samurai," says Hayashi, "someone of inner worth and upright conduct, who has moral principles and mastery of the arts."[37]

The Hagakure manual, convinced that Bushido "consists in dying," as mentioned before, encourages daily meditation on death to keep life "straight and simple." Unwavering focus on the fragility of life, then, ought to plunge the practitioner into the cherished immediate moment, the simple beauty of everyday fleeting things, stripped of all pretense. Haiku poems, song, and painting arrest our attention on favorite images of twilight, pastels of fading seasons, the fall of blossoms, the brevity of love and human life. This mood is caught best in the tea ceremony, described in the Shinto tradition as a ritual encounter "once in a lifetime." Such a fleeting instant must be endowed with spiritual intensity, for it might be the last moment together.

An obvious parallel to the aesthetics of fragile impermanence is the samurai's life, so mobile and expendable in service. Habits of military preparedness may condition people to prefer a frugal, disciplined style in art. An emphasis on devoted achievement for one's lord had in postfeudal times led to a rigorous achievement-oriented economy. In a similar way, many today view their career, family role, sports, and art as a Tao discipline demanding endless improvement. Examined in this manner, then, the motifs of loyalty, self-denial, military vigilance, a refined artistic vision, and the skills of peace and war all somehow interweave — a link between the disparate worlds of Sergeant Yokoi and of my sumie artist friend.

The Higher Loyalty

Two of the four vows emphasized in the Hagakure handbook — loyalty to your lord or the nation-state and loyalty to your family — form an uneasy juxtaposition. A potential collision between loyalties must raise anxiety for every sensitive Confucian. For instance, the People's Republic of China in 1964 published a communist party booklet entitled "The Correct Handling of Love, Marriage, and Family Problems." This study guide for local cadres tries to reinforce traditional parental authority against bourgeois youth-culture erosions of the family structure. Yet parents are forbidden to view their offspring as personal property or to encourage children in the grab for selfish careers and money. "To determine whether or not parents' love is true or false," it concludes, "we must see if their opinions accord with the Party's demands upon us."[38]

As an official solution, such a statement bears a definitive tone, but it does not dispel the agony of a Confucian conscience trying to balance two loyalties without subordinating one to the other. Facing a comparable dilemma, Akio Morita, founder of Sony Corporation, writes in his autobiography in defense of the effort to inspire a business loyalty "within the Sony family" that transcends the mere lure of high pay and leisure. He distrusts employees' self-centered attitudes prevalent in Europe and the United States, working just for "yourself and your family to the exclusion of the goals of your co-workers and the company."[39]

True to this emphatic Confucian heritage, Bushido loyalty cannot be separated from filial piety. Threading together random attitudes unique to contemporary Japan, the social psychologist Takeo Doi brings some coherence to them by examining pervasive attitudes of *amae.* This word connotes a need to be protected, loved, indulged,

to feel at home in one's surroundings, to snuggle up to someone, to find the lost symbiotic mother-child envelopment. Doi takes note of Japan's indulgent child-rearing
system and also the tendencies in adult society to differentiate a warm inner circle of
friends from an outer cold periphery of strangers. As expected, he does not overlook
the spiritual and social alienation felt by a nation left "fatherless" with the emperor's
humiliating defeat in the Second World War.

In his best-selling *Anatomy of Dependence,* Doi concludes that emperor and ancestral spirits and the Kami all exist "in a realm beyond the anguish of unsatisfied
amae — which is where . . . the essence of the Japanese concept of divinity lies."[40] According to the logic of amae, then, Shinto and specific patterns of culture and history
mutually fortify each other. Those trained in the Bushido heritage will instinctively
cast about to find an object worthy of absolute loyalty — their family living and
dead, their birthplace, nation, emperor, or the entire world. Yet a dependency or positive transference so intense, I am certain, is vulnerable to idolatry — mistaking some
conniving guru or politician for the ultimate mother and father.

A distorted loyalty of this sort finds apparent support in the Hagakure itself:
"Every morning one should first do reverence to his master and parents and then to
his patron deities and guardian Buddhas. If he will only make his master first in importance, his parents will rejoice, and the Gods and Buddhas will give their assent."
An even clearer inversion of priorities is encouraged by the following passage: "A
devotee of the Nembutsu recites the Buddha's name with every incoming and outgo-
ing breath in order never to forget the Buddha. A retainer, too, should be just like this
in thinking of his master."[41] In this spirit, the Tokugawa dynasty imposed a model
of unquestioning military obedience on its religious minorities. When "Kirishitan"
villages refused to pledge the shogun a loyalty they believed suitable only for God,
entire populations headed for immediate Christian martyrdom.

In contrast, the Hagakure's fourth vow, more inclusive than the first two, commits
a samurai to act with great compassion in the service of humanity. I have rummaged
through Bushido literature to find support for the rare moment of heroic dissent, an
appeal to some transcendent value that passes judgment on both national and family
interest. One unusual anecdote in this tradition tells of a young samurai's decision to
die rather than renounce belief in Buddha at the whim of his lord. The lord surprises
everyone by praising the man's fidelity to his spiritual teacher, surely the best forecast
that such a soldier will show genuine loyalty to his feudal lord.

Ignazo Nitobe wrote *Bushido: The Soul of Japan* in 1899 as an introduction to
Bushido for Europe and America. Yet he spent his later years trying to clear up recurrent misunderstandings between Japan and America. He was impatient, too, to
preserve this Bushido ideal from Japanese militarists who misapplied many passages
from his earlier book. A fervent Quaker, active in the League of Nations, Nitobe
tried, despite a developing conviction of failure, to erect a synthesis between Bushido,
Quaker spirituality, nationalism, and internationalism. Individual persons must each
shape their own deeper personality and not merely conform to some external ethic
or guide. Nitobe prods samurai military obedience to develop into a more authentic
Shinto loyalty, which he identifies with the Inner Light of Quakerism: "The samurai
standard of right and goodness was too often decided by outward human relations,
rather than by the inward voice of the Spirit."[42]

This genuine inward Bushido spirit can be exemplified in the celebrated feminist Fukuda, mentioned already. The anarchist Sugako Kanno also comes to mind, with her fearless Humanist conscience, though I do not side with her ideology of casual violence. Condemned to death in 1911 for an attempted bomb plot against Emperor Mutsuhito, she explained that protests expressed by waving red banners cannot match the effectiveness of protests expressed by a string of random assassinations. "Those who sacrifice their lives for a cause are accorded the highest honor and respect by later generations. I shall die as one of the sacrificial victims." When the Buddhist prison chaplain offered to pray with her while she awaited hanging, Kanno responded, "It is ludicrous for an anarchist who is against all authority to turn to Amida Buddha for peace and security simply because she faces death....I have my own beliefs and peace of mind."[43]

To head my list of model samurai dissenters I have chosen three unlikely warriors, each brave in an unpretentious way and faithful to what Nitobe calls an inward spiritual voice. The first is Yukichi Fukuzawa — pacifist, teacher and writer, translator and publisher, and founder of Keio University — who mediated between the cultures of Asia and Europe in the last decades of the nineteenth century. Raised in a middle-class samurai family, he witnessed all the inept bureaucracy and arrogant violence of the Tokugawa Shogunate in its final decline. He decided early in his career that no worse government could exist on earth, and one's major goal must be just to escape alive. Thus, disposing of his samurai long-sword by selling it, he refused the summons to war in defense of either his Nakatsu clan or the nation. "It was as if my mind," he says, "were washed clean of what people call the yearning for honor." When the army tried to draft students taught by Fukuzawa, he prompted them all to feign an excuse of illness. "For this kind of absurd war,...the lives of my students were too precious. Even if they were not to be hit by the bullets, they might hurt their feet on thorns." In 1868 he formally renounced his samurai rank and became a commoner.[44]

Completed thirty years later, his celebrated autobiography offers an explanation why Fukuzawa at his newly established private college abolished the Confucian tradition of ceremonial bowing. "The Japanese people had lived under oppressive social restrictions for centuries, and had acquired the habit of passive obedience. In directing these people into a more active life, the injunction against bowing was one step." Challenging the slavish tendency throughout Japanese history to fall back on Chinese and Confucian precedents, his school would aim at fostering "spiritual independence." Blaming "the dregs of Confucian philosophy," too, for Japan's sterile civil bureaucracy, Fukuzawa defines his own vocation: "If I could do nothing toward improving the condition of politics, I could at least attempt something by teaching what I had learned of Western culture to the young men of my land, and by translating Western books and writing my own."[45]

"I have always remained a private citizen," he says, "avoiding all political connections. I have often expressed my own ideas on political matters both in speech and in writing, and they were sometimes in opposition to the government." Repeatedly declining a government post, he remained intolerant of civil officialdom, during the Shogunate most of all, but even throughout the later reformist Meiji regime. "The titles of nobility should have been given up with feudalism, but the men in office were bent on keeping them, thus contriving to place distinction between officials and ordinary people as if the former belonged to a nobler race of people." A consistent egalitarian since his own student days, he declares, "I paid due respect to elderly people with white hair, but if they seemed to exact homage because of their title and office, I lost interest in conversing with them.... It was impossible for me to seek an official career which necessitated the bending of my knees before other people. Nor did I ever entertain the idea of rising high above everyone, for I did not care to hold my head above others any more than to bow down before my superiors."[46]

As my second ideal samurai, I have tracked down the agent behind an extraordinary deed, with motives so hidden or bland they trigger endless conjecture. If the crimes of Adolf Eichmann demonstrate the banality of evil, the generosity of this Japanese might have to be explained by the banality of good. Chinune Sugihara, the Japanese vice-consul in 1940 at Kovno, Lithuania, managed to authorize an estimated ten thousand exit visas for Jewish refugees. He stamped visas for all Jews who applied, even those without any identification papers, and continued this openhanded policy after he and his family were transferred to Nazi-occupied Prague. While other consulates throughout Europe were shutting doors, Sugihara issued transit permits that launched Jews through a dangerous exit route, across the Soviet Union by the Trans-Siberian and Manchurian Railroad into Japan. There the refugees were to sail allegedly for the United States, Israel, and various countries in Latin America.

Shortly before his death in 1986, Sugihara was honored as a "Righteous Gentile" by the Israeli government for his sacrifice and risk. He recounts how Tokyo authorities had grown alarmed at the Jewish multitudes pouring into Japan, most of them processed in Lithuania. Three times Sugihara sought permission to continue issuing permits anyway, but his superiors in Tokyo refused with mounting vehemence. However, he disobeyed these orders and was dismissed when he returned to Japan after the war.

What motives can account for Sugihara's act of defiance? Crowning him a Japanese Schindler, the press continues today to speculate about the reticent depths of Sugihara's generosity. Among possible influences they point to his White Russian first wife, a Russian Orthodox, or his friendships with particular Jews, or his lifelong cosmopolitan education and exposure that helped him transcend the heartless, fixed boundaries of nationalism. Or perhaps this modern samurai took the Hagakura fourth vow with the utmost seriousness — manifesting great compassion, to act for the service of humanity. At any rate, Sugihara himself offers just a few plain words of explanation: "I acted according to my sense of human justice, out of love for humanity." His wife Yukiko's rationale sounds even more matter-of-fact: "Hundreds or thousands of lives depended on us.... It was impossible for us to leave them behind."[47]

Perhaps my third illustration of genuine samurai dissent, centered on an inward battle in one individual life, has less cosmic impact than the first two, but I refuse to minimize it. A few years ago, a vaguely familiar Japanese face appeared suddenly, and the man asked to talk with me. Older, heavier, and balder than the young Japanese undergraduate I had once known at the University of San Francisco, he began to tell of the punishing eight years he had just left behind in Tokyo. Employed as a sales agent and translator for a small export company, he had been asked at first to room for a few months with the boss and his family, so that they could form a close father-son relationship as the nucleus to this new company.

His work routine after this consisted in launching a series of phone calls during night hours to shops in different time zones throughout the world. He would survive each day by snatching a few afternoon hours of sleep, resting his head upon a dictionary on the floor. Each weekend he traveled two hours by train to his parents' home, there to drink compulsively, stare at late night television, and sleep off hangovers. Laboring so hard for a minimal salary, at times he summoned the courage to beg for a raise in pay. However, the owner would delay, reminding him about their bond of intimacy, the need for mutual sacrifice, and their company's reliance on this indispensable adopted son.

The narrator interrupted his narrative now and then with self-deprecating jokes about Japanese workaholics — seven-to-eleven ghosts married to their corporation, with no space left for love or the soul. He grieved to find his life turned into a parody of Confucian or Shinto loyalty. Months piled up and became eight years, yet he had not been able to face the potential shame of quitting or even protesting his brutal work conditions.

My friend's mind eventually turned back to a single moment in earlier life, when he had found the courage to dissent. Seijin No Hi, "the day of grown-ups," is celebrated each January 15 in every community for all those reaching twenty. This is the Shinto rite of passage to adulthood. Unlike any of his peers, this young man had thought himself still immature at twenty. Despite pressures from his disappointed family, he refused to take part in such a lie. Now a decade afterwards, recalling and reviving the spirit of his bold adolescent refusal, he decided to phone a travel agency and book an impulsive flight to San Francisco. For him this U.S. city symbolized freedom, an innocence he had left behind, a reprieve, perhaps even a healing. Moments before departure at the terminal, he faxed back to the office this message of explosive ambivalence: "I hate you. You have ruined my life. Forgive me for letting you down. I never want to see you again."

One stereotype of traditional Japan — and also of both precommunist and communist China — implies a ruling class seldom tolerant of any civil dissent enacted in the name of a more universal principle. Yet I am convinced that the Confucius of the Analects, though upholding consistent deference to parents and civil authorities, recognizes nothing higher than loyalty to the Tao itself: "How can someone be said to be truly loyal, who refrains from admonishing the object of one's loyalty?" In another context he says, "What I call a great minister is one who will only serve his prince while he can do so without infringement of the Tao, and as soon as this is impossible, resigns."[48]

It is no surprise to find this advice of Confucius reinforced by the Taoist Chuang Tzu: "If you are willing to regard the ruler as superior to yourself and to die for him, then how much more should you be willing to do for the Truth."[49] The notion of loyalty in Confucian ethics should never be understood just as personal fidelity toward parents and rulers. It reaches beyond the person exercising authority to the symbolic office itself, and beyond this to all humanity. It is self-devotion, the duty of conscience prompted by the innermost Tao.

An image of Shiva, ecstatic Lord of the Dance, stamping out evil in a circle of flame, and thus ever creating a new cosmos. Seven-inch bronze. Madras.

3

The Hindu Way

The disparate religions of the world can be sorted into distinctive family units sharing more or less a common historical legacy. The Tao traditions just discussed, Confucian and Taoist and Shinto, illustrate one such configuration. In the following five chapters, roughly in historical sequence, two important units will be explored. First, the Indian Wisdom heritage will appear, consisting of Hindu and Buddhist Ways, and then the Abrahamic Prophetic heritage, namely, the Jewish, Christian, and Muslim Ways.

The Hindu religious tradition is often compared to an ancient sprawling banyan tree, with myriads of unrelated animals seeking a fixed or temporary home in its shade. Rooted in the Vedic scriptures, it covers the overlapping rituals and beliefs of various Indus valley peoples, most of them now settled in present-day India and Nepal, with huge diaspora communities in Pakistan, Bangladesh, Afghanistan, Sri Lanka, Bali, and the Pacific islands. No simple unifying scheme can bring order into the millions of Hindu Gods, the colliding religious sects, or the crowded stage of gurus and swamis. When asked to identify their religion, many Hindus prefer to call it not Hinduism, the term used in textbooks and by outsiders, but just the Dharma.

The Dharma has some rough parallels with the Tao described in chapter 2. The term "Dharma" comes from the root *dhr,* meaning to uphold or hold together. The term shows wide flexibility, now narrowed to indicate a particularist Hindu heritage, now expanded into the universalist core of all world religions, a *philosophia perennis.* Some Hindus define their heritage as just an ethnic religion, like the Jewish tradition, not geared for proselytizing. Yet other Hindus, notably in the twentieth century, see their legacy as an exportable global religion, sending forth Indian missions especially to the United States and Europe. Movements such as Transcendental Meditation or the Self-Realization Fellowship, for instance, even prefer to tone down their specific Hindu origins.

The devout Hindu will ask: What must I do to be saved? Or how can I be freed from the soul's endless reincarnations? Lacking an official church organization, and citing various sacred scriptures, many of which claim no exact authoritative canon, swamis tend to handle these questions in either of two ways. The particularist would say: follow the Hindu common law tradition, the *varnashrama-dharma,* which apportions moral responsibility depending on your specific hereditary *varna* or caste and your specific *ashrama* or developmental stage of life. The ancient Laws of Manu and later legal codes, for instance, sift through accumulated customs to piece together an ideal norm of behavior — how young students should serve their guru, or how higher caste newlyweds should pray before spending their first night together, or whatever taboos ensue after unavoidable contact with someone outside one's caste.

The universalist, however, would handle the same questions in another way: discern your own unique Dharma, find a suitable yoga, follow your conscience. Draw inspiration from the life of your selected guru and from myths about your chosen God-image. Because this individual quest is common to all human beings, Dharma means *sanatana-dharma,* or the dynamic cosmic order itself — what Thomas Aquinas calls eternal law or natural law. Swami Aurobindo describes it as the law of the Absolute within us, the ideal pattern of social relations enabling each being to realize its divine capacity.

Those who search for a balance between particularist and universalist polarities of the Hindu Way might look for someone living with self-critical selectivity as a traditional Hindu. An excellent illustration is Mahatma Gandhi, who called his religion Vaishnava Dharma, and usually followed strict Hindu prayer and diet conventions. He spoke at times as a confirmed particularist. Though using the nonpartisan term God, he seemed unaware that his idiosyncratic Hindu God-image and spirituality might alienate many Muslims. For example, his favorite mantra, a prayer based on the name of Rama, survives as his last spoken words. And his political speeches often looked forward to an Indian millennium called Rama-raj, a royal title from the Purana Scriptures.

When particularist tendencies in the Hindu tradition heighten, they veer toward ultraorthodox Hinduism, and at the extreme, a Hindu fundamentalism. For instance, since March of 1998, the Bharatiya Janata Party has led a minority coalition government under Atal Vajpayee as prime minister. In the recent past this party identified its platform with *hindutva,* meaning Hindu pride, or even Hindu supremacy — one of the many recurrent campaign catchwords used to justify the restriction of full Indian citizenship only to Hindus. The BJP's membership overlaps with the RSS and its VHP offspring, nationalist groups responsible for the riots a few years ago over the Babri Mosque in Ayodhya. From a Hindu militant perspective, that mosque had been located centuries before by Muslim conquerors to desecrate the temple birthplace of the Hindu God Rama. Some historians still hold these same groups responsible for inciting Gandhi's assassination because of his alleged favoritism toward Muslims.[1]

Yet Gandhi himself, outraged by narrow Hindu particularism of this sort, most often spoke the language of aggressive universalism. As a reformist Hindu, he denounced the long-condoned practices of child marriage, animal sacrifice, and all discrimination against untouchables. His own individual religion, he would always say, transcended Hinduism, Islam, and Christianity. Without replacing other traditions, it harmonized them. He insisted that error can claim no exemption, even if supported by quotations from the Vedas, Bible, and Quran. Gandhi counted nothing true unless it conformed with reason and could be spiritually experienced.[2]

This particularist-universalist dialectic, I recognize, is common to the history of most world religions. It will act as a clarifying framework in the present chapter. Singling out a few branches from the amorphous Hindu banyan tree, I shall trace two modern religious movements, Advaita Vedanta and Krishna Consciousness, universalist and particularist polarities, cool religion and hot religion, back to their roots in the central Hindu tradition. My third section will examine the controversial guru-disciple relationship, which these two movements, and almost all Hindus, consider crucial for genuine spiritual growth.

THE ONE AND THE MANY

Some years ago I attended a Catholic wedding ceremony for an Indian-American Hindu and his young Catholic bride. A former student in my world religions class, the groom had often expressed his Hindu tolerance for religious viewpoints other than his own. These lines from Gandhi had become his favorite motto: "Religions are different roads converging to the same point. What does it matter that we take different roads, so long as we reach the same goal?" The couple asked that a few distinctive Hindu touches be added to the traditional Catholic wedding ceremony, such as a banner displaying the sacred mantra "Om" and a red *tika* painted on the bride's forehead. They were eager to give their future children an ecumenical exposure to all major religious traditions.

The man's Hindu parents, however, from their first introduction to the fiancée of their only son, could not reconcile themselves to either a non-Indian or non-Hindu bride. Yet just a few weeks before the wedding itself they were shocked to find the swami at their local Indian temple unwilling to support this opposition. Instead he imposed a month's harsh fast on the parents as punishment for their intolerance and urged them to open their hearts to a new daughter. By fasting and prayer, the swami told them, maybe they could purify their house of all this hate. Later confiding his feelings to me, the groom watched with sympathy during the wedding banquet as his penitent mother and father substituted orange juice and a salad for the rich meal served to everyone else.

Today after eight years of marriage and a few children, this Hindu-Catholic alliance has taken an unpredictable new turn. I notice she now surrounds herself with more distinctive Catholic symbols than before, such as a crucifix and rosary, and attends Mass more often, but alone. Reacting perhaps to his wife's inflation of religious differences, he has set aside his own separate shrine alcove in their home, where he performs daily *puja* or worship to an image of the God Krishna. He now yearns for the day his entire family will take part in these standard bhakti rituals, presided over by the brahmin head of their home.

Though communicative with each other on most else, my two friends claim they now scarcely mention religion. I have been unable to pin down the reasons for this drift away from the universalism inspired mostly by the husband's earlier expansive Hindu vision. Maybe religious plurality and harmony were just naive catchwords. Or husband and wife each found a later need to connect lofty abstractions to some specific familiar ritual. Or society itself and their families of origin pressed a separate religious identity upon each of them. Or they could not agree about the extent to which each child would be initiated into both Catholic and Hindu traditions. Or routine marital differences were translated into religious power-trips, and the couple had to compromise by respecting the integrity of two spiritualities, separate but equal. At any rate, each party has now recovered a particularist legacy, long dormant.

This shift from universalism to particularism, illustrated by the surprising religious change in this young Hindu, suggests important parallels in the modern Hindu tradition. The Ramakrishna Movement, for example, adapted itself in just this sequence, as it gradually found a public voice in the United States and Europe. From a magisterial Vedantist philosophy, without images or ritual, it evolved into Vedantist worship, with mantras and incense before an image of the guru and avatar Ramakrishna.

On a more cosmic scale, almost all the major Hindu-Buddhist traditions have followed this same progression in exporting their teachings to the West. For instance, the initial Chinese Taoist impact on Europe came from the tao chia, its lofty moral aesthetic teaching; the second influences followed much later, from tao chiao, its specific ritual and devotional practices. The first modern historical period of Hindu-Buddhist influence was largely philosophical — the Idealist metaphysics of Coleridge or Schopenhauer or Emerson, the mind-power of Christian Science, the self-transformation guidebooks of Theosophy. The prevailing scenario in the second period was a private session of meditation and spiritual advice at the feet of a guru, usually Asian and trained in a certified guru lineage. The third phase, especially in the United States, coincided with the 1960s counterculture, alienated enough from the mainstream to welcome a transplanted culture of Indo-chic dress, food, poster art, dance, yoga, and religious images.

The Vedanta Universal

In 1993 many religious scholars met for a centenary celebration of the famous Parliament of Religions, first convened during the 1893 Chicago World's Fair. That earlier world congress was dominated by a dynamic figure in turban and orange robe, Swami Vivekananda of the Ramakrishna Order, whom the American press and lecture halls continued to acclaim a decade afterward. As a brilliant apologist, he brushed aside the disparagements of Indian culture by Christian missionaries and vindicated the tolerance, nonviolence, and spiritual depth of his people.

The religious message of Vivekananda was candid and clear-headed, alert to the era's fascination with scientific method, progressive social reform, and the quest for new varieties of spiritual experience. Coming from a country which is a "hotbed of religious sects," he explained, he had learned that the highest spirituality had little to do with buildings and public worship. True religion could be reduced to inner self-realization, a goal reached by meditation and yoga. It also implied an activist service of the poor, which had prompted him to establish the hospitals and schools of the Ramakrishna Mission. When asked by reporters if he intended to introduce America to Hindu practices and rituals, he said, "I am preaching simply philosophy."[3]

The religions of the world are not contradictory, Vivekananda taught, but various phases of a single eternal religion. Thus, he could claim to worship God in all the forms in which the various religions clothe their God-images. "I shall go to the mosque of the Muslim. I shall enter the Christian's church and kneel before the crucifix. I shall enter the Buddhist temple, where I shall take refuge in the Buddha and in his Law. I shall go into the forest and sit down in meditation with the Hindu, who is trying to see the Light which enlightens the heart of everyone." The notion that there exists only a single religious path that everyone must follow is "injurious, meaningless, and entirely to be avoided.... Your way is very good for you, but not for me. My way is good for me, but not for you.... How can people preach of love who cannot bear another person to follow a different path from their own?"[4]

Can truth be one and yet many at the same time? Vivekananda thinks that people may have different visions of the same truth, filtered through different cultures, different individual character traits. "Knowing that as long as there are different natures born in this world, the same religious truth will require different adaptations, we shall understand that we are bound to have forbearance with each other. Just as nature is unity in variety — an infinite variation in the phenomenal — [and just as] in and through all these variations of the phenomenal runs the Infinite, the Unchangeable, the Absolute Unity, so it is with every person."[5]

By introducing the term "phenomenal" here, Vivekananda wants to affirm an important cross-cultural parallel between ancient Hindu teaching and mainstream European philosophy. "This same conclusion," he insists, "was arrived at a later date by the great German philosopher Kant." Just as Brahman the Absolute must be distinguished from its many playful maya disguises, so Kant's unknowable noumenon must be distinguished from its phenomenon-categories of time, space, and individual differences. Vivekananda describes his own theology as Advaita Vedanta. By Vedanta, he means to center his teaching on the Upanishads, those philosophical dialogues that climax the Vedic revelation. Advaita, based on Shankara's ninth-century Upanishad commentaries, implies pantheistic monism, or more accurately, a metaphysics "beyond dualism." Throughout this chapter *Vedanta* and *Vedantist* will refer to Vivekananda's Advaita Vedanta movement.

Even a cursory outline of Advaita Vedanta, just one among six major historical Hindu schools of philosophy, will help indentify the source of today's accepted textbook simplisms about all Hinduism. Brahman is the only reality. From Brahman's viewpoint, your empirical self, as distinct from your transcendental self or atman, is just an appearance. The world's multiplicity, too, is only an appearance. However, from the viewpoint of the empirical self — especially that of a person socialized in an era of positivism and utilitarianism — the world and your self strike you as real and independent. Actually, all these sense data are only maya, meaning a dream or projection that your ignorance treats as reality. If you could only realize it, the human condition is actually estranged, cut off from the Brahman-atman unitive experience. The goal of your life must be to penetrate beyond your empirical self and recover that original sacred unity by following various *margas* or paths, adapted to each individual's temperament or vocation. In reaching God-realization or salvation, you will add one more step to Brahman's own evolving circular return from apparent multiplicity to cosmic unity.

Vedanta's major strength is a sweeping inclusive viewpoint; it is not just tolerant of religious differences but generous and affirming, often capable of summoning forth the highest potential in people and in the world. It offers a flexible path to the interior life for those disillusioned by sectarian religious rivalries, by the idolatry of ritualism, legalism, and dogmatism. Vedanta's first apparent limitation, however, is the chasm opened up between the transcendental "higher" realm of meditation and the empirical "lower" world of social action. And thus, people may be tempted to escape social problems by spiritual solipsism. To counter this threat, Vivekananda, touched by the same activist Hindu reform movement that produced Gandhi, hoped to translate Vedanta's heady cosmology into an ethic of engaged service: "Know through Advaita that whomever you hurt, you hurt yourself. They are all you. Whether you know it or not, through all hands you work, through all feet you move. You are the king enjoying life in the palace, you are the beggar leading a miserable existence in the street. You are in the ignorant as well as in the learned, in the weak as in the strong. Know this and be sympathetic."[6]

If this Vedantist framework is kept in mind, Vivekananda's exuberant lectures can be read with more discernment. Speaking in the poetic mode of Whitman or some other romantic seer, he often intends his words as a literal metaphysical assertion: "All minds are mine, with all feet I walk, through all mouths I speak, in everybody I reside." Or again, "I am the infinite spirit, I am that I am.... I enjoy the good and I enjoy the evil, I was Jesus and I was Judas Iscariot." Brahman the Godhead is "the reality behind all that exists. Brahman is the goodness, the truth in everything. We are Brahman's incarnations."[7]

When Vivekananda commends religious tolerance, then, his words seem irenic, welcoming as many religions as possible, treating each with equity. However, to promote religious pluralism, he yearns to speed up the very process that most other religious leaders deplore — a self-destructive splitting into countless sects, until "each individual is a sect unto himself. Again, a background of unity will come by the fusion of all the existing religions into one grand philosophy,... leaving each at liberty to choose his teacher or his form as illustrations of that unity." Yet Vivekananda goes much further than this. He thinks Christ and Allah and Krishna are mere concessions to our need for humanizing the Impersonal Principle. "The Personal God," he admits without ambiguity, "is the Absolute looked at through the haze of maya-ignorance." Bibles and Gods "are but the rudiments of religion, the kindergartens of religion.... The hour comes when great people shall arise and cast off these kindergartens of religion, and shall make vivid and powerful the true religion, the worship of the spirit by the spirit."[8]

In Madras over a decade ago, a brahmin family invited me one evening to a tasty vegetarian meal. Held captive for hours at the table, I listened with polite docility as the host, a refined barrister in his late fifties, and his son expounded these very passages and others from their family collection of Vivekananda's complete works. A Hindu particularist in his fondness for the conventional rituals, the man guided me before dinner to a small chapel reserved only for family puja. Though non-Hindus could not enter this chapel, I was invited to observe from the doorway as he chanted mantras, bathed the feet of a Rama statue as a gesture of hospitality, and decorated the God devoutly with flowers.

My brahmin hosts, despite reassuring me of their admiration for Christian spirituality, and quoting from Vivekananda, persisted in viewing my own tradition through their Vedantist filter as just a handful of archetypes and moral parables. As Vivekananda observes, all the other religions besides Vedanta "have been built around the life of what they think a historical man. And what they think the strength of religion is really the weakness, for disprove the historicity of the man, and the whole fabric tumbles to the ground.... Our allegiance is to the principles always, and not to the persons.... If the principle is safe, persons like Buddha will be born by the hundreds and thousands."[9] Like Vivekananda, my brahmin friends interpreted Jesus not as a particular historical man but as a symbol of all humankind, or just one of the Absolute's many avatars. Citing the passage in John's Gospel where Jesus says, "Whoever sees me sees the Father," the brahmin lawyer went on to interpret this remark as applicable to everyone, each capable of God-realization. New Testament phrases such as

"Kingdom of God within" or "worship in spirit and truth," quoted alongside passages from the Quran and Vedas, all came out sounding like the same Vedantist message.

I am convinced that Advaita Vedanta theology, as taught by Vivekananda, though using the vocabulary of tolerant pluralism, sets up an actual hierarchy of religions. Certainly he perceived his own religion as the hidden core of all other religious traditions. Furthermore, this Vedantist vision is the spiritual pinnacle toward which all other religions will evolve, once they free themselves from delusions about their own exclusive particularity. "Would to God," he says, "that the whole world were advaitist tomorrow, not only in theory, but in realization. But if that cannot be, let us do the next best thing. Let us take the ignorant by the hand, lead them always step by step just as they can go, and know that every step in all religious growth in India has been progressive. It is not from bad to good, but from good to better."[10]

More recently, the popular writings of Aldous Huxley, Ananda Coomaraswami, Alan Watts, and Deepak Chopra have repeated this influential Vivekananda thesis. They propose that at the core of each world religion, especially the mystics everywhere, is a philosophia perennis, affirming that God and the self, Brahman and atman, are a single reality. The particular individual is not fully real. Inner realization is the pivotal expression of religion. Perhaps the most lasting influence in this school comes from the orientalist Frithjof Schuon, with his popular distinction between the esoteric and exoteric dimensions of religion. The esoteric is this same archetypal core, whereas the doctrines and rites unique to each religion are exoteric manifestations of the core. The path to religious universalism consists in downplaying crude exoteric particularities and winnowing from all those quarrelsome sects a future Vedantist elite.[11]

The Secret God of Vivekananda

In a letter written from the United States to a monastic house of the Ramakrishna Order in India, Vivekananda sums up his distaste for religious ritual: "What I am most afraid of is the worship room. It is not bad in itself, but there is a tendency to make this all in all, and set up that old-fashioned nonsense over again." Vedantist communities had tended to get mired in "these old effete ceremonials." Vivekananda says that disciples crave "for work, but having no outlet, they waste their energy in ringing bells and all that." Besides distracting them from active service, rituals seem regressive obstacles to a mature Vedantist spirituality. For those attaining the highest knowledge do not "worship God — having realized and become one with God. God never worships God." Or expressed in another way, "It is the big Me, the real Me, that the little me is worshiping." Thus, Vivekananda hoped the ideal Vedantist would prove "philosophically religious without the least mystery-mongering."[12]

Yet a year later Vivekananda writes from England to record a dramatic reversal of attitude. Two prospective English converts, by asking their teacher to identify the rituals of his creed, and expecting to be admitted into a new church, triggered a sudden moment of truth. "This opened my eyes," Vivekananda confesses. "The world in general must have some form. In fact, in the ordinary sense religion is philosophy concretized through rituals and symbols." Without such particularity, he concludes, Vedanta "will never have a hold on Western people." So he urges one of his disciples: "We must fix on some ritual as fast as we can. . . . We will fix something grand, from birth to death of a man. A mere loose system of philosophy gets no hold on mankind."[13]

Curious about the consequences of Vivekananda's change in attitude, I twice visited a famous Vedanta temple in Santa Barbara and spoke with sisters of the Sarada Convent there. Sarada Devi, from whom the community takes its name, was the Hindu mystic Ramakrishna's spiritual wife, who after her husband's death comforted and guided the earliest disciples. When I explored it a few years ago, this Vedanta temple in the Santa Barbara hills was a plain circular chapel, dark and unadorned except for three paintings facing the congregation — Ramakrishna in the center, Buddha and Jesus to his left and right. Though Jesus is pictured here as the Good Shepherd, I had been expecting "Jesus as a Yogi," the famous Vedantist print featured in their bookstore. The Yogi-Jesus image, with its allusions to Jesus' long desert retreat, conjures up tales about a legendary Hindu-Buddhist journey by Jesus in his twenties and an apprenticeship under Indian masters.

Current liturgies at the Sarada Convent consist first of Vedanta readings and group meditation, but they also include the customary Hindu puja of mantras, incense, perfume, flowers, and food offerings before the painting of Ramakrishna. Besides traditional Hindu feasts, this particular Vedanta community celebrates the birthdays of Ramakrishna, Buddha, and Jesus. For example, one year I knelt alongside a number of Sarada sisters attending midnight Christmas Mass at the nearby Jesuit novitiate chapel. This event was preceded by Christmas Eve vespers at their own temple, where they would also perform a special puja to Christ next afternoon and sing Christmas carols. A Vedantist commitment, then, may complement and enhance, not necessarily rival, a person's former religious identity. Or many followers treat their new faith as the matrix of all other religions and thus believe they are entitled to borrow compatible myths or rituals.

As Vivekananda's mission to America and Europe gained stability, he began to distinguish more openly between official Advaita Vedanta teaching and his own private spirituality. From the instant of his first Chicago address, I suspect, he had taken a shrewd measure of his audience. Shaping the gospel of Ramakrishna for the U.S. melting-pot, Vivekananda was prompted to strip it of immigrant Indian particularities and emphasize its Unitarian, Christian Science, or Transcendentalist kinship. In his lectures and private letters of later years, he admits a different but plausible explanation for his bold editing. He had kept silent about Ramakrishna's impact, he said, because he did not want the universal message of the Upanishads dismissed as the offering of just one more Hindu sect, focused on some new saint.

His encounter with Ramakrishna himself had been the crucial religious experience of his life. As a young law student he first met this gentle visionary in the Kali temple, and for months afterward, Vivekananda returned in mounting fascination. Ramakrishna's words would cause him to question his own arid skepticism, and the mere contact with Ramakrishna's hand or foot would throw him into a trance. Years later, no longer reticent about details of this conversion, he proved eager to defend the growing bhakti cultus that by then surrounded his master. If Vedantists can tolerate puja offered to Christ, Krishna, or Buddha, as incarnations of Brahman, then why not worship Ramakrishna, "who never did or thought anything unholy, whose intellect only through intuition stands head and shoulders above all the other prophets, because they were all one-sided"? Vivekananda felt embarrassed when others expressed love for a mere disciple like himself. "But they little dream that what they love me for is Ramakrishna. Leaving Him, I am only a mass of foolish selfish emotions."

Vivekananda's own spirituality centered not just on his master but more surprisingly on Kali, Shiva's double, the Goddess of Destruction, who pervaded the imagination of Ramakrishna. Vivekananda's final letters seem almost to invite Kali as a third into any conversation: "Mother knows best," he interjects, or "Glory unto Mother!" "Whatever of Mother's work was to be accomplished through me, She made me do, and has now flung me aside, breaking down my body and mind. Mother's will be done!" Yet as a disciplined spiritual director, Vivekananda knew better than to impose his own idiosyncratic spirituality on anyone else. "The Upanishads teach us all there is of religion. Kali worship is my special fad. You never heard me preach it, or read of my preaching it in India.... If there is any curious method which applies entirely to me, I keep it a secret and there it ends."[14]

According to Vivekananda's final assessment, Ramakrishna had all his life been nothing but an incarnation of Kali. However, it took the earlier Vivekananda six years of inner conflict before he could at last accept the Goddess as his own *ishta* or personal God-image. The master dedicated himself to Kali as her "slave," and only out of loyalty to Ramakrishna could Vivekananda at last agree to serve her. "At that time I thought him a brain-sick baby, always seeing visions and the rest. I hated it. And then I, too, had to accept Her!... You see, I cannot but believe that there is somewhere a great Power that thinks of Herself as feminine, and called Kali and Mother.... It is Brahman. It is the One. And yet — and yet — it is the Gods, too!"[15]

MANY GODS OF BHAKTI

The Indian press handled Vivekananda's triumph abroad with a mixture of applause, envy, and scorn. True, he deserved applause for proving spiritual India had something to teach the materialistic West. Yet he scandalized orthodox Hindus by violating caste taboos against travel outside India and, more important, by ordaining non-Indian women to leadership positions in the Ramakrishna Order. According to a few editorials, he had flirted with cheap success by mirroring back to the West an exotic version of its own favorite moral abstractions, mostly a doctored-up Hinduism. For instance, he liked to extol Hindu tolerance. But in the real India, "we know with what great acrimony and intolerance one Hindu sect hates another and all of them hate the Muslim or the Christian." He had converted not one person to a specific Hindu devotional tradition, which demands at least the choice of Vishnu or Shiva rather than Christ. "A Christian never becomes a Hindu by accepting only Hindu philosophy." Vivekananda's "dry philosophy, in which the growth of man is based upon poverty and celibacy, is not likely to catch the fancy of any large number of people in the land of modern civilization. We want something emotional."[16]

I can imagine the dismay Vivekananda's American and European disciples must have experienced on their first trip to India, much like the vertigo of Adela Quested and Mrs. Moore in E. M. Forster's *Passage to India*. Lifted from a quiet Vedanta reading room or lecture hall, they plunged now into the overwhelming sounds and smells and heat, swarming markets and temples, the parade of statues and banners, the hideous remains from animal sacrifices, and the line-up of emaciated fakirs and beggars. Some of this wonder and confusion struck me, too, the six months I lived in India, Bali, and especially Nepal, a land less urbanized and secular than India. In all these countries I often felt inspired by the presence of a religion other than my own, a force that seemed to animate the daily work and leisure of an entire society. The Gods surfaced everywhere, even on giant "Bollywood" movie ads. Wandering through crowds in various Tamil Nadu towns, for instance, I would pass by the Shiva Cement Company, Lakshmi Footwear, or Saraswati Bookstore. In many homes during those months, families were absorbed each night in TV serial installments from the great Ramayana and Mahabharata epics, with preternatural special effects.

At a rest stop near Kathmandu, I was invited a few times by drivers of huge diesel trucks to examine their dashboard altars and the sketches hand-painted on the sides of their trucks — Gods in pious and amorous poses from the epics and Purana myths. An electrician's shop displayed a calendar print of Krishna above the computer fixtures piled on an old work table. A few steps from my home in Kathmandu was an outdoor shrine to Shiva, centered on a polished stone phallus visited daily by many neighbors with flowers and food offerings, garbage that at night provided a meal for packs of local dogs. In Nepali election campaigns, each candidate was represented by a logo painted on fences and walls everywhere. When a Nepali friend once belittled these clever symbols as suitable just for an illiterate electorate, I compared them favorably to the slogans and one-liners of average American TV political commercials. I noticed that a sketch of a broom, shovel, and rubbish bin — meant to suggest a political clean-up — included other images, most interestingly that of a man-elephant who stood for Ganesha, the God who removes obstacles. This is the very God-image credited by the world press with recent miracles. If during puja to a Ganesha image, a spoonful of milk is held near his mouth, the liquid disappears.

Henotheist Perspective

Any reflective Hindu is challenged to make sense of all these Gods, numbered at three hundred million or more. A Vedantist, of course, can condense them all into the personified attributes of a single Brahman-atman principle. Or one can adopt the approach of brahmin theologians, whose *trimurti* concept still survives in most textbook introductions to Hinduism. This three-faceted formula picks out a few prominent Gods and relegates all others to the margins. Brahman, "the Lord God," states the Vishnu Purana, "though one without a second, assumes the three forms respectively of Brahma, Vishnu, and Shiva for creation, preservation, and dissolution of the world." Brahman the Absolute can be approached from either a pantheistic or panentheistic viewpoint — as identified with oneself or as distinct from oneself. Each God of the trimurti is assigned a female counterpart, his personified Shakti or power source. All these Gods, of course, adopt an avatar identity, such as Vishnu's Krishna or Rama incarnations. The trimurti formula, however, has limited usefulness. For instance, in my opinion, the formula attempts to insert Brahma, a brahmin God of the Vedas, into the company of two extracaste, non-Vedic Gods, Vishnu and Shiva. Further, according to historical record, Brahma has left almost no imprint on classical Hindu worship and art. And even if defensible theologically, Brahman's three manifestations do not mirror the three foremost public groups in contemporary Hindu worship. These are the Vaishnava, Shaiva, and Shakta movements — followers respectively of Vishnu, Shiva, and of all their female counterparts distilled into a single Mother Goddess. In common practice, each personal God may or may not be perceived as an emanation of the One Brahman.

Less doctrinal and uniform at worship than these theories suggest, and cherishing their own favorite Gods, most Hindus do not hesitate to call themselves polytheists. They enjoy imagining ranks upon godly ranks — numbers piling up endlessly, hinting that you will never find names enough to pin down the sacred mystery. One advantage of a polytheistic viewpoint is to set aside a unique Dharma and a unique God-image for each individual devotee. A second benefit is suggested by William James in *Varieties of Religious Experience.* An orderly monistic and monotheistic system, he fears, might succumb to a craving for logical coherence. It could trim away the mystery and rich ambiguity essential to a complete religious experience. For some temperaments, the ambivalent gentleness and savagery of fate can be imagined effectively in a Godhead split into personified attributes, sometimes at war, sometimes in shifting alliance.[17]

It is important to recall that most world religions make room for two distinctive uses of the imagination. First is the apophatic Path of Negation, the *Via Negativa.* This perspective is favored by many mystics, especially Taoists and Vedantist Hindus. Abandoning human love and any human facsimile, this approach seeks communion with the Absolute, a source beyond all personal or even impersonal attributes. Since it perceives the Sacred, a presence utterly beyond our reach, as Im-mutable, In-finite, and In-effable, its characteristic tactic is the disclaimer, "*Neti, neti*" — not this, not that. Ramakrishna compares such a quest for Brahman to a thief's search in some dark chamber for a cask of jewels. Brushing up against article after article, the thief murmurs, "Not this," but by means of these negations converges at last upon the treasure.

The second type of religious imagination is more prevalent, the kataphatic Path of Affirmation, offering intimacy with a personal God or Gods. Some traditions encourage, others forbid, the representation of this personal factor by human images. Even Hindu prophets, from one of the richest kataphatic traditions, never cease their warnings against idolatry. In R. K. Narayan's short story "Such Perfection," a sculptor labors five years to carve a lifelike image of Shiva as creative-destructive Lord of the Dance, with a ring of flames around him. Horrified at a glimpse of the completed work, a brahmin priest warns the sculptor, "This perfection, this God, is not for mortal eyes. He will blind us. At the first chant of prayer before him, he will dance, and we shall be wiped out. Take your chisel and break a little toe or some other part of the image, and it will be safe." But the sculptor refuses to comply. Soon whirlwinds, lightning, and floods pummel the village, and there is no peace until the providential crash of a tree, uprooted by the storm, happens to snap off a toe of the sculpture. By this time, even the sculptor has concurred, "The image is too perfect."[18] If the image becomes Shiva's rival, it will take on a destructive reality of its own, as part of Shiva's cosmic devastation.

These paths of both negation and affirmation have their own distinctive logic and grammar. Sin in the apophatic style, for instance, tends to be any ignorance that clouds an unfolding spiritual enlightenment and liberation. In the kataphatic style, sin tends to be an alien love that disrupts the love relationship with a personal God. Shankara, founder of the Advaita Vedanta movement, coined his own terms to describe these two approaches to the Sacred. For the advanced believer, Brahman is *nirguna* or beyond attributes. But for the uninitiated, Brahman is *saguna* — with the features, for instance, of Creator and Lord. In his famous prayer, Shankara apologizes for his own weakness, prone to visualize in contemplation the formless Brahman, to praise in hymns the ineffable Brahman, to visit in shrines the omnipresent Brahman.

Perhaps the term "henotheist" describes better than "polytheist" the tendency of most Hindus to adopt a single personal God-image without excluding the existence of alternate God-images. As a sort of serial monogamist, the henotheist is accustomed to pray, for example, "Kali, I love only you!" But at special shrines or on feast days, this loyalty may switch focus to the prayer, "Krishna, I love only you!" Scarcely any interest is shown in constructing an orderly pantheon of Gods. For centuries each God's attributes have been so expanded to match the claims of rival Gods that perhaps a single monotheist source is worshiped today under a few different traditional names. This syncretist accumulation of attributes, a measure of religious tolerance, and the Hindu passion for superlatives fuse to produce an exuberant art and mythology. No doubt the average God-image, created by artists unwilling to temper their completeness of vision, can end up bombastic and disjointed. Yet the image often attempts a bold *coincidentia oppositorum,* or what the Tao traditions call a yin-yang dialectic.

Mythmakers of the world strain to capture the vital dialectic in theologian Rudolph Otto's description of the Sacred as *mysterium tremendum et fascinosum,* simultaneously an object of shuddering awe and of loving ecstasy. Stretching ordinary language to describe her first Christian mystical experience, Julian of Norwich called it a "strange harmony of contrasts." It was "living and vivid and hideous and fearful and sweet and lovely." A recurrence of mad, stunning events is the usual way to show the Sacred cannot be contained within the normal framework of human kindness. In the Bible, God's loving fidelity guarantees any covenants, but God's wrath, irrational and terrifying, sometimes erupts to make God regret and smash all guarantees. The Book of Job's dramatic dialogue, for instance, portrays a kindly Creator, confronted by a doubting, manipulative satanic Double. Both dimensions combine to form one complete Godhead that imposes the suffering that we think Job does not deserve. By immersion in these tragic antinomies that underlie God's interactions with the world, you are summoned to take a trusting leap to the horizon beyond them. There you encounter what Scotus Erigena and Nicholas of Cusa call the sacred "opposition of oppositions, the contrary of contraries."

Hindu iconography and myth handle this religious dialectic with remarkable imagination. The benign Vishnu holds a conch shell in one hand to summon devotees, a flaming discus in the other to demolish those who turn away. Even the affectionate young Krishna is first a darling but mischievous child, then a trickster adolescent teasing his lovers and disrupting marriages. Kali, for example, may be the gentle mother cherished by Ramakrishna, but she is also the dark lady with four arms, two raised to bless worshipers, two holding weapons and the severed head of a giant. With a necklace of skulls and earrings of infant corpses, she dances out of control, threatening to destroy the cosmos. Shiva, the paradoxical God of both fertility and celibacy, savior and destroyer of the cosmos, haunts cremation grounds, dresses in skins of wild animals, and smears himself with ashes. The Shiva Purana tells how he once destroyed demons with fire from his third eye, the eye of visionary meditation. But this healing fire soon took on a life of its own, raging out of control in the villainous guise of Jaladhara, who returned as Shiva's destructive Double to undermine Shiva the redeemer.

The most numerous of Hindu devotional traditions, as remarked before, are those centered on Vishnu, Shiva, and the Mother Goddess. Chapter 1 has explained how a complete experience of the Sacred is marked by attitudes of passionate commitment, awe, moral seriousness, and ecstasy. Vishnavas tend to emphasize the fascinosum or ecstatic aspect, Shaktas the tremendum or uncanny. Shaivas fix on the compelling synthesis of both these polarities, either in a riot of images or in bare aniconic design. Any exploration into actual Hindu practice has to begin with a study of these wide-spread bhakti traditions and their God-images. It is essential to value them for their own particularity, not merely as impermanent steps to higher Vedanta enlightenment.

An Apologia for Bhakti

As described above, Vivekananda explains religious plurality by tallying different circumstances of geography, race, culture, and also each person's unique character traits. In one individual, "religion is manifesting itself as intense activity, as work. In another it is manifesting itself as intense devotion, in yet another, as mysticism, in others as philosophy." His examples here correspond point for point with the three ancient Hindu margas — the three paths to the Sacred, comprising the spiritualities of action, contemplation, and affectivity.[19] Throughout popular Hindu iconography, the Path of Action is represented by the *karma yogi,* an activist with busy gestures managing liturgical, family, and civic duties. The Path of Contemplation is personified in the silent *jnanin,* seated in a solitary yoga trance. The Path of Affectivity belongs to the *bhakta,* an ecstatic troubadour chanting and dancing for the Gods.

In the markets of Kathmandu, I found many paintings of a standing or squatting Hindu yogi, his stylized X-ray body marked by implied symbols for all three margas. Tantric or kundalini yoga views the full-fledged Contemplative Path as a late developmental stage in yoga practice. You are asked to imagine shakti energy acting like an uncoiling serpent, expanding in the body through consistent meditation and bodily exercises. It rises progressively through various chakras or gauges, activating the spinal column like a thermometer, from its base to a spiritual point above the head. As each dormant spiritual potential awakens, consciousness gradually shifts its center from the ego to the world, and finally to the Sacred.

A beginner might fixate early in spiritual growth, for example, on material concerns or sexuality, symbolized by the anus and genitals. Some may soon reach the third chakra, located symbolically at the navel, center of ambition and the will to power. This level is a matrix for the karma marga and its shortcomings. The fourth chakra, associated with the heart, offers a foundation for unselfish love and higher values — developmental roots for the bhakti marga. As energy ascends through the throat, eye, and brain skyward, the jnana marga emerges, the first in many expanding phases of higher consciousness.

This tantric chart has definite teaching advantages. First, by intertwining body and spirit, it avoids an ethereal spirituality or an unbalanced mind-body dichotomy. Second, by connecting all three margas in a developmental sequence, it encourages each individual to test out and combine all three. Yet the tantric blueprint is flawed at one crucial point. It subordinates the Path of Action to the Path of Affectivity and treats both as inferior to the Path of Contemplation. The advaitin Shankara had required that all untouchables and women, forbidden by caste law to study and meditate on the Vedas and Upanishads, should follow only the imperfect margas of bhakti and karma. His disciples argued that most of us in the present materialistic Kali-yuga era can cope only with the scaled-down demands of karma marga. Applying this same unquestioned premise to himself, Vivekananda, I suspect, fails to appreciate his own distinctive spirituality. "As soon as I find that bhakti feelings are trying to come up to sweep me off my feet," he complains, "I give a hard knock to them and make myself adamant by bringing up austere jnana." By overvaluing his own version of Ramakrishna's temperament, Vivekananda underrates his own unique spiritual gifts: "Outwardly Ramakrishna was all bhakta but inwardly all jnanin. . . . I am the exact opposite."[20]

It is ironic that despite years of close friendship, Vivekananda apparently misread the complex Ramakrishna as a disembodied jnanin. According to most Vedantists, Ramakrishna progressed at last to the highest jnana after long years of tantric and bhakti apprenticeship. Yet careful reading of the "Mahendranath Diary" in the *Gospel of Shri Ramakrishna,* prefaced by Nikhilananda's thorough biography, I think, provides a richer, more accurate portrait. "Once I fell into the clutches of a jnani," Ramakrishna complains, "who made me listen to Vedanta for eleven months. But he couldn't altogether destroy the seed of bhakti in me. No matter where my mind wandered, it would come back to the Divine Mother."

As a fervent Vaishnava, eager to befriend Rama as closely as the monkey servant Hanuman, Ramakrishna tells of spending months perched in the trees, eating only roots and fruit, and with part of his loincloth dragging like a tail, hopping instead of walking. Or cuddling a statue of the child Rama, he dances with it and gives it piggyback rides. "A million salutations to the knowledge of Brahman," he cries. "Give it to those who want it!" And "O Mother, let me remain in contact with men! Don't make me a dried-up ascetic. I want to enjoy Your sport in the world." These constant references to Kali and Mother have been mistranslated as the generic term "God" by some advaitin editors. Yet his final words were actually, "Kali, Kali, Kali!" Ramakrishna's tantric identification with Kali and his passionate yearning for Krishna and Rama, I am convinced, are no mere preludes to Vedantist culmination, but permanent features of his bhakti spirituality.[21]

To demean bhakti as an inferior spirituality, I think, is just an elitist bias, commonplace not only to Hindu contemplatives but to most mystics everywhere. Discounted and harassed by activist organizer types, perhaps the contemplatives of this world are tempted to retaliate by fantasies of otherworldly self-importance. At root the margas themselves are just three options, varying according to temperament, culture, particular religious custom, and individual experience. To evoke the best creative influences in all three, you must first discover a marga suitable for yourself. Then adopting it as principal aim, you subordinate the other two margas as essential means. In years ahead, the marga that dominates energetic youth may yield, of course, to a different marga during the final twilight. I think the margas should not be ranked; nor should one marga be pursued in isolation from the other two.

Among Vivekananda's many tributes to Ramakrishna, I find the following passage his most balanced appraisal: "Jnana is all right, but there is the danger of its becoming dry intellectualism. Love is great and noble, but it may die away in meaningless sentimentalism. A harmony of all these is the thing required. Ramakrishna was such a harmony."[22] In other words, the highest action and contemplation should be permeated by affectivity, or devout action must be the fruition of a most unwavering contemplation. Any one marga, lived with balance or integrity, can serve as a comprehensive spirituality.

Although the basic impulse to devotional self-surrender has never been absent from the Hindu tradition, the bhakti movement at its most vigorous extends from the eleventh to the eighteenth centuries. A common phenomenon in the history of religions is the sudden revival of spiritual feeling after a long period of dry ritualism, legalism, and dogmatism. For example, during the eighteenth century, once Lutherans and Anglicans had become a prosperous established church, they were rocked by new Pietist and Methodist upheavals. In an earlier period, an era of Muslim and Rabbinic orthodoxy triggered a prophetic rebuttal from Sufi and Hasidic mystics. And the decline of medieval Christian theology into academic debate spurred Abbot Joachim's apocalyptic visions, the utopian social protests of Spiritual Franciscans, and a popular movement called the Devotio Moderna. A product of the latter movement in the fifteenth century, *The Imitation of Christ,* the most widely read Christian book after the Bible, in a single line sums up the spirit of any bhakti reform: "I'd rather be able to feel contrition for sins than to define it." In the same vein, Luther exclaims, "It is not by reading and studying that you become a theologian, but by living, dying, and being damned."

For centuries in India, brahmin leaders had been supporting a Hindu revival, first to counter the Buddhist moral reform born within Hinduism itself and second to defy the Muslim religious and cultural forces encroaching from outside. As an alternative to Buddhism, Shankara had established his Advaita Vedanta communities of intellectual ascetics. To withstand Muslim influence, brahmin priests had reaffirmed the caste taboos and exacting rituals that tightened the distinction between Hindu and non-Hindu. What this restoration lacked was a vital touch of religious feeling. When the bhakti movements erupted in protest, they reached out with fervor to everyone, no matter what caste, race, or gender. New bhakti leaders, many from brahmin families, would base their authority no longer upon a hereditary priesthood but upon a spiritual lineage of gurus. Bhakti theologians Ramanuja and Madhva taught that God and your individual soul are inseparable but distinct — panentheism, in contrast to Shankara's pantheism — and therefore capable of a mutual loving relationship. With this sort of theological backing, prayer could now be a personal conversation, expressed not only in meditative study but even in dance and song before the Lord.

The central text for bhakti has always been the Bhagavad Gita, a brief segment of the Mahabharata, longest of all world epic poems. Bhakti is defended here as the most accessible and trustworthy of all three margas. Since Shankara, Gandhi, and almost all major Hindu thinkers have written their own partisan commentaries on this most influential of all Hindu scriptures, it may be useful to summarize my own interpretation. As Arjuna gets ready for a civil war against his own relatives, he cannot help but question the meaning of life, especially any sort of direct combat. All his misgivings are packed into a single question addressed to Krishna: "If your thought is that jnana marga is greater than karma marga, why do you enjoin on me the terrible action of war?" Concerned more about the margas themselves than the justification for war, Krishna takes a number of chapters to explain his answer.

First, Krishna claims that jnana or the Path of Contemplation is an excellent spirituality, but only for those capable of living it in depth. Second, jnana can be distorted by a purely negative or one-sided pursuit: "Not by refraining from action do people attain freedom from action. Not by mere renunciation do they attain supreme perfection." Third, not by the Path of Action or karma marga alone, but also by *nishkama* karma, one can reach all the aims of jnana. Nishkama means karmic action detached from the selfish desire for results and reward, somewhat similar to the Taoist concept of wu-wei. Centuries later, Gandhi, the contemplative activist, would pick nishkama karma as the name for his own distinctive marga. Gandhi's spinning wheel, the symbol still prominent on the Gandhi memorial in Delhi today, stands for a meditative jnana at peace with the spinning rhythm. At the same time it represents a militant karma marga — weaving India's own clothing, an act of rebellion against England's manufacturers and cultural dominion.

At this step of his argument, Krishna returns to Arjuna's question as first stated. By stressing only his own unaided efforts at jnana and karma, Arjuna has been overlooking a more crucial issue — the need for God's grace to prompt and sustain any initiative that is merely human. In the spirit of later Mahayana Buddhists and Augustinian Christians, Krishna commends the "yoga of union," a bhakti loving surrender to God, as the indispensable basis for both knowledge and action. "Those who set their hearts on me and ever in love worship me with unshakable faith, these I hold the best yogis.... If you are not able to practice yoga concentration, ... then take refuge in devotion to me, and surrender to me the fruit of all your work." Here the Sacred is not an impersonal Absolute but a loving personal God. Whenever suffering overwhelms us, whenever the world needs saving, God is ready to enter this life as a human or animal avatar.[23]

Krishna Consciousness

Just as the Gita expects the Way of Action to be stripped of all selfish desire, so it lifts bhakti also to the heights of nishkama. You must love Krishna not to reach a better rebirth or final salvation, but just for the sake of Krishna. Unless this motif of loving self-surrender is taken seriously, no one can appreciate a figure like Krishna Caitanya,[24] the famous sixteenth-century Bengali ecstatic who stands first in the guru lineage that underlies the contemporary Krishna Consciousness movement. As a young man, after the deaths of both his father and first wife, Vishvambhara Mishra had a religious conversion that left him intoxicated with the love of Krishna. This experience occurred at a shrine containing the huge stone footprint of Vishnu, a mark of God's incarnate presence on earth. The name Krishna Caitanya was given to him by his guru, and it means literally "Krishna Consciousness." With his eyes full of tears, Caitanya would now talk about nothing but the name of Krishna. His feet in a gentle dance step, eyes uplifted, arms flailing, hands holding wooden clappers to beat a tempo to the march, Caitanya would lead wild street parades that upset sober brahmins and especially their Muslim rulers. His Vaishnava followers danced and sang to the music, chanting "Hare Krishna, Hare Krishna, Hare Hare!" again and again in a crescendo of sound and speed, until many could feel an explosion of religious frenzy.

Whereas Vedantists view spiritual growth as an unfolding knowledge of the Absolute, the Caitanya tradition identifies growth with deepening levels of intense feeling.

Once you experience Krishna as a shakti force pulsing through your blood, you can be certain God's love is healing you. Ordinary love for your mother, child, spouse, or friend is only a slight foretaste of the love you will someday feel in God's embrace, once you reach salvation. In the meantime God does not wait for you to find God, but as an avatar descends into the world to seek you out. Before even the impulse to love God occurs to you, God has been loving you from the beginning. It is understandable that many disciples would soon focus their loving worship on Caitanya himself. They thought him the reincarnated Krishna or saw in his frequent swoons, tears, and laughter a lovesick Radha yearning for the presence of Lord Krishna. Now the divine lover, now the human beloved, Caitanya himself represents God's immersion into our complete human condition. God becomes human in order to experience how it feels humanly to love and be loved by God.

The Caitanya movement has also been called a Hindu musical revolution, mostly because love songs, mantras, and dance rhythms take the place of traditional Vedic sacrifice. Most Vaishnavas had already known *kirtan,* a form of congregational song praising a God-image by listing the God's attributes and glorious deeds. Through *nama-kirtan,* the only form of organized worship in his particular community, Caitanya would sing each name of Krishna with such intensity of feeling that he could induce in himself and his hearers an ecstatic trance. For most Hindus, the mantra "Om" — the first word of the first prayer in the Veda collection — sums up all the power of the Vedas and, when chanted, evokes in a sacramental way, or somehow brings about, the unity of all being. Its very sound contains within itself or incarnates God's power. For Caitanya, the various Krishna mantras had this same efficacy. For him the words and rhythm actually *are* the Real Presence of Krishna. Often at nama-kirtan meetings Caitanya would tremble and weep, stiffen and drop into fits, or suddenly run outside and clamber up a tree. As a broader spirituality, Krishna Consciousness has meant the infusion of this ecstatic bhakti moment throughout daily life, so that it permeates drama, poetry, painting, even eating and working.

For myself and most non-Indians today, experience of the Caitanya tradition has been limited to contacts with the Hare Krishnas, or the International Society of Krishna Consciousness. My first encounters with them in the 1960s proved an annoyance — the manic joy of bouncing acolytes, hairless and saffron-clad, book-selling or panhandling at sidewalk stalls or air terminals. Hare Krishna beginnings in America paralleled the quick growth of other religious communities, such as Scientology, Children of God, and the Unification Church, all accused of shady recruitment tactics and brainwashing. Soon newspapers reported a series of lawsuits — now Krishnas being sued for kidnapping, then Krishnas themselves in countersuits defending their First Amendment rights to proselytize. Then a few Krishna communes were investigated for allegedly stockpiling weapons, drug-peddling, and even compiling a hit list to kill off disenchanted ex-members. Today after three decades, with numbers declining, their world organization is split into leadership factions, quarreling over doctrine and spiritual authority.

Yet at the charismatic peak of this movement's growth, I explored a few Hare Krishna restaurants to try out inexpensive, tasty vegetarian dishes and came to respect the kind, vibrant disciples who cooked and waited table there. In San Francisco's Golden Gate Park, I joined a parade to celebrate the Krishnas' annual Chariot Festival, designed to replicate Caitanya's favorite Jagganatha feast at Puri. Amid delirious chanting and dancing, flowers and incense, the images of Krishna and Radha were displayed alongside Jagganatha statues on gigantic carts, a sort of dignified state-visit or a recreational outing for the Gods. Later, paging through their literature, I recognized the conventional bhakti pedigree for much that first looked so improvised and eccentric.

The founder of the Hare Krishnas was Swami Prabhupada, a retired businessman, commissioned at the unlikely age of seventy by his Vaishnava guru to convert America and Europe. Arriving at New York in 1965 with almost no funding, he rented a loft in the Bowery and began chanting and lecturing on street corners. His success was immediate. Attracting thousands of disciples from the counterculture, he raced through his last dozen years of life to found hundreds of communities and then a world organization. Despite suspicions to the contrary, his message was not packaged to attract a fashionable hippie audience. Prabhupada denounced the preachers he called "show-bottle spiritualists." No one can reach genuine Krishna consciousness without a life of austerity. Yet "if there are restrictions, rules, and regulations, people will not become attracted. Those who want followers in the name of religion, just to have a show only, then, don't restrict the lives of their students, nor their own lives. But that method is not approved by the Vedas."[25]

From his candidates Prabhupada asked a life of hard work for others, the submission of one's own will to the common good, and abstinence from meat and drugs and promiscuous sex. By chanting Caitanya's great mantra all day long, anyone could develop genuine Krishna consciousness and reach salvation. As his disciples multiplied, however, this simplified spirituality expanded to reinstate, one by one, familiar traits of the classical Hindu Way. Motivated perhaps to qualify for U.S. tax-exempt privileges, the movement gradually emphasized the trademarks of a Eurocentric-style church, with ordained sannyasins and fixed congregational ceremonies. Disciples were introduced to the major Vaishnava scriptures, trained in meditation, and taught to perform traditional Hindu puja each morning before an image of Krishna.

It is clear that Caitanya and Prabhupada both share the same bhakti tradition, but the circumstances of their mission differ sharply. Caitanya preached to a sixteenth-century Indian audience, Hindus and mostly Vaishnavas, familiar with kirtan, mantras, and the bhakti style. Prabhupada began as a poor, solitary immigrant in New York City, facing an audience mostly of drop-outs, drawn from secular or nominal Christian backgrounds. Though perhaps hankering unconsciously for the authority of a genuine spiritual leader, the crowds he faced often had religious vocabularies that were limited to words like "freedom," "individuality," and "rebellion." Ignorant of India and the Hindu tradition, indifferent to cultures other than their own, many of his hearers would have described themselves as too cool for bhakti emotional fireworks.

If asked to gauge the intensity of devotional commitment, most people today would consider Advaita Vedanta a cool religion and Krishna Consciousness a hot religion. Yet despite this contrast in style and mood, both movements stem from similar bhakti roots. Just as Prabhupada and Caitanya worship Vishnu and Krishna his avatar, so Vivekananda and Ramakrishna worship Shiva and Kali his shakti. As recounted before, Vivekananda began his mission by preaching a Vedantist moral philosophy — the gospel of Ramakrishna, cleansed of its Hindu oddities. This mission, of course, took place a century ago, in a more insulated Eurocentric era than at present. Later,

Vivekananda decided to restore a touch of ritual, Hindu or otherwise, to satisfy his public's immature craving for play and color.

Prabhupada, later spiritual counterpart to Vivekananda, stepped into an American milieu far less confident of its own religious identity, during a major cultural upheaval. From the beginning, he apparently planned to integrate traditional bhakti ritual into his Hindu teaching. Prabhupada's intent was favored by the rapid exodus of so many Krishnas from their city lofts and storefronts to form isolated rural communes, where the accustomed Hindu family rituals could be lived in their integrity. More important, stripped of its magic — the original Indian music, gestures, poetry, and rich connotative names — little of Caitanya's unique bhakti would have been left to transplant.

THE GURU-DISCIPLE VOCATION

The Hindu tradition, as explained before, disclosed itself to modern America and Europe in three historical stages. The first and third have been illustrated by the theology of Advaita Vedanta and the bhakti spirituality of Krishna Consciousness. Overlapping these two, the middle phase has been less permanent and organized — random scenarios of individual discipleship under a guru or of membership in a guru-centered ashram community. Vivekananda, for instance, gradually emerged as the guide of a small circle whose members had each been meeting or writing him for private spiritual direction. After offering advice to a friend, he writes, "You need not thank me, for this is only a duty. According to Hindu law, if a guru dies, his disciple is his heir. . . . This is, you see, an actual spiritual relationship, and none of your Yankee 'tutor' business!"[26]

Vivekananda's appreciation for the guru vocation has found parallels in the Krishna Consciousness community. According to various surveys, what attracts and sustains most of their candidates is not the chanting, temple worship, or doctrine, but the nurturing relationship with a particular guru. In a central passage of the Bhagavad Gita, Krishna gives Arjuna this advice: "Through your submission, the questions you ask, your service, those who have knowledge and see things as they are will teach you knowledge." Such knowledge, Krishna explains, is "passed on from teacher to teacher in an unbroken line." Prabhupada often cites this chapter as a proof-text demonstrating the link between Krishna-realization and finding an appropriate guru. "The Lord therefore advises," Prabhupada argues, "to approach a bona fide spiritual master in the line of disciplic succession from the Lord Himself." Such a master "should be accepted in full surrender." Disciples must be able "to pass the test of the spiritual master, who when he sees their genuine desire, automatically blesses them with genuine spiritual understanding." Today no follower can reach Lord Krishna directly except through the guru as "transparent medium, although it is true that the experience is still direct. This is the mystery of the disciplic succession. When the spiritual master is bona fide, then one can hear the *Bhagavad-gita* directly, as Arjuna heard it."[27]

The Sanskrit term *guru* means someone who dispels ignorance. For almost every Hindu, there can be no authentic spiritual training without a guru. As the principal mediator, "the guru brings the human individual and God together," says

Ramakrishna, "even as a matchmaker brings together the lover and the beloved. ...The disciple sees guru and God as one and the same." Vivekananda reinforces this same approach. Spiritual knowledge cannot be authentic unless it is mediated "through an apostolic succession from disciple to disciple, and unless it comes through the mercy of the guru and direct from his mouth....The guru is the bright mask which God wears in order to come to us. As we look steadily on, gradually the mask falls off and God is revealed."[28]

The Hindu guru must not be mistaken for a mere teacher, mentor, or psychotherapist. To appreciate this exalted spiritual figure, it is helpful to gauge the guru's influence, first within the conventional brahmin ashrama structure, and then within a typical guru-centered community or ashram.

Traditional Rites of Passage

The ancient Laws of Manu divide each life into four ashramas or developmental stages, the first two implying gradual involvement in the world, the last two gradual detachment from it. An adolescent male from one of the top three castes is expected to pass through the first ashrama. This apprenticeship in the guru's home is a twelve-year period of celibate student life, where the apprentice begins to study the Vedas, develop a mature moral identity, and train for a profession. The householder stage follows next, a time to marry, become a productive citizen and parent, and support generously those in the other three ashramas. Stages three and four, the phases of detachment from the world, are far less institutionalized. The third ashrama marks retirement to intensify the contemplative life — a solitary individual or married couple pledged now to celibacy, ceding career and family responsibilities to the next generation. The fourth ashrama demands *sannyasa* or complete renunciation, where you give up home, possessions, caste, ritual duties, and even your personal name, in prayerful waiting for death, alone or within some religious community.

An ordained sannyasin himself, Vivekananda after a few years in America began applying ashrama titles to his followers, notably his division of women into *brahmacharini* novices in the first ashrama and sannyasini professed religious. These same terms surface, too, in many Hare Krishna communities, distinguishing especially between second and fourth ashramas, the married householder and the vowed celibate sannyasin. Yet how pertinent is the ashrama sequence to the average Hindu in contemporary India?

Today the ashramas apparently survive in many rural joint-family systems and among orthodox brahmin families almost everywhere, but with less frequency in urban settings. Most students enroll not in a guru's quarters but in large state schools, and the rites marking their ashrama progression often shrink to the predictable routine decisions when to marry or retire. Yet even this fading tradition has left its imprint. For many Hindus, the developmental stages in their life cycle at least tend to be separated by recognizable rites of passage, sacraments that link these transitions with the primordial time of the Vedas. Contemplative styles of life become plausible options alongside those of wealth and workaholism. And in that society, I suspect the homeless ascetic, adolescent student, or retired grandparent are badgered less to justify their usefulness.

The ashrama sequence also introduces coherence into the laughter and tears, and

ongoing rites of death, puberty, marriage, and childbirth occurring almost simultaneously within the extended family structure. This collage of differing rhythms in
life is presented with mastery in the *Apu Trilogy* films of Satyajit Ray, which trace
a boy's climb toward adulthood, with each gain along the way accompanied by loss,
including the deaths of all five people closest to him. A characteristic scene in the
first film centers on the expanding consciousness of young Apu, surrounded by three
generations of women — his mother scrounging for meals, his sister eager to marry,
and his parasitic grandaunt. Here are four destinies at differing levels, separate but
somehow entwined.

An American adaptation of the ashrama tradition caught my attention two decades
ago, when my Hindu colleague invited our entire theology department one evening
to his suburban Detroit home. At dinner, we all listened in surprise as he and his wife
announced their agreement to enter jointly upon the third ashrama. Both pledged to
set aside more time for solitude and the spiritual life. The time seemed right — with
the birth of their first grandchild, the couple's son and daughter were now settled in
careers and homes of their own. This act of spiritual renunciation brought to mind
a comparable moment in the modern Anglo-Indian novel *The Vendor of Sweets* by
R. K. Narayan. The widower Jagan, after days of meditating on the Gita and sitting
at his Gandhian spinning wheel, decides finally to bequeath his candy shop and house
to an irresponsible son and join his swami-sculptor friend in a deserted park. This
resolution is greeted in the village of Malgudi as something traditional and matter-
of-fact. "I will seek a new interest different from the set of repetitions performed
for sixty years," he says. "I am going somewhere, not carrying more than what my
shoulder can bear. . . . I am a free man. . . . Everything can go on with or without me."[29]
Crossing the threshold of both the third and fourth ashramas in a single gesture, Jagan
now needs only a staff, begging bowl, and ocher garment to identify himself as a
traditional sannyasin.

Just as the third ashrama launches a training in withdrawal from the world, so its
exact converse, the first ashrama, starts training the young candidate for spiritual engagement in the world. The first ashrama is entered by a unique Hindu ceremony
called Upanayana, Rite of the Sacred Thread, with parallels to the Jewish Bar Mitzvah and the Christian Rite of Confirmation. Visiting the brahmin home of a student
friend near Madras, I once listened to an insightful family commentary about pho-
tos from a huge Upanayana festival album on permanent display next to the sofa.
Whereas many families enjoy introducing visitors to a comparable album of wedding
pictures, this home focused on the oldest boy's initiation a few years before. Proud
to describe the lavish ritual, to estimate the crowds and costs, and to laugh about
mishaps and confusion, members of the family replayed every stage of my friend's
initiation at the age of fifteen into his first ashrama. Again, at a Kathmandu center
for homeless boys, I once observed this same initiation ceremony, performed by two
elderly brahmin priests. After a few weeks of instruction on rudiments of their faith,
a group of about two dozen young men received the Sacred Thread. At one dramatic
moment in the three-hour ritual, each candidate donned a new Nepali hat and jacket,
further symbols of a fresh twice-born Hindu existence.

The scripture texts that accompany initiation into this first ashrama are especially
meaningful. In the classical Hindu tradition, a boy is dressed only in a loincloth when
introduced by his father to the guru. Calling him by name and commending him to

the care of various Gods, the guru touches the boy's head and breast to signify his full acceptance of him as a student. By investing him with a thread over his left shoulder, the guru establishes a bond between them. "May your pure heart ever hold me dear," the guru prays. "Under my direction I place your heart. Your mind will follow my mind. In my words you will rejoice with all your spirit. May God unite you with me." I once surveyed mature Hindu friends and random youngsters at a San Francisco community swimming pool, asking with deadpan naïveté why they wore this ragged thread on their shoulders, even when swimming. I got different explanations, most of them overlapping and plausible: a tie to your guru, a magic charm for protection, a chain binding yourself to a new caste identity, or a badge that must be stripped off before performing any future actions that might endanger caste purity.

The Laws of Manu, representative of society about 200 B.C.E. and after, give an idealized scenario of the way a disciple ought to live at his guru's home during the first ashrama. Under his guru, the young man studies and meditates, tends the sacred fire, and helps the guru's family with housework. Manu gives quaint directives on proper gifts for the teacher, methods of Vedic study, and many cautions against seductive women, masturbation, and standard frivolities. A true disciple even anticipates the commands of his teacher, obeying him as "the image of Brahman, . . . as his father and mother." He should never dress more fashionably than his teacher, nor rise later and go to bed earlier than he. "Controlling his body, speech, senses, and mind, let him stand with joined hands, gazing at the face of his teacher." The boy gets amusing warnings against coining nicknames behind the guru's back or doing parodies of the man's walk and speech. Even if he hears proper criticism spoken against the guru, "he must cover his ears or depart to another place. By censuring him, even justly, he will in his next incarnation become an ass; by falsely defaming him, a dog; . . . by envying his merit, an insect."[30]

The next two injunctions in this text seem to stretch the tradition beyond narrow boundaries of caste and fixed authority. "One who possesses faith may receive pure learning even from a person of lower caste. . . . Even from a child, good advice. Even from a foe, lessons in good conduct." And if the disciple commits himself deeply to his training, he might even surpass the learning of his master. "As one digging into ground with a spade obtains water, so an obedient student obtains knowledge which lies hidden in his teacher."[31]

However, as the Primal traditions have always recognized, sacred wisdom must not be profaned by reckless dissemination. As teacher of the Vedas, the guru should "rather die with his knowledge than sow it in barren soil. . . . Unless asked, he must not explain anything, nor answer someone who asks improperly." The guru must try to teach with "sweet and gentle words" and "without giving his student pain." Most important, how the guru lives, as well as what he teaches, must be exemplary for students. He merits their reverence only for his wisdom and holiness, not for white hair, wealth, or status.[32]

The Sadguru Option

In India an alternative guru tradition has long existed, parallel to the ashrama sequence just described, and today is poised to replace it. Instead of the bond between the brahmin Veda teacher and a young male novice in the first ashrama, this other bond between the guru and adult disciple cuts across distinctions of caste, gender, and formal ashramas. India has no shortage of names for this enlightened guide — *pandit, sadhu, sannyasin, rishi, swami, babaji, fakir.* I prefer the title *sadguru,* which combines the role of guru with that of sadhu, someone aspiring to *samadhi* or deep spiritual enlightenment. Today outside India the sadguru has become a familiar symbol of both reverence and scorn, especially after the Beatles' pilgrimage thirty years ago to the ashram of Maharish Mahesh Yogi in northern India and, later, the controversial expulsion of Bhagwan Rajneesh from his Oregon commune. A favorite target in cartoon editorials, the lone guru doling out answers from a Himalayan ledge has been replaced today by the bearded guru chauffeured in a fleet of Rolls Royces.

For many Hindus, finding just the right guru can be the most important decision of their life. At its best, this relationship promises an intimacy they might never experience within marriage, the family, or same-gender friendships. Such an option becomes a safety valve, too, in the tight ashrama social system. Joining a voluntary ashram community, some young males can avoid an arranged marriage or career, predetermined by family or caste. Strict, conventional, older brahmins, liberating themselves as sannyasins from burdensome hours of daily ritual prayer, can develop their own unique spirituality. Parents after retirement can escape confinement within an extended family or abandon a loveless marriage they had never freely chosen.[33]

Some gurus come from a formal lineage of gurus, with explicit ordained authority. For example, in the foreword to his Bhagavad Gita commentary, Swami Prabhupada, founder of the Hare Krishnas, lists his guru genealogy — a line of thirty-one gurus, with the God Krishna as first, Lord Caitanya as twenty-second, and Prabhupada as thirty-second.[34] In contrast, some gurus are of anonymous background and have improvised their own unique tradition. Thus, some gurus are also founders, or as avatars they may reincarnate the founder or even God.

I tend to be suspicious of gurus who stretch their avatar claim and, leaping over a doubtful or nonexistent lineage of gurus, attempt to merge directly with the founder or God standing at the origin of that lineage. Sathya Sai Baba, for instance, at the age of fourteen fell into a trance, from which he emerged as proclaimed avatar of the earlier guru Sai Baba of Shirdi. This more recent Baba is guru founder of a large movement known throughout Asia. At a meeting of his disciples in Singapore, where I was once invited to talk on the unity of world religions, the audience set aside a fervent half-hour chanting a mantra of five names, each word repeated eight times, accompanied by drums, clacking finger cymbals, and clouds of incense. Chanted up and down a musical scale, each name evoked a different world religion, all somehow blending into one universal vision — Allah, Krishna, Buddha, Jesus, and Baba.

Under a chosen guru, you may decide to combine the traditional first and fourth ashramas into vows of lifelong service. As described above, in the Advaita Vedanta and Krishna Consciousness movements, this commitment may involve renunciation of the world to live in a quasi-monastic setting. It is also possible to preserve the third ashrama or married option, which still implies partial commitment to the guru — a life of active family and professional duties, with periodic retreats and conferences at the guru's ashram to reinstate contact. Ashrams that feature a specific rite of initiation into a guru's fellowship often borrow motifs and rituals of rebirth from the ancient Upanayana rite. Gurus may invest disciples with the sacred thread or garlands and prayer beads. Some assign the ocher robe and staff associated historically with sann-yasin hermits. Some confer a secret mantra, or merely a significant touch or glance, somehow transmitting the gift of God-consciousness. In fact, many disciples recount experiences of a miraculous *shakti-pat,* an electric shock of power radiating from the guru at this instant in the ceremony.

As perceived today, the guru is no longer just the Vedic guide from an earlier ashrama tradition. That ancient figure had been a brahmin teacher, honored for his moral life and knowledge of the Vedas. Living out the Vedas, he could expect to re-ceive almost the same reverence as the Vedas themselves. Respect for the guru shows itself in the Upanishads — a term that literally means "sitting down at someone's feet," implying a philosophical dialogue between guru and disciple. Yet by the time of the bhakti revolution, recounted above, this veneration had heightened into worship. Gurus would now be respected not for a brahmin pedigree, nor Vedic knowledge, but for their inspiring spiritual endowments. In the tantric literature, rites tend to be secret and so complex that they need an extraordinary guru to embody and commu-nicate the proper training — someone superhuman, almost God-like. In the epics and Purana literature, the Absolute is humanized, now as a personal God, now as a range of avatars that even include the person of the guru.[35]

Among Caitanya's disciples, introduced earlier, many were said to worship Cai-tanya as an avatar of Krishna or of Krishna and Radha united. A few years ago I observed a devout Vaishnava at daily puja in his home. Removing a Krishna statue from the home altar for bathing, feeding, and worship, he then unfolded a white cloth containing the mark of his guru's footprints and kissed them in veneration. Today Vaishnava, Shaiva, and Shakta disciples often erect in their temples an image of the guru founder alongside their patron God-images. Even Vedantists at the convent in Santa Barbara, as I explained before, have focused daily puja before a painting of Ramakrishna, guru and founder. It is understandable how a loving puja intended for God could be redirected toward God's living symbol, the person most profoundly united with God. Thus, in guru-puja you bow, prostrate yourself, offer flowers, or burn incense before your guru. Testing the limits, you may even feel prompted to drink water that has washed the guru's feet or take into your mouth a betel cud which the guru chewed.

Though repugnant to the aniconic temperament, and also to my own personal taste, these extravagances do seem compatible with *bhakti kirtan,* dancing, and rap-ture before a loving personal God. Yet it is paradoxical that Vedanta intellectuals like Vivekananda could endorse this bhakti preference for guru avatars. In a pas-sage quoted earlier, he treats the sadguru as a mask of God and, more important, his own guru Ramakrishna as a Kali avatar. Although the public Vedantist message of Vivekananda removes the impersonal Absolute beyond all personal imagery, ritual, and historical religions, his private feelings grant the mere human guru a privileged deification.

According to most Hindus, anything can function as a symbol of the One Brahman-Atman, or anyone might prove to be a secret avatar of Vishnu. Thus, it is consistent that ordination rites in some ashrams culminate in a guru's prostration before the trained candidate. Before bestowing a final mantra, some gurus address the disciple: "Now you have become a God, and now I am worshiping you." Granted that God alone deserves worship, I support the gesture of bowing to God's presence in a disciple, at least to counterbalance the more misleading refrain, "God speaks only through the guru's voice," or "Our guru is greater than God."[36]

The spiritual intimacy between guru and disciple, as described so far, touches mostly the commonplaces of world spiritual traditions. The traditions share a common pattern of lay retreats, spiritual direction, monastic fellowship and obedience, even the twice-born rite of solemn religious vows. Yet today, conditioned by the outrages of Jonestown and countless investigations into exploitative cults, critics have been conditioned to view any guru relationship with sharper scrutiny. Perhaps it is no longer possible to glimpse with resolute openness the halo of exclusive attachment, even slavish worship, distinctive of the traditional Hindu guru. Yet on reflection, Hindu rhetoric about avatars and self-annihilation seems liable to no more abuse than the clichés of Christian monasticism — obey blindly, submit like a dead body or a cane, bow to God's will in the superior's command. Claims like "God sent me," "I am God," and "God is my guru" can function in any culture as the psychopath's criminal alibi, the hype of megalomania and solipsism, or a sound affirmation of faith. The words must be weighed each time in their concrete psychological and religious context.

The ambushes and challenges that await both parties in a guru relationship pervade the fiction of Anglo-Indian novelist Ruth Prawer Jhabvala. They can be illustrated best in her story "A Spiritual Call." Daphne leaves England to join an Indian ashram led by Swamiji, a bearded, ugly man with laughing eyes who radiates spiritual serenity even as he gorges himself on ice cream and candy. His message to the world is basic but sound: look into yourself, cleanse yourself, instill inner and outer harmony in your life. Located at a sacred pilgrimage site in India, his ashram centers on a nucleus of ordained male disciples, then an outer circle of people joining him for temporary training in meditation. Daphne and her roommate, Helga, are two of these latter visitors, both eager to qualify for more lasting membership.

Fascinated by Swamiji's words, and especially his eyes, after first meeting him, Daphne had taken off on a spiritual search. Dropping her secure secretarial job in London, she also left her mother, a woman convinced Daphne must be permitted to make her own mistakes. Besides plans to found a new ashram under wealthy patronage in California, Swamiji hopes also to write a book on his teachings. Yet his rhetoric and grammar are so crude that he needs Daphne's skills at editing, which tend to be uninspired but correct. With growing jealousy, Helga watches the guru devoting an unsuitable amount of time to his secretary, and Daphne stinting on meditation and sleep in order to labor over Swamiji's manuscript. Helga first teases then scolds her for feigned unawareness about triggering the guru's affection. Daphne has to admit that her motivation for coming to India has changed from mystical communion to something excessively personal.

One afternoon Daphne tells Swamiji the myth behind her name — how a fleeing girl is turned into a laurel tree in order to avoid the Greek God's advances. Reacting to this story, he encourages her not to be so shy about love. His advice before and now is this: "You must relax. You must trust and love. Give." Too sensible and cerebral, she is ordered by Swamiji to try relishing a leisurely walk, instead of showing up so punctually with her notebook. Soon after this, aware of the two women's rivalry, Swamiji, with one arm hooked around Daphne and another around Helga, at last invites them both to become permanent members of his new California ashram.

Then he invests both women with a sari uniform to mark their initiation into his community. Long before this moment, Daphne had already found spiritual completion, resigned to whatever her guru might decide for her. She could not imagine herself returning to London and her family. "But if that was what he intended her to do, then she would; propelled not by any will of her own, but by his. And this was somehow a great happiness to her: that she, who had always been so self-reliant in her judgments and actions, should now have succeeded in surrendering not only her trained, English mind but everything else as well — her will, herself, all she was — only to him."[37] The words leave an aftertaste of disturbing irony on the reader.

This story maintains a sensitive balance in unfolding the Swamiji-Daphne relationship. It avoids the heavy satire of *A New Dominion,* Jhabvala's novel about Hindu religious frauds who now manipulate Westerners, an ironic reversal of earlier British dominion over India. One renowned female guru, after welcoming an Indian college student into her ashram, promptly falls in love with him as a Krishna-image and reincarnation of her own son. Popping candy into his mouth, fondling him on her lap, she makes him her regressive prisoner. Nearby, a rival male guru reduces three alienated American women to serfdom: the first becomes a mousy robot; the second, who is dying of hepatitis, is unwilling to seek medical help without her master's permission; the third is repelled but enthralled by the guru's effort to tame and rape her.

The Daphne and Swamiji characters from "A Spiritual Call," on the contrary, are not simply rapacious or gullible, but more nuanced. Daphne had been living a satisfactory but passionless existence before India, but she chooses to renounce that life. Now she feels happy as never before. Though her personality still remains too dutiful and repressed, she seems capable of analyzing her feelings about Swamiji and making an informed free decision. Swamiji himself knows how to bring out the hidden fire in her and give the right advice and encouragement she needs to become more complete. He also links Daphne and Helga together, probably to keep his affections at a manageable distance and to limit the grounds for jealousy. Yet despite these merits, the guru seems too greedy for food, money, and control, a weakness Daphne spots even as she continues to love him. Yet most important, his disciple Daphne seems too quick to surrender, hankering for someone to find peace for her, anything to take away the anxiety of choice.

Search for the Inner Guru

In September 1995, Indian newspapers pounced on the arrest of Chandraswamy, the guru of Prime Minister Rao. Described as a spiritual adviser, psychic, faith healer, and rags-to-riches millionaire, Chandraswamy was accused of hiding an alleged killer in the pink, granite, three-story pavilion that he calls his ashram. Like a Delhi Rasputin, the "controversial godman," according to the *Indian Express,* had been exercising "enormous, extra-constitutional clout in the higher echelons of power and public life." Given habitual access to the prime minister without a security check, he had been observed consulting with Rao before major cabinet shuffles. His insider's knowledge roused suspicions of blackmail and illegal investment schemes. Prompting a general outcry in the media against superstitious trust in gurus, the arrest of Chandraswamy led to a march of protest and support, not by his disciples, but by a chance gathering of his spiritual peers, more than a thousand New Delhi saffron-robed gurus.[38]

This story emphasizes a few important motifs. I think the editorial reactions stem not from just a small, literate secular minority but from growing numbers of committed Hindus everywhere. The protest march shows that even though Hindu gurus prize their autonomy as isolated individuals, many also consider themselves part of a large professional consensus. More crucial than this, they are learning that much of Indian society no longer takes their spiritual authority for granted, but will expect them to earn respect. Also, the public is wary about excessive guru power and its potential abuse. This power must not edge its way from the realm of private Hindu spiritual direction into the public realm of a secular, pluralistic society. In a comparable situation a few years earlier, the American press, first amused that President Reagan and his wife would phone their California psychic and astrologer for private guidance, soon took serious alarm about this influence on public policy decisions.

The Hindu tradition prides itself on a complex psychology of the spiritual life, developed long before the modern psychoanalytic revolution in Europe. Drawing upon this legacy, some current Hindu psychologists argue that unique features in their culture and temperament make Indians unsuitable clients for Eurocentric psychotherapy.[39] Whereas bourgeois European and U.S. societies prize mature autonomy, India and other Asian peoples prefer the dependency or interdependency characteristic of life in a close, extended family. As discussed in chapter 2, psychologist Takeo Doi offered a similar observation about the widespread yearning among many adult Japanese to be mothered or indulged. Given this cultural difference, the guru-disciple bond is also much deeper than the psychotherapist-client relationship. Contrast the permanent commitment to a guru with a formal hour of psychotherapy in an office, perhaps one paid session a week for a few years at most. The guru teaches not just by verbal therapy but by living out the teaching, which the disciple is present to witness in all the behavior of daily life. The psychotherapist at best helps the client face up to inherent weaknesses and improve character defenses. But the guru is privileged to help mold a human sculpture so that it better expresses the soul or God concealed inside.

These differences conceded, meaningful similarities still exist between the guru and psychotherapist. First, the live-in relationship between guru and disciple is less unique when compared not with a formal psychoanalysis but with healing or training sessions guided by therapists trained in a more holistic, humanistic, or religious tradition. The clearest illustrations would be milieu therapy, especially Morita and other so-called Japanese "quiet therapies," which involve prolonged residence in a clinic or hospital. I recall taking part in a large group-therapy session one evening in suburban New Delhi under two transactional analysts, where various Indian couples responded with the candor and enthusiasm I could expect in many suburban American communities. Sessions resembled *darshan* or an active encounter between disciples and their guru, with the guru presiding by turning questions back upon the questioners, mirroring back to people their distorted attitudes, prompting one group member to advise another. Working at their best, both the guru and therapist do not instruct so much as train, creating situations that help disciples ask the right questions and try out for themselves the best solutions.

A second similarity between these two professions is the avatar complex, an occupational hazard common not just to Chandraswamy and other gurus mentioned above but also to psychotherapists. It is no surprise that the average healer will prove vulnerable to fantasies of self-importance. Freud himself compared the analyst to an X-ray technician handling radioactive matter, no less dangerous than the subtle transference projections that arise in almost every therapy relationship. To guard against contamination, Freud advised even veteran analysts to welcome ongoing supervision from colleagues. Jung, too, warned of continuous onslaughts from clients yearning to locate a savior.

Most psychotherapists work in unvaried isolation, seated for hours a day, focused mostly on a clientele very limited in number, social class, and ideas. The alleged rate of depression and suicide in the therapy profession is ominous. As a trained listener, you do not get many chances to share your own spontaneous opinions and inner life. Yet one way to compensate for boredom or despair is to savor the uncritical gratitude expressed by those you have helped. Soon this adulation tempts you to range beyond limited professional competence. You show up on media interviews to chart the profile of a hunted psychopath, or advise those coping with a hurricane disaster, or analyze foibles in the stranger whose views differ from your own.[40]

In a similar way, gurus are tempted to find themselves worthy of the flattery and worship surrounding them. I am convinced the claim to be God incarnate hampers anyone's otherwise admirable usefulness as a spiritual guide. A guru of this sort, presumed to have permanent enlightenment, will be prompted to conceal ignorance and any human vulnerability. Then the disciple will be conditioned, too, to overlook the most outrageous selfishness and abuse, all faults unlikely in a God. Recent newspaper analyses of fallen religious leaders often play up this "elephant in the living room" syndrome. Like families troubled by substance abuse or co-dependency, disciples will tend to connive with their leader's behavior and attitudes and unconsciously bracket out any wrong. Those with excessive dependency needs will often escape from one co-dependent family into another. Latching on to God or guru, they may bask in a counterfeit solace there or uncover new ways to manipulate their protectors. In my experience, both the shepherd and the flock within any religious setting are tempted to lock themselves into a conspiracy of mutual polite deception — each concealing doubts and peccadilloes from the other, reluctant to shock or disappoint.

Many prophetic voices within the Hindu tradition support the misgivings I have summarized. Critics demand that a sound, interdependent relationship with a guru be distinguished from its regressive counterfeits. Some feel embarrassed at India's deterioration today into a land of almost no disciples, only gurus, itching to commercialize one more unique religious formula. And whenever disciples surface, too many want a guru no different from themselves, to give them instant enlightenment without discipline and prayer, to drink and take drugs with them, to practice therapy on them. Swami Amar Jyoti of Pune believes an outer guru is needed only by some people, and then perhaps just for a time, in order to animate the inner guru dwelling in everyone. He recommends the modest attitude his own teacher adopted: "If anybody has the feeling that I am his guru, then, yes, I am. But I am nobody's guru. I am of service."

What begins here as apparent diffidence within Jyoti's master ends in a deep redefinition of role. Forming an implicit pact with a guru, one agrees to leave the everyday world and enter the guru's visionary world to reach enlightenment. Yet the disciple and the guide both must be responsible partners in a relationship that could prove harmful because either or both might have chosen unsuitably. The wise disciple must resist projections from those with the distorted need to dominate. The wise guru must resist even more subtle projections from those with the distorted need to submit. Swami Ananda of New Delhi calls this inner guru the power of guru-shakti. "I could not take my guru as God. I took the guru as a friend and guide," he says. "The physical person is not the guru. The guru is a power. The guru-shakti lives in the particular person who at some time was a disciple of a guru, and thus now knows the psychology of a disciple. . . . There are very few gurus who really want to realize themselves and who truly want to develop the divine potentiality of their disciples. Very, very few."[41]

The ideal teacher has been defined as someone able to awaken the self-teaching process in students, and also one who never gets in their way. Similarly, a famous guru, celebrating his own master's feast day, once explained to his colleagues, "Because this man refused to be my guru, I began to learn. And now I venerate him." The fiercely independent Gandhi thought it wiser to grope in the dark alone and wade through a million errors to Truth, rather than entrust yourself to those ignorant of their ignorance. In his autobiography he tells of Raychand, a young Jain poet and jewel merchant who befriended him on their return from England to India. Gandhi felt an impulse to take him on as a spiritual guide. Yet "in spite of my regard for him I could not enthrone him in my heart as guru. The throne has remained vacant and my search still continues."[42]

Gandhi gives an insightful explanation for walling off the outer human guru from this empty inner sanctuary. First, only God is the perfect guru. Thus, "the quest for such a guru is the quest for God. . . . Today we practice non-Dharma in the name of Dharma. We cherish hypocrisy in the name of Truth, and degrade ourselves as well as others by pretending to be possessed of spiritual knowledge and usurping all kinds of worship. At such a time Dharma consists in refusing to accept anyone as guru. It is doubly sinful, when a true guru cannot be found, to set up a clay figure and make a guru of it. But so long as a true guru is not found, there is merit in going on saying 'Not this. Not this.' And it may one day lead to our finding a true guru."[43]

Memorial to his ashes and absence, a stupa symbolizes the Buddha's presence. The lid of this miniature stupa lifts to disclose a *dagoba* or reliquary. Viewed from above, the stupa suggests a mandala; viewed from the side, it suggests a lotus rising pure from the mud, a lingam, the seated Buddha in outline. Four-inch hand-carving in ebony. Kandy, Sri Lanka.

4

The Buddhist Way

Few facts are certain about Siddhartha Gautama, the historical figure who later became the Buddha of sacred narrative. His search, conversion, ministry, and death have become the blueprint for an ideal human life. And this life has been interpreted variously by Theravada disciples in Southeast Asia; Mahayana in China, Korea, and Japan; and Vajrayana in Tibet, Nepal, and Mongolia. Born in the sixth century B.C.E., of a ruling military caste in northern India, Prince Gautama abandoned his wife and possessions to seek out *bodhi,* the deepest ecstatic awakening, which is achieved only after years of meditation. Then he began gathering a sannyasin fellowship, called the Sangha, to live out the spiritual path derived from his own enlightenment experience. At the moment of his death, he had reached final Nirvana, ultimate extinction of all selfish craving.

No doubt Gautama and his earliest disciples perceived themselves as faithful Hindus. Even his most radical attacks against brahmin ritualism, his acceptance of women and noncaste members into the Sangha, the novel emphases in his teaching — such differences had always existed among rival Hindu spiritualities. Within a few generations, however, these reforms hardened into a separate Buddhist identity. Meanwhile, as the schismatic group gained a popular following, Hindus were prompted to initiate a counter-reformation of their own. With great flexibility, the philosopher Shankara and many others tried to reincorporate the best features of Buddhist reform, and even the figure of Gautama himself. Because of this counter-reform's success, and especially after subsequent destruction of Buddhist monasteries and libraries by Muslim invaders, later Buddhists left few traces on the present Indian landscape.

In later Hindu history, reactions to the Buddha have varied dramatically. Representing the Hindu bhakti movement at the crest of its influence, Krishna Caitanya refused to associate with Buddhists, whom he viewed as heretics and atheists. However, he preferred their honest rejection of the Vedas to the alleged deceit of other Hindu heretics. The Vaishnava legacy that culminates in Caitanya had found an especially shrewd tactic to neutralize the Buddha's popularity. He was transformed into one of Vishnu's many avatars, and thus a Hindu secret agent. For instance, the Vishnu Purana, a sacred text dating from the fourth century C.E., demonstrates how this avatar schemes to defeat Vishnu's enemies. Approaching them with gentle words and dressed in red monastic garments, Buddha seduces these people to renounce their brahmin customs, such as animal sacrifice and most of the Vedic rituals. Thus weakened by their loss of Dharma armor, and exposed as traitors, they are now easily defeated by Vishnu's forces. This Purana treats Gautama's disciples with shameless intolerance. No Hindu ought to dine or talk with Buddhists, nor even to look at them. If a Buddhist observes a Hindu at puja, the ritual itself is rendered fruitless.

Modern Hindu reformers, in contrast, have tended to co-opt the Buddha as first among the major Hindu prophets. Gandhi, for instance, thought "Buddhism, or rather, the teachings of the Buddha, found its full fruition in India and it could not be otherwise, for Gautama was himself a Hindu of Hindus. He was saturated with the best that was in Hinduism, and he gave life to some of the teachings that were buried in the Vedas and which were overgrown with weeds. . . . The Buddha never rejected Hinduism, but he broadened its base. He gave it a new life and a new interpretation." Vivekananda in his famous World Parliament of Religions address treats Buddhism as the fulfillment of Hinduism and insists that neither Buddhist nor Hindu can be complete without the other. Commenting in a later letter, he wants to preserve Gautama, "the greatest soul that ever wore a human form," from the travesty of his teachings, which for some years filled India with too many temples, statues, and bones of saints. "In spite of its wonderful moral strength, Buddhism was extremely iconoclastic, and much of its force being spent in merely negative attempts, it had to die out in the land of its birth. And what remained of it became full of superstitions and ceremonials, a hundred times cruder than those it was intended to suppress."[1]

Seated near Vivekananda at the Chicago parliament, and representing the Theravadist Sangha of Sri Lanka, was a twenty-seven-year-old Buddhist student, the Anagarika Dharmapala. Paging through Dharmapala's speech before that assembly a century ago, you can now spot immediate parallels to Vivekananda's more celebrated address — an aggressive rebuttal against misreadings by Christian missionaries, and the ethical and rationalistic updating of an ancient religious tradition. In his later memoirs, Dharmapala summarizes the purpose of his mission to Chicago: "I have come to the West, a humble follower of the Buddha, not to convert Westerners to Buddhism, but to bring some knowledge of a religion that, for more than 2,000 years, has quickened the peoples of Asia to higher achievements in ethics, industry, and art." During one question period at the parliament, Dharmapala asked his audience how many had ever read the life of Buddha. Only five raised their hands. How many had read the Quran? Only four. "And you call yourself a nation — and a great nation!" he said. "And only four or five have ever read of the faith that 475 million people follow. How dare you judge us!"

In one printed synopsis of his Chicago speech, Dharmapala tells the parliament, "I have sacrificed the greatest of all work to attend this Parliament. I have left the work of consolidating the different Buddhist countries, which is the most important work in the history of modern Buddhism." In fact, this American visit had interrupted an urgent fund-raising campaign in Burma for restoring the central pilgrimage locations in India to international Buddhist control. Only a few months remained to confirm a down payment on land at Bodh Gaya, the alleged Indian site where Gautama reached enlightenment under the Bo tree. "Bodh Gaya is to the Buddhist what the Holy Sepulcher is to the Christians, Zion to the Jews, and Mecca to the Muslims," he explained years later. "I was filled with dismay at the neglect and desecration about me. The mahant, the head of the Hindu fakir establishment, had disfigured the beautiful images. At the end of a long pilgrimage, any devout Buddhist was confronted with monstrous figures of Hindu deities....On May 31, 1891, I started the Maha Bodhi Society, to rescue the holy Buddhist places and to revive Buddhism in India, which for 700 years had forgotten its greatest teacher."[2]

Dharmapala initiated the postcolonial modern era of Buddhist activism, with its own new perspective on Gautama's life and gospel. Besides Dharmapala, the present chapter will center on other prominent Buddhists, such as Giro Seno'o, U Thant, and the current Dalai Lama; then U Nu and Bandaranaike, initiating experimental socialist regimes in Burma and Sri Lanka; and later, the contemporary spiritual teachers Buddhadasa, Thich Nhat Hanh, and Aung San Suu Kyi. This wide perspective, faithful to both Theravadist and Mahayanist traditions, an integration of both contemplation and action, will offer a contemporary reinterpretation of meditation, Nirvana, and the Four Noble Truths.

FACES OF THE DHARMAKAYA

At its most profound, the word "Dharma" — or *Dhamma* in Pali, the early language of Theravada scriptures — means the dynamic order of the universe. The term first surfaced in this book in chapter 3, as the name preferred by most Hindus to identify their religion. Buddhists use the term for these same reasons, but add particular nuances from their own history. Dharma stands for the entire body of Buddha's teaching, beginning with the Dhamma Vinaya, rules governing monastic common life in the Sangha. His full teaching is often pictured as a dharma-wheel, the famous eightfold path, opening with a set of moral commandments, then offering a sequence of ever more demanding meditative steps to Nirvana. Your destiny, programmed for an endless cycle of rebirths, can be reversed by getting aboard this liberating wheel, which will teach you how to eliminate selfish desire.

Rather than Dharma, many Buddhists prefer the term "Dharmakaya," meaning the Dharma-body, or "Buddhadharma," a term emphasizing the virtual identification between Buddha's teaching and the teacher himself. In perhaps the most quoted passage from the Theravada canon, Gautama says, "What is there, Vikkali, in seeing this vile body? Whoever sees Dhamma sees me, whoever sees me sees Dhamma."[3] Thus, when you ponder the best classical images of Buddha, you are invited to study the precise way he sits, reclines, or walks. You cannot miss the serenity in this face, the disciplined cast of the lips and eyes and shoulders, the hand gestures of invitation or assertiveness or quiet. These details teach the right posture and attitudes for meditation. In the many famous Buddhist temples I have visited in Asia, I usually draw close to examine the central Buddha statue. Often you can trace small dharma-wheels engraved on the hands, torso, or an exposed sole of the foot. If you penetrate beyond Gautama's mere physical form, the Gautama-body, you will discover Dharmakaya, the truth-body, the body of his teachings.

On the one hand, for strict Theravadists of Southeast Asia, those adhering only to the canonical Pali scriptures, Gautama was just a saintly human being, and no more. In Nirvana now, dead and transformed, the physical Gautama is simply absent. He is present only through his Dharmakaya, which his disciples must each try to internalize in their own lives. On the other hand, for the Buddhist majority — Mahayanists and Vajrayanists in North Asia, but also many Theravadists — the transformed Gautama now functions as far more than a human being. A legend occurs in the Anguttara Nikaya about a brahmin disciple trailing Gautama on the road and discovering on each of his footprints the image of a thousand-spoked wheel. "These cannot be the footprints of a human being!" the man concludes. In Hindu iconography, giant blank footprints are a familiar aniconic reference to Vishnu. As Buddhists meditated on the mystery of the Buddha, they would eventually develop a more transcendental approach to both the teacher and his teaching. Dharmakaya would now mean the essence of Buddhahood, the Buddha-reality, the Absolute, the Sacred. And Gautama is just one among many avatar embodiments of this transcendental Buddha-nature. With parallels to the early Docetic view of Christ's humanity in Christian history, the physical Gautama functions as just a canvas depicting a spiritualized humanity, the Sacred.

Given their two contrasting theologies of the Buddha's nature, Theravadists and Mahayanists tend to differ also in other ways. Theravada, the Path of Elders, implies Southeast Asia, a contemplative spirituality centered mostly on the monastery, and rigorous fidelity to the ancient Pali scriptures. Mahayana, however, the large raft of salvation, implies North Asia, and an inclusive spirituality — both contemplative and active, monastic and lay, a movement that ranges from the florid tantric rites of Tibetan Vajrayana to the aniconic simplicity of Japanese Zen. With echoes of the Protestant-Catholic dialectic in Christian history, Theravada tends to emphasize the scriptural, iconoclastic aspects of Buddhist reform, whereas Mahayana tends to reintegrate much of what earlier Buddhists abandoned from their Hindu legacy.

Buddha's Gospel

It is instructive to listen to the reasons given for a boycott by Theravadist monks in Sri Lanka during Pope John Paul II's visit early in 1995.[4] A large banner, with a hundred monks behind it, registered the following protest: "Pope, withdraw your distorted comments on Buddhism. Apologize to the Buddhist world before you arrive here!" Checking the few remarks about Buddhism in the pope's latest book, readers cannot miss the sharp dichotomy he sketches between true Christian teaching and the "almost exclusively negative" Buddhist doctrine of salvation. These words echo Vivekananda's complaint about destructive Buddhist negativity, cited at the beginning of this chapter. What does the pope mean by the term "negative"? He explains that the Buddhist system, which he calls "atheistic," teaches only detachment from an evil world, without offering a new positive alternative, such as a personal God and savior. On the contrary, the Christian West, says the pope, "is marked by a positive approach to the world. . . . For Christianity, it does not make sense to speak of the world as a radical evil, since at the beginning of the world we find God the Creator who loves his creation."[5]

Buddhists have other reasons to suspect that the pope's misinterpretation of Buddhist teaching signals a bias permeating top levels of the current Vatican administration. Two years after this controversial visit to Sri Lanka, Cardinal Joseph Ratzinger, prefect of Rome's Congregation for the Doctrine of the Faith, gave an interview with the French weekly *L'Express*. Repeating his earlier prediction that Buddhism will replace Marxism as the Catholic Church's greatest challenge by the year 2000, Ratzinger allegedly stated: "If Buddhism seduces, this is because it seems possible to attain the boundless and blissful without having concrete religious obligations. In that sense, it is an auto-erotic spirituality."[6] Though he might have unmasked contemplative distortions in every religious tradition, even in some Christian stylites and holy anorexics, his words singled out Buddhists alone. Widely quoted and parodied, such a blanket reduction — promulgated from a casual secular pulpit, with innuendo about moral irresponsibility and sexual regression — could only offend Buddhist sensibilities.

Contributing to further misunderstanding about Buddhist nihilism, some Buddhist delegates at the 1993 centenary World Parliament of Religions shocked their fellow representatives by refusing to join assembly prayers addressed to God. However, this exactitude about religious language should come as no surprise from most thinking Buddhists, with their known preference for indirection and paradox, their iconoclasm, their apophatic spirituality or Path of Negation. A century ago, the Anagarika Dharmapala anticipated these misinterpretations of Buddhism by the pope and others and tried to correct them. Did critics find Theravadists agnostic and negative? First, Dharmapala never heard anyone complain that Mahayanists are anything but positive. "Even with regard, however, to what has been called Southern Buddhism, it is not quite correct to regard it as negative. The Pali Canon contains the grandest possible descriptions of Nirvana, which is described as 'uncreated' and 'immortal.' It is this positive Nirvana to which the Buddhist aspires. But inasmuch as it is really beyond speech, it must be indicated as 'not this' and 'not that' if one is to avoid misleading." Understood in this sense, Nirvana is not negative, but the only thing positive and real.[7]

The Buddha himself, in my opinion, should be interpreted as first a moral pragmatist, dodging insoluble theological arguments about an immortal soul, cosmic origins, or existence of the Gods. As Dharmapala observes, "the only ground on which agnosticism can be predicated of Buddhism is the fact that Buddha never favored speculation on transcendental and abstract problems." The Majjhima Nikaya introduces a charming dialogue in which an elderly sannyasin, directing these very questions to Gautama one by one, threatens to defer entering the Sangha until he gets every doubt resolved. Buddha compares this fussy questioner to the man dying of a poisoned arrow wound. The patient stubbornly refuses surgical aid until he can track down the racial and caste pedigree of his assailant, or the exact design of arrow feathers and bow. But why waste time on a question that makes no appreciable spiritual difference? It is "not useful. It is not concerned with the principle of religious life. It does not conduce to aversion, absence of passion, cessation, tranquillity, supernatural endowment, perfect knowledge, Nirvana. And therefore I have not explained it."[8]

In chapter 3, I described the faith of an average Hindu as henotheistic. This functional monotheism centers worship on one preferred God-image, without denying the existence of other images. By their consistent negations, I think Gautama and his disciples are just slapping down all theological labels imposed on them by outsiders. Throughout their early history especially, they tried to sidestep futile sectarian disputes. But more important, the disciples wanted to protect their founder from a henotheistic reductivism, with its eagerness to insert Gautama into an already crowded Hindu pantheon.

For six weeks in Thailand, I visited a few of the forty thousand Buddhist monasteries scattered throughout the country. Yet I regret missing a pilgrimage to the monastery founded by Bhikkhu Buddhadasa, acclaimed Theravada reformer and writer. Located far south of Bangkok, Wat Suan Mokh means the Garden of Empowering Liberation. In a film documentary featuring the work of this monastery, I once observed monk artists painting and carving panels representing scenes from various world religions, many of the pieces copied from books of religious iconography. The countless Buddha-images on display represent a variety of artistic styles and theological interpretations, from the eighth to the twentieth century. This art is used by monk guides to teach crowds of visitors the basic ingredients of Gautama's Four Noble Truths, a message shaped into an easily memorized sales pitch characteristic of medicine peddlers. First, what troubles you? Suffering or alienation. Second, what illness lies underneath these symptoms? Selfish desire, the predatory instinct, the will to power. Third, what is the aim of the cure? Nirvana, or extinction of this selfish desire. Fourth, what is the specific means of cure? The Buddha's eightfold path.

The entire Buddhist gospel can be capsulized in this instant formula, ready for preaching, easy catechesis, and global export. Another summary occurs in the famous mantra, "I take the Buddha, the Dharma, and the Sangha as my refuge." Guiding visitors through their rural gallery, the monks urge them to study all these images taken from the major world religions. Here are savior parables about Vishnu, Jesus, Moses, Muhammad, and a multitude of bodhisattvas from the Buddhist heritage, each trying to heal the guilt, pain, and selfishness common to every human being. Take responsibility for your own salvation, and help others, too. Don't imagine hell as a kingdom of otherworldly misery, but as the Bangkok nightlife and pollution today. More than this, meditate on the inferno within your own heart, the hell of *tanha* or selfish desire. Like Buddha's eightfold path, the same moral rescue from hell is taught by every religious tradition — no lies, murder, injustice, fornication, or substance abuse.

Self-evident though Buddha's message may sound, it calls for a profound revolution of consciousness. Less a new religion than a new religious perspective, it measures all spiritual paths according to one single-minded criterion: To what extent does this tradition liberate you from selfish desire? As Buddhadasa, the founder of Suan Mokh monastery, tells his visitors from various religious backgrounds, "the goal of all religions is salvation, and throughout history all religions have shown the way to salvation.... In Buddhism the Dhamma is the path, the journey, and the realization of the goal of the journey. A similar claim could be made for such terms as God and Tao. Buddha, Jesus, and other religious founders are all simply media for manifesting this central truth to humanity, so that human beings can escape suffering."[9] Thus, a religious tradition other than one's own is not rated for its degree of closeness to a particular church, to Christ, not even to God. It is valued only for its spiritual capacity to liberate, not only people, but all living beings.

One's religious focus is expected, then, to shift from a personal God, the Supreme Being "out there," to an apophatic Nirvana within. Delighting in his negative paradoxes, Buddha introduces this condition of soul as the "Isle of No-beyond, where there is No-thing to be grasped." You catch hints about this moment of self-transcendence only by attempts to imagine what it is not. Some Jews and Muslims, and Christians especially, approach God as Wisdom, Light, or the Beatific Vision, metaphors that highlight the inner experience of someone at worship. Hindu Vedantists describe Brahman as *sat-cit-ananda,* the source of truth, consciousness, ecstasy, all words that imply one's own inner completion. With a similar partiality for psychological language, Buddhists will often refer to the Sacred as Nirvana, the extinction of selfish desire. It is the Buddha-nature, the internalized Dharmakaya.

The Wisdom-Compassion Balance

Gautama's life story centers on an act of dispossession, a progressive deepening of spiritual mindfulness, and most important, the hovering between self-liberation and a compassionate decision to save others. This heroic pattern is reenacted today among Theravadists in the popular Shinbyu Rite. Young boys are tonsured in Sri Lanka, for example, and given saffron robes and begging bowls. Then for a brief or sustained period in the monastic Sangha, they identify sacramentally with Gautama's renunciation.

In Thailand two of my former students, consecrated by this same rite of passage, entered the local Sangha for three summer months after completing their graduate business studies in San Francisco. Their motives to become monks, they told me, were gratitude to their parents and a hope that good karma from this renunciation would benefit the family and also their own fledgling business careers. They later recounted their intensive training in meditation, the ordeals of community living and austere diet, the early morning ritual begging expeditions each day through the neighborhood. A rite of closure, festive and public, marked the men's expected decision to leave the Sangha at summer's end. As far as I could tell, both Theravadist laity and monks in Thai society accept these ready monastic entrances and exits with equanimity. Returning to the lay condition, both men now had an available guru and new friends, more knowledge about their Buddhist heritage, and most of all, a heightened respect for the contemplative life.

Though less noticeable than a public communal ritual, Gautama's life pattern shows up, too, in the disciplined, silent self-abandonment of a Zen disciple in sitting meditation. It is also present in the shocking bonfire self-immolation of activist Vietnamese monks three decades ago during the crumbling Diem regime. The Dalai Lama in 1956, on his first pilgrimage outside Tibet to the Indian Buddhist shrine at Bodh Gaya, sought his own distinctive participation in Gautama's transfiguration. He prayed for guidance, trying to decide whether to seek political asylum in India or return to Chinese communist guardians in Tibet. "Now I stood in the presence of the Holy Spirit who had attained maha-parinirvana, the highest Nirvana, in this sacred place, and had found for all mankind the path to salvation. As I stood there, a feeling of religious fervor filled my heart, and left me bewildered with the knowledge and impact of the divine power which is in all of us.... So after a few more days, I had to drag myself back to the world of politics, hostility, and mistrust."[10]

I suggest the Dalai Lama in his act of Buddha-puja as the first of two exemplary images guiding any effort to balance the dichotomies of textbook Buddhism — Theravadist and Mahayanist, monks and lay people, meditation monks and ministry monks, philosophical Buddhism and folk Buddhism. Like Gautama, distended between spiritual completion in Nirvana and a summons back to activist leadership of his people, the Dalai Lama had somehow to reconcile the polarities. His life represents a balanced, comprehensive tradition shaped by long training, which he once described as an immersion in the moral guidance of Theravada and also in the more esoteric meditation methods of both Mahayana and Vajrayana. "Tibetan Buddhists do not separate these teachings," he insists, "but pay equal respect to them all."[11]

In Tibetan liturgies of mantra chanting, monk participants hold a ringing bell in the left hand and a *vajra* thunderbolt scepter in the right. With rhythmical tantric gestures, the monks oscillate the bell and vajra. The rite symbolizes a yin-yang union of the feminine and masculine, wisdom and compassion, *prajna* and *karuna* — the heritage of both Theravada and Mahayana, the meditative and the active life. I have witnessed the same symbolic use of bell and vajra in pujas celebrated by *vajracarya,* married priests in Nepal. For the four months I lived west of Kathmandu, I used to haunt the nearby pilgrimage center of Swayanbhunath, which claims to be the world's oldest Buddhist stupa. Though its monks are Vajrayanist, they have welcomed Theravadist monks to build a retreat house near a steep purgatorial stairway up the mountain toward its stupa pinnacle.

My second guiding image in this chapter is a huge Chinese cliff-carving at Longmen that portrays Gautama, old and serene. Buddha is flanked by the severe, detached jnanin Kasyapa on his left and by the passionate bhakta Ananda at his right — in other words, by the Hindu paths now of contemplation, now of affectivity. Each disciple mirrors a single facet of the master's plenitude. A common distortion, I think, pervades the work of Max Weber, Carl Jung, Joseph Campbell, and many Eurocentric students of world religions. They divide spiritualities into Eastern and Western. The East specializes in mysticism, contemplation, a world-denying asceticism; the West specializes in compassion and a world-affirming social activism. According to its proponents, an East-West dichotomy can be confirmed by the many conversions of Western young adults today to Eastern religions. Their busy, one-sided Western religious heritage cannot fulfill the heart's deep contemplative needs.

Counter to this East-West bias, I have already stressed a more comprehensive view of Hindu spirituality in chapter 3. Paths of action, contemplation, and affectivity can be exemplified respectively by Hindu giants like Gandhi, Ramakrishna, and Krishna Caitanya. Moreover, later chapters in this book will not slight the contemplative side of the three Abrahamic traditions — Kabbalists and Hasidim, the Sufi, or the Rhineland and Spanish mystics. I think West and East are geographic misnomers for the deepest currents in everyone, no matter what the person's religious tradition. One polarity or the other may prevail in a culture, an entire era, or phases of an individual life. Yet no spirituality can be complete without a yin-yang interweaving of contemplative and active strands, distinct but complementary opposites. At its most authentic, the Buddhist tradition reveals a unique interplay of wisdom and active compassion, a dialectic which the rest of this chapter will now explore.[12]

COMPASSIONATE ACTION

One reason I have tried to restore an activist dimension to the Dharmakaya is my own long disregard for Buddhist activism itself. Before 1975 the only American Buddhist families I met had been Asian immigrants, adapted to a congregational-style parish life. I also knew the retreat and meditation centers managed by Japanese and Tibetan monks and the drop-out Zen popularized by Beat poets and the psychedelic counterculture. Yet this exposure did not prepare me for the Buddhists I would encounter on the island of Guam.

After the fall of Saigon, I worked the summer of 1975 as Catholic chaplain at a relocation camp in Guam. Unlike the island's larger centers that funneled refugees to the United States, this particular camp was a barbed enclosure designated just for a few hundred refugees, almost all male and ex-military, returning to their families in Vietnam. They had fled Saigon in panic, hoping their families could later join them abroad. Though offered liberation and new citizenship in the United States, these men now opted instead for return to communist Vietnam. Such a choice, of course, provoked some hostility in their U.S. wardens and the local people. From my perspective, most men in the camp had been tormented by this burning decision, forced to weigh the tempting promise of work and freedom against existing responsibilities toward their families. Each day I would drift from one group to another, sharing in their meals, witnessing incomprehensible card games, and counseling. I had to rely on translators, simple body language, and crucial limited English words like death, love, work, hope, and God.

Here for the first time I met some articulate young militants who challenged my premises about Buddhism. Offering Mass for Catholics or Bible discussions for all Christians, I felt encouraged to venture beyond these familiar religious boundaries. Perhaps I could help a few of my dispirited Buddhist friends organize their own meditation and support groups. For this purpose, with the aid of translators, I photocopied classic texts from the Pali canon, such as Gautama's Fire Sermon or parts of the Dhammapada. To my surprise, after skimming through these readings, everyone turned them down resolutely.

I discovered that some of the Buddhists, and Catholics too, openly distrusted me as a potential CIA spy. Others seemed to resent this patronizing gesture from a meddlesome priest, spokesman for a religion identified with the former anti-Buddhist Diem regime. The more informed, too, perhaps disdained my ignorance, which misled me to hand out Theravadist texts to people shaped all their lives by Mahayanist teaching. However, the actual words accompanying this gesture of rejection had a plausible ring to them. As my translator helped me recognize, the monkish Buddha of these texts sounded irrelevant, even detrimental, to their own contemporary Buddhist convictions. These men honored various brave religious kings in Asian Buddhist history. They wanted to build a new postcolonial society where all citizens could develop their own Buddha-nature, without excessive dependence on religious institutions, customs, or scriptures. They felt the colonial invaders had taken cynical advantage of their gentle Buddhist faith. Europe and America had snatched from them the very wealth and functions of government which a docile style of Buddhism had once taught the Vietnamese to renounce. Admiring Gautama's insistence on democratic process and caste equality in the Sangha, they now preferred an engaged but cautiously restricted role for the modern Sangha in education and politics.

Though these Buddhists were Mahayanist, they typified an emphasis I now perceive cutting across all Buddhist cultures. Even in Theravadist countries of Southeast Asia, Sangha candidates are sorted today into traditional meditative monks and the ministry monks engaged in teaching and social work. I shall identify the latter current — which is relatively new — as ethical and activist, at times antiritualistic. It is a lay movement — its progressive branch somewhat secular or even anticlerical, its traditionalist wing eager to preserve the Sangha's integrity yet insert it into contemporary life. It is also Ashokan, a term evoking Ashoka, the great Buddhist missionary emperor, the Constantine of India. In other words, today's Buddhist activist aspires to be a genuine bodhisattva.

Vow of the Bodhisattva

A bodhisattva is literally a bodhi-being, someone already enlightened, or on the threshold of Nirvana. This person delays Nirvana to help others reach it. "Let them hate or love me, accuse or wrong me, but let them share in enlightenment." This is the prayer of the seventh-century poet Shantideva. "May I be a protector for the unprotected, a guide for wanderers, a boat or bridge for those desiring the other shore, a lamp or bed to those in need, a slave for those who need a slave." The world is trapped in a net of craving, ignorance, and pain. The bodhisattva resolves to set all living beings free, even in worlds beyond this one. "It is better that I alone suffer than that all beings sink to the worlds of misfortune. In those places I shall give myself into bondage, to redeem all the world from the forest of purgatory, from rebirth as beasts, from the realm of death."[13]

Once while answering questions from a Singaporean student about my personal meditation methods, I asked him to be more specific about his own style of prayer. On impulse he suddenly moved a chair in my office, prostrated his entire body face-downwards along the rug, propped his steepled hands at an angle in front of his face, and after a few moments of silence, uttered this moving prayer: "Lord Buddha, graciously receive me and what I do. Let it not be to my credit, but help toward the enlightenment of every living creature." I have never forgotten this burst of religious serendipity. A few years after this, on a research trip through Malaysia, I came across the following similar bodhisattva prayers from a child's Sunday School catechism in Penang. The first prayer opens: "I am a link in Lord Buddha's golden chain of love that stretches around the world." And the second prayer begins with the following affirmation: "We surround all people and all forms of life with infinite love and compassion."[14]

In a ritual setting, often in the presence of images and sutra texts, with a bow to their guru or to the abbot in a monastery, Buddhists of all traditions can turn these simple dedicatory prayers into a formal bodhisattva vow. The implications of the prayers are momentous. Like the Flying Dutchman, you chain yourself to perpetual samsara or rebirth on earth and even in future cosmic purgatories. For the sake of others, you forfeit whatever karmic merit and wisdom you can ever acquire. Nothing seems further removed from this radical selflessness than the merit-grubbing in late medieval European piety — the bank account of Indulgences for a commuted jail sentence in purgatory. Yet comparable distortions can be traced, even in the Theravada tradition. Average Buddhists cannot imagine themselves becoming fully enlightened monks, rich in karmic merit, nor outlasting the countless purifying rebirths required to reach Nirvana. With Nirvana dropping out of sight, they tend to focus instead on some more familiar topography, not the cessation of rebirth but a better earthly rebirth. Bhikkhu Buddhadasa complains that devout people often support temples and monks just to gain a better rebirth. "Such people know nothing about Buddhism at all, for they are acquainted only with how to get and how to take. That is not

Buddhism.... The heart of Buddhism is not getting things but getting rid of them. It is, in other words, nonattachment, not seizing or grasping anything, not even the religion itself, until finally it is seen that there is no Buddhism."[15]

It is instructive to contrast two rock inscription prayers from Pagan in eleventh-century Burma. Though both voices belong to Buddhist queens, only one shows a bodhisattva heart. "Before I reach Nirvana," says Queen Caw, "by virtue of the work of merit I have done on such a big scale, I wish virtue and prosperity if born again as a human being. If I am born a spirit, my wish is to be ... beautiful, sweet-voiced, well-proportioned in limbs, the beloved and honored darling of every human being and spirit.... May I have lots of gold, silver, rubies, coral, pearls.... Wherever I am born, may I ... not know one speck of misery. And after I have tasted and enjoyed the happiness of human beings and spirits, ... may I at last attain the peaceful bliss of Nirvana." On the contrary, entombed nearby, Queen Amana wants her own merit showered upon the king and all his subjects. She asks that even "Yama, king of death, and all creatures also share it.... I pray to cross samsara full of the good graces — modest in my wants, even-tempered, compassionate, wise, conscious of causes, large-handed, unforgetful, and affectionate."[16]

The bodhisattva figure has roots in Gautama's active years of ministry, viewed as a prolonged deferment of his own parinirvana. The Mahavagga Vinaya contains perhaps the earliest legend preserved by his disciples about Gautama's pivotal decision to postpone Nirvana and share the Dharma. His first impulse had been to give up teaching the Dharma. "With great pains have I acquired it. Enough! Why should I now proclaim it? This doctrine will not be easy to understand for beings lost in lust and hatred." But he was soon persuaded otherwise by an inner theophany, or perhaps the personified compassion in his heart. "Alas, the world will perish," the God Brahma argues, if the Buddha's mind "decides to remain in quiet, and not to preach the doctrine. As a man standing on a rock, ... look down upon the people lost in suffering, overcome by birth and decay — you, who have freed yourself from suffering!" Gautama's compassion later became characteristic of his gracious dialogic method of teaching and recurs as a major Dharma theme in such sayings as the following: "If you are not concerned for one another, monks, who is there to be concerned for you? If you want to tend me, tend the sick."[17]

The Lotus Sutra and other basic Mahayana scriptures tend to stretch the margins of Gautama's earthly life ahead to a timeless afterlife scenario at Vulture's Peak, where he engages in dialogue with heavenly bodhisattvas. The Theravada tradition, on the other hand, extending these margins backward before Gautama's birth, seeks its bodhisattvas within the mythical realm of once upon a time. In Buddhist Southeast Asia, the Pali scriptures most familiar today, especially among children, are the Jataka tales. If Gautama could achieve Nirvana within a single lifetime, many Buddhists argue that his Gautama-incarnation must have climaxed a long evolving preincarnation of heroic earthly bodhisattvas or Buddhas-to-be. Thus, these five hundred narratives about Buddha in his earlier animal, demigod, or human forms center on some crucial act of renunciation. As colorful variations on a limited set of themes, the animal characters stun you with their eagerness to be sacrificed. Each story opens with a dialogue between Gautama and his disciples, setting the teaching context. Then the tale is introduced as an exemplum and concluded invariably by a formula like the following: "After this lesson, the Master summarized his theme and specified his incarnation:

'At that time the human king was Ananda, the monkey's retinue the Sangha, and the monkey king myself.' "

Among their many purposes, these animal tales stir the moral imagination to recognize solidarity between people, animals, and the rest of nature. For example, the monkey king stretches his body between two trees on either side of a river so that other monkeys can tread across his back to safety from pursuing hunters. Yet his own body becomes so exhausted he cannot escape. A deer king persuades a pregnant doe to let him replace her at the slaughtering block. An elephant permits a destitute forester to dig out and sell his prized ivory tusks. A rabbit shakes himself loose of fleas to spare their lives and surrenders his own life to the flames so that a fasting brahmin can enjoy his meal without having to violate the taboo against killing. "Offering his whole body as a free gift, he sprang up, and like a royal swan, alighting on a cluster of lotuses, in an ecstasy of joy he fell on the heap of live coals."

A hermit in another Jataka story is so intent on caring for animals ravaged by drought that he almost starves. Or a man of low caste persists generously to share his food with a fastidious brahmin, who would rather starve than eat something contaminated by the other's touch. In his ten final preincarnations, Gautama's second-to-last embodiment is Prince Vessantara, whose alleged first words as a child were, "Mother, what gift can I make?" His life becomes almost a parody of bodhisattva self-abandonment. He gives away a kingdom, then his two children, and even his wife. Like the Book of Job, this tale ends with the Gods restoring all his gifts a hundredfold.[18]

From a later Mahayanist perspective, the Buddha and the Dharmakaya, as I have explained, are exalted into a single transcendental principle. According to this teaching, you already possess the Buddha-nature or the bodhisattva-reality within yourself. Even now, samsara is really Nirvana itself, if you could only become aware enough to get beyond appearances. Once a meditative approach to life has become second-nature, your bodhisattva potential stirs to life. You can expect to feel the tensions between wisdom and compassion — between awareness of your shared Buddha-nature and empathy for the more tangible misery and ignorance impeding any individual's Buddha-realization.

In rich images of the Mahayana cosmos, the attribute of compassion is personified in various heavenly bodhisattvas, each often sketched with countless hands and eyes and heads, alert to everyone's needs. The most famous of these is Avolakiteshvara. This bodhisattva surfaces among Chinese Buddhists as Kuan Yin and among Japanese as Kannon, often portrayed in a gender-shift as Goddess of mercy, even a Madonna with child. The most uncanny image of Avolakiteshvara I know is the stylized face painted on the Swayanbhunath Stupa peak near Kathmandu — eyes like glaring horizontal question marks, peering from four corners over the countryside.

Modern Bodhisattvas

Asked to account for his spiritual identity, Nganang Gyatso, the present Dalai Lama, defines himself as "just a human being, and incidentally a Tibetan, who chooses to be a Buddhist monk." This is his own candid self-perception. However, as a child he had been certified by his community a *tulku* or reincarnation of the previous Dalai Lama. Today his people revere him as a "God-king," but more important, "a living Buddha, the earthly manifestation of Avalokitesvara, bodhisattva of compassion." For the Dalai Lama this bodhisattva ideal is not just his own privileged Avalokitesvara identity but a power available to us all — "the aspiration to practice infinite compassion with infinite wisdom."

Though trying to pray and study over five hours a day, he remarks that "as a Buddhist, I see no distinction between religious practice and daily life." It is the duty of religion to serve humanity and never ignore reality. "It is not sufficient for religious people to be involved with prayer. Morally, they are obliged to contribute all they can to solving the world's problems." His morning routine begins with mantra chanting and prostrations to all the Buddhas. His next ritual is an arresting illustration of the contemplative in action: "From 5:45 A.M. until 8:00, I meditate, pausing only to listen to the 6:30 news bulletin of the BBC World Service. Then, from 8:00 until noon, I study Buddhist philosophy." With disarming candor, he admits, "I consider myself to be very much in the primary grade of spiritual development."[19]

In 1980 the Beijing *People's Daily* published a contentious piece of fiction, "The Story of a Living Buddha," written by Malquinhu, a Mongolian communist. It offers a Marxist challenge to the Tibetan and Mongolian Vajrayana tradition of political and religious leadership, preserved by the reincarnation of each Lama within his successor. The tale introduces a normal mischievous boy, snatched from his playmates to become a monk, then pampered and venerated as a sort of living Buddha. After some years, once the monasteries are shut down by the communist revolution, this monk becomes an itinerant medical doctor, ministering to the poor. Returning to visit old childhood neighbors, he explains his new-found Humanism, his new sense of vocation. To find "something in which they can place their hopes, men create Gods for themselves. . . . And the man converted into a God then assumes the manner of a God to make fools of the people who have deified him. We have passed many thousands of years in this comedy of mutual trickery."[20]

The real-life Dalai Lama would support both Malquinhu's Humanism and the writer's protest against this snare of deification. "I am still half-Marxist," the Dalai Lama explains. "I have no argument with capitalism, so long as it is practiced in a humanitarian fashion, but my religious beliefs dispose me far more towards socialism and internationalism, which are more in line with Buddhist principles. The other attractive thing about Marxism for me is its assertion that man is ultimately responsible for his own destiny. This reflects Buddhist thought exactly."[21] Bernardo Bertolucci's recent film *Little Buddha* offers still another version of the search for a reincarnated child Lama. It is reported that when asked by Bertolucci if such a title might offend Buddhists, the Dalai Lama laughed and replied, "There's a little Buddha in all of us." In fact, according to Mahayanist teaching, the Buddha-nature or bodhisattva charism shines everywhere like the moon, reflecting itself differently on each unique surface, whether it illuminates the Dalai Lama or anyone else.

The Dalai Lama can stand as the most recent and compelling embodiment of bodhisattva values. He shows a determination to protest against the Chinese oppressors of his nation, yet to do so in a forgiving, nonviolent way. A disciple of Gandhi, he refuses to bear hatred in his heart for any specific Chinese person. He thinks it a particular madness of this present era to blame nations for the crimes of individuals.

"We should not seek revenge on those who have committed crimes against us, nor reply to their crimes with other crimes. We should reflect that by the law of karma, they are in danger of lowly and miserable lives to come, and that our duty to them, as to every being, is to help them to rise toward Nirvana, rather than let them sink to lower levels of rebirth."[22] Thus, his forgiveness is grounded firmly in Buddha's Four Noble Truths, applied even to his enemies.

I was astonished by the same quiet capacity for forgiveness a few years ago when a group of Tibetan monks spent a week at the Asian Art Museum in San Francisco, laboring in microdetail to construct a huge mandala of colored sand. The creative process itself, exacting and prayerful, was so marvelous to observe that I brought a few of my world religions classes along to experience it. The masterpiece was nearly complete when a deranged onlooker, screaming about death-worship and Satan, leaped onto the sand design and defaced it beyond recovery. The Buddhist reaction to the rampage of this woman left reporters and police speechless. The monks had originally planned to dismantle the sand work after a final dedication liturgy. Such an act of destruction, whether it be her gesture or their own, would underscore the Buddhist belief that all is impermanent, especially our works of beauty. They intended to pray for the woman and asked that no charges be brought against her.

A more profound illustration of Buddhist compassion occurred in July 1994, after nine Buddhist monks were robbed and murdered in the Wat Promkunaran Temple of Arizona. Under Arizona's victims' rights law, the family of an injured person can appear in court to demand harsh punishment. Instead, the guilty teenager, already convicted of the murders and facing possible execution, was stunned by a courtroom plea for clemency made by monk delegates from the Phoenix temple and also from the founding monastery in Thailand. The Buddhists also tried to locate a new defense team for an appeal and asked the United Nations to review possible human rights violations. "We don't believe in revenge," they said. "Respect for life is the first precept in Buddhism."[23]

The second bodhisattva exemplar I have selected is a more abrasive figure than the Dalai Lama. Giro Seno'o was a leading socialist dissenter in Japan before the Second World War, decrying every omen of fascist militarism and imperialism. To understand his character, it is helpful to line him up alongside the historical prototype he most resembled. Early in his life, Seno'o won the epithet of "Today's Nichiren." Nichiren is still revered today as the Japanese founder of a thirteenth-century Buddhist reform called Nichiren Shoshu, which has a modern lay offshoot called Soka Gakkai. His teaching centered on chanting the name of the Lotus Sutra, which he believed the only true Dharmakaya. Chapter 24 of this famous sutra is a lyrical ode to Avalokiteshvara, the bodhisattva of compassion, whom many disciples believe reincarnated in Nichiren himself. Combative and intolerant, denouncing all rival Buddhist prophets, Nichiren at first seems an unlikely bodhisattva, unless his compassion is interpreted as the "tough love" shown by a Japanese father, rather than the forgiving unconditional love shown by a mother.[24]

A few years before the First World War, after a youth of poverty and chronic sickness, Seno'o happened to read the Lotus Sutra. Then abandoning the Pure Land Buddhism of his family, at the age of twenty-two, he became a Nichiren priest. Within a decade his ministry to people became radicalized. At first his Buddhist vocation consisted of chanting sutras before dawn and late at night and cleaning toilets in a Tokyo youth hostel. Next he tried to teach the poor a Buddhist gospel of pious endurance in their misery. At last, he began to identify with protest movements of tenant farmers, factory workers, Korean aliens, and *burakumin* untouchables in Japan. Capitalistic greed proved to be his target, and Marxist analysis his guide. "If the light of the Buddha did not shine for me," he confessed to his diary in 1927, "I would probably be a Marxist. But even if I am not quite a Marxist, the way society is now, how can I not give Marxism my tacit approval?" A year later, he wrote, "Religion today is useless, idle — no, you can even say it is a vice." People must be freed from both spiritual suffering and material suffering.[25]

Though Seno'o in his own lifetime met the ironic fate of proving too Buddhist for his Marxist friends and too Marxist for his Buddhist friends, his distinctively Buddhist critique of oppression cuts deeper than the Marxist critique. For the fundamental cause of alienation is tanha, the selfish ego and its lust for wealth and power, both among bourgeois oppressors and among the romanticized proletariat. "The struggle to liberate the emergent [proletarian] class cannot be our sole end. It must be accompanied by the struggle to liberate humanity." His model of the socialist millennium is an egoless life of interdependence, social equality, nonviolence, and sharing of property. "The life ideal of Buddhists is the life of the Sangha purged of desires for private property."

Seno'o initiated or joined a succession of antifascist protest movements and minority parties throughout the early 1930s. As expected, his campaign for social justice and international peace collided repeatedly with state Shinto and state Buddhism, neither of which could tolerate a whisper of dissent. After his bold condemnation of Japan's aggression in Manchuria and further abroad, he was harassed by increasing police surveillance and interrogation. Worn down finally from torture in prison, he signed an admission of conspiracy in 1937 and two years later was sentenced to a five-year prison term that lasted through most of the Second World War. He never forgot the shame of his forced prison confession. He later called it the inexcusable act of a "weak character." "I should have died in prison. . . . My cowardice and meanness were pitiful." After Japan's surrender, hunting for some constructive way to expiate his guilt, he immersed himself in the Japanese peace movement.

To the Dalai Lama and Giro Seno'o, I shall add the name of a third modern bodhisattva — differing from both other figures, someone with the attributes of a steady, self-effacing administrator. This is U Thant of Burma, third secretary general of the United Nations, its first non-European leader. Convinced that the Soviet Union and the United States were Cold War prisoners of their respective pasts, he presided with serenity and diplomatic finesse during the Cuban and Nigerian crises. His memoirs hint at the legacy of racial discrimination that burdened him and his Burmese colleagues. For instance, in their own nation they had long been excluded from prestigious British clubs, simply because they were Burmese. "Although I have been trained to be tolerant," he admits, "it is difficult for me to shake off unhappy memories of servitude." As a spokesman for the nonaligned Third World, Thant brought personal experience to the unjust divisions of the globe "into the rich and the poor, the master race and the abject poor," the North and South, First and Third Worlds. He found this dichotomy far more explosive than the ideological war between capitalism and Marxism.

Thant preferred to define himself as an ethical Buddhist or even a Buddhist Unitarian. Albert Schweitzer the Humanist, Teilhard de Chardin the Jesuit, and the Buddha are three models he chose as a sound ethical basis for international dialogue. "As a Buddhist, I was trained to be tolerant of everything except intolerance," he said. "Human life is one of suffering. Hence, it is the duty of a good Buddhist to mitigate the suffering of others. . . . I was taught to control my emotions through a process of concentration and meditations, . . . cleansing the mind of impurities such as ill will, hatred, and restlessness." Acknowledging profound grief at the death of his only son and exultation three years later at his nomination for the Nobel Prize, he strained to keep reactions like these from overwhelming him. U Thant felt it necessary to meditate daily in order to nourish a mood of equanimity. "To contemplate life, but not to be enmeshed in it, is the law of the Buddha."[26]

The Buddhist Millennium

In the first three chapters, I have painted differing visions of utopia, an idealized society projected by each tradition, where its great verities shall flourish. The Huichol people of Mexico, for instance, plan an annual pilgrimage to Wirikuta, the sacred land from which their ancestors first emigrated, where everything is the reversal of present time and pain. Confucius often contrasted the moral chaos of his own era with the golden age of Yao, Shun, and Yu, exemplary wise men and rulers in the past. This is not a historical past but a legendary timeless situation, which might as readily have been projected into a Marxist classless society of the future. Gandhi, too, spoke of his Rama-Raj ideal, a coming restoration of the ideal Hindu kingdom, a reenactment of the king's return to his throne in the Ramayana epic.

Buddhists have their own version of the perfect society, a messianic era of peace and equality which brings back the grandeur of an idealized past. Half a century ago, most of these millennial hopes seemed close to fulfillment in Southeast Asia. New postcolonial independent states had emerged on the horizon — Burma, Sri Lanka, Laos, and Cambodia. Further, 1956 was the year of Buddha Jayanti, the twenty-five-hundredth anniversary of Buddha's parinirvana. According to some Buddhist traditions, the Dharma was destined to last five thousand years after Gautama. Yet the dramatic midpoint in this time-span would mark the end of decline and the beginning of a momentous spiritual renaissance. As 1956 approached, campaign speeches and press editorials from all these nations renewed the dream of Dhamma-samaja, a reign based on Dharma. With a final turn of the wheel, the Buddhist golden age, a vision pieced together especially from the folk history of Sri Lanka and Burma, would reappear.

That year, to celebrate Buddha's anniversary, Premier U Nu of Burma staged a huge ritual in Rangoon. At his signal, twenty-five hundred men in uniform donned the garb of Buddhist monks, a gesture to indicate the millennium had arrived. As promised in many legends, the state was expected to dissolve into the monastic Sangha, with its standard of shared community property. Throughout earlier campaign speeches, U Nu had often referred to the Wishing Tree myth, a perennial theme in Buddhist apocalyptic literature. This tree blossomed during the golden age, before the origins of private property. "The inhabitants of the world found on it enough perfect, healthy, and comfortable things that were sufficient . . . and used them without clinging to them." When people first began to build fortunes in excess of minimal needs, they descended to greedy aggression, then extortion, hatred, murder, and the Wishing Tree vanished. "We wish to establish a socialist state," U Nu concludes, "to bring back successfully the era of the vanished Padeytha Tree."[27]

The year 1956, the acme of U Nu's regime in Burma, was also a significant year in another Theravadist nation, the island of Sri Lanka. Though the full-moon day of May had been chosen as the exact time of Buddha Jayanti, festivities began a few years before. During this period Solomon Bandaranaike vaulted to political power on a double platform — Sinhalese as the national language, Buddhism as the national religion. His candidacy was supported by a radicalized group in the Sangha called the United Monks' Front and by the neglected rural Sinhalese-speaking majority, eager to exchange places with the English-educated elite in civil service. In one characteristic speech, he stated: "The adoption of Buddhism as the state religion will usher in an era of religio-democratic socialism. More than two-thirds of the population of Ceylon are Buddhists, and it is therefore inevitable that Buddhism should be the state religion." Invoking the Buddhist mythical past, his populist strategy was directed less against the non-Buddhist invaders in recent centuries and more against the cultural changes they had left behind.[28]

Modern histories of Sri Lanka state that King Ashoka sent the first Buddhist missionary monks there from India. Later, after Buddhism disappeared in India, the Theravada tradition and its Pali canon would be preserved in Sri Lanka. A more colorful account is given in the Mahavamsa, a Sinhalese folk history. The Buddha circled over Sri Lanka on three different visits from India and left his footprint on top of Sri Pada, a sacred mountain there. During one visit, he got rid of the original demon inhabitants by hovering over one of their settlements in central Sri Lanka and terrorizing them with darkness and a rainstorm. He eventually designated the island a sanctuary where his Dharma would be kept in its purity, in case it should decline or disappear elsewhere. Since this sacred mission underlies Sri Lanka's very purpose as a nation, it is consistent that Bandaranaike could claim that Dharma and the Sangha must be reinstated as the linchpin of a new, liberated Sri Lanka.

In contrast to Sri Lanka and Burma, the United States has a unique founding myth, the story of a postbiblical chosen people searching for the Promised Land, a new frontier and new beginning. However, for many of the new nations in Southeast Asia, their national myth has been one of restoration, the return to an earlier indigenous civilization before its ravage by outsiders. The single moment of history they all idealize is the Indian kingdom of Ashoka. This saintly figure is immortalized today as one of the few kings to repent publicly of his bloody climb to the throne. In the third century B.C.E., history handed him a fortunate power vacuum after Alexander's invasion of the Persian Empire. A fresh Buddhist convert, he now renounced further war and violence, set up welfare funds for the poor and aged, and built schools, monasteries, hundreds of stupas, and some of the world's first hospitals. He sent Buddhist teachers throughout Southeast Asia and left behind him rock inscriptions describing the vision and achievement of an ideal ruler.

"Thanks to the instructions of religion spread by the king," one of the texts states, "today there exist a respect for living creatures, a tenderness toward them, a regard for relatives and for teachers, a dutiful obedience to father and mother and elders, such as have not existed for centuries. The teaching of religion is the most meritorious of acts and there is no practice of religion without virtue." The people of Ashoka's kingdom, drawn from so many different religious backgrounds, are reassured that the king will "honor members of all sects.... There is no better deed than to work for the welfare of the whole world, and all my efforts are made that I may clear my debt to all beings." A Buddhist sovereign's duty, Ashoka believes, is to fashion a society where mature conscience and meditation can flourish. "Mankind has been given as many blessings by previous kings as by me. But I have done this with the intent that people may practice the Dharma."[29]

Ashoka's example offers a credible basis for the Buddhist Dharma-king ideal, as opposed to the Hindu God-king. Granted the two ideals' frequent similarity in actual history, the second model had absolute authority over his people, whereas the first found himself just as answerable to Dharma as were his subjects. More important, the Buddhist monarch enjoyed a close reciprocal link with the Sangha as its patron and servant. Thus, the kingship and wealth that Gautama abandoned would in later eras be preserved and exercised wisely by Ashokan-type rulers to relieve misery and to protect the Sangha and the Dharma. Ashoka can be seen as a sort of Lenin or St. Paul, translating the Dharma, geared originally for the Sangha, into a more detailed blueprint for the contemporary state.

Experiments in Socialism

The addresses of U Nu to the Burmese people contain shrewd folk wisdom, an evangelical eagerness to expound his Buddhist beliefs, and a sound critique of both Marxist and capitalist fallacies. Establishing an early reputation for translating into Burmese *Das Kapital* and *How to Win Friends and Influence People,* he hoped to reconcile and transcend Marxism and capitalism by his own Middle Path strategy of Buddhist socialism. Before the military coup by Ne Win in 1962, U Nu attempted a number of measures to strengthen the Buddhist Sangha and redistribute wealth. For instance, he convened the Sixth Great Buddhist Council, gathering monk delegates from all five Theravada nations, which launched a new edition of the Pali canon. At the same time, he released for annual retreats and daily prayers those civil servants promising to meditate, and he paroled the criminals who passed exams on the Buddhist basic catechism.

The major obstacles to U Nu's economic reforms were two distortions by Buddhists of their own ethical tradition, fallacies which he took every opportunity to correct. Too many of the rich tended to justify current superiority to the poor as their rightful destiny, earned by karmic merit from past lives. In rebuttal, U Nu urged the affluent to become voluntary bodhisattvas, laboring to heal sources of social misery in their present incarnations. Second, Nirvana was too often imagined as a remote, individualistic goal of the spirit. Yet instead, he argued Nirvana must become Marx's classless society, the Christian heavenly banquet, a fellowship based on wisdom, compassion, and freedom, all of which begin here on earth. Your goal should be a corporate Nirvana for future generations, among whom you can number your own probable rebirth.

Worst of all, the Burmese renaissance was paralyzed by Sangha militants, who tore through streets, trashing shops, overturning automobiles, and bludgeoning their political enemies. At first they had supported U Nu in his climb to power. Yet once he became premier, he alienated most Buddhist exclusivists by showing moderation toward non-Buddhist interests. In 1961 he had forced the passage of an amendment decreeing Buddhism the state religion, yet on second thought, he introduced a later amendment to protect the rights of religious minorities. In a pattern widespread throughout many new postcolonial nations, the formerly oppressed had now become oppressors, even brandishing the same intolerant slogans once used against themselves.

U Nu's final months in office can be examined from the pitiless viewpoint of his critics. This leader was disappearing more frequently from the administrative sinkhole widening around him to meditate in a hut built on his estate or in a hermitage on Mount Popa. Finally, he announced his solution to the crippling economic and political crisis. Throughout Burma, sixty thousand sand pagodas would be constructed simultaneously at an astrologically fixed hour, nine Buddhist monks would be offered gifts, and sutras would be recited for three days. At this point, convinced that U Nu lacked a lay vocation to politics, his wily opponents urged people not to vote him back into leadership, for worldly power might impede his achievement of complete Buddhahood.[30]

During this same period, Bandaranaike became prime minister of Sri Lanka, supported, like U Nu, by radical factions within the Sangha. He now proceeded to set up two Buddhist universities "for the promotion of Sinhala and Buddhist culture." Yet his regime was shaken by Sinhalese-Tamil riots caused by the preferences granted Buddhists and Sinhalese over the English-speaking Tamils, who were mostly non-Buddhists. Then he quarreled with the vice president of his party, Bhikkhu Buddharakkhita, also secretary of the United Monks' Front. By 1959, convinced that the prime minister had diluted or betrayed his campaign pledges to this front, a monk under Buddharakkhita's influence assassinated the prime minister.

In subsequent decades, provoked by the religious and cultural separatism ignited under Bandaranaike in Sri Lanka, the Sinhalese-Tamil rift widened into civil war and pogroms, which continue even today. On my visit to the island in 1985, I interviewed a number of people — Buddhist, Hindu, Muslim, and Christian. Almost all told of murdered family members, disrupted careers and education, their lost faith, their bitter intolerance against anyone on the wrong side in this conflict. A Sinhalese lawyer friend of mine regretted I might carry away from Sri Lanka an impression of schizophrenia or hypocrisy — the police barricades and violence, juxtaposed next to those unreal Buddhist words about gentleness and tolerance.[31]

The experimental socialist regimes, the programs of land reform, and the painful nationalization of foreign-owned schools and businesses in Burma, Sri Lanka, and elsewhere are still too recent for careful assessment. It is impossible to determine, too, the spiritual authenticity of this Buddhist rhetoric, for it surfaces during a postcolonial milieu of shrill nationalism, when leaders tend to grope for any ploy available to unite a people. Sometimes crowds do get the leaders they deserve and the promises they deserve, for leaders and their promises tend to mirror the hidden values of a people. To the outsider, most of the millennium slogans sound merely cosmetic.

Young monastic gangs in Burma and Sri Lanka managed to alienate their more traditional Sangha colleagues and, more important, the laity they claimed to serve. A more persuasive model for activist cooperation between Sangha and laity, I am convinced, can be found in the Thai countryside today, where many monks help alleviate poverty, sickness, and patterns of dependency in nearby villages. A 1981 survey of five monasteries in the Chiang Mai region listed the following characteristic outreach projects by the monks: temple repair, sanitation, medical treatment, crop improvement techniques, construction of community wells, and business advice. As a specific example, in an interview at one Bangkok government agency, I asked the manager of a national drug rehabilitation program about the celebrated work of Phra Chamrun, abbot of the Tham Krabok Wat. She explained that in his remote treatment sanctuary, he incorporates drug patients into the monastery as part of his community. His program weans them from heroin abuse by a combination of monastic seclusion, herbal diet, and sustained training in Buddhist meditation.[32]

Today the most widely known Buddhist development project is called the Sri Lanka Sarvodaya Movement, which I have followed on a few recent TV documentaries. In 1958, the year before Bandaranaike's assassination, a Buddhist high school teacher named A. T. Ariyaratne started work camps in the poorest outcaste villages of Sri Lanka for his students. Not run by the government, and attempting to stay clear of party feuding, these camps have increased to thousands today throughout the island. Because Sarvodayans work in Buddhist and non-Buddhist communities and refuse to be polarized, they have sometimes earned trust as conciliators in the Sinhalese-Tamil civil war.

The movement's full name means "everybody waking up by working together." Each village decides on its priorities — roofing a school, digging latrines, repairing a road, a program of nutrition or medicine. Village members are expected to work alongside Sarvodayans, to give and not just get. The modern concept of "development," whereby one nation offers dams or steel mills or computers to raise up the economic or cultural level of another nation, is here reinterpreted more comprehensively. Social change involves "waking up" on all levels, spiritual and physical. Even the poorest families contribute their labor, or crops for a communal meal, or maybe a few work songs and insights. In this way, everyone participating in a work project can complete it with a sense of pride and co-responsibility.

The socialist reforms of U Nu and Bandaranaike never had time to be tested by programs as concrete and well-planned as the Sarvodayan process. Perhaps nothing in this movement outlined thus far sounds distinctively Buddhist. Yet if you look closely, you can find Buddhist axioms and techniques. Any planning session with villagers or work-related meeting begins with a few minutes of centering-meditation. Buddha's Four Noble Truths are stretched into activist slogans, painted sometimes on walls of village centers. One sign reads: "There is a decadent village, there is a cause for its misery, there is a hope for its regeneration, and there is a path."

On this sign, each of the Four Truths is illustrated with drawings, including a picture of the selected local project as the specific fourth truth. Tanha or selfish desire, the second truth and cause of misery, is often portrayed as a wheel of interdependent ingredients — egotism, ignorance, poverty, disease, oppression, intolerance, all factors reinforcing each other in a ruinous spiral. In pictures of the third truth, offering hope for the village's reawakening, this wheel's arrows are reversed. Here bodhisattva qualities of egoless compassion, generosity, and cooperation all find their seedbed. For the average Buddhist, Sarvodaya offers one convincing preview of the Ashokan millennium, or the elusive mystery called Nirvana.[33]

WISDOM, ENGAGED AND DISENGAGED

In the last decade Taiwan has experienced a noticeable religious renaissance, especially in Buddhist practice. Numbers of registered Buddhist temples have grown from 1,157 to over 4,000, monks and nuns from 1,000 to 3,470, and the estimated Buddhists from 800 thousand to 4.8 million. Among the reasons suggested for this increase is the widespread sense of anomie and isolation over a loss of Confucian family values. But the Buddhist Way itself has changed its shape dramatically. Television, magazines, and self-help books tell of a new so-called Worldly Buddhism, contrasted with traditional Buddhism, sometimes given the derisive label of Forest or Jungle Buddhism. As philosophy professor Yang Hui-nan says, "Instead of staying passively behind temple walls chanting and meditating, monks and nuns are traveling the streets to publicize their religion. You see them giving speeches, teaching meditation, and publishing books." Buddhist practice, he explains, has always adapted to oscillations in the public attitude. For instance, monks retired into distant monasteries when persecuted and suppressed in mainland China. Yet during the ninth and tenth centuries, for instance, when people wanted them back, monks emerged and took part in the world.

The Worldly Buddhism of Taiwan bears many traces of the Protestant Social Gospel Movement in the United States a century ago. Innumerable organizations, such as Buddhist Compassion Relief or the Dharma Drum Foundation, are sponsoring drug rehabilitation, disaster relief, ecological awareness, and antinuclear protests. Like the U.S. movement, such agencies offer sincere one-dimensional remedies applied to complex social issues, a similar moral zeal, a fondness for committee work and communal tasks, at times an impatience with ritual and with the recent spiritual past. Yet one ingredient that stamps this renaissance as distinctively Buddhist is a revitalized interest in prayer and meditation. Groups of monks and nuns show up to chant sutras at public funerals and comfort the mourners; sales representatives attend Zen retreats to gain discipline and serenity; and school children frog-squat and fidget in week-long summer camps to learn skills in meditation. Almost a tenth of Buddhist adults have undergone a rite known as *kuei-yi*. This involves a formal profession of faith, promising to live the Dharma and accept a particular monk or nun as one's spiritual director.[34]

It is risky to generalize from a shift in measurable religious externals, especially if sampled from Buddhists in one nation and not another. But I suspect Taiwan's Buddhist revival will soon be matched throughout Asia. One unmistakable feature in Taiwan's meditation training centers is a bold eclecticism. Though masters attracting the most followers identify themselves with Zen, they tend to incorporate practices of other Buddhist schools, especially the Pure Land, and thus create their own Buddhist mixture. This same Buddhist eclecticism also prevails in America. For example, I was amused to hear of the culture shock experienced by a few non-Asian friends, converts to Zen, on their first visit to a local immigrant Buddhist temple. How could an austere yuppie Buddhist contemplative, accustomed to meditate with silent concentration in a room stripped of images, feel any kinship with the cluttered devotional life of poor Cambodian-American Buddhists? The temple was congested with food offerings and incense, many pictures and statues, and the sound of endless mantra chanting. In one corner, some people bowed to an image of Amitabha Buddha, with the hope that just by invoking his name, they could reach the Pure Land to enter Nirvana. In a comparable religious context, perhaps just as alien to the Zen temperament, a Vietnamese-American Buddhist family from Kansas phoned recently to ask my Christian prayers for their dying father. The family had found solace from monks at the local temple, who promised to chant Pure Land sutras for the sick before a statue of Kuan Yin, bodhisattva of compassion.

Viewing similar Buddhist adaptations recently in his native Thailand, Buddhadasa voices a Theravadist disquiet. Like most traditionalists, he fears a meltdown of the rich Buddhist heritage into pseudo-Nirvana — self-therapy, a few bustling good deeds, and a meditation black-belt in four easy lessons. Why must people reify Nirvana into a land of crystal, a city of immortality? "This sort of personification is a kind of elementary propaganda suitable for those who do not yet have the intelligence to understand the true meaning of Nirvana." Yet he can tolerate such a myth if it is taught clearly as just a visualization technique in meditation. The name of Amitabha Buddha means infinite light, in no way an individual object or place. It must refer to a condition "whose light can illumine those depths that even the light of the sun cannot reach, whose light can pierce through the curtains of ignorance and reach the mind and heart of the true practitioner."[35]

In contrast, the Mahayana and Vajrayana Buddhist majority have welcomed almost any aid to meditation, from Zen paradoxes to the most exotic tantric imagery and ritual. In eleventh-century Vietnam, for instance, Thao-Duong urged his Mahayanist disciples to follow the Chinese custom of adapting different methods to different people: "Though you may practice Buddhism in many ways, in summary there are three main methods — meditation, visualization, and Buddha's name-recitation." And if strict meditation requires too much effort, then chant Buddha's name, the easiest and most certain Way.[36]

Meditation and Mindfulness

In the countryside near Bangkok, I once attended an audience held by a celebrated Buddhist monk, who seated himself cross-legged on a raised platform in the crowded monastery meeting hall. My guide and translator was the sister of a former student of mine in world religions. Traveling some distance each month to buy white mushrooms from a famous monastery greenhouse, she would then drop by these sessions. Visitors sat in a hushed semicircle some distance from the monk, flanked by his robed disciples, more or less in the style of Hindu *darshan* facing their guru. Asked to introduce me, the only apparent non-Asian present, my friend mentioned I was a Catholic priest and professor. After an hour of insightful answers to problems raised by his listeners, which my friend kept translating for me, the monk suddenly fixed his attention on the two of us and sent a disciple down with two glasses of orange drink. "Do you meditate?" the monk asked me through my interpreter. In the Theravada canon, as I understand it, the Buddha adapts various techniques of meditation to the spiritual maturity and temperament of each hearer. Buddhaghosa and later commentators have tried to outline a single coherent method. Thus, tainted by just enough pedantry to complicate a simple yes or no, I could not give an accurate answer until I asked him, "What do you mean by meditation?"

Unable or unwilling to define the term, he just repeated his question, "Do you meditate?" After our exchange recurred a few more times, I realized this crazy dialogue had not stemmed from faulty translation. At last I said, "Yes, if you mean spiritual exercises or formal meditation or intensive reflection. I meditated at least fourteen consecutive years for at least an hour or more each day. Now I meditate formally only on occasion, but informally throughout the week." At this response, he smiled and added, "Give me two weeks with you, and I'll teach you really how to meditate!" Was this boast, I wondered, a Thai-boxer equivalent of the Zen master's slap to make me aware? Then one of the monk's female disciples intervened to offer an explanation. Her master knew that *vipassana,* a form of intense imageless meditation favored by his own Theravada tradition, must lie beyond the grasp of all those uninitiated in its practice. After this, my dialogue with the monk resumed. He clarified his attitude. He presumed the inferiority of my own meditation methods, no matter how I might translate or explain them. This challenge left me in two minds. First, ready to waive his apparent condescension or smugness, I was still willing to try out a few weeks of training with him. Yet at the same time, could anything so far beyond my unaided skill now be inculcated in just two weeks? I guessed that behind his smile lurked the sort of trainer for whom even two years would not be enough.

Though turning down this monk's offer, I determined to read up on vipassana and experiment with it someday, perhaps under a more trustworthy mentor. As I see it, each Buddhist school of meditation has mined its own distinct specialized vein of the original deposit. The classical model upon which all Buddhists draw can be outlined as a meditation process in three stages.[37] The first is a phase of calming, a withdrawal from distractions and sensory bombardment. Second is the sharpened observation of this sensory flow, viewed from progressively deeper states of trance and mindfulness. The third stage is a moment of decisive reentry, where newly empowered, you take a fresh look at each situation that requires changed attitudes or action. Some prayer traditions emphasize only one or two of the three stages. Though some insist on an exact sequence of steps, others adapt the sequence to needs of each unique temperament.

In Theravada, strict traditionalists focus only on the first two phases. For my own experiments at the first level, called *sanatha* or calming, I would try to become absorbed in a single object of experience, perhaps my own breathing process, a great blank circle, a pane of glass. Making gradual forays into the second stage, called vipassana or insight, I would try to direct moment-to-moment attention toward whatever images, feelings, or thoughts passed through my mind, and then descend slowly into the undifferentiated flow itself. Buddhists call this attention strategy "bare awareness." Such relaxed consciousness, I think, resembles Freud's notion of evenly suspended attention or free association, which helps both the therapist and client uncover half-remembered and repressed experience. Suspending many conventional ego functions, trying not to distinguish between inner and outer, morally acceptable or unacceptable, you simply note whatever arises in the mind or senses.

Exercises like these can dispose you to a more habitual mindfulness, alert to your surroundings and what you and others are really doing. As Gautama said, "Whenever you see a form, simply see. Whenever you hear a sound, simply hear. Whenever you smell an aroma, simply smell. Whenever you taste a flavor, simply taste. Whenever you feel a sensation, simply feel. Then 'you' will no longer exist. Whenever the 'you' does not exist, you will not be found in this world, another world or in between. That is the finish of suffering."[38] In this same spirit, an oft-cited Zen tale depicts a man pursued by a tiger. Cornered near a precipice, he grabs hold of a wild vine and swings himself down over the ledge. The tiger sniffs at him from above. But far below, another tiger waits to eat him. With only the vine to save him, he watches as two mice gradually gnaw away at the vine. Suddenly he spots a ripe red strawberry nearby. Grasping the vine with one hand, he plucks the strawberry with his other hand. How sweet it tastes!

By yielding to the flow of consciousness, and blurring the distinction between subject and object, the person at meditation should now be open to de-reify the self, the world, anything given public validation as a separate *the*. For this purpose, Buddhists offer an assortment of linguistic tools to unfreeze the fixed conventional notions of your mind. Any Buddhist primer contains Sanskrit words like *an-atman* or no-self, *an-itya* or no-permanence, *a-vidya* or no-knowledge, and *sunyata* or emptiness. Citing parallels to quantum field theory, Fritjof Capra in *The Tao of Physics* interprets Buddhist emptiness and impermanence, for instance, just as indications that reality transcends conventional forms. The fallacy of no-knowledge means the mind's tendency to divide the perceived world into individual and separate things, and to view oneself as an isolated ego. Most resourceful of all Buddhist linguistic aids is the concept of *pratitya-samutpada,* interexistence or an evolving interdependence, which emphasizes the relational aspect of all reality. To grasp the implications of this concept, Mahayanist prayer masters suggest a visualization exercise I find helpful. Imagine a net stretching throughout the universe. It extends vertically in time and horizontally in space. At each point of connection between threads is a crystal bead, standing for an individual existence. When you examine any single bead, you catch also every other bead reflected, and then reflections of reflections, all forming an endless shimmering totality.[39]

These paradoxical notions all catch different facets of a single phenomenon — in nature and the psyche, life is a continuous process of becoming. My experience of the world will always be painful and alienated until I let go and merge peacefully with the ongoing stream both within and around myself. Of course, this sudden shift in consciousness must become habitual, transforming my entire life. Then tanha and its supports — the conventional self, the hankering for me and mine — all will be extinguished. This is what Nirvana means to many Theravadists. And even the climax of self-conquest will sustain itself, ever more deeply, through a series of reincarnations until parinirvana.

Buddhist masters have designed many techniques to leap directly toward this culmination without delaying over the slow-charted journey. Even under careful spiritual guidance, there are two popular crash-courses in meditation I think especially hazardous. The first is Sunlun Vipassana, named after the Burmese city of Sunlun, where an unschooled farmer first perfected it. Called the "rough-breathing method," it requires you to hold your breath after each of a hundred or more deep inhalations, until the torment grows unendurable. Geared for combat, plunging yourself into the painfulness of existence almost to the breaking point, you grope toward an eventual release into egolessness and ecstatic trance.

The second crash-course has become known among Zen Buddhists, especially those of the Rinzai school, as the Great Doubt or Great Death. It is customary to assign each spiritual novice a custom-built koan, a nonsense mantra planned to render the ordinary, discursive mind impotent. Though it may take months or even years of koan practice to reach this so-called death, some Zen masters, hankering for a dramatic eureka, tend to impel and foreshorten the process disastrously. For days of intensive focus, you wrestle only with your koan. Shattered by the inability to apply conventional distinctions between subject and object, ego and the Buddha-nature, samsara and Nirvana, the mind breaks down in surrender. This moment can prove itself a free and expanding breakthrough into satori or enlightenment only if integrated into a context of balanced, seasoned spiritual training.[40]

Harsh spiritual shortcuts like these cannot suit everyone, especially those with fragile or unstable ego-boundaries. Like experiments with drugs or self-induced trance, a misguided use of the meditation process can spark a psychotic break or moods of unyielding depression and despair. From my own years of Jesuit novitiate training decades ago, I remember a few zealous spiritual athletes in our group. Caught up in marathons of fasting and meditation, they often complained of crushing headaches, insomnia, and obsessions.

A wise adaptation of the attention strategies described above can help anyone, even those with severe mental disorders. For example, one minor disorder common to Japan is called *shinkeishitsu,* a condition marked by feelings of inferiority and awkwardness in forming relationships. Under treatment by Morita therapy, patients usually begin with a week of lonely bed rest in a clinic or hospital, without any distractions but their own thoughts. An orgy of self-focus, which at first delights them, in a few days turns to ashes. For the next weeks, they eagerly displace this concern from themselves onto details of some assigned task, such as gardening or chopping wood, then a few games, and finally some conversations. Behind Dr. Morita's techniques of re-socialization lies a specific Buddhist teaching. You stop, flood, or redirect the flow of self-consciousness and consciousness itself, in order to precipitate a breakthrough beyond the conventional ego. The goal is a spirituality of the immediate and particular, the art of being fully present in each task and personal interaction at hand.

Buddhist friends of mine often relate stories about saintly lamas or roshis who float in the air, bilocate in places separated by miles, or walk on hot coals. My first impulse is to wonder how some graphic visualization exercise in meditation or a metaphorical peak-experience happened to get misread as a physical event. Yet Patanjali and other Hindu yogis have always made hyperbolic claims like these. At an advanced stage of yoga, lifted beyond conventional distinctions between subject and object, you are taught to externalize this spiritual experience for the advantage of all around you. By transforming your inner vision and imagination, you change the "objective" world. Taking a near-Vedantist Hindu approach, many Mahayanists hold that consciousness itself is not a product of the world, but the world a product of consciousness. You live in just the universe you have created, and thus deserve. The art of life consists not in escaping the world or saving the world but in reaching a profound self-enlightenment. Buddhist manifestos for nonviolence, environmental ethics, and political change presume a direct link between reform of outer structures and a self-conversion within.[41]

The Active Reentry

The third and final stage of a completed meditation is the moment of active reentry into the world. An oft-cited Zen koan addresses this comeback from enlightenment to the immediacy of everyday life. "At first tea is sheer tea; then it is no longer tea; but at last it is indeed tea." Thus, you begin with a meditative departure from the prosaic "sheer tea" to some transcendental experience — tea is the Dharmakaya, the Buddha-nature. But what still remains is the completed return, reincorporating this deeper awareness back into the concrete particular "tea indeed!"

Meditation has been leading up to this moment of compassionate application — a moment pivotal for all Mahayanists, but also for many contemporary Theravadists. For instance, writing from his rural Thai monastery, Ajarn Buddhadasa speaks as a convinced Theravadist: "Why were we born? We were born not for me-and-mine, but rather to help one another free this world from suffering." And again: "Acquiring knowledge is just a preparation for practice. Only when we actually apply that knowledge in living according to our religious principles are we practicing our religion. Only then can we realize real benefits. Only then are we religious in the fullest sense of the word." Elsewhere, he argues also for a more activist interpretation of the Sangha: "Buddhist monks are wanderers, not hermits.... Their duty is to help the people of the world in whatever way is suitable so that they do not have to suffer, or in the words of a Thai proverb, so that they can know how to eat fish without getting stuck on the bones."[42]

Among Mahayanist Buddhists, the life of early Zen master Tetsugen emphasizes the same primacy of action. Traveling throughout Japan for ten years, he collected money to publish the first wood block prints of Buddhist sutras, translated from the Chinese. Just when he had enough funds to begin printing, a famine struck the countryside. Then years later, a plague. During each of the two calamities, Tetsugen gave up all his money to the needy and then started a fresh funding campaign. After twenty years, he at last published the famous sutras that can now be viewed in the Obaku monastery of Kyoto. It has been said that Tetsugen printed three sets of sutras. And the first two invisible sets are much more beautiful than the last.

Throughout the meditation process, you have plunged deeply into the source of human misery and its cure. You come to recognize what blinds and traps so many others, those people who deserve compassion. So you determine to share your vision with them. In other words, self-discovery or self-denial is too joyful to be contained, so it spills out into relationships with the world. Hard-won compassion for oneself, uncertain of its direction, can eventually sweep away boundaries between self and others. Yet this particular sequence of attitudes can also be reversed, especially among Mahayanists. World-denying phrases somehow reappear on the lips of many world-affirming activists. A life of compassion toward others has been prized as the best way to extinguish the ego and reach contemplative wisdom.

Am I my brother's keeper? More than this, says the perceptive Buddhist. Somehow I *am* my brother and sister. According to the early poet and philosopher Shantideva, the crown of meditational practice consists of thought experiments to remove the boundaries between separate selves. "Whoever wishes to give protection quickly to both oneself and other beings," he says, "should practice that supreme secret — the exchange of self and other." Thus, first dissolve your conventional self-definition as a separate monad. Once this is accomplished, then learn imaginatively to exchange identities between yourself and others. A common visualization exercise among Mahayanists is called the Great Compassion meditation. You try to imagine the sufferings of all living creatures, one by one, engulfed in flames of terrible sadness. And then singling out particular individuals and their pain, you try to feel for them, the way you would feel for your own suffering children or parents. Then you ponder how you could help them find release.[43]

Instead of "compassion," I prefer the term "empathy," to sidestep the demeaning overtones often attached to misunderstood gestures of pity and sympathy. Moreover, from a balanced viewpoint, I share not only in the suffering of others but also in their joy. As explained in the prologue to this book, empathy means literally the ability to feel into, or feel inside, another situation. Thus, feeling-into the life of others, I enter into their life and worldview and try to feel, value, and believe as they do. From the Buddhist perspective, this solidarity is backed by the concept of *pratitya-samutpada* or interdependence, which I explained before. Because of the weblike interconnections between inner and outer worlds, whatever thought or action I initiate will trigger results beyond imagining. This belief gives me a basis for fellowship with all sentient beings and also for hope that my least action, even just a prayer, will somehow influence the destiny of others.

Buddhadasa has constructed a modern Buddhist rationale for social ethics on the simple foundation of this interdependence. If I am interwoven somehow into the good that others do, now or in the past, why should I get trapped now by envy or greed? According to his version of the original Sangha, Buddhist society today must be socialist, in a broad sense of the term. It was once the custom for farmers cultivating rice paddies to make willing allowance during the harvest, leaving a portion behind for stray people and animals. Monks were permitted no more than one rice bowl, nor any more cloth in their robes than necessary. Poverty cannot be eradicated until there is an end to excessive hoarding, which leads to the scarcity that causes poverty. Each must cooperate for the good of others, one village with another. "If we hold fast to Buddhism," Buddhadasa says, "we shall have a socialist disposition in our flesh and blood. We shall see our fellow humans as friends in suffering — in birth, old age, sickness, and death — and hence we cannot abandon them. . . . The socialistic ideal of Buddhism finds expression in the concept of the bodhisattva."[44]

Buddhists widen their socialist community to include not just other human beings but also all sentient creatures, and thus, the total environment. In a splendid prayer from the Anguttara Nikaya, Buddha prays: "My love to the footless, my love to the two-footed, my love to the four-footed, my love to the many-footed." May none of them prove harmful. "All sentient beings, all breathing beings, creatures without exception, let them all see good things, may no evil happen to them."[45] No doubt such a prayer once functioned to protect people from venomous snakes and other predators. Today, on the contrary, the animals and their environment need to be protected from us. "The earth's resources are being dug up in unnecessarily large quantities," Buddhadasa says, "only to be used carelessly and wastefully. Not only are they often not put to any constructive use, but they are turned into instruments of harm. . . . If we were to use the earth's resources according to the laws of nature and within its limits, we would not need to use as much as we do now."[46]

Central to this solidarity with all living beings is an ethics of nonviolence and peace. During recent decades, the three outstanding Buddhist figures in the global peace movement have been the Dalai Lama of Tibet, Thich Nhat Hanh of Vietnam, and Aung San Suu Kyi of Burma or Myanmar. Nhat Hanh is an elderly Vietnamese Mahayanist monk, now exiled in France, where he has founded a meditation community called Plum Village. Known today from his many books and meditation workshops, he first gained worldwide attention for leading a nonpartisan Buddhist movement in Vietnam during the 1960s that sought a peaceful end to civil war. After his banishment from Saigon, he chaired the Buddhist delegation to the Paris peace talks. It is touching to learn that in his friendship with Martin Luther King, each found much to respect in the other. King the Christian Baptist nominated Nhat Hanh for the Nobel Peace Prize, whereas the Buddhist monk saw King as a genuine bodhisattva.

Nhat Hanh has coined the term "engaged Buddhism" to describe his particular message, an artful blend of basic meditation, political responsibility, and awareness in every life. If you cannot serve your spouse or parents, he says, how are you going to serve humanity? It is not so much by going out for a demonstration against nuclear missiles that you can bring about peace. It is principally by smiling peace, breathing peace, and being peace, that you can make peace. His own Buddhist activism opens him to solidarity with peace-activists from every imaginable religious and nonreligious background. In his book-length dialogue on nonviolence with Father Daniel Berrigan, for example, he enunciates his cardinal rule for the new monastic movement he once initiated in Vietnam: "One should not be idolatrous or bound to any doctrine, any theory, any ideology, including Buddhist ones. Buddhist systems of thought must be guiding means and not absolute truth."[47]

Lacking empathy, people find it easy to discount, hate, and kill one another. Thus, in his meditation workshops, familiar now in many countries, Nhat Hanh hopes to train his followers for a life of empathy. He proposes a few vivid exercises in visualization and gesture. For example, in the so-called hugging meditation, he suggests that you take someone aside you truly love, and give the person a warm embrace. As you breathe with full awareness, you are asked to reflect in detail how precious that person is. A more demanding exercise, already summarized in my prologue, has been devised to elicit empathy for the person you most despise. "Contemplate the image of the person who has caused you the most suffering. Regard the features you hate or despise the most or find the most repulsive." Then imagine what makes this enemy happy or sad each day, what patterns of thought or reason this person follows, the extent to which this enemy is victimized by others. "Continue until you feel compassion rise in your heart like a well filling with fresh water," he concludes, "and your anger and resentment disappear. Practice this exercise many times on the same person."[48]

Like Buddhadasa, Nhat Hanh bases his teaching on the major Buddhist premises, such as disciplined mindfulness, the annihilation of the selfish ego, and especially the interexistence or dependent co-arising of all living beings. "I have a pile of orphan applications for sponsorship on my desk," he once wrote. "I translate a few each day. Before I begin to translate a sheet, I look into the eyes of the child in the photograph, and look at the child's expression and features closely. I feel a deep link between myself and each child, which allows me to enter a special communion with them. . . . I no longer see an 'I' who translates the sheets to help each child, I no longer see a child who receives love and help. The child and I are one: no one pities; no one asks for help; no one helps. There is no task, no social work to be done, no compassion, no special wisdom." Given this perspective, identifying himself not only with the person victimized but also with the person victimizing, he was able in the Vietnam War paradoxically to side with both sides in their humanity, and at the same time with neither in their violent deeds. Once the war ended, as one unforgettable gesture of healing and reconciliation for both sides, he led a number of his American friends on a slow walking meditation around the Vietnam War Memorial in Washington.[49]

Engaged Buddhism, active compassion, a spiritually infused politics — these are recognizable Nhat Hanh terms adopted by Burmese activist Aung San Suu Kyi. They describe her years of dedicated Buddhist dissent against one of the most oppressive military regimes in modern history. Mother of two children, daughter of the celebrated war hero General Aung San, she proved a major embarrassment to her government by receiving the Nobel Peace Prize in 1991. Though winning popular elections a year before, her political victory had been canceled immediately, many of her party colleagues imprisoned or executed, and Aung San herself sentenced to years of house arrest. Celebrated today in the world press as a Burmese Joan of Arc or a second Nelson Mandela, she is often identified by her extensive Myanmar following as a female bodhisattva. "I'm nowhere near such a state," she comments with a modest smile. "I would love to become a bodhisattva one day, if I was capable of such heights." Concerned about her unmanageable temper, however, she must use every Buddhist meditative resource to purify her heart of bitterness and vindictiveness toward her adversaries. Knowledgeable since childhood about her rich Theravada heritage of meditation, she admits, "I never meditated very much. My real meditation only began during my years of house arrest. . . . While we can't all be Buddhists, I feel a responsibility to do as much as I can to realize enlightenment to the degree I can, and to use it to relieve the suffering of others."[50]

As mentioned above, Nhat Hanh finds ever new applications for Gandhi's principle of separating the criminal deed from the person of the criminal. In a similar way, Aung San Suu Kyi, even in the act of denouncing the policies of her enemies, hopes never to lose her compassion and respect for human beings who after all claim to follow the Buddha just as she. Murdering someone does not make you only a murderer; you still remain much more than that in your humanity. She is even ready to sacrifice her life, if this gesture could awaken her oppressors to recognize their blindness. "When the Buddha tried to stop two sides from fighting each other," she recalls, "he went out and stood between them. They would have had to injure him first before they could hurt each other. So he was defending both sides, as well as protecting others at the sacrifice of his own safety."[51]

Nhat Hanh and Aung San Suu Kyi in their writings and more so in their lives show an exemplary integration of Buddhist prajna and karuna, wisdom and compassion, contemplation and action. The source of the Dalai Lama's serenity and nonviolent activism, too, stems from these same meditative roots. Speaking of his daily practice, the Dalai Lama says, "To engender altruism, or compassion in myself, I practice certain mental exercises which promote love towards all sentient beings, including especially my so-called enemies. For example, I remind myself that it is the actions of human beings rather than human beings themselves that make them my enemy. Given a change of behavior, that same person could easily become a good friend." He has tried to make the classical bodhisattva prayer his own: "For as long as space endures, and for as long as living beings remain, until then may I, too, abide to dispel the misery of the world."[52]

Seder dish marked in Hebrew and English for ingredients used in the Jewish Passover, annual meal to reenact Israel's liberation and its covenant. Copper of seven-inch diameter, painted in brown and gold. United States.

5

The Jewish Way

For minds accustomed to neat East-West dichotomies, Buddhists and Jews appear to have little in common. Yet a few years ago the Dalai Lama spoke to a group of Jewish theologians about the diaspora of his Tibetan people. The Hebrew motif of liberation, exodus, and search for a Promised Land has always dominated the imagery of America's civil religion. It has proven even more central to African-Americans' reflections on their own historical diaspora out of Africa. Aware of these parallels, the Dalai Lama knew that once China turned Tibetans into refugees, "our struggle would not be easy. It would take a long time. Generations. Very often we would refer to the Jewish people, how they kept their identity and faith despite such hardship and so much suffering. And when external conditions were ripe, they were ready to rebuild their nation. So you see, there are many things to learn from our Jewish brothers and sisters."[1]

When Buddhists in the twentieth century tried to translate their millennial dreams into a modern socialist state, they turned again toward Israel as a model. On her 1962 visit to Burma shortly before U Nu's fall from power, Golda Meir, Israeli foreign minister, met some unforgettable surprises at a small northern airport — enthusiastic socialist slogans, Hebrew songs, and Israeli flags, all of them presented by Burmese wives and children who had once lived in Israel. Seven years before, large groups of demobilized Burmese soldiers and their families had been flown to work a year on Israeli kibbutzim. These socialist experiments in combined agricultural and military training had then been imported back home, transposed into cooperative village settlements along Burma's disputed China border. Meir was astonished, too, by the success of other Burmese-Israeli enterprises, such as the pharmaceutical industry, irrigation projects, the training of many Burmese doctors and nurses.

In their turn, Buddhists have been helping contemporary Jews recover an appreciation for the Judaic mystical tradition. David Ben-Gurion, for example, first Israeli prime minister, was persuaded by U Nu to make an eight-day meditation retreat at his Rangoon palace temple. Recently, the Germantown Jewish Center in Philadelphia sponsored a conference entitled "The Jew and the Lotus." The center had been finding that many young Jews today, inspired mostly by Zen books and gurus, show hunger for an inner life. As Rabbi Abraham Heschel once observed, Jews who cannot pray may still be craving to pray. Many who claim to be no longer reverent at least feel a reverence for reverence. They need, most of all, an education in reverence.

Participants in the Germantown symposium agreed that Judaism in this century has unwisely neglected its spiritual tradition. Its teachers first had to cope with destructive critiques from modern logical positivism, then with the community's survival after the Holocaust. Perhaps Jewish spirituality could be enhanced today by combining traditional rituals and biblical formal prayer with more impromptu forms of meditation. For instance, one rabbi told of a dying Jewish woman in a convalescent home, upset that her daughter, a student of Buddhism, would read aloud to her from the Tibetan Book of the Dead. He suggested both women read and meditate together from a work unknown to most contemporary Jews — Yavoor Yabok, the medieval Jewish Book of the Dead.[2]

I have singled out Golda Meir as someone responsive not so much to religious Buddhism as to people in Burma who happened to be Buddhists. Her own background illustrates a dialectic between the religious past and the secular present — tensions familiar to most contemporary Jews. Recounting the memories of her childhood in Kiev and Pinsk, she idealized the extraordinary piety of her grandfather, who had been inducted at thirteen into the Russian army. During his decade of military service he refused to eat cooked food because it was not kosher. After discharge he slept for years on a bench in their local synagogue, with a stone for his pillow, in order to atone for any sins he had unknowingly committed while among Gentiles.

In the next generation, her father studied Torah at a yeshiva and grew up "no extremist in religion, but traditionally observant." Golda Meir belonged to a family that celebrated each Sabbath meal with hymns, and gathered for all the major Jewish festivals, first in Russia and Poland, then in Milwaukee after they immigrated there. She admits that in her teens "I would often have theological arguments with my mother. I wanted very much to explain to her that everything ultimately came from nature, that there was science and science has laws." With the Meirs' concerns seldom narrowed just to personal affairs, their home in Milwaukee became a center for many social causes, especially those of various labor and socialist organizations in the First World War era. Soon caught up in the Zionist movement, Meir and her sister left America for a kibbutz in Palestine. Later, her parents joined her in the new state of Israel, and the extended family again resumed its patterns of religious observance.

Meir often asked herself why Jews of such various national origins had survived as a single people. Once modern Israel had been established as a nation, immigrants from Europe, from the caves of Libya and hills of Morocco and Yemen, now lived beside Israeli-born youngsters. What united them all? "Not language," she said. "Certainly not a way of life. Certainly not standards of education. Certainly not adjustment to the technology and science of our age. . . . In my mind there is no doubt that religion, not only general religious concepts but minute and detailed observances, contributed to this endurance." Later, she tried to pin down her own concept of the Sacred. Anytime you probe life's deepest questions, you eventually reach "the unexplainable, the ultimately unknowable. It really is not important what you call it. Let us assume that for the sake of common agreement we call that something 'spirit' — the spirit of this people — which has no limitations and is indestructible. This spiritual strength is eternal. It is transmitted from generation to generation, almost unwittingly. This is the most important factor in our lives."[3]

Thus, a major religious transformation can be traced within three generations of the Meir family. The Meir heritage begins in the strictest orthodoxy of Russian and Polish ghettos, secured against assimilation. It adapted in America to a loyal but flexible religious observance, which interweaves with Zionism, socialism, and various national or international movements that speak for oppressed people everywhere. In its most recent Israeli stage, blurring the margins between the Sacred and secular, transcendence and immanence, it often adopts the rhetoric of messianic secularity. Prime Minister Meir's phrases match the basic tenet of Reconstructionist Judaism, as formulated by its founder, Rabbi Mordecai Kaplan: "Mythological ideas about God give way to the conception of divinity immanent in the workings of the human spirit."[4] To some Jewish traditionalists, of course, Meir's credo sounds like an idolatrous civil religion, deifying the Jewish people or, worse, the modern state of Israel.

These differing Jewish options within the Meir family provide a framework in the present chapter for a dialogue — Theodor Herzl and Golda Meir and David Ben-Gurion on one side, and Martin Buber and Rabbi Abraham Heschel on the other. First it is essential to examine the religious upheaval two centuries ago that initiated all three positions represented by the Meir family. Climax to centuries of diaspora, the so-called Jewish Emancipation transformed hidden colonies of the Jewish counterculture into a recognizable major global religion.

EMANCIPATION AND ITS DISCONTENTS

Moses Mendelssohn, father of the Haskalah, or the Jewish Age of Reason, once began a letter: "Moses the Mensch writes to Herder the Mensch, and not the Jew to the Christian preacher." By the late eighteenth century, grand visions of friendships and societies based on a shared human nature seemed closer to realization than ever before. This was the era of Jefferson's self-evident human rights. Flocking to prestigious salons, an international gathering of trendsetters invoked the moral axioms of Confucius, Socrates, or even Ben Franklin. Such giants of reason struck their admirers as too massive to fit within the petty margins of either Christian or Judaic orthodoxy.

A vivid illustration of openness during this Age of Reason can be found in the dramatic poem *Nathan the Wise* by Gotthold Lessing. Moses Mendelssohn, Lessing's close friend, inspired the title character of a wealthy Jewish seer. Alongside Nathan, the play introduces an impulsive Christian knight and the pragmatist Muslim Saladin, each showing the others an empathy and friendship that seem to transcend their three sectarian traditions. At the exact center of this drama is the adapted Boccaccio parable of three rings. Asked by Saladin to declare which of their three revealed religions is the greatest, Nathan tells of an opal ring, passed down perennially from father to worthiest son, a ring conferring the favor of God and humanity on whoever trusts its magic. At last, the ring stops with one father, who judges all three sons equally worthy. Unable to resolve this dilemma in any other way, he purchases two duplicate rings and bestows one secretly on each son. After the father's death, each son, believing himself recipient of the original ring, claims the throne.

Summoned to settle the quarrel between all three, a judge suggests that each persuade subsequent generations to test out the power of his own ring, so that at the end of time God himself can judge which was genuine. "Let each one believe his ring to be the true one. Possibly the father could no longer tolerate in his house the tyranny of just one ring." The judge declares that the father loved all three sons equally and would not show preference. The sons are told to imitate the unprejudiced affection of their father: "Let each strive to match the others in eliciting the opal's magic in his ring."[5]

This parable merits attention because it offers a Humanist perspective on the frequent incompatibility between Judaic, Christian, and Muslim descendants within the single family of Abraham — the focus of the next few chapters. Unfortunately, the reasonableness of Lessing's message did not guide subsequent history. For human reason took such an abrupt detour that afterward people found this earlier utopic dream almost impossible to reconstruct. Two centuries of demonic nationalism followed the Jewish Emancipation, with fierce battles for civil and social rights. And random outbreaks of intolerance climaxed in unthinkable horrors of the Holocaust. Imagine someone like Moses Mendelssohn reincarnated during the Third Reich, now attempting to dismiss his Jewishness and to identify himself as just a mensch!

Sartre's *Anti-Semite and Jew,* a courageous book written during the German occupation, quickly disposes of the question whether Jews are primarily Jews or human beings. Only the naive, abstract mind of eighteenth-century democrats, says Sartre, could state the problem in this fallacious manner. "They have no eyes for the concrete syntheses with which history confronts them. They recognize neither Jew, nor Arab, nor Negro, nor bourgeois, nor worker, but only a human being — human always the same in all times and all places." Whereas an anti-Semite blots out the humanity and sees only the Jew or untouchable alien, the Enlightenment democrat "wishes to destroy the person as a Jew and leave nothing there but the humanity — abstract and universal subject of the rights of human beings and citizens."[6]

Within just a decade after *Nathan the Wise,* and the deaths of both Lessing and Mendelssohn, legal equality was achieved for French Jews by the French Revolution, and it began to touch the rest of Europe through the Napoleonic Wars. Yet in various nations the trade-off for legal and social emancipation proved more costly than expected. Jewish community leaders, forced to surrender their separate ghetto courts and law to gain full citizenship, felt the loss of political, social, and religious authority over their own people. As the protective walls of many ghettos fell, Jews were introduced to a range of options — to enhance, delay, or resist social and religious assimilation into the majority culture. This fateful instant of choice in nineteenth-century Europe accounts for longstanding divisions of the American Jewish immigrant community into Reform, Orthodox, and Conservative factions. It also begins to explain the complex religious and political factions that divide contemporary Israeli society.

Modes of Separation

The shtetl or ghetto had existed for centuries in eastern Europe as a self-sufficient town within a town. Many years later, with this entire way of life wiped out by the Holocaust, it is understandable that many Jews recall the ghetto only in a haze of idealized melancholy. In each ghetto, neighboring families were interwoven into a small, tight community and linked to other ghettos by trade, annual fairs, and itinerant preachers. The Russian shtetl in Marc Chagall's paintings usually radiates an aura of warmth and magic — a tearful rabbi in his prayer shawl or a beggar in the snow, their grief eased somehow by the presence of a peaceful cow or flower or violin. Alert to an approaching catastrophe, you catch a bittersweet ache beneath the gentle humor of Joseph Stein's *Fiddler on the Roof,* a play based on selected Yiddish tales by Sholom Aleichem. "Because of our traditions, we've kept our balance for many, many years," says Tevye in the opening lines. "We each know who we are and what God expects us to do!"

Stripped of this romantic icing, the actual ghetto no doubt had its share of religious drop-outs and partly-ins. The ghetto experience at its best can be summed up accurately in the Yiddish word *mentsh.* To be a mentsh here has resonances different from the proposal by Mendelssohn to Herder mentioned before, that both friends sidestep their Jewish and Christian particularity and communicate from one mensch to another. Unlike the German, the Yiddish term first of all implies compassion. And this feature, as the Hasidic Rabbi Shelomo cautions, must never be confused with condescending pity: "If you want to raise people from mud and filth, do not think it enough to keep standing on top and reaching them a helping hand. You must go all the way down yourself, down into mud and filth. Then take hold of them with strong hands and pull them and yourself out into the light."[7] Besides compassion, the Yiddish legacy includes reluctance to harm any living being, a sense of family and social responsibility, an openness to the complete spectrum of human life. Though similar to the compassion of a Buddhist bodhisattva, it also implies self-mocking humor, a concern for individual relationships, and an unashamed capacity to weep.[8]

What does it mean to be a Jew? Without hesitation, most people in the European ghettos could have agreed upon a single answer. Jews are people of the Torah. The ideal of each traditional Jew is to study, pray, and embody Torah, and thus deepen the covenant with a loving personal God. Moral standards, ritual observance, and the entire educational system in this intimate society are regulated by the believing community. Often mistranslated as law, Torah means revealed teaching, which includes halakha or law. Torah is strictly defined as the covenant at Sinai between God and his chosen people, spelled out in the Mosaic Pentateuch, the first five books of the Bible. In expanding circles of inclusiveness, Torah covers first the entire Hebrew Bible. Second, it further embraces the various authoritative biblical commentaries and applications in the rabbinic Talmud. Third, at its most inclusive, Torah is also expressed in the legitimate custom and consensus of today's international Jewish community.

Similar to Hindu or Buddhist Dharma, Torah is an architectural cosmic plan. In rabbinic lore, it is the divine mind or will, even the personified consort or handmaid of God. By their exemplary fidelity to Torah, the Jewish people help restore sacred order to the cosmos. If properly understood, some traditional Jewish observances show colorful imagination in their attempt to summon and celebrate the presence of Torah in the heart. The mezuzah box enclosing a significant biblical quotation on parchment fulfills God's command, "You shall write the words of Torah on the door posts of your home and upon your gates." For a similar purpose, small tefillin containers are strapped around the forehead and wrists while praying. Congregations bow to the sacred Torah scroll, kiss it, and sometimes even embrace and dance ecstatically with what Kafka called these "old headless dolls."

A basic intention running through centuries of rabbinic leadership has been the development of a halakhic shield around the Mosaic Torah. This serves as a sacred protective screen of ritual detail, purifying the Jews and separating them from the non-Jewish world. Pharisees in the time of Jesus spelled out ever more exacting observances to separate Jews from the influence of their Roman colonizers, just as Hindus would later tighten caste restrictions against the reigning Muslim culture. In world religions classes, my more traditionalist Jewish students compare this Jewish shield of ritual observance with the Confucian effort to make all life ceremonial, as described in chapter 2. The intent of intricate dietary and Sabbath restrictions, for instance, or frequent blessings and prayer formulas, is to transform even the most ordinary actions of eating, traveling, or sleeping into a complete sacramental way of life. Abraham Heschel offers one devout interpretation of their purpose. God has been exiled from his own universe. "He is not at home in a universe where his will is defied and where his kingship is denied.... To pray means to bring God back into the world, to establish his kingship at least for an instant. To pray means to expand God's presence."[9]

Two centuries ago, in the Jewish Emancipation era, however, this whole rabbinic structure seemed threatened with collapse. For privileged halakhic civil and criminal law in the ghetto had been displaced by a single uniform secular code of law. Worse yet, liberal Jewish scholars had begun to question divine inspiration of the Talmud and even of the Pentateuch. As pointed out in chapter 1, the attempt to secularize religious institutions within a closely integrated traditional society invites a major risk. It could endanger the Center from which everything else derives its meaning.

Thus, the response of many ghetto rabbis was to insist on exact adherence to as many traditional halakhic observances as possible in this new open society. For example, they hoped for unchanged patterns of worship, segregated dietary regulations, and the use of Yiddish, perhaps even distinctive dress. For those quick to sell out their religious identities, "progress is the absolute and religion is governed by it," Samson Hirsch complained in 1854. "To us, religion is the absolute." If German Jews had previously stayed aloof from European civilization, the fault lay not in their religion but in the tyranny that confined them to the ghetto and denied them access to wider culture. Rabbi for almost forty years at an Orthodox synagogue in Frankfurt, Hirsch taught his congregation to be Jews in synagogue, kitchen, and factory, and not to "throw Judaism into a corner for use only on Sabbaths and Festivals.... Judaism is not a mere adjunct to life. It comprises all of life." Hirsch could not support the distinction made by his adversaries between the Orthodox and non-Orthodox. He recognized only "conscientious and indifferent Jews, good Jews, bad Jews or baptized Jews — all, nevertheless, Jews with a mission which they cannot cast off."[10]

Many Orthodox rabbis dreamed of exporting European ghettos intact to America and to Zionist locations in Palestine, Africa, or South America. In fact, some ultra-Orthodox communities today in Israel will not rest until the secular state has been converted into one huge religious ghetto. All marriages, funerals, and religious conversions would fall under the exclusive jurisdiction of the Orthodox rabbinate. Quarreling with modern culture, some extremists stage well-publicized protests against neighborhood shops that sell tendentious books or display sugges-tive posters, against traffic during the Sabbath, against archeological digs that seem to desecrate ancient Jewish cemeteries, or against the drafting of women into the army.[11] At its most uncontrolled, religious militancy of this sort, nourished in scat-tered ultra-Orthodox yeshivas, allegedly led to the assassination of Prime Minister Yitzhak Rabin.

A less abrasive version of transplanted ghetto orthodoxy can be found in Isaac Bashevis Singer's short story "The Little Shoemakers." Here the soul of the ghetto passes from East Europe to New Jersey. After years of delay, old Abba the Shoe-maker finally leaves home to join his emigrant sons and their Americanized families, but he experiences terrible disorientation. In their New Jersey synagogue, he finds the sexton clean-shaven, a candelabrum with electric lights, no faucet to purify your hands, and a congregation wearing abbreviated prayer shawls like scarves. So his sons don skullcaps in his presence, return to the old dietary laws, intro-duce Yiddish phrases, and eventually build a shoemaker's hut in their backyard, where Abba and his children occasionally repair shoes together, as they once did in Europe. Soon he recovers his old happiness: "They had not become idolaters in Egypt. They had not forgotten their heritage, nor had they lost themselves among the unworthy."[12]

A decade ago I experienced an uncommon reversal of Singer's story of religious transplants from Russia to the United States. In my world religions class at the Uni-versity of San Francisco, an earnest young face caught my attention — a newly arrived Soviet immigrant, an only child of two Jewish atheists. Once the topic of Judaism surfaced, he began to consult me in private sessions about his lost Jewish religious roots, which he showed increasing eagerness to explore. I referred him to a rabbi-professor of Judaic studies, who then introduced him into a local Conserva-tive congregation, a welcoming cohesive group of immigrant Russian families. Later I heard that each weekend this student would travel to a traditionalist Jewish home, some hours distant, for Torah study and celebration of the Sabbath.

Seeking an initiation into the Judaic tradition, the young man wanted the "real thing," which to him meant not a Russian ghetto transplant but a genuine American equivalent that his Russian ancestors could still have recognized. This Jewish reli-gious heritage, stolen from his parents and himself by state-imposed atheism, could now be recovered by his own free decision. A few months later, he surprised me with news of his circumcision, which I had expected as a much later culmination of longer study and spiritual apprenticeship. He had pleaded with the traditionalist rabbi to make an exception, letting him anticipate this sealing of the covenant as soon as possible. Fumbling for words of explanation, he told me he wanted to show God far in advance his willingness to give up everything.

Even for those Jews who have avoided the synagogue during most of their adult life, the ghetto values and ritual of an ancestral past often remain an unquestioned ideal. This spiritual nostalgia is evident in a sensitive Jew like Franz Kafka. Once Jewish religious life becomes simply one denominational option among others in so-ciety, it often declines to a series of inherited family duties. Thus, patterns of diet or synagogue attendance can be detached from the rest of meaningful daily existence, and in time misunderstood or discredited. Reflecting on family observances, Kafka complains that his bar mitzvah ceremony, the annual Passover meal, and obligatory synagogue attendance were all "a mere nothing, a joke — not even a joke." In a letter to Felice, a woman who was working with young children in the Jewish People's Home, Kafka admits: "As a boy I almost suffocated from the terrible boredom and pointlessness of hours in the synagogue. These were the rehearsals staged by hell for my later office life."[13]

In contrast, Kafka wishes the children at this People's Home could be introduced to authentic Jewish culture and spirituality. Their guide must not be progressive West European Jews of his own milieu but traditional Jews from Poland and the East. "The quality corresponding to the values of East European Jews is something that cannot be imparted in a Home. . . . But it can be acquired, earned." This priceless attribute gets associated in Kafka's mind with Yiddish culture and language. Raised in a German-Jewish community surrounded by Czechs, Kafka learned to dislike the German words for mother and father. "*Mutter* unconsciously contains, together with Christian splendor, Christian coldness also. . . . I believe it is only memories of the ghetto that still preserve the Jewish family." Although he later found it too unpolished and monotonous, the Yiddish theater seemed at first to portray "a Judaism on which the beginnings of my own rested, . . . that would enlighten and carry me farther along in my own clumsy Judaism."[14]

Voicing regrets similar to Kafka's, a young Jewish friend of mine used to complain of the tepid religious observances at home and among his Reform colleagues. Both his parents knew of his yearning to recover an authentic Jewish spiritual identity. Trained in the Conservative Jewish tradition, he had long attended Hebrew school, studying Hebrew and English — four hours of each language at every session. Moved by her son's longing, his mother responded with immediate support, offering to read through and discuss the entire Hebrew Bible with him, one chapter each day.

After some discussion with her friends, his mother turned to the same resource that had inspired Kafka — reconnection with the lifeline of an idealized East European tradition. She thought of the long black caftans, dangling curls of hair, broad-brimmed hats, white shirts and knickers of fervent Hasidim. Could the family raise funds to support her son at a Lubavitch yeshiva in Brooklyn or, better yet, some transplanted Lithuanian yeshiva in Israel itself? To his delight, he found himself enrolled a year later at the Pardes Yeshiva in Jerusalem, where he engaged in Torah and Talmud study twelve hours a day. Seasoned by a fervent year of prayer and study there, he came home, prouder of his Jewish heritage, but more doubtful than ever about what it means to be a Jew. Though in Israel the familiar American distinction between Orthodox, Reform, and Conservative Jews dropped away, these divisions were replaced by more complex debates between Ashkenazim and Sephardim, Zionist and anti-Zionist, observant and nonobservant, religious and secular.

Modes of Assimilation

By assimilated Jews, I mean those breaking decisively from the rabbinic patterns of observance. The assimilated all share in similar gestures of departure but offer differing resourceful motives for deconversion, the sincerity and maturity of which I shall not question. Some people might end up religiously uncommitted, socialized half-consciously by the values of the majority nearby. Others might convert to a non-Jewish religion or to its nonreligious equivalent, such as international socialism or cultural Zionism. From my own perspective, any of these options is spiritually plausible, depending on each individual conscience. The classical Hebrew prophets, of course, denounced the least assimilation. And according to a longstanding Talmudic tradition, apostate Jews, even those with Christian baptism, are still counted as authentic Jews. Confronted by all this semantic confusion, the Israeli Supreme Court decision of 1962 tried to set some practical limits to Jewish legal identity. It confirmed that both religious and nonreligious Jews may invoke the Law of Return to gain state citizenship, but not a Polish Carmelite priest born of Jewish parents. Though utter assimilation means a concealment or renunciation of all Jewish identity, the situations I shall now explore seldom reach this extreme.[15]

At times a lost or rejected Jewishness is clearer than what has replaced it. I know a young English teacher who describes himself as a Trotsky or Benny Goodman sort of secular Jew, "95 percent nonreligious." He speaks with certainty only about what he is not. When asked recently by his dean if he wanted an academic leave to celebrate Yom Kippur, my friend instead pretended to ask for sick leave for the day that followed this holy day. A full day afterward, he suggested in jest, was needed to cope with his guilt feelings for not observing Yom Kippur, which had been overemphasized in his childhood.

Recent American Jewish fiction contains frequent stereotypes of the assimilated secular Jew, fleeing yet cherishing immigrant roots, the trash bin of discarded religious and ethnic history. Bernard Malamud's short story "Jewbird" offers a witty yet ominous exchange between the frozen-food salesman Cohen and a skinny, Yiddish-speaking bird. Schwartz is the bird's name, a doppelgänger voice of Cohen's suppressed Jewish immigrant origins. Flying in the kitchen window, the bird begs a glass of schnapps or a piece of herring and decides to remain a few months. Yet Schwartz has the fish stink of the ghetto about him, rocks back and forth in prayer like a pious traditionalist, and whines about persecution from anti-Semitic crows, eagles, and vultures. Though Cohen's family finds Schwartz cuddly and charming, the assimilated Jew cannot handle all these reminders of despicable Jewishness and, in a final rage, slays the bird. This murder bears the marks of a partial suicide, killing off some vital spiritual part of Cohen's self.[16]

The most shocking illustration of mass assimilation occurred soon after the Jewish Emancipation — a swarm of nominal, sometimes genuine, conversions to established European state churches. Historians estimate that three-quarters of Berlin's Jewish population from 1800 to 1850 became Christian. "A baptismal certificate is the ticket of admission to European culture," the poet Heine admitted with cynicism. He could count on his new Lutheran identity to speed the completion of a doctorate. Moses Mendelssohn's son wrote a famous letter to his daughter, Fanny, in which he explained why Fanny and her celebrated brother, the composer Felix, were raised Lutheran. Fanny's father explains that he and Fanny's mother had been brought up as Jews and had not been forced to change religions. He writes: "The outward form of religion . . . is historical and changeable like all human ordinances. . . . We have educated you and your brothers and sister in the Christian faith, because it is the creed acceptable to the majority of civilized people. It contains nothing that can lead you away from what is good, and much that guides you toward love, obedience, tolerance, and resignation."[17]

On the surface, these examples of baptized membership in a Christian church illustrate some reasons for Jewish assimilation. Yet it is naive to mistake external rites for decisions of the heart. In the harshest anti-Semitic eras and locales of history, individuals have often retained their inner Jewish spirituality, despite public gestures of apostasy. Ironically, after generations of Christian observance in some Spanish or German Jewish families, individuals still had to face discrimination or death camps in the arbitrary present era, just because they bore some indelible racial or cultural birthmark from the distant past.

As more nuanced illustrations of assimilation, I can point to a few couples in Jewish-Gentile marriages, where both husband and wife share or even blend each other's religious traditions. In one situation, each attends the other's weekly religious services. An Anglican wife, a devout member of her own church, also sings in the Hebrew choir and lights the Sabbath candles each Friday night at the family meal. She does this because she fears her husband would otherwise neglect his Jewish observance in deference to her Christian faith. I know another family whose son, to the despair of Jewish and Catholic officialdom, expects to celebrate a Jewish bar mitzvah, followed by the Catholic sacrament of confirmation. In pluralistic or secular societies today, and even more so in nations committed to a single privileged religion, true inward assimilation is hard to verify.

A range of ambivalent rationales for assimilation can be explored in the lives of four renowned secular Jews — Karl Marx, Rosa Luxemburg, Isaac Deutscher, and Sigmund Freud. Marx, descendant of two rabbi grandfathers, grew up in the post-Emancipation milieu of recessive Jewishness. His entire family joined the Lutheran National Church, apparently so his father could practice law, a profession otherwise prohibited to Jews in that society. Marx's adult life shows the telltale signs of overzealous assimilation — a sprinkling of anti-Semitic humor and an uncharacteristic silence about any bourgeois discrimination directed specifically against Jews. For example, he jokes about Jews emerging from the pores of Polish society. He mentions an English summer resort spoiled by too many Jews and fleas. He mocks rabbinic legalism that makes "even the lavatory an object of divine regulation." In his early essay "On the Jewish Question," Marx separates the genuine Sabbath Jew from the greedy commercial Jew whose worldly cult is money. The latter deserves nothing but scorn: "As soon as society will succeed in abolishing the empirical nature of Judaism, huckstering and its conditions, the existence of the Jew will be impossible, because his consciousness will have lost its object.... The social emancipation of the Jew is the emancipation of society from Judaism." Unworthy of the name, this false Jewishness is just a Marxist alias for degenerate Christian capitalism.[18]

Prejudices can be capricious. Now Jews get blamed for Shylock and Fagin capitalists and, ironically, also for being the masterminds behind anarchist or Marxist conspiracies against these same capitalists. Yet disproportionate numbers of Jews during the last two centuries have led or supported movements of the radical and moderate Left. Various reasons have been alleged for this ideological preference. First, the secular messianism of Marx and other socialists draws unconsciously upon the ancient Hebrew prophets, who demanded business equity, authentic worship, and community responsibility toward resident aliens and the poor. Second, ghetto isolation and the restriction of Jewish social rights even after legal emancipation barred most Jews from experience in practical politics. As a result, many of their most gifted intellectuals were left insulated with utopian abstractions.

Most important, these alienated Jews learned to function creatively at the seams of overlapping cultures. Thus, many displaced their loyalty from a single race or nation to the wider human fellowship of labor, socialism, or other cross-cultural Humanist creeds. One of the most eloquent examples of this committed internationalism occurs in a letter by Rosa Luxemburg, Jewish founder of the German communist party. She cannot tolerate the myopic social conscience of an old friend: "Why do you come with your particular Jewish sorrows?... I have no separate corner in my heart for the ghetto. I feel at home in the entire world wherever there are clouds and birds and human tears."[19]

Luxemburg's words capture a vital paradox. By repudiating Jewish separateness, she wants at the same time to separate herself from any equivalent separateness, whether ethnic, cultural, or religious. Behind these double negatives, she adopts a more elusive assimilation — global Humanism. Isaac Deutscher, renowned teacher and activist, calls this same paradox the dilemma of "the non-Jewish Jew." Separating himself from his strict Polish Orthodox background, Deutscher offers a self-definition: "Religion? I am an atheist. Jewish nationalism? I am an internationalist. In neither sense am I, therefore, a Jew. I am, however, a Jew by force of my unconditional solidarity with the persecuted and exterminated. I am a Jew because I feel the Jewish tragedy as my own tragedy, because I feel the pulse of Jewish history." His role is that of the eternal protestant, combating every form of idolatry.[20]

The rabbinic story of Akher the Heretic has obsessed Deutscher's imagination from his earliest memories. On one Sabbath, Akher and Rabbi Meir engaged in a heated discussion. Since Meir could not ride on the Sabbath, he walked alongside Akher, who was seated on a donkey. Meir became so absorbed in the wisdom pouring from Akher's lips that he did not realize they now stood at the ritual boundary beyond which no observant Jew could cross on the Sabbath. The heretic turned to his traditionalist pupil and said, "Look, we have reached the boundary. You must not accompany me any further. Go back." Pleased to befriend and communicate with Meir, and sensitive to the rabbi's strict conscience, Akher himself, disregarding canon and ritual, rode beyond the boundaries. These are the qualities idealized in Deutscher's outsider, the non-Jewish Jew. "He appeared to be in Jewry and yet out of it."[21]

Sigmund Freud also had much of Akher the Heretic in him. Toward the end of his life, he would witness the classics written by two "subversive Jews," Marx and himself, destroyed side-by-side in Nazi bonfires. Always proud of his Jewishness, he could usually inject a Yiddish phrase or joke into a conversation. Yet he remained so attached to German language and culture that he did not appreciate Zionism. For the Palestinian landscape itself, he felt, had given the world nothing but sacred frenzies. In his youth, he once met a quaint old merchant whose face had been left unshaven to commemorate the destruction of the Temple. Writing about this encounter to his fiancée, he promised that "even if the form in which the old Jews were happy no longer offers us any shelter, something of the core, the essence of this meaningful and life-affirming Judaism will not be absent from our home."[22]

Yet Freud often called himself a "godless Jew." Though some Jews do distinguish between Judaic religious identity and a more inclusive Jewish ethnic identity, the traditionalist Jew treats Freud's self-definition as a contradiction. In a celebrated exchange of letters, Freud's friend Oskar Pfister, a Protestant clergyman, declared Freud in actuality a better Christian than Pfister: "But you are no Jew. To me, in view of my unbounded admiration for Amos, Isaiah, Jeremiah, and the author of Job and Ecclesiastes, this is a matter of profound regret."[23] With friendly inconsistency, Pfister can broaden his Christian label, even to include an atheist. Yet like a traditionalist Jew, he limits the Jewish label to exclude an atheist or anyone else unable to accept the Torah as normative. From Freud's perspective, in contrast, given some minimal cultural and racial identity, a Jew can be religious or nonreligious.

The Prophetic Middle

I have mentioned a widespread tendency, among Kafka and others, to locate the model Jew among Hasidim and other separatists of the far Right. Yet most of my Jewish colleagues, disdaining the extremes of both separation and assimilation, aim for a disciplined balance — a Judaism dialectically in the Gentile world but not of it. Though Moses Mendelssohn was introduced earlier as the tolerant architect of the Jewish Emancipation, he argued for this same exacting dialectic. Written in 1783, his major book, *Jerusalem,* offers fellow Jews this challenge: "Adopt the mores and constitution of the country in which you find yourself, but be steadfast in upholding the religion of your fathers, too. Bear both burdens as well as you can." Should both loyalties prove incompatible, if the price for citizenship be deviation "from the Law which we still consider binding, then we sincerely regret having to renounce our claim to civil equality and union." Resisting the tendency of his Deist friends to flatten all world religions into a single generic creed, Mendelssohn defends his own Jewish particularity: "Diversity is obviously the plan and goal of Providence." Not one among us thinks and feels exactly like someone else. "Why should we use masks to make ourselves unrecognizable to each other in the most important concerns of life, when God has given all of us our own distinctive faces for some good reason?"[24]

Ever since the era of Moses Mendelssohn, Jews have identified their education, family tradition, and chosen synagogue by such labels as ultra-Orthodox, Orthodox, Conservative, Reform, or Reconstructionist. Yet one limitation to these historical labels is their exteriority, registering mostly the extent of faithful halakhic observance. The names give little hint about the distinctive spirituality of each individual. Sensitive to this deficiency, Rabbi Abraham Heschel gave a celebrated address four decades ago to the Rabbinical Association of America. There he argued against the sterile "externalization" or "pan-halakhism" of Judaism. From visits to Israel, he had learned even soldiers complained that rabbis working with the military were obsessed with problems of dietary laws in the kitchen, rather than with questions of the mind and longings of the heart. "As a Jew committed to halakha, I say to you that halakha is not the central issue of this generation." Judaism is not "a sentimental attachment to customs and ceremonies. Judaism is a source of cognitive insight, a way of thinking, not only an order of living."[25]

Despite this caution from Heschel and others, some rabbis today still insist that

"Judaism has no theology" — the very motto that Heschel attributes to Spinoza and even Moses Mendelssohn, both of whom reduced Torah to halakha. On the contrary, Heschel insists Judaism is both "a doctrine and a discipline, faith and action. . . . In Judaism it is necessary to believe in God, to believe that God's revelation is in Torah. It is true that Judaism is much more than a dogma. But this is not because it has no dogmas. It is rather because there are no dogmas which can sufficiently express the depth and grandeur of its insights."[26]

When the Bible was translated into the Greek Septuagint, Jewish scholars committed a momentous error when, for lack of a Greek equivalent, they rendered Torah by *nomos* or law. Heschel believes this fatal decision played into the hands of later Christian apologists, quick to misrepresent Judaism as a shallow legalism. He prefers to define Torah as teaching. Notice the substantial nonhalakhic portions of the Bible — "the Prophets, the Psalms, aggadic midrashim," all summed up in the term *aggada*. "The Torah comprises both halakha and aggada. Like body and soul, they are mutually dependent, and each has a dimension of its own. . . . Halakha deals with details, with each commandment separately. Aggada deals with the whole of life, with the totality of religious life."[27]

For many American Jews, Rabbi Heschel's own life lends prophetic authority to his teaching — an attempt to balance moral action and vision, the modern and the traditional. Born of a strict Hasidic family in Poland, and moving to Weimar Germany, then to America, he taught and wrote for many years at the Jewish Theological Seminary of New York. In 1972, the day before his death, the rabbi waited outside a Connecticut federal prison in the snow for release of a Catholic priest friend, jailed for civil dissent. Two books were found at his bedside after death — a history of the Vietnam War and a Hasidic classic.

The juxtaposition of these two works among Heschel's effects is less incongruous than first appears. Most Hasidim in America today profess textual literalism, strict halakhic observance, and blind loyalty to the local zaddik. Aloof from most secular political controversy, zaddiks tend to emphasize the letter rather than the spirit of any law, religious and political. Yet ironically this movement first arose in European ghettos as a charismatic protest against rabbinic legalism. In Heschel's opinion, Hasidic masters, representing "the highest flowering" of Jewish literature, give surest proof that Judaism consists not only of rules but also of the deepest spiritual insight.[28]

The zaddik of Lublin, for example, when consulted one day about the best way to serve God, answered that penitence, study, prayer, and even eating are all suitable ways, depending on your individual calling. "You should carefully observe which way your heart draws you, and then follow that way with every effort." A similar openness is demonstrated by another rabbi of Lublin. Arriving to study under their new master, two prospective disciples watched him perform the New Moon ritual. Because this man officiated in a style unlike that of their previous teacher, they suspected he would prove an unreliable master and decided to leave him. Yet they soon changed their minds, once he confronted them: "A God whom you could serve in only one way, what kind of God would that be?"

Throughout most of Hasidic literature, a spontaneous act of kindness takes precedence over wooden rabbinic observance. In one story, the Premislaner Rabbi comes home to find his wife has pawned her last valuables to buy a small chicken instead of the requisite lamb for Passover. Ever ready to give away all their money to the needy, her husband wants to take even this chicken to a poor, hungry woman who has just given birth. "We can eat matzoh and potatoes," he reassures his wife. And after taking food to the woman, he returns to officiate at seder with a serene heart. In another tale, a disciple trails the Sassover Rabbi in secret, so that he can discover the perfect way to celebrate prescribed midnight rites for the Shekhinah in Exile. Each detail of this unique preparation for the rite looks more puzzling. The rabbi disguises himself in peasant attire, collects wood and chops it, then uses it to kindle the fire in a disabled woman's home. He divides up the traditional Exile rite so that each segment of prayers consecrates a further stage in his midnight labor. Then returning home, he changes clothes and commences his Torah studies.

The Riziner Rabbi, once asked why so many zaddiks were careless about the hours of prayer fixed by tradition, answered by telling a story. The king sets aside a scheduled hour just for those who come on their own business, and will meet them at no other time. Those who come not for themselves but on matters of the common welfare require no appointed hour. They are welcome at any time. In another daring story, the Riziner's teaching is matched by the flexibility of his Berditschever colleague. The master is approached by a ferryman, wondering if he should give up his profession because it makes regular synagogue attendance impossible. The Berditschever Rabbi asks him if travelers genuinely unable to pay are carried free of charge. "Yes," he answers. "Then you serve the Lord in your occupation," says the rabbi, "just as faithfully as you would by attending the synagogue."[29]

EXILE AND HOPE

Exile has been a familiar condition through most of Jewish history. Enslaved in Egypt before the Exodus, deported into Babylon after the destruction of the First Temple, scattered throughout the Roman world after the demolition of the Second Temple, Jews — in their harshest and most recent exile — were finally hauled in boxcars across Europe to the Holocaust death camps. A pattern slowly emerges from all these tragic experiences. Diaspora proves to be the norm, and brief moments of homecoming to the Promised Land are the exception.

The fate of God's chosen people, migrating from place to place, is etched in tales of the Wandering Jew. During the nineteenth century alone this myth inspired at least four hundred works of fiction in various European languages. With no permanent home, alienated and forever on the move, mistreated by everyone yet undaunted and mysteriously unharmed, this figure stirs the imagination. The title character in Hermann Hesse's novel *Demian* describes the Wandering Jew as a man condemned by God allegedly for some crime and thus branded on his forehead with the ambivalent Abraxas sign or the mark of Cain. "But that he's awarded a special decoration for his cowardice, a mark that protects him and puts the fear of God into all the others — that's quite odd, isn't it?"

The Jewish exile has two dimensions. Historians have labeled the Jewish geographical exile "diaspora." The interior counterpart to diaspora is called *galut* — spiritual exile. This latter sense of homelessness and abandonment may be experienced by Jews geographically anywhere, even in their Israeli homeland. Galut can be traced as the pivotal motif in at least three major Jewish rituals.

Vigil at the Wall

The Western Wall in Jerusalem, called the Wailing Wall, has been the principal Jewish pilgrimage center for centuries. To pray and weep here, at the site of these few remnants from the Second Temple and its glory, is to grieve in solidarity with Jewish suffering everywhere. We can learn much about the meaning of Jewish observance and vision just by eavesdropping on the different feelings stirred up in each Jew at the Wailing Wall.

The mother of a Jewish friend speaks about returning from the Wailing Wall, which she experienced as the climax to a sort of pilgrimage or spiritual awakening. "I have made aliyah," she remarks, selecting this term with fervor and precision. The Hebrew term *aliyah* means to go up, and its Yiddish derivative refers to the privilege of going up to read the Torah before a congregation. Pilgrims arriving in Jerusalem must ascend to get to the old Jerusalem sector, a noticeable climb in altitude, and this may also have something to do with the Hebrew term. Yet I presume aliyah to this woman implies more than this. Before the founding of Israel in 1948, the term meant a ritual pilgrimage to the Temple ruins. Since 1948, aliyah has referred primarily to one's oath of allegiance as an Israeli citizen, an act heavy with religious implications for any devout Jew. Thus, though not an Israeli citizen, my friend's mother felt immersed for a few moments in the total Jewish past and present. At the Wailing Wall she had reclaimed a spiritual and also a geographical Jerusalem. After flying back from Israel, she resolved she would now live out what Abraham Heschel has called "an inner spiritual and cultural aliyah on the soil of America."[30]

The famous theologian Moses Maimonides, accompanied by his father and brother, stood before this same wall in 1165. The Christian Crusaders at that time had the Holy Land again under their control, and like the Muslims that preceded them, allowed Jews to visit the Western Wall. The entire Jewish community at Jerusalem in those years consisted only of four families. For a few days the Maimon family prayed at this shrine and afterwards traveled to Hebron, where they worshiped at the Tomb of the Patriarchs. Maimonides swore he would commemorate this period at the Wall and Hebron each year afterwards as days of prayer and holiday. "God, give me strength for everything and help me fulfill my oaths," his account of the pilgrimage concludes. "On my part, I prayed there on ruins. On Your part, grant that all Israel and I shall see the Holy Land soon restored and lifted from its decay."[31]

In the diary of Theodor Herzl, often called the founder of Zionism, we meet a man unlike Maimonides in many ways, with a very different experience as he stands in 1898 before the Wailing Wall. Jerusalem at that time was ruled by the Ottoman Turks. To Herzl's irritation, the local chief rabbis had forbidden any Jew to enter the Christian Holy Sepulcher or the Muslim Mosque of Omar, under threat of excommunication. By that moment, Herzl's physical strength had been undermined after a succession of diplomatic failures to get Jewish colonies fully legalized by at least one major European nation.

"We have been to the Wailing Wall," Herzl wrote. "Any deep emotion is rendered impossible by the hideous, miserable, scrambling beggary pervading the place." Yet with little room for religious nostalgia, Herzl's mind immediately switched to plans for a modern Eurocentric city — a forecast of stunning accuracy. "If Jerusalem is ever ours, and if I were still able to do anything about it, I would begin by cleaning it up. I would clear out everything that is not sacred, set up workers' houses beyond the city, empty and tear down the filthy rat-holes, burn all the non-sacred ruins, and put the bazaars elsewhere. Then, retaining as much of the old architectural style as possible, I would build an airy, comfortable, properly sewered, brand new city around the Holy Places.... The old Jerusalem would still remain Lourdes and Mecca and Yerushalayim. A very lovely beautiful town could arise at its side."[32]

Two decades after Herzl's visit, Golda Meir first arrived in Israel as a Zionist pioneer. "When one comes to Jerusalem," she later wrote, "one goes first to the Western Wall. Who raised in a Jewish home could have failed to absorb Jerusalem into one's being, with all that the Western Wall symbolizes? I too grew up in a good traditional Jewish house, yet I was not myself pious, and I confess that I went to the Wall without much emotion." Yet later, from 1948 to 1967, Jews were forbidden to visit the Wall or even enter the Old City. Then came the Six-Day War with Egypt, the liberation of the Old City, and Golda joined some soldiers exhausted from combat and stood again before the Wall. "Uniformed paratroopers wrapped in praying shawls were clinging so tightly to the Wall that it seemed impossible to separate them from it — they and the Wall were one.... I, too, took a sheet of paper, wrote the word 'Shalom' on it, and put it into a cranny of the Wall."[33]

Meir calls this "one of the greatest moments of my life." An anonymous soldier who did not recognize Meir's identity put his arms around her and wept on her shoulder, as if reaching blindly for someone dear. The Wall for centuries had symbolized the destruction of the Temple and of Jewish independence. Now Meir and the men, however, wept not from sadness but from relief. For they "had fought a bitter battle and believed that this Wall was now a symbol of the future and the independence and dignity of Israel." They offered a "prayer of thanksgiving that we were here again, free Israelis in the city of Jerusalem."[34]

In terms of galut, Jews tend to view the Wall and Temple ruins as sites of longing, a kind of vacuum. This emptiness can never be filled until the final *kibbutz galuyot* or ingathering of the exiles. "By the rivers of Babylon we sat down and wept when we remembered Zion," says Psalm 137. "How could we sing the Lord's song in a foreign land?" Some Jews even register an outrageous denial of the Temple destruction itself. One rare passage in the Zohar, probably the most influential anthology of Kabbalah mysticism, says the Temple never suffered actual attack; its stones never fell into the hands of other nations. "God has treasured up the stones of Jerusalem and hidden them from the sight of human beings. A day will come when the ancient stones will be revealed and found in their former position."[35] Convinced that all this missing property still belonged to them, a few medieval rabbis even promised that each Jew would never lose tenure to four cubits of ground in the final Israel. Beliefs of this sort, filtering down to the nineteenth century, prompted creation of the Jewish National Fund, by which land in Palestine was bought from Jewish contributions and held in perpetuity for the Jewish people.

As these texts demonstrate, deep loss is often eased by denial or displacement.

One Midrashic commentary refuses to admit that God's holiness ever abandoned the First Temple at its destruction. Ezekiel's classic vision had given the opposite impression, that the Shekhinah or God's immanent presence departed on whirring wings. A characteristic Zoharic passage suggests that the Shekhinah, once the Temple was destroyed, "took one last look at the Holy of Holies, and left home to accompany Israel into exile." What Jews experience as galut or God's absence, then, might be just an unfamiliar new experience of God's continued presence. As the mystics in their apophatic theology attest, the Hidden God accompanies those closest to God through the Dark Night. The diaspora might have been God's strategy to diffuse a vital Jewish leaven among the nations.

Perhaps by the diaspora experience God is teaching Jews to depend more on the sacred teaching than on the person of their teacher. God may want them to uncover within the immediate community itself a new mode of the Shekhinah. This theme inspires one of the most audacious tales in the Talmud, "The Oven of Akhnai." Arguing with a group of rabbis about the correct application of Torah to Akhnai's case, Rabbi Eliezer is driven in exasperation to perform a few dazzling miracles to sanction his own interpretation. He even solicits a heavenly voice to say, "Halakhah is always as Eliezer teaches it." But Rabbi Jeremiah pays no attention to God's voice, for he is certain that "Torah has already been given to us on the mountain. We pay no attention, even to heavenly voices, because God has commanded us to decide according to the majority." Later, Rabbi Natan meets the prophet Elijah in the vicinity, who reports that God's reaction to the entire contest was only to laugh and exclaim, "My children have defeated me, my children have defeated me!"[36] Here is a teacher glad to be overruled at the hands of his disciples, struggling by their prayerful initiative to discover the true Torah.

Passover

The galut motif, of course, is central to the imagery of Passover. The annual feast of Passover or Freedom adheres to a set ritual framework. It also leaves room for many local accretions, which tend to develop their own rationale as venerable essentials. The feast's intent is to recount and reenact the liberation of Israel from Egypt. Assembled at table, the community listens first to the narrative of past slavery and salvation. Then they eat the seder meal somewhat quickly, in empathy with the wary exiles, ready to flee Pharaoh's persecution. The celebration culminates in final hymns of thanks, prayers for future liberation, and a welcome for Elijah, forerunner of the Messiah.[37]

The meaning of Passover is stated clearly in the aggada, a term that here means the rites and narrative readings: "In every generation, all Jews must regard themselves as though they personally were brought out of Egypt. . . . It was not our ancestors alone that the Holy One redeemed from Egypt, but he also redeemed us with them." Historically, Passover rites in individual homes replace the annual pilgrimage to Jerusalem, where all Jews once gathered as a single nation and celebrated animal sacrifices in the Temple. With the Jerusalem Temple destroyed, the home now becomes a portable temple. Matzoh substitutes for the temple sacrifices. A repentant heart, a ritual bath, and pre-Passover housecleaning purify the temple. And the head of the household becomes its ritual priest.

The mythical time of Passover is in-between, during the galut desert experience. Jews are released from the Egypt of darkness, sin, alienation, and are destined for the Jerusalem of completion, freedom, and eternal life. Like the finale of the Yom Kippur liturgy, Passover concludes with the cry, "Next year in Jerusalem!" As a reinforcement of this theme, the matzoh has been blessed earlier by a recitation of the following prayer: "This is the bread of affliction which our fathers ate in the land of Egypt. . . . This year we are here, next year we shall be in the land of Israel. This year we are in servitude, next year we shall be free!" The seder meal occurs in springtime, generally at home, and during the night. A Targum paraphrase of a verse in chapter 12 of Exodus telescopes the entire history of Israel into a fourfold symbolic night. First you experience the primordial darkness out of which God created the cosmos, next the night God summoned Abraham, and then the night of exodus from Egypt. "The fourth night is when God reveals himself to redeem the people of Israel from among the nations. All the nights are called nights of watchfulness." An authentic galut spirituality will always center on this Dark Night, the endless desert experience of Israel, and a hopeful, resolute vigilance.

No matter how wisely you acknowledge the necessity of galut and diaspora, the painful night and desert, it is essential you never forget the redemption and freedom to which they eventually lead. For example, I recall this distressing sign once tacked to a colleague's office door: "I feel happier, now that I've given up all hope." Fearful that Jews will find distorted pious motives for resigning themselves to slavery, many Hasidic masters underline the liberation motif in Passover. For example, Rabbi Bunam was asked why matzoh at the seder is eaten first, and the bitters second. According to the obvious symbolism, Jews suffered in Egypt first and then were freed, so why not reverse these dishes? "The traditional sequence," he answered, "implies that as long as the Israelites did not feel keenly the bitterness of their condition, they had no prospect of being redeemed. Yet as soon as Moses spoke to them of freedom, they awoke to the bitterness of their slavery." According to a related Hasidic story, a king banished his son for some crime. He hoped that by sentencing him to oppressive farmwork, the boy would be pressured to ask forgiveness and end his exile. However, the king was frustrated to learn that no matter how cruelly his son was treated, the boy resigned himself to this punishment and pleaded only to be treated less harshly. As Rabbi Henoch of Alexander once remarked, "The real exile of Israel in Egypt was the fact they had learned to endure it."[38]

Two puzzling ritual details in the Passover rite stir curiosity. The first is the *afikomen,* a matzoh portion broken off and hidden playfully, more or less for a later surprise dessert. The youngest children in the community soon search it out and surrender it only if promised a reward. Some rabbinic commentators view this as a symbolic ransoming of the enslaved people. A more certain exile theme can be discerned in the afikomen ritual as developed by some Mediterranean seder traditions. Pieces of matzoh are wrapped in a napkin and carried like a knapsack by the youngest child. "From where have you come?" The child replies, "From Egypt." "Where are you going?" "To Jerusalem." "What food will you eat on the way?" And the child responds by pointing to the matzoh bundle.

Again, a mysterious additional cup of wine is set aside at the meal, and the door is later opened to admit or release a sacred power. This rite seems a clear act of hospitality directed toward Elijah, messianic precursor, wandering from home to home, his task to encourage exiles and test out their readiness for the messianic era. It is also a symbolic sharing of wine and hospitality stretching out beyond the home enclosure, an opened door to express solidarity with Jews celebrating Passover throughout the diaspora this very evening. At any rate, once the prayers and singing are over, the Jewish community feels its part of the covenant has been completed and now awaits God's corresponding part.

A playful hunt for the afikomen, the didactic questions and answers, the repetitive spelled-out explanations for each major symbol — these traditional Passover rituals seem geared to touch the family, especially the children. This purpose no doubt succeeds, for during Passover many adult Jews, distant from home geographically or spiritually, feel an almost unbearable longing for home, the symbol of their Jewish religious past. I suppose most Christians, far from their family at Christmas, ache in a comparable way, even those convinced they have outgrown the simple faith of their childhood. Many stories dealing with the Passover theme stage a quiet seder in a room, while outside a modern, far-more-terrifying version of Egyptian oppression rages. The particular Jews in this sort of story draw upon their shared religious past to kindle one last effort at liberation or even survival — beginnings of the Warsaw Uprising, for example, or just a few more days' postponement of the Holocaust. In one story recounted by Theodor Herzl, an ex-religious Jew is somehow maneuvered into reading a Hebrew prayer at the seder. His throat tightening with emotion, he recalls his last Passover thirty years ago. Next in his life "had come 'Enlightenment,' the break with all that was Jewish, and the final logical leap into the void, when he had no further hold on life. At this seder table he seemed to himself a prodigal son, returned to his own people."[39]

The rabbinic aggada prompts the youngest child present to raise fundamental questions, such as "Why is this night different from all other nights?" Departing from the script, a child at this point may happen upon questions that prove too deep for immediate answer. As an illustration, one woman recalls a few precocious questions she brought to the seder of her early adolescence. "Why does freedom have to be celebrated by such exhaustively bourgeois preparations?" And again, "Why do we deserve to be at this table when our fellow Jews, let alone so many other members of the human family, enjoy no such plenty?"[40] Taking questions like hers seriously, some Jews today have developed their own creative aggada to reaffirm neglected motifs in the Passover event itself or to render the feast more accessible for a new era.

In America during the 1960s a few voices in the Jewish counterculture constructed a so-called Freedom Seder to express their own aspirations. Emphasizing themes of liberation, hope, and the future, this Passover combined biblical texts with popular folk songs of revolt and intimacy. Now, over thirty years later, the originator of this Freedom Seder has composed a sequel, called a Seder of Rebirth. Bold yet diplomatic, he and his coauthor recommend "that this aggada complement, not replace, one that is rooted in the seder of the rabbis."[41]

The context for this experimental seder is feminist liberation — women freed from oppression, both men and women released from fixed roles of the past. The Seder of Rebirth refers to God, not as lord or ruler, but as "Yahh," breath of the world. Against a backdrop of spring and newborn lambs and the sprouting of barley, the Exodus becomes a birthing. Egypt is a dark and narrow place, the birth canal. The first liberators are midwives. The splitting of the Red Sea is a breaking of the birth-waters. Though traditionalists, I know, find such tampering a faddish outrage, this Seder of Rebirth mirrors common Israeli kibbutzim adaptations of the Passover into harvest and fertility celebrations.

Sabbath

At Passover once a year, and at Sabbath each week, Jews simultaneously look back to the Exodus past and ahead to the messianic future. Each Friday evening, family members wash off grime from the week before, dress in their finest clothes, bring out the special silverware, and light candles. Protective rituals bracket out these hours from weekday time — for instance, a specific blessing over wine to begin Sabbath, another wine blessing to end it. Such regulations are designed to make Sabbath time feel different from ordinary time. Now relaxed and prepared, each Jew enters a sanctuary in time, rather than space — a twenty-four-hour period of prayer, leisure, and companionship, and three unhurried, substantial meals.

The Bible offers at least two rationales for the Sabbath. On the one hand, "Remember the Sabbath," says the Book of Exodus, "for in six days the Lord made heaven and earth,...and rested on the seventh day." On the other hand, Deuteronomy says, "Remember you were enslaved in the land of Egypt," and the Lord your God liberated you....Therefore, God commanded you to keep the Sabbath." The Sabbath, then, has a cosmic dimension, a contemplative pause to ponder the wonders of creation. It has a social dimension, too, reminding Jews of their solidarity with the enslaved and also of their liberation from Egypt. "By our acts of labor during the six days, we participate in the works of history," says Abraham Heschel. "By sanctifying the seventh day, we are reminded of the acts that surpass, ennoble, and redeem history. The world is contingent on creation, and the worth of history depends on redemption. To be a Jew is to affirm the world without being enslaved to it."[42]

For many today, especially non-Jews, Sabbath observance still connotes the boredom of forced inactivity, the sober legacy of Puritan "blue laws." Yet various Hasidic tales associate it mostly with joy and reconciliation — foretaste of the heavenly Sabbath at the end of time or a sacrament reconnecting each separate family to the wider Jewish community. In one story, a gloomy member of the congregation, seated near the synagogue doorway and visible to all those entering, is scolded by the rabbi: "The Sabbath is eager for joy. She has no place for sadness." Another tale sifts through the memories of an elderly family servant. In the home of Rabbi Elimelech, she could recall quarrels occurring on weekdays in the kitchen. But "on the eve of each Sabbath, we fell around each other's neck, and begged forgiveness for any harsh words spoken during the week." Is sadness appropriate at all on the Sabbath? Yes, but only if one has sinned the other six days. Someone coming out of a dark tunnel cannot endure the light. Or as another rabbi explains, "On weekdays our spirit is entirely sick. The Sabbath cures us partially, and then we realize the loss of our soul."[43]

Thus, the other six days of the week must prove spiritually consistent with the seventh day. "Even if we cannot reach a plane where all our life would be a pilgrimage to the seventh day," says Heschel, "the thought and appreciation of what the day may bring to us should always be present in our minds. The Sabbath is the counterpoint of living, the melody sustained throughout all agitations and vicissitudes which menace our conscience." This day is a moment of passive rest from labor and, at the same time, an active contemplation of the spiritual meaning of your labor. Historians have given the Sabbath credit for inspiring vital humane reforms in modern society — a shorter work week, paid vacations, retirement pensions, and even the academic sabbatical research leave. As a reminder of human dignity and the right to leisure and rest, this single day of the week has helped to sustain many Jews through the other six days of galut oppression. To be transformed once a week into a prince surely helps a slave retain dignity and pride during the other six days of humiliation. As Ahad ha-Am once remarked, "Not only has Israel kept the Sabbath, but the Sabbath has kept Israel."

According to one rabbinic legend, God must decide on each Sabbath whether or not to sustain the process of creation for the next six days. When Jews observe this day, they give God reason to continue the existence of the world. If this day were not observed by anyone, the world would end. In one sense, without a deep habitual experience of the Sabbath, the other six days would end, the rest of life would not be animated by religious meaning.[44] Again, the Talmud observes that "if all Jews were properly to observe two Sabbaths in succession, Israel would be redeemed immediately." In other words, this ritual plea for liberation, voiced by the entire community, would prove that Israel is not just ready for freedom but is already free. For as Pascal observes, "Whoever searches for God has already found God."

The Sabbath has been described as a moment of eternity in time, and thus a Sabbath spirituality can be expected to measure each minute of ordinary time from the perspective of eternity. The Bible applies this very perspective to God himself, when he rests the seventh day to contemplate his own creative activity. The poet Rilke's notion of *einsehen* contains a brilliant parallel between the artist's creative vision and this meditative Sabbath principle. Rilke describes his delight when he in-sees a dog passing by; this is different from in-specting the dog, which involves "immediately coming out again on the other side of the dog, regarding it merely as a window to the humanity lying behind it." In-seeing involves letting oneself into the dog's very center, the point where it begins to be a dog, where "God would have sat down for a moment when the dog's creation was finished, in order to watch it under the influence of its first embarrassments and inspirations, and to know that it was good, that nothing was lacking, that it could not have been better made."[45]

Some recent environmentalists have pointed out that God's mandate to Adam in the first chapter of Genesis — "Fill the earth and subdue it, rule over it" — has long given the Eurocentric hero a religious mandate for plundering the natural world. Yet most Jewish scholars, I am certain, would defend Sabbath observance and spirituality as a corrective to any exploitation of nature on the other six days. The psychologist Erich Fromm has explored this connection between Sabbath leisure and our contemporary sensitivity to the environment. For him, the Sabbath celebrates human victory over the chains of time. In Talmudic prescriptions for the Sabbath, "rest" can be reinterpreted as freedom, peace, and harmony between one person and another, between human beings and nature.

In regard to the Sabbath, the term "work," in the Talmud, has negative connotations, suggesting disharmony and galut, any creative or destructive interference with this equilibrium. The Sabbath is a hallowing of the ideal balance, a preview of paradise with its familiar biblical image of the lion and lamb together, human beings at peace with animals and the soil. "God is free and fully God only when God ceases to work. So you are fully human only when you do not work, when you are one with nature and with other human beings. That is why the Sabbath commandment is at one time motivated by God's rest, and at the other by the liberation from Egypt.... Rest is synonymous with freedom."[46]

The Kabbalists, and also many of the Hasidic masters, are responsible for the popular belief that everyone at the instant of crossing the threshold into Sabbath time is possessed by a special Sabbath-soul. This new soul arrives in a burst of light from the upper world descending into profane darkness. The Sabbath light endures throughout the next six days, gradually fading, until by midweek it is enhanced by an approaching light of the next Sabbath. According to the Zoharic literature, "a wind blows from the world-to-come.... The holy Shelter of Peace descends and spreads her wings over Israel like a mother protecting her children.... She then bestows a new soul upon each person." By performing the Sabbath rituals faithfully, you first transform your own heart. At the same moment, in a mystical sense, you begin to restore harmony between upper and lower worlds and join God in completing his creation of the cosmos.[47]

Galut is taken very seriously by the Kabbalists, who project it dramatically into divinity itself. Parallel to many Gnostic and Hindu myths of creation, this God-image creates the universe by a process of self-alienation. His Shekhinah light, shattered because of some primordial cosmic flaw, spills into fragments throughout the universe. Everyday profane life is filled with these many scattered hidden sparks, yearning to be freed from their constricting shells and reunited to the Pleroma, the completed Godhead. As the Mezeritzer Rabbi explains, "Were it not for God's self-limitation, creation would not have been possible, and his divinity would be unknown." Like a father, placing limitations on his intelligence and words so that he can be understood by the smallest child, "God limited himself in order that he might be known in his love for his creatures." The purpose of your life is to restore the holy sparks to their Source. For instance, conscience troubles you most after you commit a serious offense. This experience "shows that the holy spark is most powerful in the greatest sinner, and compels you to repent speedily with complete sincerity."[48]

Hasidic spirituality aims to uncover these sacred particles within the here and now, and release them with reverence. "For this reason," says the Medzibozer Rabbi, "you may eat the flesh of living beings as well as the food of growing plants. By reciting grace over them, you raise them upwards." By each loving deed you liberate Israel more fully from galut and restore the exiled Shekhinah. The privileged Sabbath-soul or garment of light guides you to free, on this day especially, what would otherwise remain imprisoned in the six profane workdays. "God has dropped sparks of holiness upon the world," says the Besht Rabbi. "Through his Torah he gives Israel clues regarding the place they have fallen on earth, so that Israel may return them to him."[49]

"In the Reign of Peace," a short story by Hugh Nissenson, sets up a convincing dialogue between two contemporary Jews on the meaning and importance of the Sabbath. In just a few pages, it manages to touch most of the interwoven themes just discussed. The encounter between these two men occurs in an orchard on a contemporary Israeli kibbutz near harvest time. The narrator is a secular Ashkenazi Jew, content to pick apples or collect eggs on the Sabbath, just as he would any other day of the week. Chaim is a devout, traditionalist Sephardim Jew from Morocco, hired out from one kibbutz to another as a temporary farmworker. The man's faith seems so mindless and stubborn. With the shock of self-knowledge, the narrator catches himself looking at Chaim "through the eyes of a Goy, just as my grandfather must have been seen by the Poles in Krakow, and with the same hatred."

Chaim offers his boss traditional greetings to usher in the Sabbath and shows surprise that urgent harvesting will continue without time off for worship. As the day unfolds, a few naive questions by Chaim gradually render his boss less certain about accepted kibbutz values. You personally, Chaim points out, do not own this orchard, so why work without salary for the common good? You are all Jews, but is no one kosher? Does none of you believe in God or the Messiah? Chaim is appalled that Jews in the kibbutz are able to endure this life as an end in itself, without need for a coming messianic redemption. In response, his boss can only gesture to the orchard and kibbutz, the beautiful land of Israel — "What more would you want?"

Chaim seems troubled by a fungus infection he notices on the bark of some trees, but especially, by a mouse crushed and dying on the cement, its body half-eaten by ants. Piece by piece he tells of his own background in Morocco, his gratitude now for freedom to worship in Israel without harassment. Chaim and his poor family had endured incredible hardship, culminating in the death of his daughter from deficient treatment of her illness. To keep up his own strength to work, he used to come home and eat — with his bare hands, in the Arab custom — the remains of their scanty Sabbath feast from the night before. The children's diet was so deprived that they pleaded to lick the grease from their father's hands. Heavy with fatigue, he would then try to complete Sabbath prayers before sleep overwhelmed him.

The story's title is drawn from the last rebuttal by Chaim against his employer's dream of a religionless Arcadia, where all Jews will someday work alongside each other and share the land. What more can redemption mean but this? Before the mouse dies, Chaim points to the whimpering body in its final moments of suffering. Then he wags a finger, indicating silently that the utopia of his boss still contains the dying mouse, the infected tree. These things are still happening. But Chaim's notion of redemption demands that this suffering, too, waits to be redeemed, "when the Messiah comes."[50]

NOT YET ZION

With a single voice the Hebrew prophetic tradition denounces any form of idolatry. God alone is supreme. And no human person, institution, or symbol may ever be treated as supreme. To mistake anything for God, says Abraham Heschel, is "to distort both the idea it represents and the concept of the divine which we bestow upon

it. . . . To be a Jew is to renounce allegiance to false gods, to be sensitive to God's infinite stake in every finite situation, to bear witness to his presence in the hours of his
concealment, to remember that the world is unredeemed."[51] In the Bible, for instance,
Nathan the prophet tries to deter David from building a temple because people might
treat a reminder of the living God as an end in itself. And accused of sedition, the
prophet Jeremiah urges loyalty to God before loyalty to the leaders of Israel, for their
proud self-deification will lead them to military defeat.

Sensitive to these prophetic warnings, Theodor Herzl was embarrassed on one occasion to find himself the object of worship. At a synagogue in Bulgaria, standing to
preach before the Holy Ark, he tried to address the congregation without facing away
from the Torah scrolls. "You may turn your back even to the Ark," an eager voice
shouted, "for you are holier than the Torah." As his diary records in 1896, the father
of Zionism was disturbed to recognize his legend in the making, the unreliability of
all popular acclaim, and his own unworthiness for so much trust.

After visiting the Wailing Wall in Jerusalem, Herzl joked that while traveling there
he "had avoided using a white horse or a white ass, so no one would embarrass me
with messianic confusions." The white horse was a symbol in Jewish and Christian
apocalyptic literature for the Messiah. Perhaps these hesitations in Herzl can be traced
to his prophetic Judaic heritage. More surely they arise from genuine modesty and
a shrewd guess that Jewish traditionalists would never be persuaded to support the
Zionist project if they suspected messianic pretensions in its leader. Though tenacious
in promoting his plan for a Zionist state, he learned over the years never to treat it
as an end in itself. After once receiving an ovation from students, he told them: "I
didn't want to arouse any beer-inspired enthusiasm. . . . Perhaps we shall never get to
the physical Zion, and so we must strive in any case toward an inner Zion."[52]

The physical Zion, the inner Zion — these are Herzl's own two terms, forecasting
both sides of the dialectic, the quarrels, and even the wars still raging a century later
over the modern state of Israel. I have thus far distinguished diaspora or geographical
exile from galut or spiritual exile. Conversely, in what follows, geographical homecoming will be represented by the Israeli nation-state or the term "Israel." The final
spiritual homecoming, often described as kibbutz galuyot or ingathering of the exiles, will be called "Zion." While on this earth, in either diaspora or Israel, Jews can
expect to experience galut. At best, they will live with a tension between galut and
Zion, but galut will never disappear.

To clarify the major religious issues that divide Israeli society today, it will help
to explore both sides of a pivotal debate in Chaim Potok's novel *The Chosen*. Two
American Orthodox Jewish families size up each other across battle lines on the reli-
gious legitimacy of a Zionist state in the late 1940s. Shocked by the unwillingness of
America and other nations to assist Jewish refugees fleeing Nazi persecutions, scholar
David Malter becomes an ardent Zionist after learning of the Holocaust. "Some Jews
say we should wait for God to send the Messiah," he says. "We cannot wait for God.
We must make our own Messiah. . . . Palestine must become a Jewish homeland."
Yet the ultra-Orthodox Reb Saunders, a zaddik patriarch with roots in the Hasidic
ghetto tradition, asks in heated rebuttal, "Ben-Gurion and his goyim will build Eretz
Israel? . . . When the Messiah comes, we will have Eretz Israel, a Holy Land, not a
land contaminated by Jewish goyim!" A secular Jewish state in Saunders' eyes is a

sacrilege, a violation of the Torah. He thinks it "better to live in a land of true goyim than to live in a land of Jewish goyim!"[53]

I admit, of course, that the controversies over Israel-Zion today are too massive to be summarized in this duel between two fictional personalities. For instance, two feasible Israeli positions have dominated news analyses most recently. One side cites national security reasons for refusing to yield land in the disputed occupied territories; the other side for reasons of peace will trade this land to the Palestinians or others. Within this controversy you can distinguish the perspective of traditionalist religious Jews and secular Zionists — but both perspectives are present on both sides of the contemporary issue. Some religious Jews quote literalist Bible interpretations that God promised all this land in its integrity; others cite the same Bible, ranking nonviolence and trust over military security. Some religious Jews call themselves Zionists, others militant anti-Zionists. Some Zionists argue for a more inclusive nation, welcoming non-Jewish minorities; those more nationalistic want to restrict full citizenship only to Jews. These groups and many others, Likud or Labor or various minority parties, all shift back and forth in a series of precarious coalition governments.

Although Potok's two fictional characters never probe these issues further, I shall extend their implicit debate here to illustrate a few important concepts. First, on the one hand, the Messiah has been viewed throughout Jewish history as either an exclusively religious figure — a prophet, a transcendent spirit, perhaps even God — or a combined religio-political revolutionary. On the other hand, the messianic factor can be interpreted more as an inner principle. In this sense it refers to a later millennium of global social justice and peace or to the chosen people themselves at their finale in Zion. Second, the messianic reality, however conceived, may intrude into the human situation as a transcendent gift, unmerited by religious observance; or it may be an external or internal force closely interdependent on religious observance. As mentioned before, the Kabbalah and Hasidic traditions suggest that the moment people's lives are perfected, the messianic era will begin. Saunders seems to expect a Messiah as personal savior, sharply dissociated from mere human efforts in the secular political arena. Malter's activist zeal to create his own Messiah, in contrast, sounds at first like blasphemy to an ultra-Orthodox literalist. Yet such claims simply echo much of the Talmud's bold rhetoric whenever it stresses the importance of our own observance.

To grasp Saunders' position, it would help to distinguish the religious Jew, first from the secular Jew, and second from the Goy or Gentile. Today Israel has both Jewish and non-Jewish Israeli citizens, whereas diaspora Jews continue to live abroad as citizens or noncitizens of other lands. In Saunders' eyes, the first Israeli prime minister, David Ben-Gurion, an acknowledged secular Jew, cannot be distinguished religiously from a Gentile. Saunders counts on maintaining his own Hasidic religious identity more faithfully as a diaspora Jew, clearly segregated by dress and customs from both the Gentiles and the assimilated Jewish majority. He would find it harder to remain a devout Jew and citizen in a secular state that uses the rhetoric of crypto-religious Jewish pretensions.

Perhaps what disturbs Saunders most is the Zionists' apparent confusion between galut and diaspora. He is convinced Jews exist on earth in perpetual galut or alienation from God, looking toward Zion or the moment of messianic religious salvation at the end of time. Whether a diaspora Jew in New York or an Israeli citizen, a Jew can never progress to a stage when galut and Zion cease to be an indispensable dialectic in the human situation. For Saunders, "if the dream was ever to be given concrete form, many would forget the distinction between place and dream, and having inherited the place would forget the dream." The Israeli state mistakes itself for Zion, when at best it can only be a small foretaste of Zion. To revere it as Zion is thus idolatry.

Malter's portion of the debate is easier to grasp than Saunders', mostly because Malter wants immediate political action in response to the enormity of the Holocaust. This is the heroic action most people today imagine they themselves would have taken, but only in retrospect, after half a century.

Holocaust Aftermath

One famous Hasidic parable describes a tree at the end of time which contains each person's burdens hanging from its branches. Invited to examine each burden from the inside out, you are then free to exchange your burden for any other. Yet after inspecting the others, you at length decide to reclaim your own. Now this story, profoundly wise about the love-hate feelings you have toward your own pain, downplays one crucial fact. Empathy has its boundaries. Your own sufferings are uniquely your own, and even from the superior vantage of heaven's front porch, you can never understand fully how anyone else's burden feels inside. From my experience as a hospital chaplain, I recall one patient who at our first meeting, before I offered a single word, told me in anger, "Don't remind me there's some patient in another room here suffering more than me. As far as I'm concerned, there's no misery like my misery."

The extent, motives, and organized cruelty of the Holocaust have been documented in entire libraries of books and films and photographs. Today at the learning center of the U.S. Holocaust Memorial Museum in Washington, for example, you can press a button and listen to thousands of oral histories by survivors. Perhaps listening endlessly to these firsthand testimonies is the most authentic response to the Holocaust, rather than consulting some limited data and then trying to write a history, sociology, or theology of the event. The most damaging comparison in current Israeli political discourse is to accuse any Jew of Nazi brutality or Holocaust solutions. Hateful slogans against Prime Minister Rabin before his recent assassination blamed him for designing a new Holocaust against West Bank settlers. Then, in retaliation, children of these Jewish settlers, staging militant demonstrations against the government and Arab residents, have been called Hitler youth.

Unlike Israeli Jews, American Jews have accustomed themselves to Holocaust comparisons of a different type. Living in a multicultural society, the average American finds an immediate link between the Jewish Holocaust and Pol Pot's exterminations in Cambodia, the Turkish massacre of Armenians, Mao's Cultural Revolution, and the genocides in Rwanda and Bosnia. At worst, often citing parallels with the Holocaust, each organized minority rewrites its own chamber-of-horrors chronicle about unique persecution because of race, gender, religion, or some other factor. Then again, the Holocaust is often edited to yield a Hollywood happy ending. Hitler's Final Solution becomes simply another example of global human inhumanity. And in American films such as *The Diary of Anne Frank* or *Schindler's List,* we discover that despite the outrage, there is still goodness on earth, even in some Gentiles.

Disturbed by these comparisons, some Jews have built a wall, much like the halakhic shield of ritual observance, to protect the Jewish Holocaust from being forgotten, minimized, generalized, or repackaged as a sugar-coated moral parable. One Jewish humorist has satirized this defensiveness as a competitive boast that Jewish scars are not just unique but deeper and more numerous than anyone else's. I have known Jews who will not accept your comments on the Holocaust unless you are a Jew or, more specifically, an actual Holocaust survivor. Even then, they think no one can speak of the unspeakable misery or utter anything but clichés. You must not apply the term "Holocaust" to any similar calamity, nor imply any other comparisons. Supporting this taboo, a recent article in the Jewish monthly *Commentary* regretted that films like *Schindler's List* could be double-billed alongside ordinary films and that actors in the first film could accept parts in another film.[54] The forgetful non-Jewish world is overwhelmed by this double bind: "Never forget!" Yet trying sincerely not to forget, you keep being scolded to remember just so. Then your particular remembering is considered intrusive, or anyone's remembering is considered meaningless.

More important than the scandal of the Holocaust is how each individual Jew comes to terms with it religiously. I have described the galut-Zion dialectic, the experience of God's presence somehow despite spiritual homelessness and abandonment. Praying at the Wailing Wall, many Jews are willing to juxtapose the Holocaust alongside the pogroms of Europe, the Temple's destruction, and the diaspora — and all Jewish suffering in history, perhaps all human suffering anywhere. To them, the Holocaust represents the very extremity of galut, nothing more. Is the idea of God any more unthinkable after six million Jews die than after the death of one innocent child? Yet for other Jews, the Holocaust is such a unique evil, comparable with nothing else, that they cannot accept a God capable of permitting it. Thus, many have decided, "After Auschwitz, God is dead."

One survey, on the contrary, drawn from seven hundred Israeli Holocaust survivors of various secular or religious persuasions, concludes that at least half, secular or religious, found the experience had not affected their previous religious position. In fact, the more observant that Jews had been before, the more their religious identity was strengthened. During the Holocaust experience, an atheist minority in this survey actually converted to Judaism. Yet most of the atheists can be represented by this one forceful voice: God did not set out to test his people, but on the contrary, they had tested him. "God failed the test and proved his nonexistence." One religious Jew still remains observant, "but today I just go through the motions. My heart is not in it." Yet some others reinforced their observances in the death camps and afterwards, just to deprive Hitler of a posthumous victory. Many concealed rations for days in order to celebrate a secret Passover or prayed as never before. In some situations, religious observance helped narcotize their pain, but in others, their religion energized them spiritually and even physically. For it enabled them to retain some moral dignity and a measure of independence from their oppressors. Some Jews even today accept the Israeli state as God's compensation for the Holocaust, a redemptive trade-off.[55]

At a decisive moment in Potok's novel, both Saunders and Malter have time to assimilate the first news reaching America about the unthinkable extent of the Holocaust. Saunders' reaction to it is only an agonized prayer, "We must accept the will of God. . . . Master of the universe, how do you permit such a thing to happen?" Yet Malter tells his son, "We cannot wait for God. If there is an answer, we must make it ourselves."[56] Thus, for the first time he becomes an ardent Zionist and, like Herzl, soon exhausts his weak heart in spreading this passionate vision. A conversion to Zionism parallel to Malter's can be uncovered in Isaac Deutscher, a post-Marxist and author of *The Non-Jewish Jew.* Wedded for many years to internationalism and the gradual decay of the bourgeois nation-state, he died with only the most reluctant ties to Zionism. Yet he conceded this life-raft of an Israeli state had become for some Jews a temporary historical necessity. "If instead of arguing against Zionism in the 1920s and 1930s I had urged European Jews to go to Palestine, I might have helped to save some of the lives that were later extinguished in Hitler's gas chambers."[57]

A comparable shift toward Zionism can be traced in the response of American Reform Jews to Hitler's persecutions. Throughout the nineteenth century, Jewish Reform prayer-books tended to alter traditional petitions and rituals yearning for a return to Jerusalem and the Temple. At the 1841 dedication of a synagogue in Charleston, for instance, the rabbi addressed his audience, "This synagogue is our Temple, this city our Jerusalem, this happy land our Palestine." In response to the Balfour Declaration of 1917, which promised British support for a Jewish Palestinian homeland, the Central Reform Conference of American Rabbis stated: "The ideal of the Jew is not the establishment of a Jewish state, not the reassertion of Jewish nationality which has long been outgrown." Yet a dramatic reversal in Reform Jewish policy was registered in the Columbus Platform of 1937: "We affirm the obligation of all Jewry to aid . . . in the rehabilitation of Palestine . . . as a Jewish homeland, by endeavoring to make it not only a haven of refuge for the oppressed, but also a center of Jewish culture and spiritual life."[58] Though most diaspora Jews in America had long resigned themselves to their hidden mission among the nations, now they had to readjust to the emergency of so many German Jewish refugees unwanted by the rest of the world.

Ben-Gurion himself found the connection between the Holocaust and his Zionist state hard to pin down. He had listened to Arab complaints that Muslim lands were forced to pay for persecutions carried out in Christian Europe. Muslim Arabs felt that Ben-Gurion and other Jews "without the Holocaust would never have come here as a mass and never have founded a state." Yet he himself first came to Palestine as a Zionist settler in 1906, which of course had "nothing to do with the Nazis. I think that Hitler did much to retard, not advance, our nationhood."[59]

In the middle 1930s, the expanding Jewish settlements looked ripe for nationhood, but because of immanent war, Britain cracked down on Jewish nationalist designs. For this reason, according to Ben-Gurion, "we had the greatest difficulty in helping even a fraction of European Jewry escape the gas chambers." In fact, Israel during the Ben-Gurion administration contained no massive number of direct Nazi victims or their descendants. The Holocaust, however, taught an important lesson to all diaspora Jews, "the potential danger of being without a homeland." Jews could live for centuries in peace with their neighbors, gain citizenship, and all but assimilate in that society except for a few traditions and separate religious practices. Yet one raving maniac could blame the world's troubles on 6 percent of Europe's population, and no one intervened to stop the genocide.[60]

One of my former students, now manager of a furniture business in Brazil, once explained to me why Israel plays such a crucial part in his Jewish identity. He does not intend ever to live in Israel but will continue to support it from a distance by his prayers and money. For there must exist at least one geographical homeland, even though no larger than a hen-coop, ready to welcome him and all other Jews in case the world ever surprises them with another Holocaust. Every child needs to feel so secure within a circle of familiar toys and love that any ventures away from this haven become endurable. It ought to be possible to crawl toward boundaries and beyond, and turn back anytime for reassurance. Without Israel as this ultimate safety net, my friend would find the diaspora too fearful and meaningless a place for him and his family.

King and Prophet in Dialogue

Gandhi once outraged the Jewish existentialist philosopher Martin Buber by dismissing Zionist claims to a Palestinian homeland. The biblical Israel, Gandhi observed in 1938, is not a geographical place, but mostly a spiritual symbol. The Jewish people have no right to invade the physical land of Palestine by the force of British guns, but remaining in Germany, should try to confront Nazi pogroms by the force of nonviolent civil disobedience.

In his celebrated letter of rebuttal to Gandhi, Buber begins by contrasting the nature of British tyranny in India with Nazi tyranny against the Jews. "An effective stand may be taken in the form of nonviolence against unfeeling human beings in the hope of gradually bringing them thereby to their senses; but a diabolic universal steam-roller cannot thus be withstood. . . . Testimony without acknowledgment, ineffective unobserved martyrdom, a martyrdom cast to the winds — that is the fate of innumerable Jews in Germany." Then, like my Brazilian friend mentioned above, Buber offers this argument for a Zionist homeland: "Dispersion is bearable. It can even be purposeful, if somewhere there is an ingathering, a growing home center, a piece of earth from which the spirit of ingathering may work its way out to all the places of dispersion." Though an individual may flourish in various adopted homes, a dispersed community without a living center and heart is just a dismembered corpse.[61]

Shortly after Martin Buber's death in 1965, the Israeli monthly journal *Ner* carried an article by Ernst Simon entitled "Buber or Ben-Gurion?" It suggests that both men, "the thinker and the statesman, have to share the honor of being the most famous Jews of the mid–twentieth century." Some think the first man complements what the second lacks; others see them standing for two wholly irreconcilable attitudes. "The tragic circumstances of Israel's birth brought the statesman to the fore and left the philosopher in the shade," the article concludes. "Israel's future depends on a more fruitful dialogue between the two." Fascinated by the frequent public collisions between Buber and Ben-Gurion, many Jews have viewed this dialogue as an updated biblical duel between King Ahab and the prophet Elijah.[62]

David Ben-Gurion, the founder and first prime minister of Israel, even while an impoverished adolescent in his East European ghetto, determined to migrate to Palestine at the first opportunity. "Jews in the diaspora as Jews are human debris," he would write later. A favorite contrast in his speeches begins with the image of a strong young Israeli pioneer, rebellious and creative. Its opposite is the diaspora Jew, a neurotic, cowardly parasite, cut off from the soil, oppressed and thus oppressing others, and above all, often arousing the legitimate contempt of non-Jews. Ben-Gurion could never imagine this diaspora as a sacred mission to disseminate Jewish moral ideals to the nations. Such an interpretation seemed designed just to gratify the complacent diaspora Jew. "Jews should come to Israel," his memoirs state bluntly. "In the diaspora they cannot really be Jews without an artificial self-consciousness and tension that disappears completely from their lives once they arrive here. Outside Israel, the end result for a Jew inevitably is either the ghetto or assimilation.... We offer a full Jewish life and a full human life, which, if not richer economically than elsewhere, promises greater spiritual fulfillment."[63]

It did not take Ben-Gurion long to drop this scorn for diaspora Jews and tone down his proclamation for Jewish youth of the world to abandon their families and pour into Israel. The president of the American Jewish Committee once reminded him that Israel's survival depended on diaspora Jews in America and elsewhere for financial and political support. For instance, most American Jews would resent being told they are exiles from Israel. They feel at home in America and share actively in creating a democratic society. "They further believe that if democracy should fail in America, there would be no future for democracy anywhere in the world, and that the very existence of an independent state of Israel would be problematic."[64]

Reb Saunders in Potok's novel accuses Ben-Gurion of deifying the Israeli state, mistaking Israel for Zion. In actual life, it is not easy to clear the prime minister of this charge. His political rhetoric plays carelessly with similarities between the two terms, but does not equate them exactly. For example, he takes note that "for most Jews, Israel is Zion." And again, "Jewish redemption is here and it is now. We are very privileged to live at a time when we are not forced to survive culturally on mysticism and dreams. It is not 'next year in Jerusalem' but today!" His Knesset address on the Law of Return applies the term "kibbutz galuyot" to immigration into the Israeli state. This "ingathering of the exiles," a phrase from the Book of Ezekiel and the Talmud, has always referred to the messianic era. He also says the Israeli state is not a new creation but simply a resumption of the original biblical kingdom of Israel. "The crown was restored to its pristine splendor 1,813 years after the independence of Israel was destroyed." In contrast, in this same speech, the prime minister concedes, "the diaspora has not ceased with the foundation of the state.... This renewal is not an end and conclusion, but another stage in the long path leading to the full redemption of Israel."[65] Yet notice that a fully redeemed Israel can also mean a state no longer dependent politically and financially on Gentiles and diaspora Jews. Such a culmination, I suspect, he might then mistake for Zion.

Ben-Gurion in Potok's novel is denounced also for his atheistic Humanism, for Jewishness without Judaism. Yet like Golda Meir, he does not deny so much as redefine traditional Judaic notions like God, Torah, covenant, chosen people, prayer, and loyal observance. I see him as a Jewish reconstructionist, daring and confrontational enough to bait most traditionalists. "Since I invoke Torah so often," he says, "let me state that I don't personally believe in the God it postulates. I mean that I cannot 'turn to God,' or pray to a super-human Almighty Being living up in the sky." Instead, the God he serves is the still, small voice Elijah experienced at Horeb, the unique conscience in each individual. You can communicate with this voice through Buddhist meditation, rabbinic observances, and countless other ways. Though the Bible says that God created human beings in God's image, Ben-Gurion believes human beings came into being and then created God in their image.[66]

Are the Jews a chosen people? They are not favored creatures or a super-race, but people with a unique burden of conscience, responsive especially to issues of social justice. "In the majority of Jews one finds something pushing from within to accomplish more, to do better, to follow a path of active virtue that doesn't correspond to the Christian avoidance of damnation.... I think the Jews chose their God and not, as Torah puts it, that God chose us." In mythical terms, all people were asked if they could accept God's teachings. "The other peoples said no, we said yes and thus were adopted by God.... It is our duty as a people to be a model to the God we have chosen, to conform to God's ways as we have defined them, and to devote ourselves to making the land we have settled...a prosperous land run along our moral precepts." In this sense, modern Jews are writing a new Torah, and "its best chapters are still to come. It is my conviction that they will tell the story about our taming of the desert."[67]

One surprising theme in Ben-Gurion's memoirs is his appreciation for the Hebrew prophets, fearless in reprimanding their governments. "These critics had a privileged position, allowing them to say the sort of home truths to their rulers that normally would put a man in irons or sever his head from his body.... In the modern world we know such situations. Too often peoples and governments heed only what they want to hear."[68] Ben-Gurion must have had Buber in mind, whose wisdom he respected — competent in religion but not, of course, in politics.

Martin Buber did not just philosophize about dissent but organized active protests repeatedly against a number of controversial policies adopted by the Israeli government. He denounced nuclear armament, for example, retaliatory raids against Palestinian terrorists, the public execution of Adolf Eichmann, and the Israeli-Arab wars. A nonconformist since his youth, Buber realized he had become a prickly embarrassment to modern Israel. "What the broader circles mostly reproach me for is that since 1917, I have expressly come out for cooperation with the Arabs — until 1947 in the form of a bi-national state and, since the victory of Israel over the seven states that attacked it, in the form of a Near-Eastern federation of peoples. I have led political actions supporting Jewish-Arab rapprochement."[69]

The Holocaust brought a shattering change to Buber's life. Four decades of the German diaspora had given him a genuine bond to German soil and culture. One day he woke to find this contract between cultures terminated by the host state. Yet he refused to blame all Germans for the Nazi murderers, in the manner that "the Christian church has so often done in branding the Jewish people as murderers of the Messiah." He felt one has to distinguish between the actively guilty, the passively guilty, and the not-guilty. What he does blame in most Germans of that era is the subordination of their humanity to the "political principle." By this term he means a shortsightedness common to the Nazis and now again to many loyal Israelis —

the readiness to "forgo a life of equality and dignity, personal and national, for the sake of superior economic, social, and educational conditions." In both nations, "we saw people, who were of the most scrupulous honesty in their private lives, as soon as their party had indicated to them who the (in this case inner) 'enemy' was, day after day, undoubtedly with peaceful consciences, lie, slander, betray, rob, torment, torture, murder."[70]

One group enslaved outrageously to the political principle, in Buber's opinion, was the Israeli rabbinate, too preoccupied with ritualism to confront the government on vital social issues. In the last few decades of his life, Buber settled into an attitude of "religious abstinence." In other words, committed passionately to the Hebrew Torah, he did not observe the designated days, places, and rituals of rabbinic tradition. He preferred direct private dialogue between oneself and God, with no set forms getting in the way. Like the Hasidic masters, he wanted to experience the Sacred in every moment of the profane, not as a separated realm. In a personal letter, he explains: "For instance, I cannot live on Sabbath as on the other days, but I have no impulse at all to observe the minutiae of the halakha about what work is allowed and what not. In certain moments, some of them rather regular, partly on occasion I pray, alone of course, and say what I want to say, sometimes without words at all, and sometimes a remembered verse helps me in an extraordinary situation. But there have been days when I felt myself compelled to enter into the prayer of a community, and so I did it. This is my way of life, and one may call it religious anarchy if he likes. How could I make it into a general rule — valid, for instance, for you?"[71]

In 1957, Ben-Gurion and Buber, both addressing the same conference, summarized their differences over the relationship between Israel and Zion. "Professor Buber claims that the state is only an instrument," says Ben-Gurion, who then in reply argues that the state is not merely an instrument but rather "the beginning of the redemption, a small part of the redemption." After listening to Ben-Gurion's customary toast to Israeli freedom, human rights, and other fine liberal values, Buber reminds the prime minister that these have not yet been applied to the Arab minority, living in their own diaspora within Israel. "Behind everything that Ben-Gurion has said on that point, there lies, it seems to me, the will to make the political factor supreme. He is one of the proponents of that kind of secularization which cultivates its thoughts and visions so diligently that it keeps men from hearing the voice of the living God."[72]

Though Buber takes seriously any messianic hints in Ben-Gurion's rhetoric, he finds them a "messianic ideal emptied of belief in the coming of the kingdom of God." It is messianism in "the narrow nationalistic form which is restricted to the Ingathering of the Exiles." Does Buber himself believe in the Messiah? The messianic era has not yet come, he says, "because I sense the unredeemedness of the world all too deeply to be able to agree with the conception of a completed redemption.... Standing, bound and shackled, in the pillory of mankind, we demonstrate with the bloody body of our people the unredeemedness of the world." Buber expects galut and diaspora both to continue indefinitely and the Israeli state to function as just a remote preliminary to Zion. Yet he will never give up on God and wrestles with God daily. "We do not put up with earthly being. We struggle for its redemption, and struggling we appeal to the help of our Lord, who is again and still a hiding one.... Though his coming appearance may resemble no earlier one, we shall recognize again our cruel and merciful Lord."[73]

In a reflective travel essay about a trip to Jerusalem, the novelist Saul Bellow remarks on the astounding way Israel reversed the fate of diaspora Jews. Once led to helpless slaughter, the Jews are now formidable warriors. Landless in dispersal, they are now farmers who have turned deserts into gardens.[74] Golda Meir once remarked with pride that if she and the other pioneers had accepted "the notion that we were all going to be owners of orange groves, stores, and factories, while others worked for us, we would never have achieved independence. We would have had no moral title to a land built by others."[75]

Yet as Bellow listens more carefully, he soon discovers that almost every immigrant has brought to Israel a different version of paradise. Two significant versions are those represented by Ben-Gurion and Buber. What disturbs Bellow, however, is that so many self-described friends of Israel urge it to set the world a moral example and become "exceptionally exceptional." On second thought, he wonders if "perhaps the Jews have themselves created such expectations."[76]

A cross of *milagros* or tiny miracles. The images of a cow, donkey, arm, or human face are nailed here in thanks for concrete favors granted those who prayed at the cross. Nine by eight by two inches, copper and silver plate on wood. Jalisco, Mexico.

6

The Christian Way

Heirs to the Jewish Torah, Christians at various stages of history have viewed themselves as now the finishing touch to this legacy, now its undoing. Rabbi Abraham Heschel has described these responses as periodic mood swings — from the piety of "Honor your father and your mother" to the enmity of a religious Oedipus complex.

A few Jews introduced in the previous chapter tell of decisive ventures to gain a measure of tolerance from Christians. In 1904, for example, after a wait of many days, Theodor Herzl was granted a half-hour audience by Pope Pius X. Hoping for diplomatic recognition of Jewish colonies in Palestine, the Zionist founder was treated instead to a cool dismissal. "The Jewish faith was the foundation of our own," the pope told him, "but it has been superseded by the teachings of Christ, and we cannot admit that it still enjoys any validity.... The Jews have not recognized our Lord, therefore we cannot recognize the Jewish people." In his diary Herzl mentions an immediate retort that he left graciously unspoken: "It happens in every family. No one believes in his own relative."[1]

Sixty years later, however, a dramatic change of climate had occurred. Pope Paul VI held an interview with Rabbi Heschel, the major Jewish consultant to the Vatican during preparations for the Second Vatican Council of 1965. At first Heschel had felt excitement at the impulse expressed by many bishops "to right the wrongs of a thousand years" toward the Jewish people. But now in a working draft to the document on Christian-Jewish "fraternal discussion," he caught an offensive paragraph urging conversion of the Jews, which to the rabbi implied "spiritual fratricide." Touched by the man's outrage, the pope agreed to cut this paragraph. "I have great reverence for many Christians," Heschel remembers telling the pope, "but I also have to remind them that my being Jewish is so sacred to me that I am ready to die for it.... I'd rather go to Auschwitz than give up my religion."[2]

As it reads today, the final Vatican document, endorsed by the whole council, "deplores the hatred, persecutions, and displays of anti-Semitism directed against the Jews at any time and from any source." It directs that the death of Christ should not be "blamed upon all the Jews then living, without distinction, nor upon the Jews of today." For his death was not so much a murder as a freely chosen redemptive death for all people.[3] This hatred and persecution of Jews, culminating in the Holocaust just a quarter-century before, can be documented from many pages of Christian history.

Throughout the Middle Ages, Jews and Christians and Muslims coexisted as close but uneasy neighbors. And under Christian or Muslim governments, Jews often found themselves stereotyped as a distrusted alien minority. In the Fourth Lateran Council of 1215, for example, the church required Jews in Christian nations to wear distinctive dress and be excluded from public office. Such measures, enacted long before this, had to be reinforced in the thirteenth century, which some Christians still idealize as the "greatest of centuries," the Age of Faith. It is ironic that each discriminatory Christian law against Jews could be matched by restrictions in various Muslim nations, directed not only against Jews but Christians, too. According to the Covenant of Omar during the same era, for example, Muslims should welcome the so-called People of the Book, Jews and Christians, as guests but not full citizens. Non-Muslims must not proselytize Muslims, of course, nor seek interfaith marriages with Muslim women, nor hold the highest leadership positions. Religious minorities had to be recognized by distinctive dress — Jews by yellow, Christians by blue.

A more disturbing irony is often downplayed by Christian historians. Whenever the popes during this period summoned a Crusade to liberate Jerusalem from Muslim control, often the immediate casualties were not distant Muslims but nearby Jews. To begin with, Crusaders were at times recruited with a promise that all their financial debts would be forgiven, including huge sums owed to local Jewish money lenders. Far more disastrous were the pogroms instigated by preachers like Peter the Hermit, quick to exploit the resurgence of Christian militancy: "What does it profit to track down and to persecute enemies of the Christian hope outside, indeed far beyond, the frontiers," he said, "if the evil, blaspheming Jews, far worse than Saracens, not at a distance, but in our midst, so freely and audaciously blaspheme, trample underfoot, deface with impunity Christ and all Christian mysteries?"[4]

This invective reaches its extremity in the later writings of Martin Luther. For instance, his 1543 treatise *On the Jews and Their Lies* urges the Christian state to treat Jewish subjects with "a harsh mercy," ready to "set fire to their synagogues and to bury and cover with dirt whatever will not burn.... Second, I advise that their houses also be razed and destroyed. Instead they might be lodged under a roof or in a barn, like the gypsies. This will bring home to them the fact that they are not masters in our country, as they boast, but that they are living in exile and captivity, as they incessantly wail and lament about us before God."[5]

Four and a half centuries after this, a young Lutheran student sat in my office one afternoon recounting his misgivings about Luther's anti-Semitism, his doctrine of "faith alone, grace alone," and all the baggage of institutional Christianity. Recently, this student had taken his pastor aside after one Sunday service and confessed a reluctance to pray the Apostles' Creed aloud with the congregation, for a few hallowed phrases seemed irrelevant or wrongheaded. Yet despite his indifference to the specific Reformation issues that engaged Luther, he still yearned to recover the spiritual passion of Luther's original dissent. And he felt drawn unaccountably to share the faith of this particular church, mostly because as a group they had been proving themselves responsible for the world of today and also yesterday. In 1995 the congregation had asked for a unique Passover–Good Friday service of reconciliation with a nearby Jewish synagogue. To prepare his Lutheran congregation for this cosponsored service, the Lutheran pastor mentioned a pilgrimage to the Stadtkirche in Wittenberg, famous now as the church where Luther served as pastor from 1512 to 1546.

Looking up at the rear cornice and roof line of this Wittenberg church today, you can still trace the massive sculpture of a pig. The pig's head is crowned with a stone yarmulke, in crude ridicule of the Jews. A decade ago, a Christian youth movement, hoping to raise a monument to Jews killed in the Holocaust, wanted first to tear down this offensive symbol from the church roof. However, they had to settle for a monument on the cobblestone pavement beneath the pig with yarmulke. For local Jewish authorities insisted the obscenity be left intact, so that future Germans could not erase it from memory. Though the building and its ornamentation date from a century before Luther, many of his spiritual descendants today are unlikely to forget either the pig or the violence of Luther's diatribes. Beginning with at least one Good Friday service, however, Lutherans in one particular congregation would ask their Jewish neighbors for forgiveness. This single honest gesture of repentance had given my student friend a spark of hope for Christianity.

As a recurring type in Christian fiction and religious controversy, the Jew often stands for otherness, a gauge by which the majority culture represents all that it is not. Such a symbol might hint at what Christians had once been, what they now repress, what they could yet become. For this reason, an especially self-revealing description of Christian essentials can be triggered by listening closely to the way each Christian answers the question, What is a Jew? Granted the import of this particular question, I tend as a teacher and student of world religions to apply a broader acid test: What are the barriers against empathy toward someone from any tradition other than your own?

THE CHRISTIAN DIFFERENCE

The Episcopal Grace Cathedral of San Francisco has installed stained glass portraying a bold mixture of the great Christian teachers and prophets alongside their modern counterparts. One elongated window features the towering figure of Calvin at left, followed underneath by the Lutheran Kierkegaard, the Anglican F. D. Maurice, and finally Tillich, straying beyond denominational boundaries. To Calvin's right, and matching his height, is the Anglican Thomas Hooker, with a range of nineteenth-century successors emerging underneath — Keble, Pusey, and Newman of the Oxford Movement. At bottom right, as a surprising climax to this lineage, are two theologians outside the Protestant circle, the first seated behind a pile of books at a desk, the second standing before a single book. These represent Rahner and Buber, a Roman Catholic and a Jew.

The image of Karl Rahner immersed in his stack of books suggests the German Jesuit's thousands of publications, the marvel of cramming so much teaching, research, and pastoral ministry into a single life of eighty years. Credited widely as the major theological influence behind the Second Vatican Council, he attempted to guide the transformation of today's divided Eurocentric church into the local Christian communities of a future world diaspora. On visits to Grace Cathedral I have meditated before this glass panel in gratitude, trusting that such an informed ecumenical gathering represents a true Anglican consensus, not just the taste of a particular rector, subcommittee, or donor.

The insights of Buber and Rahner have resonated far beyond their own particular traditions. The transcendental Thomism of Rahner, the biblical personalism of

Buber — both have tried to humanize the quarrels between those of differing religious traditions, especially Christians and Jews. However, their influence has not yet touched the average televangelist nor many of my Christian students. In class I still overhear the old hateful simplisms — a Jewish God of wrath versus a Christian God of love, tribal particularism versus universal salvation, legalism versus spiritual freedom, merited righteousness versus grace-given righteousness. Christian catchwords of this type date back to New Testament quarrels between Paul and his rabbinic adversaries — or at least between Paul the Christian convert and his own nagging shadow, Saul the Jewish legalist.

What I shall call the fallacy of inflated differences marks not only the relationship between Jews and Christians, and their interaction with Muslims, but especially many encounters among Christians themselves. Most Christian historians tend to map out this terrain by adopting a few unexamined dichotomies — fundamentalist versus modernist, church versus sect, Catholic substance versus Protestant protest, Christian West versus Christian East. Few can resist the symmetry of a neat antithesis, the tempting clarity of either-or. Within the numberless Christian denominations now extant, a trifling quarrel can still snowball into some new schism. Whenever progressive critics demystify an otherwise minor biblical passage, the fundamentalist is tempted to counter with a passionate literalness of interpretation, almost an idolatry of that text. As a more harmful illustration, consider what happens each time authorities condemn a timely heresy. The church risks not only belittling the nucleus of truth concealed in any error but also reaffirming the endangered tradition in an unbalanced counterclaim.

A rash distortion of this sort can be illustrated within my own Counter-Reformation tradition, now in its lingering twilight. The 1557 lecture *De Oratione* given at Rome by James Laynez, successor to Ignatius Loyola as Jesuit superior general, stages an imaginary dialogue with Luther: "Whereas you will not pray the rosary, I will pray it more often and with greater devotion. Whereas you damn Indulgences, I will esteem them more than ever. Whereas you ridicule prayers and masses for the dead, I will double their number. Whereas you condemn confession, I will confess my sins all the more frequently."[6] In hindsight, I would urge Laynez to tone down features marginal to the central Christian tradition. Instead, he ought to explore the heritage shared by both Catholics and Protestants — Luther's devotion to the person of Jesus, for instance, or ministry of the biblical Word, or Christ's Real Presence in the Lord's Supper.

A similar Christian imbalance came to my attention a few years ago in the acclaimed *Long Search* series on world religious traditions, written for BBC in the late 1970s by Ninian Smart. Most university courses in world religions today still draw heavily upon this teaching aid. Consisting of thirteen videotapes that range from the Toraja Primal tradition in Indonesia to Zulu Zion in Africa, it devotes three programs just to Christianity. Following his visits to Orthodox Rumania and Protestant America, the narrator broaches Roman Catholicism in an hour tape entitled "Rome, Leeds, and the Desert."

After repeated viewings, I still cannot decide whether this particular film distorts an otherwise balanced Catholicism or embalms a one-sided Catholicism with accuracy. I concede that the narrator, through interviews with a few talking heads, records the vital ferment and self-questioning during the early 1970s. Yet this entire presentation fixates on film-worthy Roman Catholic ingredients, many of them alien to the Christian style of Orthodox or Protestant churches — Vatican baroque statuary, vigil candles at saints' shrines, the pope carted on a sedilia around an altar, monks meditating in desert caves, a huge pilgrimage to Montserrat, and a British housewife's heartfelt devotion to Mary. To my own Christian spirituality, these images as a single gestalt remain just the colorful sidelights and accidentals of post-Reformation, pre–Second Vatican Catholicism. These are not the profound spiritual essentials — too elusive and prosaic to film, no doubt — shared by Catholics with most other Christians. To distill what makes Catholicism different from everything else is to trivialize and distort it.

The present chapter, designed to clarify not just Roman Catholic but the broader Christian essentials, will search for the unique Christian difference. At the same time it does not neglect the common ground shared with those outside the Christian tradition. The United States today is dominated by a multicultural perspective, a huge salad bowl of rich unassimilated ingredients. Countless we-they dichotomies of creed, race, and gender clamor for attention, with each competitive monad enjoying its separate newsletters, rallies, legal representation, and partisan versions of history. In this sort of milieu especially, whenever one religion is compared with another, exaggerated polarities leap immediately to mind. Instead of a Kierkegaardian *either-or* approach, however, I shall emphasize what theologian Karl Adam describes as the Catholic *and* — an umbrella wide enough to embrace such diverse Christians as Fyodor Dostoyevsky, Aleksandr Solzhenitsyn, and T. S. Eliot on the Right; Karl Rahner, Reinhold Niebuhr, Konrad Adenauer, and Eduardo Frei Montalva at the middle; Søren Kierkegaard, Kenneth Kaunda, Camilo Torres, and liberation theologians on the Left. Vital religious differences, both inside and beyond the tradition, will be acknowledged and even savored. And they will be transcended, too, whenever possible.

Borders between Two Testaments

The more you ponder the juxtaposition of Rahner with Buber in the Anglican cathedral gallery, mentioned above, the more affinities surface between them. The willingness of both theologians to clear away historical obstacles to dialogue, especially between Christians and Jews, has been noted earlier. During a series of recorded conversations in 1982 between Karl Rahner and Pinchas Lapide, an Orthodox Jewish scholar in New Testament studies, both men reaffirm a common hope. Each day the church prays for the Messiah's second coming, the synagogue prays for the Messiah's first coming. Thus, praying to the one God, Jews and Christians ask God to complete a single continuous promise of redemption. "So here therefore," says Lapide, "there is not a Jewish No standing over against a Christian Yes, but rather a Christian Yes beside a humble Jewish question mark."[7]

According to the Gospels of Matthew and Luke, troubled disciples of John the Baptist once pressed Jesus to confirm his identity as the long-awaited Messiah. He answered their question by a gesture to indicate he had been curing the blind and deaf and lame, and even raising the dead. By this unique ministry of healing and liberating, then, Jesus himself had launched the messianic era. He was the Messiah already among them, yet pledging to return a second time to complete his mission. To endorse him as the Messiah, of course, means to break decisively from traditional Judaism. I have described in chapter 5 the unbending Jewish conviction that no messianic era has yet arrived — not in the Israeli state and, with even more certainty, not in the person of Jesus. As one Hasidic tale recounts, when voices began screaming with excitement that the Messiah had arrived, Rabbi Manachem threw open the window, looked out upon the world, and said, "I see no renewal here." From a similar perspective, Buber and others, pointing especially to the Jewish Holocaust, have plausible reasons to conclude the world is not yet redeemed.

"To the Christian," says Buber, "the Jew is the incomprehensibly obdurate person, who declines to see what has happened. And to the Jew the Christian is the incomprehensibly daring person, who affirms in an unredeemed world that its redemption has been accomplished." Yet Buber wonders if such bold Christian optimism means just a belief that individual souls are saved by Christ in an otherwise depraved world. If so, then any Jew worthy of the name would be forced to reactivate the Hebrew prophets' social protest: "I will not live as a 'redeemed' soul in an unredeemed world."[8]

I have already documented Buber's efforts to unmask the messianic nationalism of Israeli secularists, especially the King Ahab pretensions of Ben-Gurion. Rahner echoes this same distrust of secular utopias. He takes for granted that Christians should not just remain neutral about "sensible planning for the future in this world, but must take up a positive attitude toward it." This includes practical economic policy and any reforms that expand the range of human freedom. "Our future cannot simply be accepted as the product of subhuman forces," he observes. "The future is also our responsible act. It cannot be passed off on anyone or anything else." However, at the same time he insists that Christianity, as "the religion of the absolute future, has no utopian ideas about a future in this world."[9]

For Rahner, the absolute future, which is God, must never be confused with an empirical, this-worldly future. Repudiating the Marxist dream of a classless millennium, he refuses to sacrifice a single human life for schemes where "every generation is always sacrificed in favor of the next, so that the future becomes a Moloch before whom the person existing at present is butchered for the sake of the person who is never real and always still to come." A more subtle utopianism, just as idolatrous, occurs whenever the church in a specific locale, at best merely a foretaste of finale, is mistaken for the definitive Kingdom of God. Rahner, for instance, dismisses as "nonsense" and "ideological fantasy" Ernesto Cardenal's claim that the Christian millennium had arrived with the Sandinistas in Nicaragua. You can discover the church's presence less in large-scale organizations than in poor, faceless groups, constituted by the Word and sacrament and practical charity. The church will always remain just a sign and promise, hoping against hope for the Kingdom-to-come.[10]

God as Absolute Future, Israel's prolonged exile, and a yearning for the final messianic era — all three biblical motifs overlap. Few Christians have taken this shared Jewish-Christian experience more seriously than Dietrich Bonhoeffer, the Lutheran pastor and theologian executed for treason under the Nazis in 1945. Bonhoeffer longed to recover the distinctive Jewish messianic hope that preceded and now flourishes alongside Christianity. His lengthy imprisonment had given him a

new experience of the Advent liturgy — four weeks of penitential longing and an-
ticipation before the arrival of Jesus at Christmas. These weeks are touched by the
theme of Jewish waiting, the long exile, and Dark Night. Just as a jail cell can be
opened only from the outside, so the world awaits the liberating intervention of God.
As the months of prison undermined his confidence, Bonhoeffer learned that his feelings and perspective were beginning to match those of the Old Testament much more
than the New. "It is only when one knows the unutterability of the name of God that
one can utter the name of Jesus Christ. It is only when one loves life and the earth
so much that without them everything seems to be over, that one may believe in the
resurrection and a new world. It is only when one submits to God's law that one
may speak of grace."[11]

A second characteristic shared by Buber and Rahner is their tendency to root all
religious questions in a thorough philosophy of the human person. Most Christians
today side with this premise of the Russian existentialist Nikolay Berdyayev: "Perhaps the mystery of God is better revealed by the mystery of the human person than
by direct search for God to the exclusion of human beings." It is axiomatic that any
theological assertion faces in two directions. Each statement about God implies at the
same time a statement about the human subject who theologizes. For instance, to describe God as Creator means to affirm at the same time that human beings are created
and contingent. Calvin, the great systematic theologian of the Reformation, observed
that since the strands of our wisdom about God and about ourselves are so entwined,
it is hard to determine which of the two precedes and gives birth to the other. Yet
saluting God's primacy, and wary of our proneness to shape God in our own image,
Calvin decided, like St. Thomas Aquinas before, to center the first chapters of his
opus on the nature of God.

The theology of Buber and Rahner, to the extent that their thought can be
systematized, intends to invert this conventional sequence. Buber first sets up a phenomenology of intimacy and encounter, modeled on the deep relationship between
two human persons. Then he interprets God's interaction with us in terms of this
I-Thou dialogue. Rahner begins his fundamental theology with an anthropology,
probing the human capacity for self-transcendence. Today the very concept "God,"
in its Judeo-Christian sense, treated by many philosophers as meaningless, needs a
fresh rehabilitation before we can speculate about God interacting with the world.
As the Anglican theologian John Macquarrie correctly advises, "we have to go back
to those situations where the everyday talking of the secular world has come to the
end of its resources and is confronted with a mystery.... This is a low-key approach
to theology, but it begins where people really are and by using the language that is
current among them."[12]

Granted this shared ground between Buber and Rahner, they differ, of course,
when confronted by the mystery of Jesus Christ. In his own Jewish spirituality, Buber
makes every attempt to find a place for Jesus. "I do not believe in Jesus," he says,
"but I believe *with* Jesus."[13] This minimal affirmation implies what Rahner calls the
initial step in a "low" ascending christology. With no compromise to his Jewish integrity, Buber stands beside Jesus the rabbi, both of them invoking "the absolute
Thou," a term Rahner adopts from Buber. By way of contrast, a second type of christology, described metaphorically as descending "from above," can be exemplified in

the Prologue to John's Gospel. The text introduces you at first to the Word as God's self-expression and next to this Word's insertion as God incarnate into human time. Pondering the God-mystery, you meet Jesus at first in his divine origins, then as fully human, too.

The "ascending" or "low" type of christology, on the contrary, begins by confronting Jesus in all his historical particularity, a perspective which Rahner finds more accessible to the contemporary religious seeker. On the initial level of historical experience, he explains, you meet "a Jewish Jesus in his natural Jewish environment. And in order to find this Jesus, I must want to encounter the Judaism of his time. . . . This encounter for me just begins an experience of encountering Jesus that only comes to its conclusion when the Christ of faith is discovered." Thus, in an ascending christology, you come across the human Jesus at first, then only gradually can you identify this figure as the incarnate God.[14]

Rahner observes enthusiasm today among the young for a fully human Jesus, the engaging street preacher and friend of the homeless, a Socrates or Che Guevara ready to grapple with civil and religious authorities. Reluctant to deemphasize this human side of Christ, Rahner hopes his own books help clarify that Jesus is indeed "a true man, and not just clothes worn by the eternal God." Yet to treat Jesus as merely human might be called "*Jesus-ism,* not taking into account the whole content of the Catholic faith about Christ which confesses, namely, that Jesus was true God and true human being in the unity of the divine person."[15]

God as Word and Spirit

Asked once in an interview for the central motif of his theology, Rahner gave this answer, his terse summary of faith: "That can't be anything else but God as mystery, and Jesus Christ, the crucified and risen One, the historical event in which this God turns irreversibly toward us in self-communication."[16]

The biblical story portrays our world springing from God's hands as a flawless utopia. Later, by an act of human disobedience, alienating the earth and ourselves from God, all creation suffers a spiritual death. According to the theology of Reinhold Niebuhr, to be developed later in this chapter, this biblical account of Original Sin implies a recognition of the selfish will to power running like a geological fault through every human motive, even the most altruistic. The only possible cure for this so-called Fall is a final intervention by God to restore the broken spiritual relationship. This drama in three acts, creation and sin and redemption, prompted Augustine's cry of *felix culpa,* for Adam's fortunate fault led God to become the divine and human savior.

However, for the French anthropologist and theologian Pierre Teilhard de Chardin, and for a longstanding tradition of the Eastern Church, this teaching makes too much out of sin and expiation. The God who first creates and only later redeems seems to act like an arbitrary God with two separated initiatives, adopting stopgap measures after our disruption of his original plan. Rahner agrees with Teilhard that such a scenario presupposes a fixed universe, where evil has to be explained as the secondary human distortion of God's otherwise perfect cosmos. Yet from an evolutionary perspective today, it seems the world did not start as paradise but as chaotic multiplicity, which will shape itself only gradually into the ultimate harmony of a paradise. Evil can be described as any hindrance, physical or moral, that impedes this progressive unification.

Rahner and Teilhard want to correct an unbalanced emphasis on human sin and humiliation or on analogies that imply a Roman legal squabble between God and his creatures over ownership. Both theologians shift the incarnate God to the center of their anthropology. Now Christ's completion in his second coming is viewed as the climax of evolutionary history. In the incarnation, matter and humanity prove worthy to become the human nature of God. Rahner expects, then, to uncover in matter itself a dynamic capacity to become spiritual, and in humanity itself a capacity or "supernatural existential" to become Godlike. In the evolutionary process, this step toward spiritualization introduces a higher unity, a new convergence inward, what Teilhard describes as a passage from cosmo-genesis to christo-genesis. Viewed in this way, creation and incarnation are "two moments and two phases of the one process of God's self-giving and self-expression."[17]

The New Testament interweaves three pivotal Greek terms for the Sacred — *theos, logos,* and *pneuma.* God, Word, and Spirit have been personified respectively as Father, Son, and Spirit-Advocate. For Christians, God's inner life is not an empty homogeneity but triune, a pattern mirrored somehow in the threefold way people experience God's presence. As Rahner puts it, "God himself as the abiding and holy mystery, as the incomprehensible ground of our transcendent existence is not only the God of infinite distance, but also wants to be the God of absolute closeness in a true self-communication. God is present this way in the spiritual depths of our existence as well as in the concreteness of our corporeal history."[18] It is possible to express this mystery in a brief credal formula. *Theos,* the ultimate mystery, communicates itself to the world — as an inner spiritual force or *pneuma,* and as an outer historical event, the incarnate *logos.*

Just as all of us are marked with a longing for God which God will someday satisfy, so the human race was first created in order that God could someday become human. Every person, then, even the self-described atheist, is endowed with a grace-inspired entelechy or tropism toward God and toward Christ — and even toward Christ's church. An explicit belief in the historical Christ, says Rahner, is "not something which comes to us from without as entirely strange, but only the explicitation of what we already are by grace and what we experience at least incoherently in the limitlessness of our transcendence." For every act of genuine self-transcendence is already an implicit opening to the Holy Spirit — or if you will, to the pervasive cosmic Christ. Whenever you "accept your own existence, that is, your humanity, in mute patience (or rather in faith, hope, and love, whatever you may call these), ... though you may not know it, you say yes to Jesus Christ. After all, when you let go and jump, you fall into the abyss that is there, not only as far as you have plumbed it." The Gospels assert that if you love your neighbor, you have fulfilled the Law. To love your neighbor is to love God, for somehow "God himself has become this neighbor."[19]

Many Christians today continue to question if and how any non-Christians can be saved. Some xenophobic churches limit salvation only to the explicit Christian accepting biblical interpretations endorsed by that specific church. Born into a tradition less exclusive than this, I can still dredge up a memorized Catholic catechism answer from my own childhood. It extended salvation to all those of goodwill, provided they remain "invincibly ignorant." A less smug explanation sorted out those capable of salvation into two categories — people undergoing a church baptism by water and people marked by that elusive facsimile, an implicit "baptism of desire." With more clarity, the Second Vatican Council states that salvation is possible for all those who, "without blame on their part, have not yet arrived at an explicit knowledge of God, but who strive to live a good life, thanks to God's grace."[20]

Rahner's notion of the "anonymous Christian" stands as a necessary corollary to an anthropology so resolutely christocentric. Those striving to live a good life, he says, are already Christian, even though unaware of their Christian identity. Rahner's intent is generous, to widen the boundaries of God's mercy so that it includes everyone freely responsive to conscience. Yet the label itself has been mistaken for just one more form of Christian imperialism trying to smuggle in the reluctant outsider. With the tables turned, Rahner could be treated as an anonymous Buddhist or Muslim, too, depending on the narcissistic viewpoint of his interlocutor. I cannot forget my high school classmate's protest long ago, after I once commended his integrity as a devout non-Catholic: "Don't call me a non-Ruland. I have a name of my own."

A friend whose husband is a Baptist minister once told me of the most discouraging church assignment in their lives, a five-year mission among the Lakota Sioux. She lamented that by the time she left, the poor heathen children still had little appreciation for the Christmas crib, the crucifixion, or the rite of Easter baptism. Throughout her account, this single-minded focus on Jesus made me increasingly impatient, filled with misgivings too serious to unload on her all at once. To begin with, why presume that the Sioux needed rescue from their own Primal religious tradition? Isn't the Christian God also Father and Holy Spirit? Sioux children learn in their tradition to worship the Great Spirit, the Creator, the womb from which all their ancestral spirits derive, the sacred forces of sky and earth. Even if you concede that Christian ministry may have a legitimate place here, why not begin by deepening in each person the experience of Creator and Spirit they already share with Christians? Only then, if someone proved curious and willing, you might consider introducing the formidable particularity of an incarnate God.

Maturely to love and respect a person means to accept that individual, not just as my own potential clone, a crypto-Christian, but as a unique *other*. To reach those beyond my own tradition, I can find no more equitable common ground than the shared pneuma or theos lying at the source of every unique religious person and tradition. A theocentric or trinitarian approach of this sort keeps christology in a balanced context — the sectarian Christ of fundamentalist missionaries, but also the elusive transcendental Christ of theologians like Rahner and Teilhard.

THE JUST SOCIETY

As the next chapter will demonstrate, Muhammad proved to be his own Constantine. For the Quran, like the Jewish Torah, offers a detailed blueprint of the model social order. A close Muslim friend of mine, by temperament a pacifist and dissenter, often jokes about his ironic birth within a tradition whose founder was both a warrior and civil ruler. In contrast, the movement that began with Jesus of Nazareth, spreading first in Jewish diaspora communities, then throughout Roman society, took three centuries to congeal into the empire's established church. The Gospels consistently stress Christ's repudiation of a political crown. In his ministry to the needy in all social classes, he tried in vain to transform popular hopes for an insurrectionist Messiah into the lofty deutero-Isaian dream of a martyr pacifist, expendable for others. The major charge levied against him before the Roman authority was sedition, usurping the loyalty due only to Caesar. Yet the Gospel of John concludes that Christ at last assured Pilate, "My kingdom does not belong to this world."

One Sunday morning in the late 1960s I squeezed into the crowded basement of a Catholic church on Chicago's Southside, where I served as a visiting priest that summer. Two polite, graying women had called for this meeting by announcing in the church bulletin their eagerness to explain why they had stolen the American flag usually propped next to the altar. Months before, on the church front lawn they had planted a few trees as symbols of peace, which now deserved to be followed up by a more explosive gesture. Christ must be separated from the immoral nation-state, which day after day furthered the Vietnam War. Who could then foresee my visit a year later to the more radical of these women in Detroit, now imprisoned for breaking into a federal office and destroying draft files? On that occasion the warden would threaten that if I insisted on seeing this subversive witch, he promised to initiate an investigation and FBI file on me.

That Sunday in Chicago, a year before her Detroit imprisonment, this woman and her activist friend confronted a series of questions in the church basement hall. One recent immigrant from Lithuania, proud of her own U.S. citizenship, praised the U.S. flag and the country as a rampart against the Bolsheviks. One laid-back teenager retorted, "It's just a piece of painted silk. Sew it on the seat of your jeans. Do what you want with it, but don't mistake it for Jesus." Next, a marine in uniform interrupted with this question: "First, was the flag handled with reverence? Second, was it folded correctly? Third, was it kept in a safe, appropriate place?" Then a neighborhood pundit offered a useful historical footnote. She learned that U.S. bishops had asked their churches during the 1930s to fly a papal flag next to the altar. Yet when Italy and the United States declared war on each other in 1941, American bishops scurried to add a U.S. flag alongside the altar for symmetry, so that no one could doubt the patriotism of American Catholics.

Though many in that room cited conflicting biblical passages to bolster their position, I found no consensus about a Christian's duty either to obey or to dissent from civil authority. These colliding approaches, of course, can be traced back to America's pluralistic milieu, but more important, to an unexpected reticence in the Bible itself. The New Testament in its moral and social teachings never spells out the distinctive features of a Christian society. Instead, the Pax Romana and stunning network of Roman law and communications are welcomed as a providential backdrop for dispersal of the Gospel. Acts of the Apostles, written in part to show that Christian faith and loyal Roman citizenship can be compatible, takes for granted that Paul's demand for a trial in Rome will place him before the most reliable civil forum on earth. Since most of the earliest Christians expected an immediate cataclysm and return of Christ, many seemed content to stay passive nominal citizens. They could take advantage of

Rome as the best temporary expedient to hold a perishing world together. However, by the late second century, Christians would find themselves persecuted for the crime of atheism, showing intolerance toward Gods dear to the Roman majority.

In the pre-Constantinian era, and during later Christian history, two scriptural texts provided the basis for debate about the limits of political loyalty. First, chapter 13 of Paul's Letter to the Romans states: "Let every person submit to the governing authorities. There is no authority except by an act of God, and the existing authorities are instituted by God. Consequently anyone who rebels against authority is resisting a divine institution.... Pay tax and toll, reverence and respect, toward those to whom they are due." This text has inspired an interesting range of interpreters, each speaking from a different political experience. On the one hand, gripped by fear of anarchy and convinced that princes, not church authorities, are the more trustworthy bastions of order, Luther read this passage as a strict religious vindication of secular authority. On the other hand, a seditious interpretation, given in Origen's second-century apologetics, trims Paul's words down to an admonition intended only for the ordinary citizen, not for the revolutionary spiritual elite.

The antithesis to this text appears in the threatening cry from the Book of Revelation, chapter 13. Written most likely toward the end of the first century, during the reign of Domitian, its imagery is cryptic and bloody. Loathsome beasts assume political power and demand to be worshiped as Gods, mouthing blasphemy and filth, at war against God's people, "deluding all inhabitants of the earth, making them erect an image in honor of the beast.... Rich and poor, slave and free, had to be branded... with the mark of the beast." Read according to apocalyptic-genre expectations, this text seems a disguised attack against the current totalitarian regimes of Nero and Domitian. Now transformed into a satanic power, Rome must be endured or overthrown.

In juxtaposition, then, the passages from Romans and Revelation pose a dramatic paradox. This disparity in attitudes toward the nation-state can be accounted for in various ways. Maybe Paul's earlier hope for cooperation with Rome dwindled to a martyr's alienation expressed in Revelation. Or maybe Paul's epistle took for granted an acculturated Greco-Roman, world-affirming, middle-class perception of the empire, while the Book of Revelation emerged from a militant, Jewish separatist tradition, speaking for the marginal and slave proletariat. Or more simply, one may conclude that the nation-state in New Testament writings has been represented comprehensively, now at its zenith, now at its apocalyptic nadir. Each explanation has its own plausibility.[21]

Referring to biblical traditions such as these, and also to scenarios of the earliest Christian communities, later reactionary, progressive, and radical platforms within the Christian political tradition seek out some basis of legitimation. These three options will now be examined as three valid patterns of genuine Christian Humanism.

By Humanism I mean the concern to humanize the world, to secure and extend human values, and by Christian I mean the sort of just society implied in Christ's prophetic teaching. Of these three positions, the reactionary option is Christian integralism or totalism, prepared at its most militant to understate the Humanist factor for the sake of a uniform, uncompromising Christian identity. Second, the progressive option is Christian democracy or Christian socialism, aiming for a Humanism that is open and pluralistic, trying to preserve both dimensions in balance. Third, the radical option will be called Christian kenoticism or prophetic self-transcendence. Here you are ready to minimize or surrender your Christian identity, and entrust it to the silent realm of vision and motive. Instead you now commit yourself to whatever seems the most authentic Humanist program, whether capitalist, communist, or some other form of revolutionary socialism.

As an oversimplified precis of totalism and its two alternatives, recall Dostoyevsky's famous credo, written in a Siberian prison: "If anyone proved to me that Christ is outside the 'truth,' and this really meant that 'truth' is outside Christ, then I would prefer to remain with Christ than with 'truth.' " In contrast, Meister Eckhart affirms his belief, no less passionate than Dostoyevsky's: "Truth — so noble a thing, that could 'God' turn aside from it, I would cling to truth and let 'God' go."

Total Christian

The clearest scenario of totalism, the first of three Christian options, can be found in the Roman Empire under Theodosius, just a few generations after Constantine's conversion. Romans had been accustomed to state-supported temples, public worship by the entire community, religious concerns interwoven with every other aspect of life. However, with this totalist framework still surviving, the pivot of a new Christian faith now replaced the old Greco-Roman polytheism. By the middle of the fourth century, a once-persecuted church had in its turn become persecutor, demolishing non-Christian temples and imposing the death penalty on those who still persisted in offering Pagan sacrifice.

As protectors of the church, enforcing canon law and theological orthodoxy, emperors gradually moved bishops into prominent rank in the civil bureaucracy. Western Europe developed a volatile juxtaposition of papal-royal jurisdictions, each given co-equal status in Augustine's City of God. The Byzantine East, however, preferred a relatively harmonious fusion of the two, so that it is hard to determine which dominated the other, the church or the state. With the emergence of nationalism and the sovereign nation-state, this Pax Christiana dream of East and West split into an assortment of Latin Catholics, Orthodox Greco-Slavs, and Protestant Anglo-Saxons. Often an entire national church adopted the incidental religious identity of its ruler.

Familiar with the national church pattern — Anglican in England, Roman Catholic in Spain, Lutheran in Sweden, for instance — nine of the thirteen American colonies passed laws to protect their own respective established churches. Some colonies restricted public office only to members of their privileged church, while others extended religious liberty to include all Protestants but excluded Catholics and non-Christians. New England Puritans, for instance, viewed themselves as the New Israel, a Christian Bible commonwealth, and not in any sense a pluralistic democracy. Twenty years ago, at Jesuit House near the University of Chicago, I used to show visitors a singular document mounted proudly in our dining room. A conversation piece, especially for my Protestant colleagues at the divinity school, it summarized a 1647 Puritan law in Massachusetts banishing any Jesuit from that jurisdiction — for the first trespass, imprisonment; for the second, a sentence of death.

One of the most literate modern apologists for the total Christian nation-state is

T. S. Eliot, who liked to describe his loyalties as classicist in literature, royalist in politics, and Anglo-Catholic in religion. This very motto echoes the triad *"classique, catholique, monarchique,"* applied in 1913 to Charles Maurras, a decisive influence on Eliot between the two world wars. Maurras founded Action Française, professing an *integrisme* so fascistic, xenophobic, and anti-Semitic that the Catholic Church later condemned it.[22]

Written at the approach of the Second World War, *The Idea of a Christian Society,* Eliot's major work on faith and culture, strained to round up every resource in the ideological war against Nazi neo-Paganism. What spiritual impact could an ideology of democracy offer England against Hitler or Stalin? "Had it any beliefs more essential than a belief in compound interest and the maintenance of dividends? Such thoughts as these formed the starting point, and must remain the excuse, for saying what I have to say." Rather than a banner of watered-down British secularity, Eliot yearns for a tough Christian social alternative. This means "a religious-social community, a society with a political philosophy founded upon the Christian faith," not "a mere congeries of private and independent sects."[23]

Within England's context, Eliot does not require an established church. However, he rules out the possibility of disestablishing the Anglican state church as he knows it. Disestablishment would prove catastrophic — a "visible and dramatic withdrawal of the Church from the affairs of the nation, the deliberate recognition of two standards and ways of life, the Church's abandonment of all those who are not by their wholehearted profession within the fold." The ideal Christian nation-state is intended not just for saints or the devout leisure class but especially for those "whose Christianity is communal before being individual.... It would engage the cooperation of many whose Christianity was spectral or superstitious or feigned, and of many whose motives were primarily worldly or selfish. It would require constant reform."[24]

Maybe Eliot invests his Christian nation-state with so much control because, like many apologists fighting a totalitarian enemy, he tends unconsciously to adopt the features of his adversary. Or perhaps he has exaggerated the scenario of a lost medieval Christian synthesis, an era of limited historical-religious horizons, of incidental religious and racial concurrence. At any rate, his conclusions are unmistakably totalist. He argues that a citizen cannot be "Christian in some social relations and non-Christian in others.... To accept two ways of life in the same society, one for the Christian and another for the rest, would be for the Church to abandon its task of evangelizing the world." More specifically, his Christian nation-state has no room for the absolute conscientious objector.[25] With even sharper clarity, in the earlier University of Virginia lectures, *After Strange Gods,* Eliot shows an obsession with the aesthetics of cultural homogeneity. The date is 1933, during Hitler's rise to power. Here Eliot complains to U.S. Southerners about the influx of foreign immigrants into cities of the North. In an ideal Christian nation-state, he says, "what is still more important is unity of religious background. And reasons of race and religion combine to make any large number of free-thinking Jews undesirable."[26]

The persona of Eliot is a network of ambiguities. Notice the jazzy iconoclastic style of his early poems, alongside the chastened prose of his literary criticism. Patriotism, which this emigrant from Missouri felt toward the British crown, at last meant loyalty only to the House of York, defeated centuries before in the War of the Roses. And the litterateur with top hat, striped trousers, and Anglicized manners often seemed a parody of British stereotypes. In this vein, Eliot might be expected to devise a social order too Christian for most Christians. His idealized Christian leader reveals an unexpected kinship with Dostoyevsky's Grand Inquisitor. Both Eliot and the Inquisitor, touched by compassion for the weakest Christian groundlings, are determined to protect the happiness of these people by a regimented uniform society. In exchange, citizens will have to pay a stiff price, the surrender of religious liberty.

"Rome and the sword of Caesar" are the two basic weapons that Ivan in Dostoyevsky's *Brothers Karamazov* gives to the Grand Inquisitor. This figment of Ivan's creative imagination, however, gradually reveals himself as Ivan's double, the satanic rebel concealed in his own heart. Dostoyevsky, like most other Orthodox Slavophiles, believed that Caesaro-papism in Europe had alienated sensitive religious minds and driven them toward totalitarian atheism. As Prince Myshkin explains in *The Idiot:* "The pope usurped an earthly throne, and took up the sword. Socialism, like its brother atheism, springs from despair in opposition to Catholicism.... Our Christ, whom we have preserved and they have not even known,... must shine forth in opposition to the West, and carry our Russian civilization to them."[27]

This same Slavophile perspective lies behind Solzhenitsyn's controversial Harvard address in 1978, which reproached the West's flagging confidence, its spiritual immaturity, and its fixation on secularity, legalism, and consumer goods. Exiled from Gulag horrors to a warm cottage in Vermont, Solzhenitsyn disappointed his Harvard audience by refusing to perform like the grateful immigrant, with testimonials to America's superior way of life. Instead he idealized his old Russian homeland, to which he would return in triumph a decade later. By contrast with soul-less Americans, the Russian soul through extreme suffering "has now achieved a spiritual development of such intensity that... it has produced stronger, deeper, and more interesting characters than those generated by standardized Western well-being." Though the political composition of Solzhenitsyn's utopia is never spelled out, it employs the rhetoric of Christian homogeneity and restricted civil rights, especially restricted freedom of the press. He identifies his enemy as the "autonomous, irreligious Humanistic consciousness," or "a Humanism which has lost its Christian heritage."[28] Dostoyevsky's adversaries, in contrast, cover a wider range — not just godless Humanists but also Roman Catholics, Jews, Poles, and Germans.

The worst Slavophile fears regarding Roman Catholic imperialism, however, can be corroborated by the political theology of Cardinal Alfredo Ottaviani, leader of the archtraditionalist forces at the Second Vatican Council. Facing the predicament of a dominated minority church in Stalinist regimes, and nearby, a dominating majority church in Catholic regimes, such as Franco's Spain, Ottaviani formulated an insolent double standard. When in the minority, Catholics should agitate for universal religious equality, or even separation of church and state. Yet when in the majority, Catholics should restrict the rights of minority religious traditions in that society, for "error has no rights." The head of a Catholic nation-state has the duty, he argued, "to protect from everything that would undermine it the religious unity of a people who unanimously know themselves to be in secure possession of religious truth." Repudiating this mind-set, the Second Vatican Council majority insisted that whereas error in the abstract may have no rights, individual persons acting in conscience do.[29]

Open Christian

"Christian Humanism," the term Eliot applies to his model society, can be redefined to include a range of explicit Christian political parties in Europe and Latin America after the Second World War. Political histories label this remarkable shift the rise of Christian Democracy. Granted that the new Christian label no longer bears Eliot's totalitarian overtones, still a Christian Democratic party, like a Christian labor union, I suppose, implies a conservative agenda. In the moral chaos after the war, governments of Germany, Italy, and France had need for breathing space and healing — a persuasive anticommunist candidate to fill the gap left by Hitler, Mussolini, and Petain, someone to restore the family, church, economy, and all the basic freedoms. Just as T. S. Eliot sought a tough Christian alternative to Hitler's atheism, so leaders like Adenauer, De Gaspari, and Schuman constructed what Adenauer called a "Christian Humanism" to withstand the "totalitarian party ideologies" of communists and ex-Nazis.

The architect of modern West Germany, elected its first chancellor at age seventy-two, Konrad Adenauer in his *Memoirs* explains the origin of his own Christian Democratic Union: "Only a great party with its roots in Christian-Western thinking and ethics could educate the German people for their resurgence, and build a strong dike against the atheistic dictatorship of communism." The party's ethical manifesto was drawn from Adenauer's background in natural law ethics and recent papal encyclicals: "The obligations inherent in the idea of good faith, the recognition of an order based on law and binding upon everyone, the rejection of state omnipotence and narrow state egotism, the affirmation of the solidarity of all people and nations and its concomitant responsibilities, the defense of the common good of an international order, the rejection of pernicious race theories, the respect for the dignity and God-given liberty of the individual — all these were ideas which had, to a considerable extent, been formed and developed by Christian thought."[30]

Adenauer hoped to establish a Christian identity strong and elastic enough to attract most segments of German society, yet ease the tensions between them. He believed "the new party had to be a Christian party, and one that would embrace all denominations, Protestant and Catholic Germans. Indeed all who knew and valued the importance of Christianity in Europe would be able to join — and it goes without saying that this also applied to our Jewish fellow-citizens."[31] Though adept in the vocabulary of reconciliation and compromise, Adenauer would often surface in political cartoons, however, as the puppet master running a chancellor-democracy, the tenacious patriarch refusing to retire after three terms in office. I think it unfair to sum up his political achievement in a single oft-cited jest, but the following remark shows he knew his own ambivalence about exercising authority: "If God had made people more clever, they could have ruled themselves better. If God had made them more stupid, I could rule them more easily. I would prefer them more stupid, of course."[32]

His socialist opponents had hoped that a society so devastated could now be overhauled radically. So they would not forgive Adenauer for launching just one more bourgeois capitalist revival, now under Christian disguise. Acknowledging this criticism, he responded: "In my view, there was need for a just social order that would enable every person to acquire property for himself and his family. I was convinced it was unnecessary to nationalize.... The concentration of political and economic power in the hands of the state was, I thought, likely to lead to undue dependence on the state." Nazism had taught him that "owing to their history, the Germans were all too inclined to submit to the power of the state." His emphasis on private ownership, family rights, and Christian values also had its usefulness in foreign policy. Adenauer was wily enough to realize that "the best way to counteract the isolationist tendencies in the United States was to keep underlining Germany's allegiance to Western civilization, to the democratic view of life and politics, and the ideal of Christianity, and to stress our community with America."[33]

A more radical style of Christian Democracy, nuanced and Chileanized, surfaced in the fragile career of Eduardo Frei Montalva, father of Chile's current president. Lawyer and professor, son of Swiss immigrants to Chile, the elder Frei became president of Chile for six stormy years before the accession of Salvador Allende's leftist regime in 1970. He described his Christian Democracy Party as "nonconfessional. ...Inspired by a philosophy which in the end is confirmed by natural right, its call goes to all — Catholics, people of other faiths, or with none at all."[34] As a middle position between the plutocratic Right and communist Left, he offered a democratic Left, attracting support from many progressives, but especially from business and church conservatives. The latter were driven toward Frei's camp in their panic to escape the unthinkable — his revolutionary friend and rival Allende, whose campaign was gathering momentum offstage.

"There are two principal roads — capitalism and communism," Frei once observed. "Neither suffices because neither understands the sacred quality of human beings." Capitalism dehumanizes a person by making work the overpowering feature of life, and communism dehumanizes by making the state superior to individual rights. The free individual must be seen as "a creature of God, possessing a soul, and therefore someone who transcends human structures." It is important to connect the evolution of Frei's political thought with an unexpected "opening to the Left" by Chile's Catholic hierarchy. The humane social philosophy of figures like Jacques Maritain, Frei's principal mentor, had left a gradual influence on the seminaries. During the 1960s, Pope John's *Mater et Magistra,* the Second Vatican Council decrees on religious freedom and acculturation, Pope Paul's *Populorum Progressio,* and especially the consensus of 150 Latin American bishops at Medellín pushed for a radical transformation of society. The Chilean bishops themselves were no longer dominated by Archbishop Caro of Santiago, who had censured Frei's party long before for "fighting the Franco regime, the most Catholic in the world, and believing in diplomatic and commercial relations with Russia."[35]

Frei alerted himself to this long-overdue shift in official Catholic self-definition. A new Christian "development ethos" was now replacing what he identified as the old "deviation...passed on to the Latin American Catholic by what we might call the Spanish stream of spirituality." Social analysts have seized upon many causes for the relative underdevelopment of Latin economies — static hierarchical societies, the climate's impact on mind and emotions, an entrenched military class, colonial exploitation that fostered an economy overdependent on imports, the lack of a Protestant work ethic.[36] To this web of influences, Frei added the strand of religious *hispanidad,* a sort of otherworldly fatalism, like the malaise that undermines the average culture of poverty. The Spanish Catholic mystique at its worst conditioned people to accept human misery and the inherited economic structure as sanctioned somehow by God's will. Catholics were expected to develop a spiritual indifference to material progress and contempt for business and manual occupations. All abuses in government could be treated as a consequence of Adam's Fall. In effect, society was pervaded by a pious "disregard for practical effectiveness and the functional value of good intentions."[37]

In contrast, the new Catholic *aggiornamento,* a "spirituality of economic development," permitted resignation to the inevitable only after you had made every effort to improve the full scope of human life, including its physical conditions. "The handling of money does not in itself degrade anyone," Frei insisted. Avoiding nepotism, true Christian charity in government had to mean that posts must be conferred on the most competent, not on those most grateful or needy. Political change should not prove threatening to the deepest values. For "Christian morality is a morality of specific replies to specific problems, which are always different. And this requires a dynamism that continuously adapts the Christian reply to problems of existence."[38]

Frei was succeeded as president by Allende, who was assassinated in the anti-communist military coup of 1973, with alleged U.S. connivance.[39] Unfortunately, Frei's programs for land redistribution, expropriation of foreign-controlled industry, and tax and education reforms eventually lost public support. These remedies proved too sluggish for his allies on the Left, too disruptive to the Right. His critics thought he promised too much for one short term, launched changes on too many fronts at once, and won listless cooperation from rival parties that had everything to gain from his impotence. The conservative bankers and churchmen who elected him president had guaranteed from the beginning that his party would lack a Senate majority to carry through any massive reforms.

Perhaps the very juxtaposition of both names in Frei's party title, Christian and Democrat, presents a self-defeating anomaly. A party pledged to tradition and modernization at the same time seems to promise a moderate half-way house, attractive especially to reactionary voters. These interests had expected to co-opt Frei in their battle against lawlessness, violence, and atheistic communism. But once the economy stalled, or his reforms veered too close to socialism and nationalization, extremists on the Right were geared, even before 1973, to risk a military dictatorship.

Kenotic Christian

In a society pervasively Catholic or Christian, the dissenter finds it hard to earn credibility without adopting the vocabulary and symbols of Christianity. The platform of traditionalist politicians often sounds like a holy war — consecration of the nation to Mary or the Sacred Heart, defense of the home and sacred family values, a moral crusade against materialism. Moderates like Frei Montalva and his party despair to see their more prophetic Christian values preempted by conservative opponents, whose own religious loyalty stands unquestioned. Against so-called Christian regimes like these, sometimes the most cogent dissent consists in rejecting Christian labels altogether. Perhaps one must also discard the vocabulary of parliamentary democracy, moderate reform, Alliance for Progress, and all the other weasel words misused to tame revolutionary passion.

The social order envisioned here is more radical than the two types of Christian Humanism discussed before. I have called it kenotic, for lack of a better English term, to capture an attitude of deliberate namelessness, silence, and self-abandonment. *Kenosis* is the word used by Paul in his Letter to the Philippians to explain Christ's surrender of his divine prerogatives — "he emptied himself, he became a servant." With this prophetic pattern in mind, the kenotic Christian, ready to sacrifice an explicit Christian identity, will search for a practical secular coalition with any true revolutionary Humanist.

It is helpful to investigate the reasons for Kierkegaard's reluctance to call himself a Christian. His 1855 *Attack upon Christendom* can be read today as a spirited protest against Caesaro-papism, Christian nationalism, and the kind of "communal" Christianity that T. S. Eliot proposed. The Lutheran Church, having extended its margins to include everyone in Denmark, seemed empty of passion and inwardness. "What Christianity needs is not the suffocating protection of the state," he remarked. "No, it needs fresh air, it needs persecution. . . . And let us again serve God in simplicity, instead of treating him as a fool in magnificent buildings. Let seriousness prevail, and stop playing a game. For a Christianity preached by royal functionaries who are paid and made secure by the state and employ the police against other people, such a Christianity has the same relation to the Christianity of the New Testament as swimming with a cork float or with a bladder has to real swimming." In the pulpit, Kierkegaard charged, civil servants preach a gospel of renunciation, poverty, and readiness to suffer for Christ, whereas the sacred words are turned into lies by the louder preaching of their lives. When Jesus returns, will he recognize any true faith behind this so-called Christendom? "Christendom is twaddle which has clung to Christianity like a cobweb to fruit."[40]

A pure sectarian idealist, Kierkegaard searched in vain for an authentic Christian in the nineteenth-century established Danish church. Instead of jaded Christian crowds, filled with illusions about a Christian land and a Christian people, he preferred one honest Pagan, or someone at least passionate enough to reject Christianity. Adopting a wise Socratic irony, Kierkegaard knew that if you want to prove others more ignorant than yourself, never presume to be smart, but first admit your own ignorance. "It has exasperated those against me that I am able to make it evident others are Christians still less than I — I who am yet so very diffident about my relation to Christianity that I truly see and admit I am not a Christian." In a society where everyone was Christian simply as a matter of course, Kierkegaard intended his own prophetic denial to ignite the same self-questioning in others, too. "My task," he concluded, "is to revise the definition of a Christian."[41]

Kierkegaard's storm over phony preachers of renunciation can be matched by the outrage of Father Rivas in Graham Greene's 1973 novel *The Honorary Consul*. Rivas had abandoned the priesthood to become a revolutionary terrorist. How could any person of conscience keep preaching "sell all and give to the poor" before pews of starving children, while his archbishop far off, "rendering unto Caesar," dines in splendor with the military elite of Paraguay? The novel gives uncanny insight into the brave but abortive effort to release oneself and others from the addictions of cultural Catholicism. When Rivas tries to persuade his wife that their marriage, though unrecognized by the official church, is truly valid, she can only respond with church-mouse docility, "If you say so, Father." He reprimands her gently, "I wish you would not call me Father all the time. I am your husband, Marta, your husband." Her final rejoinder underlines the fatal gulf between them: "I would be so proud if just once I could see you as you used to be, dressed at the altar, turning to bless us, Father."[42]

Rivas had cut his ties with the institutional church after police denounced him to the archbishop for a controversial sermon. In his eulogy for Father Torres, shot while fighting with guerrillas in Colombia, he concluded by admitting "that unlike Sodom the Church did sometimes produce one just man, so perhaps she would not be destroyed like Sodom." In fact, the historical Camilo Torres did actually die in battle, a martyr for the Colombian revolution. Professor of sociology, popular university chaplain, newspaper editor of the radical *Frente Unido,* he abandoned the priesthood and an academic career to join the Colombian Army of National Liberation. Ever impatient with barriers that separated theory from practice, he became progressively more engaged — from picket lines, prisons, barrios, at last to the soldier's routine of kitchen patrol, guard duty, and killing. Though friends among the Christian Democrats supported his weekly newspaper, most of them parted with Torres once he welcomed communists to his staff, and especially after he resigned from the priesthood. In rebuttal, Torres explained his laicization as "taking off my cassock to be more truly a priest."[43] A number of my own Christian friends, resigning from the ministry or priesthood in recent years, have offered reasons almost identical to those of Torres.

The true blasphemer, I think, must be someone who takes God seriously enough to snub or rage at God. When Kierkegaard rails against Christendom, for instance, he sounds blasphemous to the average churchgoer. Yet like Kierkegaard, when Torres abandons Christian symbols, he acts not from indifference or hatred but because he cares enough not to want them abused. Torres believes that the Mass is intended to be the profound expression of a worshiping community united by love. The sacrament of the Lord's Supper is "fundamentally communal. But the Christian community cannot worship in an authentic way unless it has first effectively put into practice the precept...to feed the hungry, give drink to the thirsty, clothe the naked, and procure a life of well-being for the needy majority of our people." Christ's Sermon on the Mount had foreseen this very situation: "If you are bringing your offering to the altar and there remember that your brother has something against you, leave your offering there before the altar, go and be reconciled with your brother first, and then come back and present your offering."[44]

In the revolution against hunger, poverty, illiteracy, and lack of shelter and public services, Torres declares himself "prepared to fight together with the communists for our common goals....I do not want to be identified with the communists alone, and thus, I have always sought to work together not only with them, but with independent revolutionaries and those of other ideologies." To discredit its adversaries, the ruling class has always resorted to tactics of name-calling — Roman emperors persecuted "barbarians," prerevolutionary France its "free-thinkers," Latin America its "communists." "I am not an anti-communist," Torres explains, "because among the communists themselves, whether they know it or not, there may be many true Christians." Moreover, "this communist charge hounds nonconformists among my compatriots, whether they be communists or not." Torres thinks that a true Christian "should not be anti-anything, just pro-humanity."[45]

Even today after the recent Soviet meltdown, collaboration between Christians and neo-Marxists in Europe and Latin America continues to test the limits of flexibility on both sides. Both parties often find themselves in surprising agreement about strategies of radical social change. This dialogue, and the renewed emphasis on basic human and international rights after the Second World War, has sparked a theology of liberation, prominent especially in Latin America. As its major priority, the movement hopes to raise the consciousness of oppressed people. More specifically, it argues that, to overcome a legacy of otherworldly fatalism, the poor need skills of decision making and participatory management. The church is expected to disidentify with the wealthy and ruling classes and identify with concerns of the poor. This social realignment will be painful and divisive, of course, but the price is unavoidable. Unfortunately, the closing paragraphs in most ecclesiastical documents on any social issue are accustomed to urge Christian love and nonviolence on all parties, almost at any price. Expressing a desire for superficial blanket-reconciliation, this pious gesture tends to placate reactionary consciences and blunt the edge of outraged cries for revolution.

Liberation Christians expect any theologian worthy of the name not merely to reflect and react but to plunge into action. You must track down the empirical causes for a particular institution becoming exploitative. Otherwise, you cannot hope to desacralize and delegitimize current social injustices. Theologians of the more detached academic type are subjected to a harsh critique. Most conventional publications in theology can be reduced to self-vindicating projections by a Eurocentric elite, often male and celibate and bourgeois, insulated from rural poverty because of their nearness to secure metropolitan power centers. The Christian theologian of liberation tries to be more self-consciously regional and political, just as Christ was political. Uruguayan theologian Juan Segundo, for instance, argues that Jesus was indeed a revolutionary, not so much against the Roman Empire as against the oppressive Scribes and Pharisees. "They, and not the Empire, imposed intolerable burdens on the weak and dispensed themselves from these burdens, thus establishing the true socio-political structure of Israel." To that extent, then, the countertheology of Jesus proves itself overtly but not exclusively political.[46]

The hazards of any political theology have already shown themselves. They include the impatient leap of Rivas and Torres from nonviolent protest to romanticized guerrilla warfare, Ernesto Cardenal's naive identification of the Sandinista regime with Christ's second coming, and the tendency to manipulate the Bible to yield concrete political solutions. I have mentioned Rahner's and Buber's repudiation of all premature utopias, a motif developed incisively by Reinhold Niebuhr, renowned prophet of American "political realism." Niebuhr scoffs at the certainties of both Christian traditionalists and Christian revolutionaries. Those on the Right tend to confuse loyalty to God with loyalty to a particular established regime; those on the Left tend to deify reason or isolated biblical quotes. "There is no Christian economic or political system," he asserts. "But there is a Christian attitude toward all systems and schemes of justice." This attitude is one of practical scrutiny, calling every political and moral system into question.

To many Christians, the classical doctrine of Original Sin has meant the literal report of a single aboriginal crime and its legacy. Yet Niebuhr reinterprets this story as transhistorical, exposing a bias toward self-interest that affects every human being, including the first man and woman. "Acknowledgment of human dignity must be accompanied in Christian thought by a recognition that these precious individuals are also sinners, that their lusts and ambitions are a danger to the community, and that their rational processes are tainted by the taint of their own interests."[47] Our will to power becomes increasingly more demonic and intense, as its perimeter widens from individual to family, race, church, and nation. Niebuhr thinks political justice can be achieved not by the futile effort to eradicate self-interest but, more wisely, by the effort to harness and deflect it. It takes humility to realize that "the forces of self-interest to be deflected are not always those of the opponent or competitor. They are frequently those of the self, individual or collective, including the interests of idealists who erroneously imagine themselves above the battle."[48]

As a convincing illustration of religious idealism, balanced by a touch of Niebuhrian irony and self-criticism, Zambian ex-president Kenneth Kaunda deserves a hearing. His friends claim that in the first twenty minutes of every political speech, Kaunda, a daily Bible reader, always gives proof that he is truly the son of a Presbyterian preacher. *A Humanist in Africa,* published in 1966, his second year as president, states his credo: "By Christian Humanism, I mean that we discover all that is worth knowing about God through our fellow humans. And unconditional service of our fellow human beings is the purest form of the service of God.... For all my optimism about our human possibilities, I do not make the mistake of forgetting that we are God's creatures, with all that this means both in limitation and in dignity. Nor do I deny the reality of sin. The besetting sin of the Humanist is pride. The significance of Jesus Christ is surely that he spells death to our pride by showing us how far short of God's design for us we are."[49]

Revolutionary founder of Zambia and its president for a quarter-century, Kaunda has now retired from office after his first loss in free elections. Still active in loyal opposition to his successor, Frederick Chiluba, he puts up with recent recurring bouts of house arrest. Among various reasons suggested for his defeat are Zambia's land-locked economy, an overdependence on copper exports, border incursions from neighboring guerrilla forces, and a bureaucracy inept if not corrupt. Confronted by so many crises during his prolonged one-party rule, Kaunda had found it necessary to modify, without betraying, the values that first shaped his rebellion against the British Rhodesian government. Kaunda the earlier revolutionist embraced Gandhian pacifism as a moral absolute, but Kaunda the later president would take up arms as a last resort in civil war. Ruling a new nation, poor and divided, a people with no tradition of democracy, he found it essential to avoid racial and tribal favoritism, and in dealing with adversaries to try persuasion rather than force. Kaunda hoped to achieve a socialist secular nation-state, racial and religious pluralism, and generous reconciliation with his former colonial adversaries. During his years as president, his moral perspective seemed progressively to widen — from the rights of Zambians, to Pan-African rights, to the inalienable rights of every human being.

"Zambian Humanism" is the specific name Kaunda has chosen for his new social order. "Zambia is a country of many religions — Christianity, Judaism, Animism, Hinduism, and Islam, and others. I did not feel it was my place as president of the new republic to adjudicate between them, to declare this religion or that 'official' so far as the State is concerned.... Because I happen to be one of those odd people who feels equally at home in a cathedral, synagogue, temple, or mosque, I recognize the power inherent in all the major faiths and urgently desire to see that power harnessed for the welfare and good of humanity." The common ground he discerns in each of these traditions is "a high view of the human person as paramount creation of the Supreme Being." They all teach a similar morality of compassion, service, and love. Zambian Humanism, however, must not be confused with Humanism of the Eurocentric Enlightenment, designed as an alternative to religion. "Humanism is neither antireligious nor some super-religion," he says. "It is only 'anti' that kind of piety in a vacuum which devalues God's world by rendering the pious unavailable for the service of their fellow human beings."[50]

The devastating imprint left by African colonialism, as Kaunda records it, matches the scars Frei Montalva observed in Latin America. "Colonialism, for all its benefits, devalued the human person. It created elite societies in which human worth was determined by an irrelevant biological detail — skin pigmentation." The settlers intended to destroy Africans' self-confidence, convincing them that they were "primitive, backward, and degraded, and except for Europeans' presence among us, would be living like animals." Too many victims were left with a withering Bwana Complex, still looking over their shoulder for the white man's approval. In the new Zambia, black Zambians may now prove slow to befriend white Zambians as equals, mostly because the black underclass were long taught by colonists to value whites merely as indispensable specialists and bosses, not as complete human beings.[51]

It must be conceded that at first Europeans had the Bible and Africans the land, but soon Europeans had the land and Africans the Bible. From Kaunda's viewpoint, people with self-respect pounded out of them by aggressive colonialism needed most of all to restore faith in their own possibilities. "This is why a Humanist outlook accords well with our temperament," he says, "while grim Marxism and the narrow Christianity which preaches endlessly about human depravity does not.... We have seen something of the very best Christianity, thank God. I myself have benefited from it."[52] At the same time, Kaunda guesses one reason for a growing Muslim impact upon Africa is its reinforced self-confidence in your humanity without minimizing your dependence upon Allah.[53]

Perhaps a Humanism truly inclusive and communal, not individualistic and selfish, may eventually become Africa's contribution to the imperialistic First World, which chatters proudly about all it has to teach others. "Let the West have its technology," says Kaunda, "and Asia its mysticism. Africa's gift to world culture must be in the realm of human relationships."[54] Recognizing the advantages of technology, he still questions how his nation can embrace this gift without being trapped by consumerism and losing its soul. His litmus test for an advanced civilization consists of one question: "How does that society treat its old people, and indeed, all its members who are not useful and productive in the narrowest sense?... How can we humanize our politics in Zambia so that the humblest and least well-endowed of our citizens occupies a central place in the government's concern?"[55]

Kaunda's model human being, of course, is the person of Jesus Christ. His description of Christ combines explicit quotations from Gandhi and Teilhard de Chardin — a nonviolent, activist Christ at the heart of an unfolding cosmos in which "humanity is thrusting like an underground seed upwards toward the light." For Kaunda, Jesus is "the Man against whom all people must measure themselves when they try to live the life of love." A pronounced characteristic of Jesus is that he does not judge people according to their accidental group membership. "To him each man, woman, and child, irrespective of color, is unique, endowed with ultimate worth and dignity.... Every person is unrepeatable, ... intended to be an end in oneself."[56]

The dedicated Christian activist, then, is foremost a "servant of humanity, ... an instrument of Christ's love which challenges people to become their true selves.... In this sense, Christian practice is not a particular brand of action appearing alongside other endeavors. Rather, it blends with human efforts...." Thus, in Kaunda's society, genuine Christian presence must not be the label of a privileged church or party, but a spiritual power diffuse and nameless.[57]

CHRIST THE WAY

The distinctive focus in Christian spirituality can be summed up in a few traditional phrases — imitation of Christ or following in the footsteps of the biblical Christ. Buddhists often imitate Gautama's conjectured posture and hand gestures in meditation and try to broach his experience of Nirvana by praying near landmarks like the Bo Tree and Deer Park. On pilgrimage to Mecca, the Muslim hopes to duplicate step-by-step the recorded rituals and spiritual attitudes of Muhammad as the Prophet passed in his own final pilgrimage from the kaaba to Mount Arafat. For the Christian disciple, spiritual identification with Christ assumes an astonishing range of forms.

Most popular of all Christian formal prayers, the Our Father is recited to adopt the mind of Christ, communing with God his Father. Jesus asked that the Last Supper, a foretaste of his approaching death, be reenacted "in remembrance of me," so that later followers could experience his real sacramental presence among them. The purpose of monastic vows is to mirror the circumstances of Christ's successive development — the routine labor and prayerful quiet of his thirty hidden years or the final public ministry of preaching and teaching. St. Francis of Assisi shares in Christ's sufferings to such an extent that his hands and feet are marked with the stigmata, and he hopes to die a martyr in Muslim Egypt. St. Ignatius Loyola, yearning to act out his fantasies about imitating Christ, takes a barefoot pilgrimage to Jerusalem. At the climax of his journey, he stands in the stone footprints allegedly left behind by Christ on Mount Olivet. Later the Muslim guards are offered his penknife as a bribe to let him return so that he can calculate the precise direction faced by each footprint.

From earliest childhood, most of my Christian friends and I have been molding a Christian imagination, each of us shaping and shaped by our own unique images about the life of Christ. At times I have eavesdropped on adults coaching young children in their night prayers or have attended dying hospital patients muttering their prayers. I catch accustomed Gospel turns of phrase, but more important, the emphases, omissions, and odd displacements in each individual mind. Our imaginations have been influenced, at times infiltrated, by the religious images that others left behind them. Raphael's Madonnas, Michelangelo's Creator, or El Greco's suffering Christ succeed so well that some people can no longer imagine these figures in any other way. In the last half-century, prominent films on the life of Jesus have added visual details wherever the New Testament is vague or silent.

Whenever I try to picture Jesus today, I cannot escape a montage from memory that combines Max Von Sydow in *The Greatest Story Ever Told* (1965), Enrique Irazoqui in *Il Vangelo Secondo Matteo* (1966), Ted Neely in *Jesus Christ Superstar* (1973), and Willem Dafoe in *The Last Temptation of Christ* (1988).[58] No film has left more graphic traces, however, than Cecil B. de Mille's 1927 silent epic, *King of Kings,* which I viewed once a year for almost a decade. During that pre-television era, for forty days of Lent, the penitential season of prayer and fasting before Easter, most Catholic families in Erie, Pennsylvania, would abstain from attending the movies. At a single matinee toward the end of Lent, one large theater offered a free performance of this film. Each scene would unfold with glacial solemnity, interrupted by panels of dialogue that listed the biblical chapter and verse, accompanied by music from Wagnerian operas and familiar Protestant hymns. As the U.S. milieu itself changed over the next fifty years, so the commercial public's image of Jesus seemed to change on film — from the reverent iconlike portrayal of Jesus, to a more humanized, average-looking Jesus in gritty surroundings. Even if the humanity of Jesus looked increasingly convincing, his miracles seemed even more plausible, mostly because of advancements in the technology of special effects.

My spiritual training as a Jesuit illustrates the contemplative explorations common to many Christians. I learned to mull over the very adverbs and adjectives used by the Gospels to surmise the implicit attitudes of Jesus — the way he treated religious authorities, for instance, children, or outcast sinners. Among the techniques recommended for Christian transformation in the *Spiritual Exercises,* a book drawn from his own experiences, St. Ignatius asks the reader to imagine Joseph and the pregnant Mary, for instance, on the road from Nazareth to Bethlehem. "Consider its length and breadth, and whether such a road is level, or passes through valleys or over hills." The contemplative aim here is to enter the Gospel scenario as concretely as possible, gain loving familiarity with every character there, and "pray for joy with Christ in joy,... or for pain and tears with Christ in torment."[59] During my novitiate I remember once uncovering a crucial detail in the Gospel of Mark, which I interpreted with naive literalism. I had evidence now that Jesus did not always take the more strenuous, self-mortifying path. For at least once during a storm alongside his disciples, he took a break, "lying in the boat, on a cushion, asleep."

Explaining his own post-Christian version of Christianity, Carl Jung points out distortions triggered by the one-sided focus just described. "Christ is an exemplar who dwells in every Christian as his integral personality. But historical trends led to the *imitatio Christi,* whereby the individual does not pursue his own destined road to wholeness, but attempts to imitate the way taken by Christ."[60] In other words, by overemphasizing Christ as a historical model for living, you can miss what Rahner called the transcendental or cosmic Christ, the inner spiritual dynamic within each person. Paradoxically, the Way of Christ is not merely a teaching but itself a personal force — Christ the Way, the Holy Spirit, an enabling presence that radiates strength and joy. My gaze should focus not only backward to someone else's life but also upon the sacred presence now within my own life.

Paul in his Letter to the Romans asserts that the transformed Christian, while in the Spirit, cries out "Abba." Commenting on this passage, Augustine says, "This 'crying' is also the gift of God.... What a mistake to believe our seeking, asking, knocking is of ourselves, and not given to us.... God's grace not only indicates what ought to be done, but helps make possible the achievement of what it indicates."[61] In a touching set of instructions for his friend Peter the Barber, *Simple Advice on How to Pray,* Luther manages to distill the Christian rudiments of prayer: "Remember that you are not just standing or kneeling by yourself, but also the whole Christian Church and all good Christians with you, in one united prayer." Luther concedes that he himself often browses so richly "on one single thought that I can let go all other petitions in the Our Father. For when that happens, the Holy Spirit himself is speaking. And one word of his is worth a thousand of our own prayers."[62]

Here Luther catches a directness and trusting personal familiarity that echo what Jesus no doubt experienced in crying, "Abba, Father!" Through our inarticulate groans, both Son and Spirit communicate with the Father, as Paul explains: "God willed that we be shaped according to the image of his Son, ... and searching our inmost being, knows what the Spirit means, because the Spirit pleads for God's people in God's own way."

Christ of Many Faces

A decade ago in Jakarta, Indonesia, I stopped by a large Catholic church, crammed with statues and paintings donated from various parishes in Holland. The four Indonesian high school students acting as my guides presumed I would be pleased to discover the finest European art, left behind after the departure of Dutch colonialism. I could not guess my guides' honest artistic estimate, for they longed mostly to share their guest's anticipated delight. Yet to my own taste, this art displayed the worst clichés of Baroque and St. Sulpice artists. Maybe the treasures had been contributed in a massive garage sale, so that churches back in Europe could renew their architecture and decor after the liturgical reforms of the Second Vatican Council.

By way of contrast, far southeast of Jakarta, I visited a Catholic chapel in Jogjakarta, with about fifty original paintings of various Old and New Testament scenes. This gallery proved so stunning I felt compelled to preserve every picture on slides. The priest had commissioned a handful of amateur artists in a Balinese village totally Hindu in population, touched by little or no contact with Eurocentric Christian iconography. For each painting, he would first read them a biblical passage, discuss it with the artists in an allegedly nondirective way, and then urge them to paint it according to their own unique interpretation. The painted characters all wore sarongs or saris, framed in a setting of jungle foliage, animals, and gathering villagers. Often you could not distinguish the Jesus figure from his neighbors except for a bright aura and expressive eyes. Though a few canvases just substituted Hindu poster clichés for predictable Christian ones, most of the art helped me toward a fresh reimagining of scenarios dulled by familiarity.

Both these situations show how the Gospel has been colored by the contact between differing cultures and differing religions. The New Testament itself, of course, gives evidence of daring adaptations — from Hebrew to Aramaic to Greek, from Jew to Gentile, from the exclusively Jewish-Christian to the inclusive Christian. Matthew's Gospel, for instance, addressing itself to a Jewish audience, centers on a Messiah-Christ, the personified New Torah. John's Gospel, in contrast, with Hellenic Jews in mind, identifies Christ with more universal archetypes such as Wisdom, Life, and Light.[63] Yet what began in the Bible as a Christian encounter with the neighboring world of Greece and Rome has widened today to include the entire earth and interplanetary cosmos. Most Christians now rub elbows with neighbors from all major religious traditions of the world.

Why has the face of Christ changed as it encounters each new culture and religious tradition? To begin with, every culture brings with it a different filter of language, logic, and social values. A shift in any of these factors will affect the unconscious mind-set of preachers, artists, and their public. The second reason, exemplified in Paul's First Letter to the Corinthians, emphasizes a resolute aim to adapt the Gospel: "I made myself a Jew to the Jews, in order to win the Jews.... For the weak I made myself weak. I made myself all things to all people in order to save some at any cost."[64] This rationale can be mistaken for just a foxy sales tactic. Yet until proved otherwise, it deserves to be taken at face value — a sincere confession of zeal and empathy.

Without devaluing Paul's hope to evangelize, I side with a third and more pivotal explanation why so many faces of Christ do and should exist. Since Christ and his Way are a mystery, the depths can never be fathomed completely. Given the filter of one particular culture, spirituality, or individual consciousness, only a few aspects of the multifaceted will show up in any one situation. Yet especially through contact between people across cultures and religions, features otherwise hidden or taken for granted can be thrown into fresh relief. My premise emphasizes the need for true catholicity — each theology partial and one-sided, each person incomplete without the others, all of us interconnected horizontally in space and vertically in time.

From the many new perspectives on Christ opened up by recent dialogue of this sort, I have selected four that show rich promise. Each will be described as a separate face of Christ, a fresh prospect in the Christian Way.

Elder and Healer: The first face of Christ to be explored arises from contact between the Christian tradition and a few of the many indigenous or Primal religions of Africa. Assigned from the United States to social ministry in Zambia for the last decade, a priest friend of mine recently picked out some highlights in his own inculturation process there. Accustomed at Mass to have his congregation stand up when addressed with "The Lord be with you," he soon realized his new audience had been taught by their indigenous traditions to sit respectfully, whenever an elder addressed the assembly. In another example, affirming the Roman canonical approach to marriage, Catholics focus on a couple's actual exchange of vows in public as the inauguration of their sacramental marriage. Yet indigenous traditions stress instead the sacred process in a long unfolding relationship. Many African couples live together for months or years before local society confirms the "final" legalization of their marriage.[65] Given this situation, the outsider is challenged to rethink the premises and borders of sacramental marriage. Maybe African folk wisdom provides a responsible middle position between strict canonical vows and the increasing number of disastrous serial or trial marriages in modern secular societies.

African indigenous ritual and moral values show surprising kinship with biblical culture, whereas at times both these older traditions strike the Eurocentric Christian as alien terrain. The Letter to the Hebrews states that Christ's task was to lead God's children into glory. It was appropriate that their elder brother and guide should die for them, then, because he and they are members of the same family. God perfected, "through suffering, the leader who would take them to their salvation.... It was essential that he should in this way become completely like his brothers, so that he could be a compassionate and trustworthy high priest of God's religion, able to atone for human sins."[66]

These particular facets of Christ — the elder brother, the leader of initiation rites, and the guide's need to share step-by-step and complete the entire ordeal so that the others will be inspired to follow — do not immediately grip the average Christian today. Yet the text speaks to a people steeped in the Primal Way, deferential to the authority of their elders, especially the elder brother, and sensitive to a persistent watchfulness of the Ancestors. According to Primal initiation rites, candidates are isolated from their family of origin and adopted into a new fellowship. At each stage of initiation they are guided by an elder. One candidate, usually the eldest, chosen to represent all the others, symbolizes or *is* the group. No one can claim adult identity until completing the entire initiation process.

Thus, by his circumcision Christ becomes a precommitted member of society. Then in his proto-initiation, Christ is separated as a teenager from Mary and Joseph in the Temple and later passes through all the stages of life, tasting every aspect of what it means to be human. The initiation culminates in his death-cry, "It is completed." He asks no one else to undertake any burden he himself has not first experienced. The bond struck between his disciples and Christ gives everyone a full share in his sacrifice and triumph. In this reading, chapter 5 of the Letter to the Hebrews takes on special poignancy. Christ's major qualification as a priest, the people's representative to God, is that "he can sympathize with those who are ignorant or uncertain, because he too lives in the limitations of weakness."

Another role of Christ, especially familiar to indigenous people in Africa, the Pacific Islands, the Americas, and elsewhere, is Christ the healer. The shamanic cure and its implications have already been explored in chapter 1 about the Primal Way. In the United States today, not only Native Americans and New Age exponents but also charismatic and Pentecostal Christians have begun to earn limited public respect for holistic medicine and faith healing. However, I side with many Christians, partial to the modern Eurocentric tradition of scientific medicine, who would prefer to whittle down the profusion of miraculous cures in the New Testament. It is easy to imagine Christ's lament about the crowds thirsting for magic, missing the true significance of his miracles. In this frame of mind, when my Korean Pentecostal friend, for example, speaks with enthusiasm about his church, I feel embarrassed by his tabloid focus on the number and details of unusual healings within the community.

Contrary to this skeptical mind-set of my own, during the public ministry of Jesus and his disciples their preaching is almost always coupled with healing. And this combined form of ministry dominates the pages of early Christian history. Jesus commonly makes little distinction between health of mind and of body. Thus, the Kingdom of God is preached without distinction to the little ones, the lost, the weary and heavily burdened, and the sick. Concerned for these oppressed, marginal people most of all, he promises hope, forgiveness, love and offers an invitation to change their lives and join his new fellowship. A true change of heart is capable of sparking the inner forces of self-healing, which then affect the entire mind and body.

Traditional African healers know that sickness represents a fissure in the family and community, no matter what its chemical and genetic causes. The cure will not be complete without rituals of reconciliation, bringing back the patients to fellowship with their ancestors and local society. In dealing especially with mental disorders, the Yoruba healer, for instance, expects those cured to confirm the ritual reentry of their sick spirit back into the body. Acting out an elaborate rite of dismissal, patients perform a blood sacrifice to ward off any recurrence of mental breakdown and immerse themselves in purifying waters to symbolize the completed process of rebirth. Then they are restored to their families.[67]

Christ provokes censure in his society for demonstrating repeatedly that a sick person in need must take priority over strict observance of the Sabbath. Like traditional African healers, he often introduces rites of exorcism into his cures and takes responsible measures to ensure the patient will be readmitted into the community. For example, Christ directs that a healed leper visit the priests so they can perform the necessary rituals of the man's reentry into society. Or after curing a possessed maniac living in isolation, Jesus asks that the patient be returned to his home. Healing at times involves touch, spittle, oil. The cures are often accompanied by important words — a blessing, a gesture of empathy, a spiritual explanation of the healing as a sign. Like the best physicians in any era, Christ aims to heal the whole person, not just the symptoms.[68]

Teacher of Wisdom: The second face of Christ, as teacher of wisdom, becomes prominent if Christ is viewed in relation to the so-called Wisdom legacy of Asia, introduced in chapters 2 through 4. For instance, chapter 4 suggested limited parallels between Buddhist and Christian forms of meditation, monastic commitment, and compassionate engagement in the world. This common ground has long been acknowledged. Yet after a few decades of conversing with devout Buddhist friends, meditating alongside them, studying their sacred texts, I can now admit an unexpected hermeneutical reversal. By this reversal I mean my questions have deepened and reversed, so that now I am the one in question. My earliest impulse had been to trim the textbook abstraction called Buddhism down to size, so that it could fit stock Christian categories. Yet sidestepping my unconscious arrogance, Buddhist friends instead have succeeded in prodding me to challenge and reinterpret my own Christian priorities.

What happened is this. The Old Testament wisdom literature, long overshadowed for most Christians by the Pentateuch, the Prophets, and the historical books, has now shifted into the foreground of my consciousness. This genre embraces Proverbs, Job, Ecclesiastes, Sirach, the Wisdom of Solomon, and by extension many of the Psalms. Frequent passages in the New Testament are touched by this wisdom style and motifs, which pervade much of Gnostic literature also and later classics of patrology such as *Christ the Educator* by Clement of Alexandria. Written in the early third century, Clement's work spells in detail how Christians should eat, dress, make friends, and live out their religious values. According to ordinary usage, the term *paidagogos* applied to Christ in its title refers to the educated household slave, a tutor and mentor, who conducts the children to school and guides their moral training.[69]

Major features of this wisdom genre show up clearly in the Letter of James. Luther scorned this book as an "epistle of straw" because it remained silent about the need for Christ's redemptive grace. Yet perhaps for Luther's very reason, among others, I have found James the most earthy and accessible of all New Testament books to readers from other religions. Theocentric rather than christocentric, it also skips over the patriarchal image of God as warrior and king and the fixation on Jewish salvation-history. True to biblical wisdom conventions, it presumes a global moral order and reaches across religious borders to address anyone seeking a mature life. The entire wisdom tradition reaches its fruition, of course, in Christ's many Gospel parables and sayings. Drawing upon chapter 24 of Sirach and other key wisdom passages, the Gospels at times identify Jesus with Torah, or the personified feminine Sophia, or a banquet of knowledge open to everyone. In Matthew, for instance, Jesus says, "Come to me, . . . and I shall refresh you." In John he says, "I am the living water," or "I am the true bread."[70]

All these portions of the Bible stand out when a wisdom filter or grid is laid over the text. Careful readers often notice Judeo-Christian parallels as they read through the Dhammapada, various Mahayana sutras, Zen tales and koans, the Taoist and Confucian classics, or Vedic hymns and Upanishadic dialogues. Approached through this lens, Jesus now assumes a more pronounced role as teacher, sage, and guru. In one famous Zen tale a disciple reads aloud from the Sermon on the Mount to Master Gasan — consider the lilies of the field, offer the wicked no resistance, and whoever seeks shall find. "That is excellent," Gasan comments. "Whoever said that is not far from Buddha-realization." Most aphorisms of Christ can be read as unsettling paradoxes. Zen masters employ the koan to drive one's mind to its limits, so that stunned and humbled, it may thus be laid open to sudden enlightenment. Similarly, Christ tells his parables to trigger an upheaval of self-searching.

Many hours of my life have been set aside for teaching rudimentary English and the art of small talk to international students, or straining to overcome language barriers in cross-cultural counseling sessions, or befriending strangers on long visits abroad. In a number of these exchanges, the other person and I have caught ourselves matching proverbs from our respective folk traditions and sacred scriptures, one metaphor more graphic than another, some of them too dense and paradoxical to survive translation. Much of a person's unique moral values, I have suspected, can be condensed to fifty or so favorite aphorisms, which guide everyday behavior in the marketplace. An elderly Chinese gentleman, whom I encounter regularly at a local swimming pool, likes to exchange a new proverb with me occasionally. The words often distill a profound religious attitude toward life — for example, Dag Hammarskjold's "For all that has been, thanks. For all that shall be, yes." At times my friend and I debate the correct interpretation of more baffling proverbs.

Accurately understood, Christ's parables are not illustrations designed to render teaching more concrete but a medium of divine revelation. First posing enigmas, trawling for the curious and motivated hearer, the story withholds an explanation until later. The Gospel of Mark portrays Christ's disciples constantly puzzled by his words and actions. They are ordered again and again to keep his messianic identity a secret. In the inaugural parable of the sower, and its subsequent explication only to the humble and well-disposed, we catch hints of his characteristic teaching method. Those who have not yet grasped its explanation "see and see again but do not perceive, hear and hear again but do not understand." The briefest of all four Gospels, Mark's original text ends the crucifixion narrative with the shocking account of an empty tomb. The ensuing short paragraph about further events leading up to Christ's ascension, the epilogue treated by most scholars as a later addition, offers a neat Hollywood ending. To conclude with the puzzling empty tomb, however, is to wrap up the entire Gospel and thrust it before the believer as a long-suspended koan, a summary challenge to faith.

Like the parables, Christ's "signs" are emphasized in John's Gospel. The sign is an event or truth charged with enigmatic reverberations, often by associating it with wisdom archetypes such as bread, life, water, or light. After a particular sign appears, Christ is greeted by misunderstandings and murmurs. A final explanation follows, which divides listeners into those ready to seek further teaching and those who cling blindly to just a material interpretation of the sign. This pattern of paradox-misunderstanding-explanation can be traced in Christ's dialogue with Nicodemus about waters of rebirth, with crowds about the bread of life, or with Jewish leaders about curing the man born blind. Christ's parables, like his signs and miracles, are a sacred revelation unfolding step-by-step, an epiphany of both his person and his Way. Disclosure of the mystery will be adapted to the particular developmental stage of faith in each individual disciple.

Transfigured Icon: A third face of Christ, the divine presence incarnate, which Rahner associates with a high or "descending" christology, gains full attention in a Hindu context. The Bhagavad Gita, presenting Krishna and Arjuna in dialogue before battle, culminates in Krishna's gentle summons: "Set your heart on me alone, give me your understanding,...come to the waters of Everlasting Life....I will reveal a supreme wisdom."[71] You can hardly discount the similarity between this Hindu paean to wisdom and Christ's wisdom invitations cited above. Arjuna at last begs Krishna, avatar of Vishnu, to disclose "the glory of your own supreme being." And Arjuna is granted a staggering vision of countless eyes, faces, stars, and the flashes of a thousand suns.

I have examined a few Hindu prints that dissolve into a flood of shapes and colors, a blend of Salvador Dali and Jackson Pollock, in their attempt to evoke this astounding moment. "And Arjuna saw in that radiance the whole universe in its variety, standing in a vast unity in the body of the God of gods."[72] After Arjuna prostrates himself in awe and bewilderment, Krishna shrinks back to his finite bodily appearance. Listening to Krishna's words, I feel prompted to revisit the Gospel account of Christ's transfiguration on Mount Tabor. Its symbols of color, dazzling light, and cloud are more understated, but it makes a comparable impact on the three shaken witnesses.

Jesus transfigured is the Christ of glory, a mystery that defies any effort to imagine or paint it. His resurrection from death occurs off-scene, out of time, an event that artists try to broach only through its symbolic effects — an empty tomb, a laser beam penetrating through rock, a spiritualized figure framed by a blinding aura and a circle of stunned guards. Powerless to render such an instant, the artist remains mortal, after all, less adept at depicting plausible saints than demons and gargoyles. Faced with a comparable challenge, Dostoyevsky throughout *The Brothers Karamazov,* for instance, inserts authorial complaints about his protagonist Alyosha. Alyosha seems undefined, a sickly ecstatic, a poorly developed creature. Yet characters like him and Prince Myshkin seem to skirt the edge of ecstasy, epilepsy, schizophrenia, almost as if Dostoyevsky cannot locate holiness at the center of human life, but only at its margins, trailing off into the subhuman or superhuman.

This same tendency to dematerialize human nature can be observed in many of the most treasured ancient icons portraying the Christ story. The earliest Buddhists approached Gautama with awesome aniconic restraint, and their later images often show a preference for stylized, elongated human Buddhas and Buddha-Dharma giants. A similar taste prevailed among the first Christians. Conditioned by a strict aniconic Jewish tradition, and left numb by the riot of henotheistic images in popular Greco-Roman culture, many Christians learned an initial mistrust of statuary in the round and of realistic portraits. Instead they turned to sacred words and letters, various cross images without the corpus, the cruciform architectural pattern of a basilica, a simple fish or lamb design. Only gradually did Christian artists accustom themselves to sculptured flat reliefs, painted icons, frescoes, and mosaics. These images often focused on a Christ towering in final judgment or, paradoxically, an enormous Madonna holding the Christ child with a toy world in his hands. The icon painter evokes an otherworldly Christ that transcends the ordinary human form — a two-dimensional distended body, with puppetlike gestures, weightless garments, eyes glaring, a diaphanous haze of light and color.[73]

A Hindu believes that Krishna, who may or may not have been an actual historical figure, is one of many avatars assumed by the God Vishnu. Taking a different perspective, the Christian believes that Jesus, an actual historical figure, is the single instance of God incarnate. In a few passages, Krishna sounds like Vishnu's highest avatar, or perhaps his only avatar: "Even those who in faith worship other Gods, because of their love they worship me, although not in the right way." Thus in a Hindu variation on Rahner's christology, any person might actually be an "anonymous Vaishnavite," worshiping a transcendental Krishna. More often, however, Vishnu seems to speak through Krishna as just one avatar channel among many: "Although I am unborn, everlasting, and am the Lord of all, I come to my realm of nature and through my wondrous power I am born. When righteousness is weak and faints, when unrighteousness exults in pride, then my Spirit arises on earth."[74]

Thus, throughout history, whenever someone truly needs a savior, Vishnu responds by assuming one of his countless avatar identities. This belief has the advantage of adapting God's face to every possible context — race, time, culture, even religion. Traditionally the number of major incarnations has been condensed to a group of ten figures celebrated in the epics and puranas. The modern theologian-mystic Sri Aurobindo uncovers a fascinating pattern in this particular set of avatars. They constitute a myth of evolution — from the fish, through land animals, human dwarf, then higher phases of humanity, culminating progressively in Buddha of the past, Krishna of the present, and Kalki of the messianic future. In other words, God continues the process of redeeming every aspect of evolving human history, from its origins to the final apogee. Thus, salvation is universal, process-oriented, and most important, linear — a characteristic not often emphasized in Hindu theology.[75]

It is difficult for the Christian imagination to conjure up vast pluralistic and cosmic implications, given only one savior and one brief life span — God's unique incarnation in Jesus Christ. Yet God's evolving process of salvation, which Aurobindo projects on the macrocosm, has been condensed by St. Irenaeus to the microcosm of Christ's one human life. A theologian of the second century, Irenaeus stands first in a line of thinkers captivated by parallels between microcosm and macrocosm. According to the disputed adage, "Ontogenesis recapitulates phylogenesis," events in a developing individual life and also events in the unfolding history of humankind can parallel each other — even sum up, climax, somehow influence each other. Paul had taught that the sacrificial death of Christ the second Adam is able to undo the fateful disobedience of the first Adam. The word Irenaeus uses to describe Christ's lifelong task of revising or revisiting is "recapitulate," which means to bring to fruition or to go over the ground again. "He moved through every stage of life," says Irenaeus, "restoring communion with God to all."[76]

Christ shared successively every aspect of human experience. "For he came to save all by means of himself — all, I say,...infants and children and adolescents, young adults and old people. He therefore passed through every age, becoming an infant for infants, thus sanctifying infants. He became a child for children, thus sanctifying those who are of this age." Boldly stretching Christ's thirty-three years to fit his theory, Irenaeus even adds, "Likewise he was an old person for the old, so that he might be a perfect master for all....Then at last he came on to death itself."[77]

A daring imagination can spread Christ's salvation beyond the evolving human race to every other dimension of the cosmos. St. Gregory of Nyssa pictures Jesus immersing himself in waters of the Jordan, which symbolize all forces of the earth. As he emerges, he sanctifies and elevates the whole world by means of the water which runs off his body. "Mighty Matter," the prayer of Teilhard de Chardin begins, "the hand of God, the flesh of Christ....I acclaim you as the divine milieu,...ocean stirred by the Spirit, clay molded and infused with life by the incarnate Word!"[78] The bond between natural forces and the cosmic Christ finds superb expression in Dostoyevsky's *The Brothers Karamazov*. The monk Zossima once pauses on a warm July night, so quiet that he can hear the splash of fish and identify each separate bird call. "Every blade of grass," he tells his peasant friend on their forest journey, "every insect, ant, and golden bee, all so marvelously know their path....Christ has been with them here even before us....The Word is for all. All creation, every leaf is striving toward the Lord, singing glory to God, weeping to Christ, even unconsciously."[79] For this reason, Zossima, Alyosha, and so many other mystics of the soil drop down in reverence to kiss the earth, beg its forgiveness, and enjoy a life of solidarity with all living creatures, even the unseen spirit world.

How can the time-bound death in Jerusalem of one exclusive individual be correlated with the salvation of people at every time and place? Unable to solve or sidestep this mystery, artists boldly enlist the imagination to evoke the cosmic repercussions of Christ's death. Some crucifixion paintings depict a skull beneath the cross, at times even identified as the remains of Adam, with Christ's blood dripping on the skull. Golgotha in legend becomes Adam's burial place; Christ's agony in the garden is transferred to the Garden of Eden. The cross that redeems mankind is extended down to cut into the earth's center as a global axis connecting heaven and earth. A tenth-century triptych of the crucifixion has the cross at its base transfixing a contorted troll, probably a river or mountain spirit, symbol of Hades.

An especially popular motif in earliest Christian history is Christ's journey to the underworld, reenacting the pattern of most Orpheus and Hercules myths — a gauntlet of ordeals, liberation of captives, a savior returning from darkness with the gift of immortality for all human beings. Applying his theory of recapitulation to every stage of Christ's life, Irenaeus imagines him completing his mission by descending to the realm of the dead, so that he can share in and sanctify these lives, too. Iconography portrays the wounded Christ battling with devils, a tradition that later culminates in the famous harrowing-of-hell mystery plays. This myth is developed graphically in early apocryphal literature, notably the Acts of Thomas, Apocalypse of Peter, and Gospel of Nicodemus. Christ is observed baptizing and preaching to Old Testament saints and even blameless Pagan philosophers, now released from prison.[80]

The Prophetic Servant: Obverse side to the transfigured icon just portrayed, the face of Christ as prophetic servant reaffirms his humanity — a mortal individual plunged into our limited historical time and space. This is Martin Buber's Jesus the Rabbi, not someone to whom but with whom a Jew is able to pray. The human face of Christ will surface even more explicitly within the next two major traditions under scrutiny, the Muslim Way in chapter 7 and the Humanist Way in chapter 8. Muslims recognize Jesus as one in a line of prophets culminating in Muhammad — all of them only human, all sent by the one God, a God for whom incarnation would be inconceivable. And for many Humanists, at least those who find the Sacred feasible, Jesus is a human seer and revolutionary, but someone no more sacred than ourselves and the cosmos.

Muslim and Humanist versions of the human Christ can be illustrated at their most controversial by sampling some popular fictional lives of Jesus. These composite efforts can then act as a grid to highlight details otherwise left vague and unemphatic in the New Testament. Like the influential Jesus films described above, such portraits try to change the plot or fill in these curious blank spaces. Their creative accounts repeat variations on a few simple patterns, so that you suspect the existence of a single Ur-source for these lives, or at least a remarkable similarity of motive prompting the storytellers in their search for a Jesus alternative.[81] Consider a few recurring ingredients. Most versions tend to edit out the resurrection of Jesus, for they do not accept him as divine. Yet a number of them also reject his death on the cross. Maybe such a death is too scandalous and brutal for the average religious sensibility. Or perhaps the authors of these lives think the New Testament connects such a death too closely with the Godlike redemptive task of Jesus. Or more likely, the crucifixion cut short the life of Jesus too early, before he could live so many other imaginable lives.

Another feature in some accounts of Jesus is a sequence of travels or ordeals seasoning him during his hidden life or after his alleged death by crucifixion. The authors prefer his redemptive purpose to touch a more universal audience than Palestine alone. He needs exposure to a more complete human existence — just as his life could be enriched by reincarnation into a series of fresh avatars or Irenaeus-styled recapitulations. Christ's added journeys also give him spiritual training under various gurus, from Qumran to India and China, a historical contact that might account for puzzling cross-religious coincidences.

To render Jesus more accessible, especially to a popular Humanist audience, the fictional biographies try to provide him with a more plausible human existence. First he must surrender or relax his strict celibacy and know sin and temptation more directly. For example, in *The Man Who Died* by D. H. Lawrence, Jesus after his purported death wanders to a temple of Isis in Lebanon. Mistaken there by his priestess lover for the God Osiris, Jesus learns the mysteries of sexual love and fathers a child. As portrayed in Nikos Kazantzakis's *Last Temptation of Christ,* the ordinary joys of love and family life remain only an alternative, the road not taken, in Jesus' imagination throughout his dying hours on the cross. Jesus dies far away from Palestine in the short story "Jesus on Honshu," by John Updike, an author usually associated with a more conventional Christian perspective. During young adulthood, Jesus wanders to Japan in response to a restlessness that he identifies as his father's voice. There he trains in yoga for years under the sage of Etchu, who teaches him such Buddhist and Taoist aphorisms as the following: a seed must die to live; only the weak are strong; an archer must focus upon the prey and not upon the bow. He carries this wisdom back to Palestine. Surviving his reported death there, he returns to marry in Japan, has three daughters, many grandchildren, and dies after a full life of more than a hundred years.[82]

Whereas Humanist accounts such as these demand a Christ-image more fallible and earthy, most Muslims, on the contrary, yearn for a more uncompromising reformer — the fiery monotheist and iconoclast, a Jeremiah slapping down all rival religious claims, including any hint of worship directed toward the human Jesus himself. For example, Nicolas Notovitch's *The Unknown Life of Jesus Christ,* written in 1894, depicts Jesus as a young adult, traveling from Tibet through India and Iran, preaching to groups representing one successive world religion after another — Buddhists, Jains, Hindus, Zoroastrians. Condemning their respective idols, he summons all people back to the one God.[83] The most controversial fictional Muslim life of Jesus, the *Gospel of Barnabas,* made its first appearance in the eighteenth century. It may have originated earlier, but not before the reign of Pope Sixtus V in the sixteenth century. A familiar text for teachers and polemicists in various parts of the Muslim world even today, the book purports to be a lost Gospel, more reliable than the canonical New Testament.

This apocryphal Gospel never duplicates Quran passages but inserts artless references to Muhammad in a compendium of interwoven excerpts from all four canonical

Gospels. For example, when Jesus promises to send the Holy Spirit, the Paraclete or Advocate, Barnabas substitutes the explicit name of Muhammad, thus establishing a conscious prophetic legacy from Jesus to his successor. At the beginning of his ministry, Jesus receives a book of revelation from the angel Gabriel in a desert cave, with presages of Muhammad's later Quranic visions. When Peter at Caesarea Philippi confesses that Jesus is the son of the living God, Jesus rebukes Peter for his idolatry. In one sermon Jesus tells the story of Adam and Eve, which concludes when Adam, "turning around, saw written above the gate, 'There is only one God and Muhammad is messenger of God.' "[84] Though this adapted portrait may strike some readers as ludicrous, its heavy-handed brush strokes call attention to unambiguous prophetic features Muslims identify in Isa ibn Maryam, the Jesus of the Quran.

Interwoven into a composite Jesus-figure, these selected Humanist and Muslim versions try to retrieve essentials believed to be missing in the canonical Gospels. Their aim is to redesign a Christ that is first more unmistakably human and vulnerable, but at the same time paradoxically more militant and single-minded — a prophet attacking every seductive religious counterfeit. I have called this composite emphasis the prophetic servant, a figure unmistakably human and activist. Reexamined alongside fantasy-critiques of this sort, the New Testament, I am convinced, has its own subtle traces of the human and prophetic, clearer now when brought into focus.

One feature that undermines the fictional plausibility of these lives, I think, is their lightweight stereotype of a true human prophet. To be human runs deeper than just the commonplace indications of sexual desire or a happy marriage. Indeed, prophets are challenged to stay human while facing the cross, the extremes of pain and death — and at that moment manage somehow to humanize the ordeals themselves. More important, to be prophetic can demand a life of moral protest so inclusive that it ranges beyond stock scenarios of trashing a polytheistic shrine or overturning the tables of money-changers in the Temple. From my own perspective, Christ led a life so pervasively countercultural that its jarring impact during his own lifetime has lost its shock value after centuries of familiarity.

Earlier in this chapter I introduced the model kenotic Christian Humanist society, responsive to the prophetic manifestos of leaders like Camilo Torres, Kenneth Kaunda, and the theologians of liberation. This kenosis or self-abandonment ideal draws upon the biblical motif of a servant Christ, someone truly of the people, a liberator as compassionate as any Buddhist bodhisattva. This Christ-image has its surest grip today on those alert to the actual political-social milieu in which he preached, the mind-sets of those he tried to free and empower, the depth and limits of his own human consciousness.

As the Suffering Servant portrayed in Deutero-Isaiah's hymns and Paul's Letter to the Philippians, Christ stands in the midst of all oppressed people and chooses freely to die with and for them at the hands of their oppressors. Too often this servant-image has been misused to force women, the poor, and the marginal into docility and resignation. "Unless you die with Jesus," such victims are cautioned piously, "you cannot reign with him. No cross, no crown. No pain, no gain." Yet each individual must learn to distinguish between passive and active suffering, between enslaved suffering under an oppressive government and self-chosen suffering for an act of dissent against such a regime. Marxists and theologians of liberation have long pointed out an axiom often overlooked. You cannot really help people and treat them with dignity if you just feed and inoculate them or dole out stop-gap loans. They have to achieve their own human liberation and social transformation.[85]

It is hard today to gauge the genuinely revolutionary impact of Christ's life and teachings. Imagine, for instance, how the first reports of Christian preaching in eighteenth-century China affected the typical Confucian sage, the sort of person Mao and his peasant revolutionaries would later scorn and persecute. Christ looks like a figure of doubtful legitimacy, oddly prone to choose his disciples from tax-collectors and fishermen, and known to dine with prostitutes and sinners. This uncouth man shows no evidence of filial piety. Not only neglecting his parents, he undermines the five Confucian hierarchical relationships in society by calling everyone his brothers and sisters. At times he even sides with women over men.[86]

"This man receives sinners and eats with them." This is one accusation that hounded Christ throughout his ministry. His oft-cited beatitudes from the Sermon on the Mount had the potential to turn accustomed social and moral distinctions in his society upside down. He promised that those denied justice would now gain it. In effect, leaders in society would have to prove by their mercy and humility their worthiness to lead. The Greeks and Romans had aesthetic criteria of their own to separate the beautiful people from chaff. To distinguish clean people from the unclean, Qumran sectarians had used the badge of ritual exactitude — the very measure adopted by Pharisee leaders, fretting to preserve the religious integrity of their people under an army of foreign occupation.

Yet Christ upset this fragile balance of social and religious priorities. He befriended foreigners such as Romans and Samaritans. And anyone could predict that this prophetic new kingdom of his would gradually open its doors to all the Gentiles. No considerations of wealth, birth, family ties, education, occupation, or physical appearance excluded a person from his following. As a prophetic activist, Christ redefined the meaning of honor and shame, the meaning of inner religious worth.[87]

Christ the prophet and servant stands at the center of Martin Luther King's vision, described in his sermon about the "drum-major instinct" preached at Ebenezer Baptist Church a few months before his assassination. The urge to be ahead, to achieve honor and reputation, a creditable ingredient in its own way, can be turned against people. You can spot the ruse of advertisers peddling a whiskey for persons of distinction or a flashy car for the envy of neighbors. Yet in a more devious way, the drum-major attitude incites snobbish churches to boast of high incomes and doctorates among their clientele. It also motivates the worst racists, stripped down to their last shreds of self-esteem, the pride of mere skin pigmentation.

Instead of materialistic success, King asks his followers to achieve loving service, transforming their legacy as enslaved servants into a self-chosen vocation to serve other people. In one simple phrase Christ once summed up his whole redemptive life, asking to be remembered as someone who came among us to serve. Genuinely to lead and win, to carry the drum major's baton, a person must take first place in love and generosity. For as Christ insists, "The greatest among you shall be your servant."[88]

"Who do you say that I am?" According to the Gospel of Mark, this is the question Christ raises near Caesarea Philippi, and I have chosen four current attempts to answer it. Favoring this or that aspect of the multifaceted Christ, most Christians basically still adhere to the balanced credal guidelines of the fifth-century Council of Chalcedon. There the church identifies Jesus Christ as one divine person in two distinct natures, human and divine. Balancing a christology from below with a christology from above, Rahner cautioned against two classical misinterpretations of the incarnate God. The first distortion he calls Jesus-ism, which views Christ as merely human. Christ is an urban guerrilla Che Guevara, a free-spirit matinee superstar, the noble Gandhian pacifist and activist servant for others, the prophetic and vulnerable Jesus-figure of the fictional lives just sampled. All this and more, but not divine.

At the other extreme, the second classical distortion worships a Christ that is just divine, not really human. Suppose that you isolate the transfigured face of Christ, the third Christ-image described above, and reduce his human reality to only a disguise or even an avatar epiphany. As a further illustration, introduced in chapter 3, the Vedanta Christ of Ramakrishna and Vivekananda implies a humanity that is sheer maya appearance. Here you can identify the ancient Docetic heresy, rejected by the early church.

The Christian imagination is challenged to ponder both the human and the divine facets of Christ separately, and only then to try balancing them in juxtaposition. First, his desolate cry in the Synoptic Gospels, "My God, my God, why have you abandoned me?" And second, his final shout of triumph in the Gospel of John, "It is achieved!"

A unique individual man named Jesus of Nazareth shed his blood on a particular few square feet of ground at an unrepeatable instant of linear time. According to the most testable historical affirmation in the ancient creeds, "he suffered under Pontius Pilate, was crucified, died, and was buried." Many viewers today may not appreciate the sentimental, overly explicit Christ-image of late Gothic and Baroque artists — an inconsolable pieta or a flayed crucified corpse. Yet this art at least confronts them with the scandal experienced by Christ's disciples right after the crucifixion, when Easter could only have seemed an improbable fantasy. In Dostoyevsky's *The Idiot,* Myshkin describes the effect of such a painting hung above the doorway in Rogozhin's room. "Why, this is a painting that might make some people lose their faith!" he exclaims. It represents Christ at the moment of removal from the cross, "a face which still retains much warmth and life. Nothing is rigid in it yet, and the suffering seems to continue in the face of the dead man as if he were still feeling it." The body is mangled and swollen from the beatings. How could the apostles and women standing there, gazing on this battered cadaver, believe it would be resurrected?[89]

Never forgetting this mortal human face of Christ, you next open the second chapter of the Letter to the Philippians, where Paul combines the Suffering Servant with a Christ transformed by resurrection: Christ "emptied himself,... and in obedience accepted even death on a cross. Because of this, God raised him up and gave him the name which is above all other names... — Lord." Thus, dying a fully human death, Christ immersed himself into the utmost suffering, darkness, and loneliness, the experience of every mortal being-unto-death. Midpoint in his rite of passage between death and resurrection, the nadir of his descent into hell transforms itself into a beginning ascent to glory, his epiphany as the transfigured cosmic Savior.

The Kaballist mystics, as recounted before, ponder implications of the Shekhinah eclipse, the night of exile. And similarly, Sufi mystics lose themselves in meditation, yearning to participate in Muhammad's night ascension into heaven. In their own distinctive way, too, Christian mystics, and also the average Christian at prayer and the sacraments, will want to share spiritually in this passage of Christ downward into death and then upward, a process which John of the Cross calls the Dark Night experience. This night is frightful and depressing because the mind's habitual functions are strained beyond their limits to grapple with unfamiliar divine light, paradoxically the deepest religious vision.

God's action upon each believer might be compared to a wise but rigorous spiritual weaning. On the one hand, at some point in spiritual development I can expect to be dropped from the arms of God and forced to walk alone. John of the Cross and other Christian mystics describe this experience as a severe wounding, loss, and burial. On the other hand, groping beyond familiar concepts and images, this abandonment proves to be just the first stage of a momentous rite of passage — a dying with Christ in order to be resurrected with Christ. What feels like painful darkness and estrangement is in fact an initiation into the incomprehensible depths of God.[90]

The Muslim credo, the *shahada* — "There is no god but Allah, and Muhammad is the Prophet of Allah" — inscribed in Tughra calligraphy by Aftab Ahmad of Pakistan for *Aramco World Magazine.*

7

The Muslim Way

Two decades ago a contingent of about twenty Muslims flew from Saudi Arabia to sign up for a few semesters of rudimentary English at the University of San Francisco. It would take them weeks to resolve the enigma of coin-operated laundromats, bus transfers, and fast food, and adapt to life in the residence halls. Once I got to know some Saudi neighbors on my floor, they persuaded me to help them find a special meeting room for *salat* group prayer five times daily, especially on Fridays.

From the start, the religious intensity of these young Sunnite Muslims left me with conflicting reactions. Touched that anyone today should care so much about God, still I was troubled by the fuss about sobriety and ritual exactitude. Some in the group, for instance, appointed themselves pleasure police, quick to reprimand their colleagues for skipping required prayers or sneaking an occasional can of beer. Some offenders told me they feared being reported back to the Saudi agency that paid their tuition and allowance. When at last allotted a mosque room by university officials, most in the group wanted it locked for their exclusive use, so that it would not be desecrated. Some asked that the call to prayer be shouted "as Allah demands," even during hours when most residents on campus were asleep. The Saudis, joined now by Muslims from Malaysia, North Africa, and Pakistan, rallied behind one unexpected single complaint — the fear of ritual defilement if forced to walk forty yards from lavatory purifications to the mosque. I tried to figure out the extent to which this excitement was triggered by clear religious law, the heady taste of cross-cultural solidarity, or a macho territorial imperative.

Then in March, the TV news suddenly reported that King Faisal of Saudi Arabia had been assassinated. That evening many Saudis gathered at my door, asking to hear the local newspaper account read aloud, followed by their own precise word-for-word translations. A tight circle formed, many of them weeping openly, anxious about their families and the fate of their country. "U.S. experts on the Middle East expect that Saudi Arabia's foreign policy will remain unchanged." Slowly enunciating these opening words, I scanned down the page, hoping to locate a single sentence of grief or compassion, no matter how trite, that did not smack of U.S. self-interest. "The new king gives every assurance of protecting U.S. business investments." The newspaper then offered a few careless observations about Muslim burial customs and the nature of Islam. But murmurs soon drowned out this myopic version of the tragedy. "To them, we're not human beings," one student groaned, "we're just oil wells and dollars."

Then the Saudi group drifted sadly toward the mosque to pray together for their dead king. For the first time I wanted to join them at common prayer. Determined from my first encounter with them to support their Muslim faith, not to win converts, I now felt my place ought to be more closely at their side. After that evening I began to attend salat at the mosque regularly, especially on Fridays. The group seemed to welcome my presence, even if I sat quietly in the rear, not taking part in the knee-drill. Though I did not understand the Arabic words, I tried to appreciate their body language and attitudes. What touched me was the symmetry in lining up and prostrating together, the energetic antiphonal prayer, the disciplined silent attention, and notably, an overwhelming sense of reverence.

THE MUSLIM CHALLENGE

This first interchange with Muslims as a large group raised a number of issues that even now I tend unwisely to forget. First and most crucial, a textbook abstraction called Islam does not confront generic Christianity, but one Christian and one Muslim at a time befriend each other. Meditating or working alongside each other, you can often form a bond of mutual respect and affection. Mere theological discussion, however, may dredge up and reinforce the old congealed misunderstandings.

Second, I can understand why many Muslims, liberated just yesterday from colonial restrictions on religious expression, or transplanted for the first time into an oasis of Christianity or secularity, would flaunt the public externals of their spiritual identity. Yet in any religious heritage the creed of some people may freeze to dogmatism, their worship to ritualism, their ethics to legalism. Literalism and one-sidedness plague every religion, but especially the scriptural Abrahamic traditions, as exemplified most clearly by some integralist neo-Catholics, Evangelical Christians, Orthodox Jews, or revivalist Muslims. Prophets arising within each tradition, almost by job description, are those chosen to smoke out such immature distortions and reaffirm the authentic Way.

Jesus and Paul denounce again and again the Pharisees' single-minded focus on the letter of religious law. And whenever Muslims mistake sheer observance for the spirit, they, too, must reclaim this central passage in the Quran: "Righteousness does not consist in whether you face toward the east or the west. The righteous are those who believe in Allah and the Last Day, . . . who for the love of Allah give their wealth to relatives, orphans, the needy, wayfarers, and beggars, and for the redemption of captives."[1]

The Sufi tradition adds color to this same prophetic reprimand. In one tale, Shibli runs through the streets with a flaming coal, shouting that he will set fire to the kaaba in Mecca. Thus, when Muslims bow toward Mecca, Shibli wants them focused not on the shrine within the Great Mosque at Mecca but on the Lord of the shrine. Attar's *Conference of the Birds* contains an anecdote about a young dervish so committed to prayer that he wonders why he has never reached spiritual perfection. The prophet Moses answers him by pointing out the hours of vanity this young man spends grooming his beard to look like that of a conventional pious Muslim. Stung by Moses' rebuke, the dervish then devotes hours to obsessive prayers of self-reproach and to the ordeal of plucking out his handsome beard, hair by hair. Appraising the whole scenario, the angel Gabriel reminds Moses that this dervish now spends even more time on his beard than before.[2]

The damaging side-effects of ritualism were brought home to me one afternoon in rural Indonesia, a nation containing the world's largest Muslim population. There on a back porch I chatted with a retired couple, members of the Dutch Reformed Church, trying to make ourselves heard over the blast from a nearby minaret. We heard not just the muezzin's summons for salat but scratchy recorded Quran readings, proclaimed over the tropical countryside for a quarter-hour at regular intervals. Conditioned by this exposure to popular Muslim habits of observance, they both admitted their Christian faith had changed over the years. By now it had cut a channel underground as a silent interior life. He and his wife were developing an aversion to all religious externals and ritual, including attendance at their own church. Perhaps in just this way, the Sufi, Hasidic, and Christian mystics through the centuries have risen in prophetic dissent against religious formalism.

The third issue raised by my experience with the Saudis was a recognition of widespread bias, not just in the milieu but also in myself. Asked to play translator between the flawed news media and these sensitive readers from a different nation and religion, I detected blind spots in my own culture and religion. Before this I had heard frequent Muslim complaints of unfair treatment from the Eurocentric secular press. Granted that the reports of King Faisal's death showed at least a bias of insular self-interest and materialism, I now began to piece together the outlines of a more pervasive anti-Muslim frame of mind. It has tainted the medieval Crusaders and Dante, then later Christians, and today the average American. In an association test, just say the word "Muslim," and my knee-jerk response today would be "terrorist," "fanatic," or "fundamentalist." My imagination is stocked with TV images of fierce, screeching faces in the Iranian Revolution, repressed Arab women anywhere veiled in black, thieves with chopped off hands in the Sudan, a Saudi princess stoned to death for adultery, and emir oil tycoons in orgies of food and sex. In contrast, revivalist Muslims have picked up no less hideous a caricature of permissive U.S. society — race riots, gang wars, porno shops, marital infidelity, and child prostitution.[3]

Mutual distorted perspectives tend to nourish each other. From their first emergence alongside Christians, Muslims could be identified only as an invasive ethnic presence — Saracens, Moors, Turks, Tartars. Later, having earned grudging recognition as a unique religious tradition, they were labeled Mohammedans, despite Muslim complaints that this name implies worship of Muhammad instead of Allah. As a Muslim student once pointed out to me, Eurocentric people, like Adam, continue to arrogate the privilege of naming all the animals, but only from their own narcissistic perspective. At the historical moment when colonial powers sorted a range of disparate nations under the single umbrella "Islam," Europe defined itself as the West. The Third World is third to the privileged First; the Middle East is east and middle to the axis of Europe and the United States. Developing and underdeveloped nations are measured according to a Eurocentric calculus of development, sanctioned by the World Bank, the International Monetary Fund, and the World Trade Organization. News media in the United States may disdain the traditional *Malay tudung,* for instance, worn by a managerial-class Muslim woman, as if this style of dress shows a fear of modernity and liberation. Yet this woman's only failing may have been to reject the miniskirt, bikini, or pants suit, all symbols of U.S. cultural domination.[4]

With the same arrogance, Christians like to describe their own civilization as Judeo-Christian. They are quick to make links to Athens, Rome, or Jerusalem, but they consistently overlook their debt to Baghdad and Cordova. In various Mexican cities an annual religious pageant is still performed in which dancers dress as Spanish and Moorish troops to reenact the historical defeat of Islam by Christian Spain. As a brutal measure to unify Spain in 1492, Ferdinand and Isabella had forced Jews and Muslims to accept Christian baptism or else leave the country. On the morning that Columbus sailed for America, the last ship of Jews expelled from Spain was leaving that same harbor, and Columbus promised to bring back enough gold to finance a final Crusade against the Muslims in Jerusalem.[5]

It is ironic that Muslims revere Jesus as a prophet, standing for social justice and nonviolence, a symbol of the spirit and not the letter. He is second in stature only to Muhammad. Yet from the Christian perspective, Muhammad is just a pseudo-prophet. And his message has seemed to spread not by its inherent spiritual worth but only by military conquest.

Getting the Last Word

It is hard to describe the Muslim tradition without reaching for an architectural metaphor. Its prophetic reassertion of belief in one God suggests empty desert vistas and transcendent space. Its finest artistic language has proved to be the mosque and minaret. And even sharia or sacred law is taught to school children today in the popular mnemonic formula of the Five Pillars. Those familiar with the notion of ethnic domain in architecture can understand how differing simulated worlds may occupy the same geographical place. In the Paleolithic Age, for instance, a mere row of upright stones might have marked off a sacred magic circle. On the same patch of ground, this arrangement of stones yielded perhaps to a later Canaanite phallic shrine, and then a Jewish temple. Similarly, Jews, Christians, and Muslims, each in a unique way, revere many of the same sacred places, prophets, and tales of creation and apocalypse.

A few years ago Jewish ultranationalist Baruch Goldstein plotted a massacre of Palestinian Muslims at Hebron on the West Bank of Israel. He chose the symbolic date of Purim, a Jewish feast coinciding that year with the Muslim sacred Friday salat during Ramadan. For an appropriate site he picked the Ibrahim Mosque, a sanctuary dedicated to the common spiritual ancestor of Jews, Christians, and Muslims. If you walk from Hebron to Jerusalem, you discover an even more obvious example of a single place overloaded with parallel but distinctive religious associations. Close to the Wailing Wall ruins of the ancient Jewish Temple stands the Byzantine Church of the Holy Sepulcher, built to memorialize the final days of Christ's fateful journey to Jerusalem. Not far from this, erected allegedly on the cornerstone of Solomon's Temple, and on the primordial site where Abraham was commanded to sacrifice his son, is the Muslim Dome of the Rock. Muhammad is believed to have come here on his visionary ride and ascension into heaven.

Jerusalem, then, is not the same Holy City for Jews, Christians, and Muslims.

Pilgrims of one creed often jostle against those of another, and one tradition's stories and prayers seem to cancel out those of another. With the same presumption shown by Christians telling Jews how to interpret Moses or Elijah in the Hebrew Bible, Muslims tell Christians the correct way to interpret Jesus and the Holy Spirit in the Christian New Testament. Yet the Muslim Ibrahim and Ismail must not be mistaken for the Abraham and Ishmael of Jewish scriptures, nor the Muslim Tawrat and Injil for the Jewish Torah and Christian Gospel, nor the Muslim prophet Isa ibn Maryam for the Christian Jesus. Every religious tradition in this common Abrahamic family has its own unique configuration. Each must be measured according to its own vision, without straining to detect causes of willful or unconscious replacement when a later prophet reinterprets an earlier one. The archaeological rubble from specific Jewish and Christian monuments, I believe, matters far less than the new Muslim edifice itself, built with inspired coherence and imagination from old remnants.

The average Muslim is distressed to page through the Jew's own Torah text or the Christian's New Testament. If Hebrew patriarchs and prophets can be portrayed as liars, murderers, and fornicators, then this disedifying text must be a corrupt version of the Mosaic original. And the scandal of four different Gospel texts — their disparities picked apart by Christian scholars today in Jesus seminars — again shows a confused transmission of Allah's transparent message. Thus, if you want to discern and obey the will of Allah, neither human reason alone nor even the combined Jewish and Christian scriptures can offer you sufficient clarity. So Muhammad was chosen in the seventh century to mediate God's final and comprehensive self-disclosure in the Quran. This revelation has the paradoxical advantage to be earlier and at the same time later than the Jewish and Christian covenants. Abraham, historically the first after Adam to receive the complete truth from Allah, lived long before God chose Moses and Jesus. He was a true Muslim before the Torah and the Gospels came into existence. This earliest revelation given to Abraham was then reaffirmed to his descendant Muhammad in the Quran. Its late arrival provides an opportunity for Muslims to learn from Jewish and Christian mistakes, and definitively to correct them.

Among Abraham's modern heirs, however, the affinities between Muslims and Christians seem less obvious than those between Muslims and Jews. From the outsider historian's perspective, strict Jewish monotheism gave rise to the Christian heresy of an incarnate God. This Christian fallacy in turn provoked a Muslim reinstatement of the original Jewish monotheism, now more militant and universalist than before. In Hegelian terms, the Muslim synthesis rises out of the Jewish thesis and Christian antithesis. The Christian label, of course, refers to an overwhelming variety of churches. Its spectrum extends from the so-called high, sacramental, iconic style of the Orthodox and Eastern churches, the Roman Catholic Church, and Anglican Church, to the low, evangelical, aniconic style of the Reformed tradition, especially Cromwell's Puritans. A Catholic church crowded with statues and candles, for instance, looks like a Hindu temple to the low-church Methodist. From the opposite viewpoint, a simple New England congregational church, stripped bare except for Bible and pulpit, looks like a Jewish synagogue or Muslim mosque to a high-church Anglican.

Yet once you place a Muslim grid over the Christian tradition, surprising new parallels shift to the foreground. Pope Innocent III, majestic twelfth-century warrior and caliph, summoning the Fifth Crusade against Saladin, presided over a Christendom that seemed almost a mirror image of the extensive Muslim empire surrounding Europe. Like their Muslim counterparts, the Crusaders treated the campaign as a jihad or holy war. Their chaplains promised that death in battle as a soldier of Christ meant the grace of martyrdom. Again, Muhammad's achievement as a religious judge and political leader finds its match later in the lawyer Calvin, his codified morality and experiments in theocratic government at Geneva, and his outrage against any intermediary intruding between oneself and God's glory. Or recall the Arians, Nestorians, and especially the early Jewish Christians, many of them alien to a Hellenized christology defined in the major Christian councils. What Rahner calls an ascending christology, the focus in these churches on Christ the prophet and human servant, veers closer to the Muslim's Isa ibn Maryam than to a descending christology, the imperial Pantocrator Christ of the basilicas.

Muslims and Jews, in contrast, despite their recent wars over the Israeli state, share bonds that few Christians can fathom. It is axiomatic that the sharpest hatred, an attitude that Freud describes as the narcissism of minor differences, occurs mostly between the closest neighbors — the Scotch and English and Irish, Tutsi and Hutu Rwandans, Serbian Orthodox and Croatian Catholics and Bosnian Muslims. Yet both Muslims and Jews share the strictest monotheism, spurning any type of incarnate God and forbidding all efforts to picture God in physical form. Their basic culture and the sacred languages of their scriptures, Arabic and Hebrew, are Semitic. Muslim and Jewish observances demand similar dietary laws, ritual purity, and the rite of circumcision. For the last century, counter to European assimilation and colonialism, both have strained to preserve their own identity as a political and religious people. And both have accepted various grudging compromises with secularism, nationalism, and socialism in building a series of modern nation-states.

All that halakha implies for a Jew, the sharia implies for a Muslim. Centered on the Law, both religious traditions seek the revealed will of God, essentially as interpreted by a line of respected legal scholars, which Muslims call the *ulama*. "Sharia" means the complete spiritual Way. Its basis is the Quran, read in two pivotal contexts. The first is Muhammad's extra-Quranic sayings, or hadith. The second context is a consensus of the worldwide believing community, or the *umma muslima*. Sharia prescriptions cover all human activities — religious belief, duties of prayer and fasting, and every foreseeable personal and juridical responsibility within a society pervasively religious.[6]

The well-meaning ecumenist tends to line up the Jewish Torah, Christian Bible, and Muslim Quran as three separate scriptures, each bearing the same authority within their respective traditions. Such an analogy is wrongheaded. For the Jewish and Christian Bible reports a revelation that happened offstage, whereas the Quran is the actual revelation itself, the uncreated Word of God, recited by Gabriel to Muhammad. The closest Christian parallel to the Quran would be God's incarnate Word, the person of Jesus Christ. Thus, through the Virgin Mary and Muhammad as crucial mediators, the Word becomes incarnated in Jesus, and the Word becomes worded in the Quran. Mary in her virginity is an immaculate vessel suitable for giving birth to the incarnate Word. And Muhammad proves himself a comparable vessel, freed by his illiteracy from secondary intellectual pollutions.[7] As to the founders of these three traditions, Christ is revered by Christians as divine, but Moses and Muhammad are viewed by all three traditions as prophets, unquestionably no more than human.

The message of their final Prophet, so Muslims teach, supersedes the message of all preceding prophets, including Moses and Jesus. Aside from other non-Muslims, then, can Jews be saved today by following their flawed Torah, and Christians their flawed New Testament? It is true that Muslim regimes in some historical periods have shown tolerance toward the idiosyncratic beliefs of so-called People of the Book. Yet Quran commentators have always debated this issue. For example, one sura says: "Believers, Jews, Sabaeans, or Christians — whoever believes in Allah and the Last Day and does what is right — shall have nothing to fear or to regret." And again, "People of the Book, you shall not be guided until you observe Torah and Gospel and that which is revealed to you from your Lord."[8]

Yet a different attitude lies behind the following sura: "He that chooses a religion other than Islam, it will not be accepted from him, and in the world to come he will be one of the lost."[9] Just as Christians vary in their readiness to extend possible salvation to the outsider, Muslims also differ among themselves, struggling to reconcile these differing suras. However, I have already pointed out a recurring universalist frame of mind, quick to uncover a true Muslim or pre-Muslim in Adam, Abraham, Moses, and Jesus. In this spirit, eventually Muslims might locate anonymous Muslims all around them.

PILGRIMAGE: THE AXIS AND THE RIM

In my bedroom I have set aside a shelf display of images and symbols from the major world religions. Just two items represent the Muslim tradition — a tiny pocket Quran in microscopic script from Iran and a thin stone disc on a chain, bearing an engraved image of the kaaba. A souvenir gift brought back from pilgrimage to Mecca, the disc is intended ideally to be worn near the heart, for there within lies the true kaaba. The great fifteenth-century poet Kabir, revered by Muslim Sufis, Hindu Bhaktas, and Sikhs, insists there is no need for pilgrimage to Mecca or Benares, nor for the guidance of gurus, nor for the words of the Quran or Puranas, if you want to reach God. "I am neither in mosque nor in temple," says God. "I am neither in kaaba nor in kailash, nor in rites and ceremonies. . . . I am here beside you." Even if Kabir's premise is conceded, still the human imagination demands at least a flicker of symbolic focus. Muslims have been given this sign in the kaaba at Mecca — an abstract compass point, a gigantic empty stone cube, as a sign of God's utter transcendence.

God speaks in the Quran: "We enjoined Abraham and Ishmael to cleanse our House for those who walk around it, for those who meditate in it, and kneel and prostrate themselves." Then Abraham and Ishmael built the kaaba and dedicated it with the prayer, "Lord, make us submissive to you. Make of our descendants a nation that will submit to you. . . . Send them, Lord, an apostle of their own who shall declare to them your revelations, instruct them in the Scriptures and wisdom, and purify them of sin."[10] This significant text shows the principal etiological story behind the Mecca kaaba. This shrine is the focus of the hajj pilgrimage, a major ritual responsibility at least once a lifetime for every Muslim capable of making the trip.

These passages describe Abraham and his son, not so much building as rebuilding. Muslims believe that Adam constructed the first kaaba on earth, patterned after an angelic kaaba in heaven, and at that time was given the sacred black stone, still revered today at a corner of the shrine. The final mention of Ishmael in the Hebrew Book of Genesis occurs after Abraham, obeying God's command, deserts Ishmael and his mother Hagar in the wilderness, both of them seeking desperately for water. "What is the matter, Hagar?...Lift the child up and hold him in your arms," God tells Hagar, as he directs her to a well full of water, "because I will make him a great nation."[11] Years later, Abraham returns to search for his adult son, according to the Muslim epilogue to this story. And digging near the Zamzam well, with mounting excitement and awe, father and son together rediscover the ruins of Adam's ancient temple, symbolic center of the earth.

The later apostle for whom Abraham and Ishmael yearn, of course, turns out to be Muhammad. In the year 630, after experiencing eight years of exile and military failure since the flight to Medina, Muhammad at last rode his camel in triumph into Mecca. With enemy clans watching in sullen helplessness, he tapped the black stone with his long camel-stick as he completed each circling, and then knocked down all 360 idols standing in the courtyard. He would not rest until all polytheistic overlay had been stripped from the original Abrahamic faith. Next he entered the massive kaaba stone cube itself and began scrubbing images off the walls, uttering the shahada prayer at each corner as an act of reconsecration: "There is no god but Allah, and Muhammad is the Prophet of Allah." Departing then for Medina, he returned again two years later, with accurate foreboding that this would be his final pilgrimage. He brought with him a young disciple on the same camel, apparently so that the boy could observe each detail of Muhammad's pilgrimage ritual. For every prayer and gesture would be devoutly reenacted by Muhammad's later disciples.

Today the empty kaaba is covered in black cloth with gold Quranic arabesques and is surrounded by the splendid Great Mosque of nineteen arched gateways. Hub of a wheel with spokes radiating throughout the earth, it is the magnetic center toward which all praying Muslims prostrate themselves five times daily and where the *mihrab* or prayer niche in every mosque is pointed. Most Muslims hope to be buried in Muslim cemeteries, where the bodies will be pointed in their graves toward Mecca. Men must dress for pilgrimage in an unstitched sheet, with one shoulder bare, a cloth that many will preserve afterward for their burial shroud. Women are expected to wear a white dress, without jewelry. Many Muslims believe that the clothes they now wear on the hajj shall be their clothing when summoned for the Final Judgment.

As pilgrims approach the city of Mecca, a sacred space restricted to Muslims only, they enter a zone of special sanctuary and consecration. This is the moment to renew their vow to abstain from sinful thoughts and actions throughout the pilgrimage, especially from harm toward any living being. After circumambulation of the kaaba, they must then confront the remaining rites — passage barefooted along the causeway stretching between tombs of Hagar and Ishmael, meditation from noon to sunset at Mount Arafat, a day at Mina on the Mecca outskirts to cast stones at three pillars, and the Id al-adha animal sacrifices on the tenth day of the month. Finally, after the optional shaving of head and beard, everyone is prompted to spend a few days in reflection and dedicated reentry, now bearing the honorary title of hajji, a green turban, or some other indication of completing the pilgrimage.

Reenacting Primordial Stories

It is possible to distinguish three overlapping religious levels that run through the entire hajj liturgy. Most important is the privileged reenactment of Abraham's original submission to God. Muslims take their name from *islam,* the act of total submission to the will of Allah. The root *slm* in words like *salaam, salem,* and *dar as salaam* connotes obedience, peace, refuge, and security. To foster the process of identification with Abraham, Mecca contains Abraham's own sacred kaaba, the precious water from Hagar's Zamzam well, and a nearby stone upon which Abraham allegedly stood to complete his task of construction. Pilgrims rush up and down the causeway to imitate Hagar's forlorn search for water. Mina is the revered place where Abraham was told to sacrifice his son, where he resisted diabolic temptations to disobey, and where he finally offered a replacement sacrifice. The Mina pillars are said to represent Abraham's devils, phallic remnants perhaps from some polytheistic temple. By stoning them in the old Semitic style of banishing evil, believers reaffirm their own jihad against contemporary idolatry. The massive communal rite of animal slaughter at Mina crowns each pilgrim's effort to recover the firm unquestioning faith of Abraham, ready even to sacrifice his son.

The famous black stone of Mecca, worn smooth by centuries of pilgrim contact, is the only surviving relic from the original kaaba. It is also a remnant that touched the lips of Muhammad. Memory of the Prophet's two final pilgrimages to Mecca adds a meaningful second nuance to the Abrahamic theme. Muslims claim not merely the unwavering monotheistic faith of the patriarchs but a faith long betrayed, now purified and reasserted in the face of rival counterfeits. Muhammad's return to Mecca gives the kaaba experience a militant neo-Abrahamic dimension.

A contemporary sheik has described his own self-questioning as he tried to interiorize the shahada credo chanted endlessly by pilgrim crowds: "When I was circumambulating the holy kaaba in Mecca, I really doubted whether I was even a true Muslim. What was I doing here? And at the time, I thought that feeling was a horrible experience to have. But then I realized it was a great blessing, because in the hajj everything was stripped away."[12] Many pilgrims insist on walking the final fifty miles from the Jidda airport or seaport to Mecca. Why must they walk? Perhaps some hesitate to pay the bus fare, yet others must fulfill a private vow. Though the exact means of Muhammad's entry is disputed, these pilgrims want to enter the Holy City on foot in humility. Centuries before, the conquering prophet himself, renouncing every trace of *shirk* or idolatry, must have entered just like this.[13]

On his final pilgrimage, Muhammad went to Mount Arafat and preached a weary farewell sermon — an event now commemorated on the ninth day in the month reserved for hajj. At sundown he fell into ecstasy and received one of his last divine revelations. Muslims today stand meditating in prolonged silence at this spot and then retrace Muhammad's footsteps as they complete the remaining pilgrimage rituals, including a recommended visit to his tomb at Medina. The night before the ninth day, many Muslims camp out in thousands of tents on the plain of Arafat, an experience that can transport contemporary urban Muslims back to the simple nomadic origins of the first umma muslima.

Besides the Abraham and Muhammad dimensions, then, the umma or pan-Islamic believing community constitutes a third religious dimension of the pilgrimage. The badge of hajji identity often serves as a prerequisite among candidates for Muslim leadership back home. It is not surprising, then, to meet strong uniformity of doctrine, ritual, and even architectural style flowing consistently from the Mecca source to the farthest Muslim outreaches. Two weeks of intensive religious renewal, the precisely monitored public liturgies, the sermons, the conversations with pilgrims from other nations — these experiences are transmitted by each pilgrim back home to help tighten a worldwide Muslim consensus. Pilgrimage to Mecca celebrates not only the origins and heroic continuity of Muslim history but also Muslims' present diversity and unity as a group, especially at the culminating Id al-adha sacrifice. For this feast day is celebrated in solidarity with all pilgrims at that moment by Muslim households throughout the world. A Yemeni Muslim has told me of yet another way the hajj strengthens solidarity. More vigorous travelers may offer to perform the hajj in place of a sick or working relative. My friend hopes someday, for instance, to make the pilgrimage in honor of his dead mother, hindered by ill health from completing her hajj obligation while still alive.

Malcolm X's autobiography gives a poignant account of his own umma experience that canceled out his Black Muslim racism of previous years. Malcolm's anger had long focused on Christians, the blue-eyed devils of white America, slave names, "house Negroes," and the violated taboo against pork chops. However, on a hajj shortly before his assassination, he discovered that "during the past eleven days here in the Muslim world, I have eaten from the same plate, drunk from the same glass, and slept in the same bed (or on the same rug) — while praying to the same God — with fellow Muslims, whose eyes were the bluest of blue, whose hair was the blondest of blond, and whose skin was the whitest of white. And in the words and deeds of the white Muslims, I felt the same sincerity that I felt among the black African Muslims of Nigeria, Sudan, and Ghana."[14] Perhaps belief in the one God could remove the vicious "whiteness" from everyone's attitudes and behavior.

According to various hadith accounts, Muhammad in his farewell address actually emphasized this crucial antiracist premise: "All of you stem from Adam, and Adam stemmed from dust. Know that no Arab has any priority over a non-Arab, a non-Arab over an Arab, a white person over a black person, a black person over a white person, except in the degree of righteousness."[15] These words sum up the Muslim ideal, even though individual Muslims complain of persistent abuses within their own societies. It is not easy to root out the myth of Arab supremacy, for example, and the subtle color discriminations pervading African and Indian folklore, long before the accentuation of this distortion by racist colonial powers.

Recently, Idris Diaz, a black Hispanic-American Muslim journalist, tells of lively breakfast conversations at various pilgrimage sites during his own eleven days at Mecca. People from various nations would argue each morning over details of how to reach a particular sacred spot at the required time. "Look, I'm here for my hajj," he would say. "I'm going to do in good faith whatever you tell me, and I'm going to hope Allah accepts it. But I'm not going to sit here and argue over these fine points." He could not stomach the recurring diatribes against Jews. "It was a Jewish guy who footed the bill for my hajj," Diaz would remind his new companions. "How can I have any problem with Jews? There are good people of every faith — in fact, isn't that what the Quran teaches?"[16]

Muslims at the Boundary

As pilgrims to Mecca, Muslims journey "to the Center, to the house of God," says Muslim theologian Seyyed Nasr. They perform the hajj to do penance and seek forgiveness for sins. In returning home, they are expected now to live devout lives. They bring "the purity and grace — or barakah — of the house of God with them. Something of the Center is thus disseminated in the periphery . . . to unify the Muslim community and spread the purity which lies at its heart to the limbs and organs."[17] Counter to this focus on the Center represented by the hajj, a number of divergent and often recusant forces are active around the perimeter of the Muslim world. To overlook these counterforces would be to mistake a bland uniform stereotype for the kaleidoscopic Muslim reality.

Perhaps the first reason these counterforces survive is the relatively meager festival life decreed by official Muslim calendars. Only the tenth day of hajj and the joyous conclusion of the Ramadan fast are mandatory traditions. Perhaps Muhammad did not want to risk idolatrous abuse in any attempt to Islamize prevalent folk customs. Yet those unable to put up with his austerity have managed ever since to smuggle in various local feasts. Examples would include *nawruz* or the Persian New Year, which is the spring fertility festival of ancient Egypt, and the various *mawlids* or birth and death dates of regional prophets and saints, especially the feast of Muhammad himself.

A further reason behind this creative diversity is the widespread reaction against tasteless hajj distortions. Recent Muslim reformers in Southeast Asia, for instance, acknowledge with distress that most of the poor cannot afford the pilgrimage to Mecca. Some pilgrims will mortgage or auction essential family property and squander most of the funds on a single Mecca junket, then return claiming their local community should support and fawn over them. In a few tourist offices of Singapore, Malaysia, and Indonesia, I have noticed vigorous hajj advertising campaigns. Travel agencies sometimes even offer commissions to respected local hajjis for enlisting new candidates. Many pilgrims return home expecting to enjoy a life of contemplative withdrawal, perhaps to preside at most local religious events, but no longer to do physical labor. Maybe they are hoping unconsciously to emulate their Buddhist monastic neighbors, accustomed to have lay devotees fill their begging bowls.[18]

Both the Quran and hadith, on the contrary, demand egalitarianism, with no room for social discrepancies, inflated titles, or a priestly caste of freeloaders. Elsewhere in the Muslim world, too, complaints recur against Wahabi purist control of the Mecca holy places. This particular school of observance has left its historical mark on Saudi Muslim spirituality. Guides appointed to ensure that visitors correctly perform the hajj rites seem at times to impose rigid Wahabi orthodoxy or a current Saudi version of Arab nationalism. To avoid any hint of idolatry toward Muhammad, for example, pilgrims are not allowed to prostrate themselves at the Medina tomb of Muhammad at conclusion of the hajj. In the early nineteenth century, Wahabi reformers destroyed the shrines of Shiite saints in the holy city of Kerbala, Iraq. That outbreak of religious iconoclasm may have had its commercial angle, too. At various times in Muslim history, pilgrim detours to regional shrines in Iraq, Iran, and North Africa have threatened to tap the flow of wealth to Mecca.[19]

The most important reason for Muslim religious disparities today is the bitter historical schism that surfaced within two decades after Muhammad's death. Shiite Muslims quarreled with Sunnite Muslims over the nature and leadership of the umma. The Sunnite majority today attribute infallible authority to the consensus hammered out by the first Muslim generation, for Muhammad in one hadith promised, "My community will never agree in error." They back the line of caliphs elected by the umma as legitimate leaders. Yet a movement of political-religious dissent — which was to become the Shiites — had gradually taken shape by the time of Ali, Muhammad's cousin and son-in-law, the fourth caliph. New non-Arab converts resented the Arab nepotism shown by previous caliphs. More important, religious idealists yearned for a charismatic moral leader like Muhammad, rather than some decadent political dynasty in Medina or Damascus like that of any non-Muslim nation. Holiness could be located more plausibly in Muhammad's nearest companions or his own blood descendants. With their religious leadership no longer centered on God but on a remote caliphate and worldly success, Muslim dissenters replaced this loss with an enthusiasm for Sufi shrines, prominent local gurus, and apocalyptic saviors.

Thus, refusing to endorse a debased majority sunna or tradition, the Shiites developed their own apocalyptic version of a pure, authentic sunna. Shiites make up almost one-fifth of the umma today — concentrated in Iran, with substantial minorities spread through Iraq, Turkey, Lebanon, the small Gulf nations, Afghanistan, Pakistan, India, the former Soviet Union, and many parts of Africa. They believe the true sunna has been transmitted underground through a succession of holy Imams, who alone possess the gift of infallible spiritual authority. This sequence extends from Muhammad to Ali to Husayn and then to their brief line of descendants, the last of which disappeared. This Hidden Imam will return someday as the messianic liberator or Mahdi. "Perhaps the most outstanding feature of Shiism," says Iranian political scientist Hamid Enayat, "is an attitude of mind that refuses to admit majority opinion is necessarily true or right." This mind-set offers "a rationalized defense for the moral excellence of an embattled minority."[20]

Shiites have earned notoriety throughout Muslim history for their doctrine of *taquiyyah* or expedient dissimulation, a controversial tactic of survival familiar to many persecuted minorities. Into your public consent to any civil or religious law, for example, you insert a subversive proviso. You demand that every law must conform to the will of the Hidden Imam. Consent can be withdrawn suddenly, rationalized by an appeal to this elusive spiritual authority. Thus, Shiites have been distrusted for taquiyyah, while at the same time respected for the spiritual teaching of their mystics, an esoteric tradition kept secret from the prying gaze of the uninitiated.

If the centralized majority tradition is best typified by the hajj, then the peripheral minority can be symbolized most vividly by the Shiite Muharram liturgy. The tragic defeat of the House of Ali, especially the martyrdom of his son Imam Husayn, has always touched deepest Muslim feelings in Iran, Iraq, Pakistan, and India. At the battle of Kerbala in Iraq, Husayn contested the claims of Yazid to the caliphate, and after witnessing the thirst, starvation, and slaughter of his besieged troops and family, one by one, he was cruelly stoned to death and decapitated. This catastrophe is immortalized in Husayn's shrine at Kerbala, a renowned center of pilgrimage, and in the famous *taziyah* or passion play.

Muharram rites extend for ten days, from New Year's Day to Ashura, a span similar to the Jewish High Holy Days that culminate in Asor or Yom Kippur, the Day of Atonement. Ashura combines Yom Kippur communal repentance with overtones of mourning the old year's death, consecrating the new. In Muslim Northwest Africa, this day is associated with sacred bonfires, derived from Primal agrarian rites, and with memorial liturgies for the dead. These overlapping motifs lie beneath the Shiite Ashura reenactment of Husayn's martyrdom, with its fierce outpouring of grief. Not just the lives of individual Muslims, but official chronicles of Muslim history, demonstrate that the umma has fallen short of what God expected it to be. The people cry to Allah in repentance and for retribution, for return of the Imam-Mahdi, for a restoration of Muhammad's idealized reign over his first community at Medina.

During Shiite Muharram rites, cafés and places of public entertainment close down in many cities, and black flags appear everywhere. Pilgrims travel far to reach the major shrines at Kerbala, Kazimayn, and Nejev, or else gather around local replicas of the Kerbala shrine. The media restrict themselves mostly to Quran readings and other explicit religious programs. Many people endure strict fasts, wear mourning garments, and do not shave. Though local adaptations vary widely, the taziyah usually occurs in two situations, at home or in public. In more intimate versions, women and children enact or give a dramatic reading of the long epic at family gatherings, the narrators at times moving from home to home.

A recent Muharram celebration at the Zainabiyyah Hall in Toronto, for instance, a gathering composed mostly of immigrant families from Pakistan and India, devoted each of the ten Muharram days to a different martyr among Husayn's companions. The battle of Kerbala was treated as a family tragedy, in which both men and women played a heroic role. Sermons centered in turn on the model behavior for a son, bride, uncle, or grandmother, all of them interacting within an ideal Muslim family. Children watched the effect of these mourning rites not on distant performers but on those nearby they respected and loved. One Shiite described how he attended Muharram as a young child and observed his father weeping. The boy would later pretend to cry in order to imitate his father, but now weeps automatically each time he ponders the implications of Husayn's martyrdom.[21]

At large-scale outdoor passion plays, in contrast, men assemble in streets for a graphic drama and procession. The pageant demonstrates Husayn's personal faith, his motives for rebellion, the unequal battles between soldiers on horseback at Kerbala, his last exchange with each of his dying family, and finally the gory head displayed before his grieving followers. Crowds witness a somber parade of huge funeral floats and a symbolic burial of Husayn's coffin. Many individual families construct their own papier-mâché coffin and cremate it in a ritual bonfire or bury it. Though the practice has been outlawed periodically, a number of zealots each year will goad themselves into a frenzy of self-mutilation with whips or swords, in order to identify with Husayn's passion and death. These graphic penances have been replaced in many South Asian and North American communities by generous blood donations to blood banks. Muslims in the streets and at home sob openly, striking their breast or head, keening in a rhythmic cadence, "Ya Ali, Ai Husayn, Husayn Shah!"[22]

Some versions of the taziyah epic reach far beyond Husayn's lifetime to portray scenes from the wider sweep of Muslim salvation-history. In one early episode, for example, the angel Gabriel visits the Hebrew patriarch Jacob, inconsolable over the loss of his son Joseph, and introduces an angel troupe to perform an instant preview of Husayn's martyrdom centuries later. Jacob gains new perspective on his own suffering, compared with the enormity of Husayn's. Or some lamentations by Husayn at Kerbala turn into broad apocalyptic forecasts of injustice, perhaps within more recent eras: "They are going to kill me mercilessly, for no other crime or guilt than that I happen to be a prophet's grandson.... All are gone! In this land of trials there is no one compassionate enough to befriend and protect the household of the Apostle of God."

One version of the passion play concludes with a remark by an anonymous elderly Muslim, as the bleeding head of Husayn is paraded past him, "On those lips have I seen the lips of the Apostle of Allah!" The epilogue to another version has proven singularly offensive to Sunnite orthodoxy. After Husayn's death, Muhammad at Allah's command entrusts Husayn with the key to paradise, lifting him to such dizzy heights that he becomes exclusive mediator for all humankind: "Deliver from the flames of hell everyone who has shed a single tear for you, ... achieved a pilgrimage to your shrine, or composed tragic verse for you. Bear everyone with you to paradise!"

Muslim history abounds with tales of conquest and glory, and at times seems to lean on the simplistic Jewish Deuteronomist premise that armies loyal to God cannot lose battles. Experiences like the Shiite Muharram contribute a crucial Job-like tragic demurral to Muslim triumphalism. Husayn's martyrdom recalls the easily overlooked years of desolate misunderstanding in Muhammad's earlier life. Perhaps at times even Muhammad could not fathom why God should decree a decade of military defeats at Medina. Ritual participation in the Husayn event is a pledge of readiness someday to die Husayn's kind of death in the midst of a hostile world, the death of a courageous Muslim witness to the faith. At the same time, it carries each believer back to the religious wellspring of the Shiite community's existence.

Wahabi purists and the Muslim majority stand far removed from popular Shiite piety, especially the near-deification of Muhammad and Husayn in these rites. The average Sunnite relishes the famous Sufi satire about a caretaker of some local shrine whose son, Nasruddin, sets off to travel around the world on his donkey. When the animal dies in the rarefied mountain air of Kashmir, the boy drops down heartbroken in quiet meditation, after raising a mound over the grave. Pilgrims crossing the steep trails eventually generate a myth of the Silent Mourning Dervish. They conclude that the relics must have been remarkably holy to evoke so much devotion. Soon a rich man builds a dome over the grave, and others begin to add it to their list of pilgrim centers. When Nasruddin's father arrives to investigate this rival shrine, he confesses to his son that their family shrine had also been erected many years before over a similar donkey grave.[23]

In an attempt to mediate between Sunnite and Shiite traditions, the Pakistani statesman and poet Muhammad Iqbal finds an unexpected symbolism in the kaaba itself: "Its end is Husayn, its beginning Ishmael."[24] In other words, the Muslim epic begins and ends in sacrificial desolation. According to Muslim belief, Ishmael, who rebuilds the kaaba, is the son offered as a bloody sacrifice by Abraham in surrender to God. At the end of this story stands the martyrdom of Husayn, Muhammad's grandson. With his death at Kerbala, the ideal political-religious regime of the early umma muslima comes to an end, overthrown by a political regime that has been religiously discredited.

THE RELIGIOUS-CIVIL IDEAL

Writing in the mid-1930s, Iqbal found a meaningful contrast between the sacred pilgrimage to Mecca and the secular pilgrimage of ambassadors to the League of Nations at Geneva. According to Iqbal, both Mecca and the league claimed the intention of uniting people, but the motto of the Eurocentric league proved to be "Divide and conquer," a policy imposed most destructively by the British upon their Muslim colonial subjects. The kaaba, on the contrary, stands for the Muslim ideal of a single pan-Islamic religious-political unity. Counter to the polytheistic idols that prevailed before Muhammad's purification of Mecca, the kaaba now symbolizes God's unity and also the unity of all humanity.[25]

Two decades after Iqbal's assessment, Egyptian President Gamal Nasser concluded his autobiography, *Egypt's Liberation: The Philosophy of the Revolution,* with a more politicized vision of the hajj: "I stood before the kaaba, and in my mind's eye I saw all the regions of the world which Islam has reached. Then I found myself saying that our view of the hajj must change. It should not be regarded as only a ticket of admission into paradise after a long life, or as a means of buying forgiveness after a merry one. It should become an institution of great political power and significance,...a periodic political conference in which the envoys of the Islamic states...lay down in this Islamic world-parliament the broad lines of their national policies and their pledges of mutual cooperation from one year to another." A few years after this statement, King Faisal of Saudi Arabia and the Shah of Iran proposed a similar Muslim World League at Mecca. Nasser by this time, however, could not accept what he judged its reactionary agenda. By including non-Arabs and stressing pan-Islamic unity, such an international summit, he thought, might undermine his own pan-Arab campaign against Israel.[26]

In chapter 4, I discussed the search by the postcolonial regimes in Burma and Sri Lanka for fresh legitimation. Both new nations have tried to harness liberated centrifugal ethnic forces under the banner of common Buddhist teaching, indigenous folk history, and the ideology of socialism. Chapter 5 outlined the imaginative modern efforts to retain a Jewish religious and cultural identity, once ghetto life opened wide to the European Jewish Emancipation. Chapter 6 mentioned the dilemma faced by any dissenter within a society pervasively Christian — those in power have preempted the very Christian symbols cited to justify revolt by those not in power. Muslims have had to confront situations comparable to these, so it will be useful to recall the many parallels.

It is almost impossible to keep pace with the diversity and unpredictable growth of the many new nation-states invoking traditional Muslim values and symbols. Instead of the bodhisattva Maitreya's return, U Nu's Wishing Tree millennium, or Gandhi's Rama-raj utopia, Muslim political leaders commonly imagine a restored golden age of the first four caliphs or an apocalypse of the Mahdi or Hidden Imam. Islam has many political languages, and the Islam to which rulers and dominant elites appeal is not the Islam of the masses or the Islam of revolutionaries.[27] Muslims in power and also those dissenting against them often label their cause a classical jihad. And many of them invoke the same Quran passages, but with conflicting interpretations.

Measuring a Muslim Revival

Ever since Egypt's defeat by Israel in 1967 and the Arab oil boom in 1973, many books have surfaced in Europe and the United States examining the threat of an Islamic resurgence, reassertion, or revival. Two distortions, I think, undermine much of this otherwise well-researched social analysis. First, the Muslim resurgence has long been in progress, and in recent decades Eurocentric interests have simply shifted the phenomenon from an unnoticed back-page column to the front pages. The creation of Pakistan as a separate nation, for instance, the Algerian Revolution, Nasser's execution of Muhammad Qutb and others in the Muslim Brotherhood, and the increasing influence gained by the Ayatollah Khomeini during his exile — all these events show that Muslim aspirations had been active before the Arabs' renewed assertion of bargaining power. The Islamic historical process is more complex and longstanding than the outsider's limited awareness of it.[28]

Second, minds accustomed to a secular, constitutional government, and the tidy separation of religion from other areas of life, tend to impose their own limited categories on the comprehensive Muslim sharia already described. They seem unable or unwilling to appreciate that Islam is not just a creed but also a community and civilization, an integral way of life. They tend to treat it as a mere ideology of legitimation, a rationale serving the political Right or Left, and isolated from vital economic and cultural forces.

In 1996 I came across a graphic example of this perspective. A *New York Times* editorial deplored Necmettin Erbekan's ascendancy at that time, with only 20 percent of the vote, from head of the Welfare Party to prime minister of Turkey. Worried about Erbekan's "Islamist," anti-Zionist, anti-Western views, the article urges support not for Erbekan and his shaky coalition government but for Turkey's military, "which sees itself as the guardian of Turkey's secular pro-western course." According to historical record, since the founding of the modern republic in 1923 by Ataturk, the Turkish army, wary of Islamic revivals, has been forced periodically to intervene in defense of Ataturk's secular Constitution. The editorial writer, a Middle East policy specialist, denounces a reckless new White House admission that "secularism is not a condition for American-Turkish relations."[29]

Classical Arabic lacks terms to express a dichotomy between the secular and the religious or between church and state, probably because the culture has always treated religious and political authority as indistinguishable. Recognizing this premise, one has to respect a complaint expressed by Khomeini at least a decade before the Iranian

Revolution. So-called Orientalists and even *Time* magazine versions of Islam, he said, mirror back to Muslims a pastoral, quiescent, and otherworldly image of themselves. Such an image then so enervates them that they permit Western imperialists to loot Muslim resources and productivity. "The propaganda institutions of imperialism have sought to persuade us that religion must be separate from politics, that the religious leaders must not interfere in social matters." This perspective reinforces a religious leadership "who do nothing but discuss points of law and offer their prayers, and are incapable of anything else."[30]

"Do not keep silent," Khomeini warns the ulama, "at a time when Islam is being wiped out, like the Christians who sat discussing the Holy Ghost and the Trinity until they were destroyed. Wake up! Pay some attention to reality and the questions of the day." The naive U.S. press, with its own tradition of church-state separation, would continue to scold clerics like Khomeini for meddling in politics. But wasn't Muhammad political? "Under his leadership, a free, vital, virtuous society came into being and won fame. Everyone had to bow before its might, even the enemy. But why should anyone bow before you, whose only activity is offering opinions on points of law?"[31]

Muhammad has been rightly called his own Constantine or Charlemagne. By contrast, early underground Christian sects, a politically inactive minority, took three centuries to develop into the sole established church under Justinian. Buddhists or Christians have never been identified as a people in the way Jews call themselves a chosen people or Muslims refer to themselves as the umma. Chapter 5 described the hope of many ultra-Orthodox Israeli Jews to incorporate the halakha into constitutional law in modern Israel. In a similar way, Muslim traditionalists — by Constitution in Pakistan and Iran, for example, or by gradual parliamentary pressures in Malaysia — have tried to get sharia recognized as the law of the land. After the humiliations suffered under colonialism and a European system of education, Muslim reformers in various nations for the past century have been trying to eliminate vestiges of the political status quo and replace it with a revolutionary Islamic ideal.

To suggest the wide range of modern Muslim political alternatives, I shall examine both poles of the spectrum. First, a more secularized and nationalist government, close to the Eurocentric model — the Turkey of Ataturk. And second, an emergent revolutionary regime more Islamic and neotraditionalist, the Iran of Khomeini.

The Secular Limit

November 1, 1922, is a pivotal moment in the history of modern Turkey. Mustafa Kemal, later to choose the surname Ataturk, abolished the sultanate. It must be remembered that Muhammad's successor, the caliph, was elected by Muhammad's closest disciples to lead the entire umma muslima. By the early sixteenth century, however, the Ottoman sultan had incorporated the role of caliph and sultan into a single office, ruling over much of present-day North Africa, the Middle East, and the Balkans. European conquest and nationalist wars for independence had gradually eroded this sprawling empire, so that its military defeat in the First World War left it ripe for dismemberment. Though mosque and state should be two faces of a single leadership according to Muslim theory, the Ottoman Turks in practice treated

Islam as a separate sphere of authority. Whereas the nation-state took responsibility for military and economic affairs, ulama clerics had control over social relationships in the family, courts, and schools. A series of reforms had been shrinking this religious sphere of administration, as more areas of social life were affected by secular legislation. After eventual military defeat and economic chaos, the secular authority lost credibility, and with it the worldly authority of the sultanate.

To his worldwide Muslim audience Ataturk pronounced the ruined sultanate a victory for Islam and the traditional caliphate. Though the Ottoman caliphate had long proved irrelevant for many non-Arabs, Muslim leaders throughout the world were now showing pride at its restoration as an independent religious presence in modern Turkey. In a comparable situation, a number of Catholics had celebrated the Pope's loss of his temporal authority, the Papal States, in 1870. For now the Papacy could more clearly exercise spiritual leadership over an international community, with headquarters in Rome. Mussolini's Concordat with the Vatican in 1929 granted it only a sliver of territory, just enough for legal autonomy.[32] For a few years Ataturk had been searching for radical precedents in Muslim history. He would often stop in local mosques, take part in Friday salat, and preach a sermon in the pulpit on his new plans for a purified Islam that was genuinely Turkish. "It was by force that the sons of Osman seized the sovereignty and sultanate of the Turkish nation," he announced to the Assembly, which included powerful ulama members. "They have maintained this usurpation for six centuries. Now the Turkish nation has rebelled and put a stop to these usurpers."[33]

Once Britain and France recognized the sovereignty of his new Republic, Ataturk for some months gave an impression of patient but futile attempts to collaborate with the new surviving caliphate. However, in 1924 he demanded its dismantling, for once deprived of political relevance, was there anything left of the caliph to maintain? Ataturk was anxious to "cut out this tumor of the middle ages," as he put it. "It is necessary to liberate and to elevate the Islamic religion...from its position of being a tool of politics, in the way that has been traditional for centuries." Intent not just to reduce but to wipe out traditional religious authority, he now made a series of lightning moves. In one month after another, the state took over mosque property, shut down dervish religious orders and religious schools, and disbanded the Ministry of Religious Affairs. People could not wear clerical garb or the fez in public. Instead of the sacrosanct Arabic alphabet, they must now use the Roman alphabet. The sharia gave way to new codes of law imported from Europe, so that Muslim customs no longer governed social relationships in the family. Women could now vote, for instance, and husbands lost the unilateral right to divorce. Even worship was transferred from Friday to Sunday.[34]

How can one account for the immediate acceptance of so many radical changes? First of all, the Turks felt pride in a new nationalist regime built by a charismatic war hero. This government rose from the ashes of a demoralized non-Turkish empire. People felt, too, a sense of great urgency. If Turks did not modernize their institutions quickly to match the allegedly superior technology and education of Europe, they were likely to be swallowed up by military or economic colonialism. Ataturk's self-assured dominance satisfied those accustomed to the monarchical style of sultan or ulama, while his intelligence and professionalism satisfied critics of an inept and decadent old regime. He had the backing of an extensive European-educated elite, and also of the many women whose rights and position he had revolutionized.

Examined in their totality, Ataturk's seemingly piecemeal reforms followed a shrewd logic. Their impact widened cumulatively from laws concerning the remote bureaucracy to those that touched the ordinary person where it mattered. A 1923 amendment added to the Constitution of 1921 guaranteed that "the religion of the Turkish state is Islam." Yet by 1928 this article was dropped from the constitution. Most likely such a separation between mosque and state had been Ataturk's secret target from the beginning. Because he has left behind little indication of his developing mind, you cannot determine whether his alienation from traditional Islam intensified over the years or had hardened early, remaining hidden for political reasons. His biography, however, does yield evidence of early disaffection. Ataturk could never stomach his mother's exaggerated Muslim piety, but he relished his father's liberal, anticlerical bias. Obeying her plans that he attend a religious school to be trained as a Quran lector or teacher, he made himself so intractable that school authorities delighted when he left for the military academy of his daydreams.

Two early encounters with Muslim extremists affected him deeply. At the age of sixteen, Ataturk and a friend happened upon a group of sheikhs and dervishes at a railway station in Salonika. Dressed in long conical hats and billowing robes, these figures churned up the crowd by their drums and flutes, so that people began to shriek and faint from hysteria. Both young observers reacted with disgust, shamed by the way foreigners must view this Turkish freak show. Later in his life Ataturk would call religious fanaticism "a poisonous dagger which is directed at the heart of my people."[35]

In another incident, sent on a mission to Damascus during his young adulthood, Ataturk for the first time experienced a traditional Arab city, almost untouched by cosmopolitan life. After dark it was a city of the dead, with no night diversions. One evening he tracked down the source of unexpected mandolin music floating from a café, only to discover it came from a group of migrant Italian railway workers, singing and dancing with women of their own families. Retreating to quarters, he exchanged his officer's uniform for European-style clothes before returning to share in their uninhibited enjoyment. Perhaps the real enemy of Turkey was not European colonialism, he reflected, but Turkey's own Muslim-sanctioned culture of repression and hypocrisy. The Ottoman Empire, he once remarked, had become a place that reserves the torments of hell for Muslims, the joys of heaven only for non-Muslim residents and tourists.[36]

Ataturk's favorite poet, Namik Kemal, once wrote: "Death passes over us in a minute, but traditions are eternal. They aim at the way one sits, walks, reads, cuts one's beard.... The traditions have reached such a point that a man cannot be in command of his own beard, not to mention his family." According to Ataturk, no modern Turk could be free until stripped of this oppressive Muslim folk culture, centered in the local mosque and café, manipulative especially in the smaller towns. To replace this tyranny, Ataturk could offer only a blend of Turkish nationalism and a secular regime modeled on successive constitutions of the French Republic and the writings of Rousseau, Durkheim, but especially Comte, the father of positivism. "For everything in the world, for civilization, for life, for success, the most important factor is science," Ataturk affirms repeatedly.[37] Comte, Freud, and other modernists outlined the progress of civilization from a childhood of religious animism through philosophical adolescence to the utopian adulthood of modern science.

One refrain keeps recurring in Ataturk's various speeches for reform, a disdain for religion as a childish phase of human evolution. A people "come of age" do not need dervishes or sheikhs, he says, any more than they need fortune-tellers or witch doctors. This same Comtean premise goes unchallenged by Jamal al-Din al-Afgani, writing a few generations before Ataturk's reforms. Revered today by many neotraditionalists as the comprehensive Muslim revolutionary, the much-traveled al-Afgani wrote his famous *Reply to Renan* in 1883. There he makes the shocking concession that Muslim history begins in antiscientific superstition, then must still struggle through a phase of Quranic dogmatism before it can evolve toward an age of scientific reason. "Muslim society has not yet freed itself from the tutelage of religion," Afgani says. "Yoked like an ox to the plow, to the dogma whose slaves they are, Muslims must walk eternally in the same furrow that has been traced for them in advance by the interpreters of the law.... What would be the benefit of seeking truth when they believe they possess it all?"[38]

As Ataturk himself saw it, Turks could not be truly civilized until they learned to dress like European grown-ups. "Boots or shoes on our feet, trousers on our legs, shirt and tie, jacket and waistcoat — and of course, to complete these, a cover with a brim on our heads."[39] In a comparable way, the Meiji restoration in Japan decades before had enforced a code of Eurocentric dress as the symbol of profound social change. For Ataturk, borrowing a presupposition that looked self-evident to many in his milieu, civilization means a blueprint of twentieth-century Eurocentric modernism. Reason means submitting all religious experience to the strict reductivist measure of the experimental scientific method. The Eurocentric secular nation-state today, of course, means the right to a private religion, to a free interior commitment, much like the scenario implied in the U.S. Constitution. But for Ataturk such a society requires a separation of mosque and state in the style of militant secularism fashionable during the French Third Republic, an anticlerical animus against specific religious institutions and public symbols.

Ataturk strained impatiently to lift his people from their religious stupor. If asked in his later years whether he still considered himself a Muslim, he would probably have replied that faith must be rational, and Islam can be accepted to the extent that it does not contradict reason and science. However, by the time of his death in 1938, he no longer gave any indication of Muslim observance. "Throughout history the Turk has respected all beliefs cherished as sacred," Ataturk said. "The Turk's religion is neither this nor that particular religion."[40]

Yet in hindsight now, it appears that Ataturk's secular revolution scarcely touched people outside the urban centers. And its fatal aftermath was to drive underground a vital Muslim dimension of Turkish life, forbidden for at least a generation to reveal its face in public. After the Second World War, in a new climate of human rights, the Democratic Party rose in opposition to Ataturk's Republican People's Party, and part of its platform consisted of attempts to reinstate this suppressed religious dimension. Once in power during the 1950s, the Democrats introduced required classes in religion for all Muslim children, established special schools for Muslim clerics, and built about fifteen thousand new mosques. Eventually the new Constitution of 1960 tried to tone down Ataturk's virulent secularism. First, defining Turkey as a secular nation-state, it ruled out any attempt to base "the fundamental social, economic, political and legal order of the state on religious dogmas." Then in careful balance, listing a Turk's essential human rights, it promised that "every individual is entitled to follow freely the dictates of one's conscience, to choose one's own religious faith."[41]

After 1960, periodic military coups have erupted to deter alleged religious fanaticism or coercion and to restore the principle of constitutional secularity. However, it is significant that the text cited in each coup is not Ataturk's original 1923 Constitution, but the Constitution of 1960, which maintains a more just and open secular basis for government. During Ataturk's administration, Hagia Sophia in Istanbul, built first as the mother church of Christian Orthodoxy, adopted later as a central mosque for the Ottoman Empire, was transformed at last into a secular museum. Yet in 1996, speaking for an increasing number of Muslims, Prime Minister Erbekan prayed openly that Hagia Sophia might be reinstated someday as a mosque. His shaky coalition government would last for just twelve months.

The Islamic Limit

The high noon of Turkish secularity has been idealized in more recent decades by various reformers, many of them even more resentful than Ataturk toward their Muslim past. An official Syrian army magazine in 1967, for instance, featured an article by one young officer proclaiming the advent of the "new Arab Socialist, who believes that God, religion, feudalism, capitalism, and all the values which prevailed in the pre-existing society were no more than mummies in the museums of history." This new pan-Arabic credo relies not on heaven or hell "but only on yourself and your own contribution to humanity.... We have no need of people who kneel and beg for grace and pity." Reactions by religious and civil authorities to this manifesto were decisive and punitive. Radio Damascus repudiated the article immediately as an American-Zionist conspiracy against Islam. Police confiscated all copies of the edition. And courts sentenced both the author and editors to life imprisonment.[42]

In Egypt, by contrast, the socialist regime of Nasser managed to engineer drastic secular reforms while retaining a semblance of Muslim continuity. Intent to hover near the Soviet orbit without formal alignment, Nasser would often cite Muhammad as the first socialist. Yet as early as 1954, sharia courts and statutes were replaced by a uniform secular legal system applied to all Egyptians, no matter what their religion. Ulama clerics became a salaried branch of the civil service. Even Friday sermons consisted of an official text composed by the government and read by a cleric at each mosque.

Throughout these innovations, however, Nasser took pains to show himself an observant Muslim, and he guaranteed that each step of his revolution would be sanctioned by ulama leaders at al-Azhar, the famous Cairo world center of Muslim learning. To support his quarrel against Muslim Brotherhood militants, for instance, he had them condemned as heretics by the sheikhs of al-Azhar. His successor, Anwar Sadat, in the same spirit, pressed the ulama to issue a decree validating his controversial peace treaty with Israel.[43] Yet how far could such an ingratiating Muslim seal of approval be stretched? Bitter Egyptian critics would cite the ironic proclamation issued by Napoleon in 1798 during his invasion of Egypt: "I worship God (may He be exalted!) far more than the Mamlukes do, and respect His Prophet and glorious Quran.... The French also are sincere Muslims."[44]

What fostered Ataturk's and Nasser's initial success was the combination of a society carefully primed for change, and leadership by a military hero endowed with unusual political sophistication. These ingredients, however, seemed lacking in the ill-fated regime of Muhammad Reza Pahlavi, Shah of Iran. Just as Ataturk drew upon a pre-Islamic Turkish heritage to legitimize his nationalistic republic, so the Shah tried to revive the alleged pre-Islamic Persian or Zoroastrian foundations of his "peacock throne." And like Nasser, the Shah for a time gave the impression of an observant Muslim, deferential toward ulama clerics. As his great antagonist Khomeini would later concede, this son echoed the strategy of his father, the previous Shah, "by professing loyalty to Islam initially and using Islam as a weapon. For example, he commissioned a printing of the Quran, visited Mashhad once or twice a year, and prayed upon occasion.... But gradually he came to feel there was no longer any need for deceit, and began to rule by pure force and, at the same time, to rob the people of all their wealth and resources."[45]

On the surface, Iran during the 1970s appeared the most thoroughly modernized, if not Westernized, of all Muslim nations. Oil revenues had financed the building of gigantic nuclear power plants, a modern telecommunications system, and an army equipped with the latest U.S. missiles and supersonic planes. Yet with the rapid expansion of industry, Iranian schools could not be built fast enough to train the needed engineers and managerial class. Thus, in 1976 American universities alone numbered at least thirty-five thousand Iranian students, just a fraction of a vast student exodus sponsored by the Pahlavi regime. When many of these young people returned to Iran, they brought back a disturbing medley of Marxist, existentialist, and pragmatist catchwords. Besides radical attitudes about feminist rights and sexual permissiveness, these graduates now questioned most other traditional values supported by their parents and the ulama. Meanwhile, American workers had been imported to manage the new technology, many of them lured by posh housing, diplomatic immunity, and wages often scandalously larger than those paid to the best Iranian professional. Flaunting its foreign music, dancing, casinos, cinema, television, drugs, and alcohol, a transplanted culture of secularity soon collided directly with Iran's religious and family tradition.[46]

The Iranian economy was now scarred, too, by ugly disparities — a familiar prelude to any revolution spurred by rising expectations. "The people that live right on top of our oil deposits are suffering from hunger and thirst," Khomeini complained, "and cannot even clothe themselves." Yet the petroleum wealth was leaking out elsewhere, "into the pockets of foreigners, particularly the Americans." In return, "America gave us the military bases it constructed for itself in our territory," as a shield against the Soviet empire. The Shah had become just an American stooge, propelling Iran's youth away from Islam and their homeland and brainwashing his people with Eurocentric propaganda. Repressing all critics by his notorious secret police, he soon alienated almost every segment of the population. Facing certain prison, medieval torture, even murder, dissenters soon included an increasing number of Muslim seminarians and teachers. "The Shah cared only for the upper echelons of the army and security forces," said Khomeini, not the ulama or other religious institutions. "He despised everyone else."[47]

Blind or even hostile to Muslim sensibilities, Shah Pahlavi muddled into an incredible act of arrogance. He had long been trying to incorporate the ulama into his state machinery as a so-called Religious Corps.[48] Then during pretentious ceremonies in 1969 and 1972, costing a hundred million dollars, the Shah staged his self-coronation and marked the twenty-five hundredth anniversary of the Persian Empire at Persepolis. By this last gesture, he tore Islam away from his own redefinition of modern Iran. At the same time he decreed a change in the official calendar — years would no longer be computed from the beginning of Muhammad's flight to Medina, but from the alleged date that Cyrus ascended the throne. Besides this new chart of sacred time, almost a replica of the traditional Zoroastrian calendar, many other symbols of pre-Islamic Persia were paraded everywhere in the years just before the 1979 revolution.

Dreaming that Iran would become the "Japan of the Middle East," the Shah and his American financial advisers had no premonition of catastrophe. Even years later, those responsible for a steadily increasing GNP and so many consumer delights felt baffled how they could be denounced as the Great Satan. "Driving through the city of Meshed in an open car only four months before the situation became desperate," the Shah wrote later in his memoirs, "I was acclaimed by 300,000 people. . . . I can recall nothing in the history of the world — not even the French Revolution — to compare with what happened subsequently."[49]

"This diabolic celebration of the 2,500th anniversary of monarchy," Khomeini called it. "God only knows what calamity for the people and what source of bribery and extortion for the instruments of colonialism it entails. Had the stupendous budget for such despicable events been spent on feeding the empty stomachs and providing a living for the miserable, some of our calamity would have been alleviated."[50] This critique brings with it the added moral authority of Khomeini's own life, marked by an austerity that challenged the Shah's decadent pretensions. In contrast to snapshots of the Pahlavi coronation, or the royal family at ski resorts and Italian villas, you can picture a gaunt bearded elder, clothed in sober black. Instead of a garish peacock throne, imagine Khomeini's bare monastic cell at Qum, the Iranian seminary where he taught and wrote for many years before his exile to Turkey, Iraq, and France. After the fall of Shah Pahlavi, *Time* magazine devoted a lengthy cover story in 1980 to Ayatollah Ruhollah Khomeini, the man of the year — an icon symbolizing triumph of the fanatical and irrational, a fresh menace to American foreign interests. Scheduled for an interview with Khomeini, *Time* correspondents were kept waiting, seated beside rural petitioners and important politicians at Qum in a crude antechamber, lit only by a naked bulb dangling from the ceiling. Within the new Islamic Republic, here was the true center of power, a prophetic reproach against the Shah's wasteful government complex in Tehran.[51]

Thus, Khomeini's own life made him a persuasive adversary against all that was wrong with Iran. Whenever his followers listened to a Quranic phrase on his lips, they felt certain it arose not from mere political expediency but from a mature life of prayer. And this faith was not otherworldly but engaged, activist, and thus also political, a theology of liberation in the best sense. He tended to speak in a disciplined monotone, without humor, avoiding affect even when uttering words of grief or ecstasy, so that speech seemed a gesture of selfless witness to the truth. Though details about his early life are still obscure, Khomeini had established himself as a poet and teacher of speculative mysticism at the Qum seminary by the 1940s and had published defenses of Shiite orthodoxy. His writings argued for the legitimacy of praying to Muslim saints, pilgrimage especially to shrines of the Imams, and also the right of the Muslim ulama to veto proposed state legislation. His lectures at Qum grew increasingly political and thus more popular, followed by public speeches even more outspoken, so that he was eventually banished from Iran.[52]

In addition to the integrity of Khomeini's life, a second factor in his favor was his shrewd command of the media, combining a fundamentalist's yearning for the past with a televangelist's eye for the latest sales tactic. Earlier I mentioned his recognition of how Eurocentric Orientalists and magazines had fed back the image of a docile, nonpolitical Islam to the average Muslim. The revolution of 1979 has been aptly dubbed a revolution by audio-cassette. Exile from Iran did not silence the Ayatollah's voice of protest, but rendered it even louder, far more compelling and awesome by its absence. During the late 1970s I became teacher and counselor to a number of Iranian students, at that time the largest international group on campus. Arguing with excitement about the impending revolution, wary of the Shah's informers, circles of Iranians would huddle for long evenings in dorm rooms to hear recorded lectures by Khomeini and the radical sociologist Ali Shariati. Though eager to paraphrase these ideas for me, Iranian friends often complained of my inability at that time to appreciate either the message or the peculiar charism behind it.

During his Paris exile especially, Khomeini had access to first-class recording equipment, which was used to tape his speeches and many of the four hundred interviews granted to newspapers there. Evading police censorship, a tiny cassette could be smuggled back easily into Iran. At the same time the tapes shaped a powerful consensus among Iran's worldwide student diaspora. Khomeini knew the language of everyday life, not just that of the classroom or mosque, and he knew how to manipulate the news media. I cannot forget the year-long barrage of TV images showing American hostages from the U.S. embassy in Tehran, the shrieking mobs and rifle-toting young monitors — all registered on a lens hypnotized and trapped. This act of guerrilla theater was orchestrated with mastery by Khomeini, now by an abrupt intervention, now by a stagy reluctance to oppose the will of the people.

Most important, Khomeini and his disciples proved creative in reinterpreting Muslim history to support the Ayatollah's own prophetic mission. Street cartoons from the revolution portrayed him as Moses leading the desert Exodus, hounded by Pahlavi in the role of Pharaoh, with the face of President Jimmy Carter pasted on the false idol worshipped by Pharaoh. Carter more often plays Yazid, the caliph responsible for Imam Husayn's massacre at Kerbala, and Pahlavi is Shimr, the caliph's general. Khomeini found ready historical precedents for his own situation in exile. When Muhammad could not wipe out the immorality and polytheism at Mecca, he retreated to Medina for many years to build an ideal community and wait his chance to return from exile. Like Muhammad, Khomeini, remote and silenced by persecution, could scarcely be distinguished from the Hidden Imam of Shiite salvation-history.

Paradoxically, Khomeini and the long-awaited Mahdi became more present by their very absence.

Counter to the Shah's reinstated pre-Islamic calendar, Khomeini publicized three sacred calendars of his own. Iran's prerevolutionary Muslim calendar centered on a cycle of Shiite feast days — the birth of Muhammad, the date he chose Ali to succeed him, the date of Ali's death, Imam Husayn's massacre at Kerbala, and the Twelfth Imam's birth. To this cycle Khomeini's revolutionary calendar added a mounting series of government atrocities, the date of each martyrdom succeeded by its commemoration forty days later, which in turn triggered demonstrations, crackdowns, and further martyrdoms. His postrevolutionary calendar celebrated the June 1963 uprising, the day of Khomeini's return, and a succession of triumphant highlights from the new Islamic Republic.[53] In the Muharram parades and passion plays, a crucial shift in emphasis had emerged in years immediately before the revolution. Now instead of weeping passively over sufferings of the Kerbala martyrs, crowds filed through the streets with upraised fists, shouting "Down with the Shah," ready to imitate the active defiance of the martyrs. Husayn in the seventh century died resisting a tyrant caliph so that he could provide an example for later revolutionaries everywhere. There cannot be a middle ground between the good Husayn and the wicked Yazid. As one recurring banner would now express it: "There were no spectators at the martyrdom of Husayn."[54]

In Iran today, since his death in 1989, Khomeini is popularly called Imam Khomeini, even at times the Twelfth Imam himself. At first he used to sign official portraits with a more exact qualification, *Nayeb-e Imam* or aide to the Imam, a title that flourished during the nineteenth century, applied to those of exceptional spiritual charism. In prerevolutionary Iran, the capitalized title of Imam was reserved exclusively for Ali, Husayn, and their successors in the imamate. Yet by the closing years of the Ayatollah's exile, fervent crowds could be expected to blur distinctions, often acclaiming him the Hidden Imam. Ayatollah Shariatmadari among others warned his colleague Khomeini that to acquiesce in this title was blasphemous.[55] After the revolution, perhaps more sensitive to this ambiguity, Khomeini did not claim the traditional infallibility attributed to a living Imam. When asked by a cocky *Time* reporter, for instance, if he had ever erred about anything, Khomeini replied, "Only the Prophet Muhammad and other saints have been infallible. Everyone else makes mistakes."[56]

A central preoccupation in Shiite theology is the authoritative role of the *faqih* or jurist, which was Khomeini's preferred title for his ulama position. Though every orthodox Muslim regime tends to cite precedents from the Quran and sharia, the Shiite tradition, as explained before, invests immediate decisions of the Imam himself with a unique, infallible authority that can challenge most other precedents. Yet whether Khomeini was called Imam or the Imam's standby, I think, made little functional difference — as either faqih or Imam, his decisions carried tremendous authority. Khomeini justified this power by arguing that during the prolonged disappearance of the Twelfth Imam, Muhammad would not have left his people without detailed guidance, a guidance provided by leaders like Khomeini. He explained: "100,000 more years may pass and conditions may not permit that His Holiness the Twelfth Imam come back. Should the Islamic laws during this period remain idle? . . . Did God limit the execution of His laws to only 200 years? Did God let go of everything after the Lesser Occultation?" Today the power to interpret and administer these laws rests with the "just jurists." And Khomeini numbered himself such a jurist, first among equals. "The jurist is the deputy of the most noble Prophet, and in the period of Occultation, he is the leader of the Muslims, the supreme figure of authority in the nation." Though reluctant to become actual political ruler of Iran, Khomeini cherished the role of principal mentor on the sidelines, a voice of visionary moral authority, ready to advise, and if necessary, to intervene and veto.[57]

The Islamic Republic designed by Khomeini must never be mistaken for a secular constitutional democracy. Law in the Islamic Republic is not based on the decisions of an executive or parliamentary branch, nor does it depend on approval by the majority of citizens. "It is constitutional or conditional in the sense that those who govern are subject to a set of conditions in their reign that are specified in the Quran and the traditions of the most noble Prophet." The republic needs no elaborate bureaucracy, just "two or three agents, a pen and an ink box" to govern a city. "Our only basis of reference is the time of the Prophet and the Imam Ali.... The entire system of government and administration, together with the necessary laws, lies ready for you." For example, "if the administration of the country calls for taxes, Islam has made the necessary provisions. And if laws are needed, Islam has established them all." Whereas a secular government concerns itself only with the political and social order, a genuine Islamic regime has "commandments for everybody, everywhere, at any place, in any condition. If you were to commit an immoral dirty deed right next to your own house, Islamic governments have business with you."[58]

At the present moment, Iran's Islamic Republic is still an experiment too recent for seasoned appraisal. During the first decade of its existence, Iran went to war with Iraq, a development that united Iran's internal factions against a common enemy and thrust a virtual dictatorship upon Khomeini, a military and executive role for which he had probably never planned. From his long heroic opposition to the Shah, he seemed the only recognizable symbol of Muslim righteousness and national unity that almost all Iranians could endorse. When finally in power, he proceeded to interpret the Quran and sharia one moment with single-minded literalness, yet the next instant he would fall back upon his own resourceful improvisation, sanctioned by the authority of faqih or Imam, just as Muhammad no doubt had to improvise in shaping his government at Medina or Ali and Husayn had improvised in the later imamate. And like Calvin at Geneva, or the Puritans in New England, he took on the responsibility to enforce divine law on everyone, even in the intimate hideouts of their lives.

The emergence of Khomeini's faqih theocracy, spartan and intrusive, shocked many secular liberals, Marxists, and Muslim moderates as a vicious betrayal of the revolution. To them, Khomeini, the idealized dissenter, had proved himself just another Ataturk, even more cunning than themselves. During exile he had always cited the Quran to oust the Shah, but seldom to specify in detail the Shah's replacement. He had even hinted that a new "Islamic-Humanistic" era would follow, a phrase interpreted hopefully as a pledge of compromise and collaborative leadership.[59] Many of his adversaries were executed. Those still alive continue to wonder about the man. Had the Ayatollah contrived from the beginning first to lure secular liberals into his camp and then, once in power, to spring his repressive theocracy on them?

Perhaps the secular militants themselves, however, eager to locate any effective anti-Shah banner, paid selective inattention to Khomeini's obvious agenda, for many of them no doubt counted on discarding all this Muslim window-dressing after the revolution. Yet it is true that revolutions commonly begin in the consolidated strength of generic complaints but end in later schisms over dividing of spoils. In fairness to Khomeini, I think an inventory of his extant books and speeches proves he held to a single, consistent Muslim political vision. Piece by piece, this vision evolved whenever he had to test the implications, for example, of an obscure precedent in the reign of Muhammad, Ali, or Husayn, and try to turn it into workable legislation.

Khomeini felt the Islamic millennium would remain incomplete until it spread to all Muslims across national boundaries. The hajj of 1982, for example, included a core of activists among thousands of Iranian pilgrims. After a number of stormy demonstrations proclaiming the message of Khomeini and his revolution, they were expelled from Mecca. In response to this bullying treatment, a Khomeini spokesman denounced the Saudis as a nation of "pleasure-seekers and mercenaries." "How long," he asked in anger, "must Satan rule the House of God?"[60] He then demanded that a council of representatives from all Muslim nations replace Saudi control of the sanctuaries at Mecca and Medina. In situations like these Khomeini soon had to deal with militant opposition, then, not only from the United States but also from Iraq and Saudi Arabia.

The average Muslim anywhere must have cheered Khomeini's holy war against the American Satan, this latest broker of the secular dream. Yet at the same time, few Sunnite majorities throughout the world could side with Iran's particular grievances and frame of mind. First of all, ulama leaders in most Muslim nations had not experienced the damaging alienation between mosque and state that plagued the Shah's regime. Also, much of Khomeini's Islamic state seemed overidentified with the parochial rhetoric and imagery of the Kerbala martyrs, the imamate, Shiite theology, and — more ominously — with the limited charism of this one man.

TOWARD A MUSLIM SPIRITUALITY

Like all true Muslim activists succeeding him, Muhammad lived a comprehensive Muslim life — not just the warrior statesman but also a unique ecstatic, at times praying far into the night. Allah tells him, "All night keep vigil, wrapped up in your mantle, . . . and with measured tones recite the Quran, for we are about to address you words of surpassing gravity. It is in the watches of the night that impressions are strongest and words most eloquent. In the daytime you are hard-pressed with work."[61]

In my interactions with different Muslims mentioned above, at times I have been escorted behind the armor of correct religious observance to discover a vital spirituality. My visit with one unforgettable student from Yemen in his apartment is representative enough to deserve retelling. Married and thirty years old, this man since childhood had been reciting salat formal prayer five times daily. When asked if he ever used his own words at prayer, he described some favorite mantras and short prayer formulas learned from his parents and also from his sheikh or spiritual mentor whom he still consulted periodically. In addition, he would engage in frequent *dua* or informal prayer, sharing his desires and regrets with Allah as an understanding friend.

My few evenings with this Muslim and his family were spent listening to his expressive readings from Arab poets and the Quran, with indispensable translations. At these visits, by the way, I grasped for the first time the striking rhymes, assonance, and cadence patterns of the recited Quran — a chanting or musical recitative, almost a liturgical reenactment. To perform salat or to recite the Quran with suitable reverence, you are expected to measure out sacred space — with or without a prayer rug — at home, in a mosque, or any other selected area. Then you perform the prescribed ablutions, recollect yourself meditatively, and turn toward Mecca. A zone of holy ground emerges, a prayer space with boundaries to exclude profane and evil forces.

"My grandmother," he explained, "always used to encourage me to read some of the Quran each night before going to sleep. That way, I would dream of the angels. I believe she was right, for I still dream of them." Throughout childhood he committed almost the entire Quran to memory, feeling it in his pulse, and by now he is just beginning to understand it. Today he meditates, too, in the sense of resting quietly in God's presence. But his primary sense of prayer consists in chanting and pondering the sacred text, engaging in it with body and mind, letting it seep into his bloodstream. He is trying to shape a unique Muslim imagination, to stock it with images and phrases from the Quran. "Whenever I read the words," he says, "I feel I am watching the lips of Allah. And I hear Allah speak these words to me." This praying style strikes me as a genuine faith searching for insight — *fides quaerens intellectum.* For the mystery must first be experienced and lived before it can be fathomed intellectually. Trying to understand it can only be gradual, but a process left ever incomplete.[62]

After I got to know this Muslim better, I once asked if it disturbs him when his heart strays from or doubts the salat rite or the Quran words on his lips. I explained that often in counseling sessions, especially during hospital chaplaincy, I have listened to people unable or unwilling to lean back on their traditional prayer formulas. Depressed or alienated, they may see no meaning in just a wooden recitation. For such an effort seems hypocritical, and many people want their words to match only what they sincerely feel right now. Recognizing this dilemma, my friend expressed a hopeful attitude, almost identical to that of Abu Uthman al-Hiri, an early Sufi mystic. "I recollect with the tongue," a disciple once complained, "but my heart does not become friends with the recollection." Then al-Hiri advised him, "Be grateful that one of your limbs obeys and one of your parts is led aright. Maybe later your heart too will come into accord."[63] This approach matches the Confucian advice, developed in chapter 2, to try acting like a father in order to elicit the inner nature of a father.

The Sharia Bedrock

Every Muslim must try to live out the sharia, or more specifically, to perform the basic Five Pillars — the shahada creed, the salat daily prayers, the *zakat* alms tax, in addition to hajj and the Ramadan fast. Whoever follows these essentials shall be saved. Yet if understood in depth, each sharia external duty contains within itself a challenging inward path, open to anyone wishing to go further. As my Yemeni friend explains it, the ordinary believer is invited to move beyond the outer ritual deed. Reinforcing this same approach, one popular introduction to Islam gives the following summary of basic Muslim spirituality: "The salat means to awaken from one's dream of forgetfulness and remember God always. The fast means to die to one's passionate self and be born in purity. The pilgrimage means to journey from the surface to the center of one's being, for as many Sufis have said, the heart is the spiritual kaaba. The zakat also implies spiritual generosity and nobility. . . . Sharia is the necessary and sufficient basis for the spiritual life."[64]

An interiorization of the sharia — this phrase sums up the spiritual process just described. The words can also identify the aim of most Sufi mystics, especially in earlier formative centuries of Sufi history.[65] "To kiss the threshold of the sharia" is how one sheikh depicts a Muslim's first duty in the spiritual life. Another says, "Sometimes Truth knocks at my door for forty days, but I do not permit it to enter my heart unless it brings two witnesses, the Quran and the Prophetic tradition." I shall use the term "sufi" to designate first the monastic communities, lay orders, or political brotherhoods prominent in Muslim history, most of them centered on a charismatic sheikh. The word's etymology refers to a garment of rough cloth, a lifestyle of simple poverty — sign of an ascetical counterculture, zealous to reaffirm Muslim essentials during an era of materialistic and political expansion. By the twelfth century, a wide range of organized Sufi communities, similar to Christian religious orders or Hindu ashrams, had emerged to foster a life of contemplative prayer and to preach the sharia.

In and beyond these Sufi communities, many of them still vigorous today, Sufi spirituality means any sort of training relationship in spirituality under a sheikh guide with a certified lineage. More broadly, the name can be extended to embrace the full range of ordinary Muslim spiritual self-renewal. Though rejecting the sharia cadaver dissected by jurists and theologians, most of the classical Sufi masters did try to remain orthodox Muslims, faithful to a living sharia that towers over any other knowledge. At their most iconoclastic, these masters would claim that Muslims need only enough astronomy to locate the direction of Mecca for salat and enough mathematics to calculate the legal amount of zakat. In short, Muslims should discard any books or sheikhs or other props that distract them from a direct encounter with Allah.

Just as the Five Pillars yield a hidden path for endless spiritual advancement, so the Quran itself can be mined for countless levels of revealed meaning. If God is infinite, so is God's Word — transcending yet accessible to every possible allegorical and symbolic interpretation. According to an important hadith, Muhammad taught that each verse of the Quran has an inner and outer meaning. One early mystic boasted the discovery of at least seven thousand different interpretations for every verse of the Quran. And some Sufi groups have preserved a few key esoteric interpretations of their own, disclosed step-by-step only to their disciples. Even today, many Muslims try to find hidden meaning in the number of Arabic letters in each sura or in the numerical value of the letters, in the same Kabbalistic manner that some Christians pour over mystical numbers, words, or images in the Book of Revelation. Special importance has been attributed to reciting a repeated number of Quranic verses — three, seven, fifteen, fifty, or seventy, for example. Some people pronounce specific words or passages of the Quran to heal the sick, or chant and dance out Quranic mantras to induce trance. Like Catholics praying the rosary, a number of my Muslim students are accustomed to finger their prayer beads, reciting a famous litany of Allah's ninety-nine attributes selected from the Quran.[66]

On the wall of my office is a large montage, each fragment displaying the sha-hada in one of sixteen different calligraphic styles. It is significant that a tradition whose mystics delve into hidden Quranic meanings has at the same time developed the art of Quranic calligraphy. These marvelous designs try to achieve a visual effect as unique as the audial experience of God's Word. Script becomes a sort of visual sacrament, symmetrical and pure, sharing in the very speech and writing of God. It adorns mosques, minarets, prayer rugs, and personal jewelry and melts into creative floral, lace filigree, and more abstract geometrical designs. The familiar arabesque is a tendril that creeps along endlessly, drawing the eye onward with a hint of God's infinity.

For Muslims, the arts of calligraphy and architecture displace decorative painting or sculpture of the human and animal image. In earlier chapters, I have explored different motives for iconoclasm. It is not difficult to understand the moral iconoclasm of the classical Hebrew prophets. This attitude has been reinterpreted by most contemporary Humanists as a challenge against every pseudo-religion that undermines human maturity. Or like many religious people, you may prefer the apophatic spirituality of silence and emptiness, favored by mystics in various world traditions. Recall, too, the disciplined aniconic caution of early Theravada Buddhists, fearing that the mortal Gautama might otherwise be inflated into just one more garish Hindu avatar. In addition to all these convincing reasons, the Muslim reluctance to use human and animal images may have more specific historical motives behind it. First, exuberant art had become associated with exploitative privileged classes, whereas Muslims from the beginning tried to eliminate luxury and caste from their message. Second, unable perhaps to compete with rival civilizations in their skill at religious painting and sculpture, Muslims decided simply to change the game rules. Identifying themselves mostly with the mobile international business class of the Middle Ages, Muslims developed a sober bourgeois morality, pragmatic and impatient with the ornamental, aesthetic, or whimsical. These features had no place unless they could serve some clear didactic purpose.

Motives of this sort, however, scarcely begin to explain Muslim iconoclasm. Like today's abstract and nonobjective schools of art, Muslims may have learned to dismiss recognizable images in order to stress color masses, pattern, and direct emotional impact. Similarly, their religious sensibility might have strained unconsciously to achieve an immediate spiritual evocation, without reminding the viewer of other experiences. Most important, to concentrate on the Quran as their exclusive sacred icon, Muslims determined to eliminate all other symbols that might drain or divert religious attention from Allah's one definitive revelation.[67]

The Unitive Experience

A few distinctive Sufi motifs can be illustrated by examining an outstanding classic, *The Conference of the Birds* by Farid ud-Din Attar. Translated today into many languages, this twelfth-century work has inspired centuries of poets and mystics. The story describes a huge array of birds assembled for pilgrimage in search of their king, the Simurgh. The kingdom they seek lies beyond seven valleys, which stand for seven major obstacles to spiritual progress. Their elected leader, a hoopoe bird, strikes up a dialogue with one species of bird after another, each pouring out various misgivings about this quest. Though the hoopoe inserts many convincing short parables in her advice to each hesitant pilgrim, the number of her followers dwindles gradually to a mere thirty birds. The journey unfolds, with many strenuous challenges. At its climax, Simurgh the king, his name based on an outrageous pun in the Persian language, turns into *si-murgh* or thirty birds. Thus, search for the Sacred is reinterpreted as a quest for the deeper self. "The sun of my majesty is a mirror," the Simurgh at last explains. "Seeing yourself there, you see your body and soul completely. Since you have come as thirty birds (si-murgh), you will see thirty birds in this mirror.... Annihilate yourselves gloriously and joyfully in me, then, and in me you shall find yourselves."[68]

The mirror analogy serves many purposes in Attar's story. The Simurgh proves elusive — now inviting, now warding off those who seek him. This unpredictability of response indicates he loves as he wills, not because any individual pilgrim may deserve this love. By withholding himself, he tests the loving resolve in them all and intensifies their spiritual yearning. They endure great pain and despair in the Valley of Death, their last ordeal before knocking at the door of the Simurgh. After some moments of anxious delay, a chamberlain steps out, and "having tested them, opened the door. And as he drew aside a hundred curtains, one after the other, a new world beyond the veil was revealed. And now was the light of lights manifested,... and a new life began for them in the Simurgh." Long before this moment, the hoopoe bird tells about a king of such beauty that he must veil his face on the street, or else people would faint and their businesses shut down. The king's people could neither endure his direct presence nor exist without him, so he chanced upon a paradoxical compromise. He installed a mirror which refracted his image, so that each could gaze according to that person's capacity. In other words, this is a God both hidden and revealed. And a mature spiritual life consists in making peace with all the shifting moments of light and shadow in the soul.[69]

In charting out the stages of spiritual transformation, this classic explores an ambiguity common to many Sufi prayers and lyrics. It opens with the following invocation: "Admire then the works of the Lord, though he himself considers them as nothing. And seeing that his essence alone exists, it is certain there is nothing but him.... God is all, and things have only a nominal value. The world visible and the world invisible are only himself." Based on this same approach, the hoopoe explains why God decided to create the universe: "If the Simurgh had not wished to manifest himself, he would not have cast his shadow.... The different types of birds seen in the world are thus only the shadow of the Simurgh.... By his abounding grace he has given us a mirror to reflect himself, and this mirror is the heart. Look into your heart and there you will see his image."[70]

Denying the existence of anything other than God, these passages are filled with the lofty imagery of pantheism. The unitive experience is conjured by a string of metaphors commonplace among mystics of all traditions. Veering ever closer toward the flame, the moth at last plunges into it and disappears. The journey's goal and the journey itself are two surfaces of one mirror. God is an ocean in which the individual vanishes like a drop, or a desert with depths hidden underneath ever new sand dunes. Identification with God is closer than chemical ingredients transformed by alchemy or lovers utterly lost in each other. Attar and Rumi both introduce an ardent dialogue in which a lover knocking at the door announces, "It's me," and is turned away. But after long meditation on this rejection, there is a second attempt to knock. "Who is it?" asks a voice beyond the door. And the one knocking now responds, "It's you." At this word the door opens.[71]

Alongside the passages cited thus far, Attar inserts a few sober qualifications, which sound like a nod to the nonpantheist, the orthodox Muslim reader. Each bird is urged to polish the mirror of the heart by ascetical training and then sink "into the immensity of the Simurgh, though you must not think you are God on that account.... You will not be God, but you will be immersed in God." And again, "Learn from my mouth the true doctrine — the eternal existence of Being. We must not see anyone other than him. We are in him, by him, and with him."[72] This is the cautious, more exacting language of panentheism, which affirms that God and I are distinct, but intertwined inseparably with each other.

Pantheism remains the standard charge trotted out against Sufi teaching. From the perspective of a strict Muslim jurist or theologian, to deflect the worship designed only for God toward anyone or anything less than God is to commit *shirk* or idolatry. This indictment has hounded spiritual masters in all monotheistic traditions, especially Christian mystics like Meister Eckhart, whose approach is apophatic rather than kataphatic — the so-called mysticism of infinity rather than the mysticism of personalism. In the history of Christian spirituality, the apophatic spiritual style can be traced back to Plotinus, Pseudo-Dionysius, and later Neoplatonists, but it flourished more vigorously among Hindus like Shankara, Vivekananda, and modern Vedantists, as explained in chapter 3.

It is unfortunate that one of the first influential introductions of Sufi thought to Europe happened to be entitled *Sufism, or the Pantheistic Theosophy of the Persians,* a treatise published in 1821 by the German Protestant theologian F. D. Tholuck.[73] Reacting with shock or delight, readers of Sufi literature today tend to project an unmistakable pantheism into descriptions of mystical union and of God as an emanating light, force, or diffuse sacred presence in all things. This bias is nourished by popular anthologies of Sufi tales, trimmed and jazzed up, ripped out of context, almost indistinguishable from tales by Zen Buddhist or Taoist masters.[74]

The Sufi mystics deserve a more informed reading than this. It is important to concede from the start that a particular master may have been a strict or marginal Muslim, orthodox or heterodox. Just as Sufi techniques of yoga, trance-dance, and mantra-chanting derived from traceable Hindu and Buddhist sources, so to varying degrees, the imagery and insight of a particular Sufi writer may also lean on these influences. However, written within a monotheistic context, the text demands first a broader panentheistic reading, unless compelling evidence directs otherwise. Perhaps any ecstatic utterance sounds monistic at first. Yet it could refer to a duality of lovers who are interdependent but retain their distinct identities. It could also suggest a duality of yin-yang complementary polarities, each distinct factor needing the other for completeness.

In listening to the account of a unitive experience, it is crucial to distinguish between the phenomenon perceived and its metaphysical interpretation. First, the experience of spiritual union with God can be described as a sheer phenomenon, expressed in the grammar of metaphor, poetry, oracle, or presentational symbols. Second and at the same time, the mind of the visionary or observer, pondering this experience, may conclude something about the nature of God and the universe, an affirmation usually expressed in ontological language, discursive prose, or representational symbols. The thirteenth-century Sufi theologian Ibn al-Arabi has called these two distinct perspectives the unity of contemplation or *wahdat ash-shuhud,* and the unity of Being or *wahdat al-wujud.*[75]

It must be acknowledged, however, that no Sufi can be identified exclusively as poet, visionary, philosopher, or theologian. Masters like Attar, Rumi, and Ibn al-Arabi blend or slide back and forth unconsciously between all these roles, genres, and perspectives. Misunderstanding arises inevitably if one isolates, for instance, the unity of contemplation and tries to approach it and judge it by criteria suitable only to the unity of Being. Any Sufi poet, interpreted by a single-minded prosaic Muslim jurist or theologian, will end up sounding like the poet Walt Whitman, as mocked by D. H. Lawrence: "Walter, what have you done with your individual self? For it sounds as if it had all leaked out of you, leaked into the universe.... It's all empty. Just an empty Allness. An addled egg."[76]

These efforts to give ecstatic utterance a fair hearing, however, may skim over a profound religious paradox that has preoccupied Muslim theologians for centuries. It is ironic that within the most focused, disciplined monotheist lies a dormant tendency that like a geological fault threatens at any moment to widen into full-blown pantheism. In American intellectual history, for example, how could the distant sovereign God of New England Puritans be replaced in just a few generations by Emerson's immanent Nature and the Oversoul? W. E. Channing, the father of Unitarianism, suggested an intriguing continuity between these two God-images, the God beyond and the God within. He attacked the Puritan theologian Jonathan Edwards for making God the only active power in the universe. Channing then proceeded to blame Edwards for annihilating God's creatures, and thus for prompting us to question whether any such thing as matter exists.[77]

In a comparable way, a Sufi disciple yearns for the one God, meditates only on God, and submits meanwhile to a strenuous training in self-denial and self-annihilation, treating the self and the world as nothing. Thus, in one's consciousness, the supreme ineffable God gradually crowds out every other reality and can easily become the All. "The eyes are blind," says Attar in his invocation, "even though the world is lighted by a brilliant sun. Should you catch even a glimpse of God you would lose your wits, and if you should see God completely you would lose your self.... There is none but God."[78]

This risk of pantheism was addressed boldly by an unlikely poet and theologian, Jalaluddin Rumi. He divides the shahada creed into two affirmations. The first part states, "There is no god but Allah." Then the second adds, "And Muhammad is the Prophet of Allah." To believe only the first half could lead to pantheism, a fusion and confusion of all world creeds. The second half, as Rumi interprets it, is calculated to destroy this first temptation. It limits the inclusiveness of Muslim faith. It distinguishes Allah from other Gods and Muslim faith from other professions of belief. To reaffirm the historical reality of the sharia and Muhammad's prophetic mission is a pivotal test for every Muslim monotheist.[79]

Muhammad's Night Journey

"For those who look to Allah," says the Quran, "there is a good example in Allah's apostle."[80] The popular Muslim imagination has surely fallen in love with the Prophet Muhammad, for so many prayers, songs, and poems extol his gentleness, sunlike face, and handsome black hair. His very name has been treated almost as a prayer. It is the common basis for oaths and the pattern for names of many males. To be a convincing model for every human being, however, Muhammad could not be a withdrawn celibate, and surely not the incarnate God. He had to pass through every phase of human life, sharing all affliction and joy, to show the Way.

This comprehensive human being has often been belittled as a crude polygamist and imperialist by non-Muslim critics. For instance, a recent children's book about the lives of world spiritual leaders, published by Simon and Schuster, was recalled from circulation after protests by the Washington-based Council on American-Islamic Relations. The text disparages Muhammad as a man preoccupied with beautiful women, perfume, and tasty food. "He took pleasure," one passage says, "in seeing the heads of his enemies torn from their bodies by the swords of his soldiers. He hated Christians and Jews, poets and painters, and anyone who criticized him."[81] Muslims themselves, on the contrary, view Muhammad as a tender exemplary father and husband. They single out his military campaigns as a paradigm of all morally just warfare, especially in his compassionate treatment of prisoners. Ready to forgive his enemies, he showed them tough love by first defeating them.[82]

The manner and extent of emulating Muhammad have led to many quarrels within the umma. Influential scholastic theologian and mystic al-Ghazali expects disciples to imitate Muhammad "in all his comings and goings, motions and rests, even in his manner of eating, rising, sleeping, and speaking." He then picks a few loving, punctilious examples, which parallel the impassioned guru emulation practiced by many Hindu bhaktas. Like Muhammad, "begin with the right foot when you put on your shoes. Eat with your right hand. In cutting fingernails, begin with the forefinger of your right hand, and end with the thumb. Begin with the right little toe and end with the left little toe."[83] It is easy to parody this piety of the itsy-bitsy. Quick to attribute an obsessive personal quirk of their own to some imaginary hadith or fable about the prophet, some of my Muslim friends, I think, have abused this approach. Yet in such observances you can discern the momentous weight of the past, a badge of group solidarity in minuscule but perceptible detail. Such details reveal an attempt to sacralize ordinary life, much like the Confucian kowtow or the Jewish diet rituals.

It is possible to commit shirk or idolatry in veneration of Muhammad. A long tradition of theosophical reflection about his superhuman powers was triggered by just a few central hadith. The following words are attributed to Muhammad: at the beginning of time, "the first thing God created was my spirit," or "I was a prophet when Adam was still between clay and water." Or Allah addresses him, "If it had not been for you, I would not have created the heavens." Most Muslims today count on him as the principal witness to intercede for his Muslim community at the Final

Judgment. According to speculations of many Muslim philosophers, each individual's power of intellectual insight, the capacity to abstract a universal concept from sense data, is activated by God's mind or the soul of the universe. In this context, Ibn al-Arabi and others identified the sacred light of insight with Muhammad. He is archetypal humanity, the source of light. Whereas Justin and other early Christian apologists described Jesus as the incarnate Logos, so some Muslim theologians identified Muhammad with the Logos, the rational principle of God's creation. As Attar exclaims, "The origin of the soul is the absolute light, nothing else. That means it was the light of Muhammad, nothing else."[84]

To Wahabi Sunnites and most other Muslims, nothing could be more contradictory and blasphemous than a deified Muhammad. As described before, the Wahabi Saudis prefer to exclude even a hint of worship at his Medina burial site and celebrations of his birthday. The orthodox Muslim will always resist the demonic urge to deify, much like the urge to ingest all reality into a pantheistic equation. These are simply more recent variations on the polytheistic idolatry Muhammad had to combat all his life. However, zealous efforts to suppress a cultus centered on Muhammad often seem to nourish the very devotion they discredit. For example, religious authorities may forbid actors from taking the role of Muhammad in plays or movies and painters from portraying his features in paintings. Persian and Moghul miniatures often contain a blinding flame or faceless blank to represent Muhammad's presence. In a comparable situation, early Buddhist art wiped out Gautama's image from group scenes and left only an empty throne or footprint. Though the original purpose of this artistic convention was to avoid idolatry, its effect can be just the opposite — a sacred apophatic silence. Like the Hidden Imam, present in his very absence, the faceless or invisible Muhammad for some Muslims elicits a response of even more ardent religious worship.

The incident in Muhammad's life that surfaces most prominently in Sufi poetry and art is the *miraj,* his literal or visionary night ride from Mecca to Jerusalem and ascent into heaven. This popular story can be traced to a few controversial Quran passages, difficult to construe with certainty. Allah, says one sura, made him "go by night from the sacred temple to the farther temple, . . . that we might show him some of our signs." The other sura refers ambiguously to either Gabriel or Muhammad: "He stood on the uppermost horizon. . . . He saw some of his Lord's greatest signs." From these two suras, a number of hadith anecdotes, the eighth-century biography of Muhammad by Ibn Ishaq, and a few later accounts, an outline of the basic story emerges. Within the framework of a journey, the narrative extracts the kernel from countless intermittent visions given Muhammad as he gradually recorded the Quranic revelation.[85]

Muhammad is awakened one night by angels near the kaaba. The angels split open his body, take out his heart, and purify it in Zamzam water. Then placing him on a winged horse called Borak, Gabriel carries him to the Temple in Jerusalem, where Muhammad greets an assembly of prophets, including Abraham, Moses, and Jesus, and leads them in prayer. He and Gabriel next climb a ladder to heaven and gain entry only after Gabriel vouches that Muhammad has been given a special divine mission. Rising up through the seven heavens, Muhammad at every level meets a different prophet from the past, each repeating the same questions to Gabriel, "Who is with you?" and "Was he called?" After Gabriel's reaffirmation, each figure always concludes, "Please welcome Muhammad. His coming here is good."

Then Muhammad and Gabriel progress upward from Adam, through Jesus and John the Baptist, Jacob's son Joseph, Enoch, Aaron, Moses, and finally to Abraham at the entrance to paradise. The finale to more popular versions of this tale presents a flash encounter with Allah, followed by a debate with Moses about the number of required salat periods to be imposed daily on all Muslims. Allah asks fifty at first, but Moses tells Muhammad, "I tried out people before you,... and it did not have the desired effect." With Moses nagging him, Muhammad returns to Allah again and again and gets the burden reduced. Eventually he is ashamed to ask that it be curtailed further than five times daily. A divine voice finally calls out, "I have established my divine commands, and have made them easy to my servants."[86]

Like every great creative narrative, the night journey of Muhammad accomplishes many purposes. First, his revelations, inward and so hard to imagine, are here given a colorful time-dimension. His Quranic experience has a vertical cosmic scope and a horizontal range back through history. Second, his inaugural call to be a prophet draws on the familiar shamanic symbolism described in chapter 1, above. He receives an angelic incision, a baptism into the kaaba-Zamzam heritage of Abraham, and a shamanic winged horse and ladder to enter wider unconscious realms. In a heavenly naming ritual, Muhammad is again pronounced the Prophet, and his mission is reaffirmed by everyone present. Third, step by step, he sets up continuity with Jesus, Moses, and others and gives a new configuration to the prophetic historical past. In the act of opening doors and welcoming him, each prophet at that moment surrenders some previous status. In Jerusalem it is Muhammad who leads them all in prayer. Fourth, an etiological sketch foresees and answers the average Muslim's complaints about the salat obligation, contrasted with relatively lighter duties in the Jewish prayer tradition.

Tales of Muhammad's night journey and a few Christian epics, such as the *Purgatory of Saint Patrick,* probably influenced the structure of the cosmic journey in Dante's *Divine Comedy.* According to Dante's aggressive Christian theology, of course, Muhammad ends up disemboweled in the inferno simply as a traitorous Christian who dismembered the church. Dante is guided through the inferno and purgatorio by Virgil, who is later replaced in the paradiso by the archetypal Beatrice. Most readers of Dante interpret Virgil at this moment of leave-taking as a symbol of unaided human reason, impotent to guide the soul in its highest reaches. Similarly, in most versions of Muhammad's night journey, Gabriel takes his leave before the final meeting with Allah. "If I went one step further, my wings would get burned," the archangel sighs. According to Rumi's interpretation, discursive reason cannot draw any nearer to the mystery of divine love. Or even the highest created being is still a veil that must not intrude between Muhammad and the Creator. In one hadith, Muhammad says, "I have a time with God in which no created being has access, not even Gabriel who is pure spirit."[87]

Abu Yazid al-Bastami was the first of many Sufi masters to use the imagery of Muhammad's night journey to describe his own religious visions and thus to introduce a new literary genre. "I dreamed I ascended to the heavens," Bastami begins. As his flight on a green bird lifts him through one angelic realm after another, he identifies them with graduated psychological stages, the familiar purgative-illuminative-unitive odyssey toward God. At one pause in this climb, he cries out, "O Lord, with my egotism I cannot reach you nor escape from my selfhood. What am I to do?" God answers, "O Abu Yazid, you must win release from your thou-ness by following my beloved Muhammad. Smear your eyes with the dust of his feet and follow him continuously." Many Sufi theologians were convinced that the ordinary spiritual Way unfolded by stages of more intensive identification or, paradoxically, phases of self-diminishment. Ibn al-Arabi calls them annihilations — first lose your self in your Sufi guide, then next in Muhammad, and third, the rarest achievement of all, in Allah.

Prayer and growth in the interior life, no matter how rudimentary, are viewed by many Muslims as a participation in Muhammad's night journey, especially in its stages of spiritual yearning, the Dark Night ordeal, and eventual delight. At each spiritual crisis, Muhammad's example and intercessory power are promised as a guide. Some years after writing his popular epic on the birds, Attar recounted a dream where Muhammad showed up to press him, "Do you love me?" And Attar responded, "Forgive me, but the love of Allah has kept me busy from loving you." Muhammad, however, then leaves behind this unforgettable last word of challenge: "Whoever loves Allah, loves me."[88]

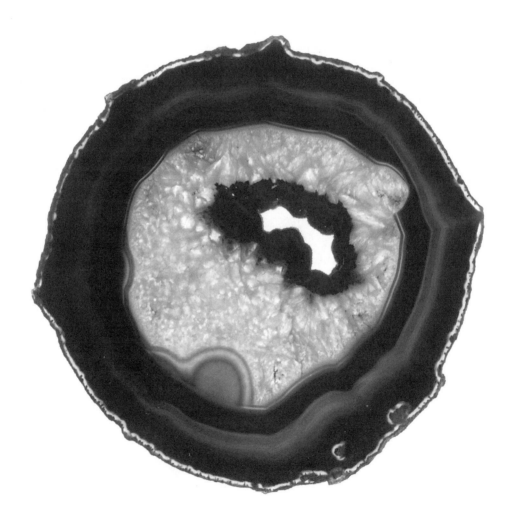

Mandala cross-section of a geode in blue and translucent white, selected to suggest marvels of nature concealed within the rind of a common boulder. Northern California.

8

The Humanist Way

Millions of religious people live outside boundaries of the principal extant traditions selected for study in the preceding seven chapters. Some groups have a long distinctive historical identity, such as the Zoroastrians, Jains, or Sikhs. Many have surfaced in more recent history — for instance, Bahais, Mormons, or Christian Scientists. Others are still emerging movements, branching off from more recognizable traditions or steering toward fresh syntheses — such as current disciples of the New Age, New Thought, Ritual Magic, Wicca, and neo-Paganism. Somewhere beyond and between all these public creeds and rites is an uncharted flow of individuals, their religious identity too unaware, improvisational, or intricate for any sort of labeling. Many people, too, define themselves only by their aversion to any religious earmark whatsoever.

One remarkable feature of the seven major religious traditions discussed in previous chapters is that each claims its own distinctive form of Humanism. Muhammad Ali Jinnah, founder of modern Pakistan, for instance, saw himself as a Muslim Humanist. "In the Quran," he used to say, "humanity itself has indeed been called God's caliph." For to each Muslim's faith the Quran applies a single acid test of practical service — out of love for Allah, you must share your wealth with the family and with orphans or anyone else in need. Jinnah's colleague and occasional adversary Muhammad Iqbal expressed a similar ideal in a few lines of poetry: "There are many who love God and wander in the wilderness. / I will follow the one who loves the persons created by God."

Leaders of Hindu reform like Vivekananda and Gandhi both defined religious activism as a life permeated by God-consciousness, worship offered to the divinity in every human being. "If I could persuade myself," said Gandhi, "that I should find God in a Himalayan cave, I would proceed there immediately. But I know I cannot find God apart from humanity." The contemporary Vietnamese monk Thich Nhat Hanh preaches what he calls an "engaged Buddhism," an artful blend of contemplative awareness and nonviolent political responsibility. And the Dalai Lama has tried to model his own life on the traditional bodhisattva prayer — "For as long as space and living beings remain, may I, too, endure to dispel the misery of the world."

Faithful to the Hebrew prophets, one Hasidic master after another brushes aside exact rabbinic observance to perform a spontaneous act of kindness toward the stranger. As described earlier, the Jewish communist Rosa Luxemburg has no separate corner in her heart for the Jewish ghetto. "I feel at home in the entire world," she says, "wherever there are clouds and birds and human tears." And social activist Isaac Deutscher, from a family of Polish Orthodox Jews, could identify himself as a Jew only "by force of my solidarity with anyone persecuted and exterminated." "Christian Humanist" is the term Kenneth Kaunda of Zambia uses to describe his spirituality: "We discover all worth knowing about God through our fellow human beings. Unconditional service of them is the purest form of the service of God." And the priest revolutionary Camilo Torres refused to say Mass for his congregation until they first obeyed the Gospel precept to feed and clothe the needy majority. "I am not an anti-communist," he insists, "just pro-humanity."

It is paradoxical that such diverse cultures, temperaments, and spiritualities should end up with almost an identical contemporary Humanist ethic. Parallels like these recall the stunning convergence in moral and spiritual insight during the so-called Axial Period around the fifth century b.c.e., described in chapter 2. That era encompassed Kung Futze and Lao Tzu in China, Zoroaster in Persia, Gautama Buddha and Upanishad philosophers in India, Plato and Aristotle in Greece, and the major Hebrew prophets. Within those five civilizations, believers were stirred in comparable ways to reinterpret the old dying religious symbols and integrate them into a life of moral responsibility.

Among major religions the more recent consensus about a few Humanist truisms, however, may lack the depth of this Axial Period convergence. For the politically correct Humanist slogan or sound bite has often been contradicted by the anti-Humanist deed. I hope future historians of the twentieth century will keep track of all the high-profile catchwords, both sacred and secular, used to justify Pol Pot's killing fields, Khomeini's crusade against the Bahai, Argentina's extermination of the "disappeared," and the indelible bloodshed in Tibet, Bangladesh, East Timor, Biafra, Rwanda, Northern Ireland, and Bosnia.

As mentioned in the introduction, I side with Gandhi's insight that there exist as many religions as individual people in the world, each spirituality unique though often overlapping with others. You can anticipate that two or more individuals, agreeing now to adopt a credal formula, now a particular moral platform, will tone down these idiosyncratic inner differences. However, the discontinuity between religious vision and moral action has always puzzled me. For instance, you and I may pray the same Christian creed but contradict each other on such vital moral issues as abortion and nuclear disarmament. Yet again, someone else may support my basic moral position on the environment but deny all my Christian premises. The more complex a moral issue, I suppose, the less likely will your ethics derive in a simple logical line from a recognizable official religious premise. The way you perceive a concrete problem will be conditioned by half-aware factors such as your individual temperament, morally sensitized to some issues more than others, and the prevalent moral consensus that crosses religious boundaries.

In my own relationships with others, I was prone for some years to reach out, expecting resonance with fellow Catholics and other Christians, less by degrees with Jews, Muslims, Buddhists, and perhaps least with the random atheist. But experience itself has disrupted this tidy chart of intimacy. Today someone in the peace movement, Amnesty International, or the International Rescue Committee, perhaps unchurched or agnostic, often shares deeper values with me than do many Catholics and Christians. In this spirit, once you place a Humanist grid over each of the principal world religions, new priorities emerge in sharp relief, and also the chance to track down new affinities. The agnostic is accustomed to be sized up as an anonymous Christian or Hindu, depending on your imperialistic religious perspective. With equity, then, the Humanist asks for a reversal — to view the humane Christian or Muslim as an anonymous Humanist.

A HUMANIST CREDO

One reason most religious traditions sound more humanistic today is obvious and humbling. They may be learning from the modern secular climate of humanitarianism, equity, relativity, and pragmatism. Theologians are prodded daily to rediscover neglected footnotes in their own religious legacy about tolerance, love of other people, and love of the earth.

Mark Twain once drew a shrewd comparison between religious monopolies and drugstores. While doling out repulsive nostrums for centuries, pharmacists left their soothing medicines untouched on the shelves. Not the physicians, but patients themselves rebelled at last against this system, abandoned the drugstore, and began to devise their own remedies. Then to restore business, physicians prescribed ever weaker doses of the worthless drugs and started emphasizing cure and compassion. Likewise, people were kept "religion-sick for eighteen centuries," until they began abandoning the churches. To restore business, the clergy then began prescribing weaker doses of hell and damnation and started emphasizing empathy and love. The churches had long condoned slavery and witch-burning on the basis of just a few biblical citations. Now suddenly today preachers have changed their message about slavery, witchcraft, hell, and damnation of the unbaptized. "More than 200 death penalties are gone from the law books," Twain says. But "the text remains. It is the practice that has changed. Why? Because the world has corrected the Bible. The Church never corrects it. It also never fails to drop in at the tail of the procession — and take credit for the correction."[1]

In the present Age of Secularity, religious authorities still totter in late to take credit — for instance, by offering a long overdue, grudging exoneration of Galileo or Darwin. You can overhear trendy voices from almost all religious traditions addressing their communities, now by a borrowed socio-political tract on unjust structures in society, now by the latest psychological wisdom about how to love or even how to die. One day, polishing the draft of a Sunday homily, I was interrupted by the visit of a friend who considers herself agnostic. Glancing over a few of the sermon's better moments, she was able to dig into her Humanist imagination and match my practical applications of the Gospel with anecdotes and insights far more insightful than my own. During her long drive that afternoon she had been listening to various motivational tapes, most of them self-help and twelve-step programs, with no explicit religious language. All the advantages of Humanism struck me at that moment. In a casual motivational style, without getting sidetracked by cumbersome religious symbols and doctrines, you could reach people directly about what really matters to them.

However, instead of the one-sided dependency caricatured by Twain, it is more accurate to acknowledge a subtle mutual influence between secular and religious mind-sets. For instance, on the one hand, late nineteenth-century Catholic papal teaching on the rights of labor unions was surely prompted by competition with Marxist organizers for souls of the proletariat. Yet, on the other hand, in exhaustive detail Marx's *Das Kapital* cites parliamentary committee reports of social injustice, compiled by British activist reformers, many of them from an Evangelical background. In fairness, the religious impulse must always be treated as potentially dialectical. One moment it may support, even absolutize, the fashionable verities of a particular time and place. But next moment it can turn into a religion of the oppressed, offering people in that society an ultimate basis on which to question and overturn any penultimate certainty.

A touching exchange in Camus's *The Plague* occurs during a brief swim taken by Tarrou and Dr. Rieux as respite from their work with plague victims. "What interests me," Tarrou confides, "is learning how to become a saint. . . . Can you be a saint without God?" Rieux replies, "I feel more fellowship with the defeated than with saints. Heroism and sanctity don't really appeal to me, I imagine. What interests me is being a human being." The two men's shared code constitutes a Humanist compendium. They treat the plague, whether it be physical microbes, the taint of Nazi collaboration, or some other moral flaw, as something within every person. They are vigilant not to contaminate others less infected and "while unable to be saints, but refusing to bow down to plagues, strive their utmost to be healers."[2]

Among the most respected secular saints of the twentieth century is the British Humanist Bertrand Russell, who publicized his message through books, TV interviews, and protest marches. The opening lines of his three-volume autobiography sum up the values that guided him through a long, energetic career: "Three passions, simple but overwhelmingly strong, have governed my life: the longing for love, the search for knowledge, and unbearable pity for the suffering of humankind. . . . Love and knowledge, so far as they are possible, led upward toward the heavens. But always pity brought me back to earth. Echoes from cries of pain reverberate in my heart."[3]

One day in 1901 he had a sudden taste of lonely futility, much like the shock of death and misery that first met the young Gautama outside his protected royal garden. Russell would later refer back to his own shattering awareness as "not unlike what religious people call conversion." "Having for years cared only for exactness and analysis," he explains, "I found myself filled with semi-mystical feelings about beauty, with an intense interest in children, and with a desire almost as profound as that of the Buddha to find some philosophy which should make human life endurable."[4] He saw humanity doomed to extinction in a dying solar system. It seemed everyone ought to face this tragic verdict without flinching and then at least help those suffering nearby with sympathy, encouragement, and affection. Russell's conversion drove him from contemplative mathematics into a career of militant public advocacy, especially against war.

With apparent endowments of a traditional bodhisattva, Russell is tolerant except for one vehement reservation, which he expresses with his usual force and clarity: "I think all the great religions of the world — Buddhism, Hinduism, Christianity, Islam, and Communism — both untrue and harmful." And "what the world needs is not dogma but an attitude of scientific inquiry, combined with a belief that the torture of millions is not desirable, whether inflicted by Stalin or by a Deity imagined in the likeness of the believer."[5] Russell's sentiment here matches the uncompromising moral proviso of Gandhi: "For me God and Truth are convertible terms. And if anyone told me that God was a God of untruth or a God of torture, I would decline to worship God."

This animus against religion has been traced by Russell himself back to a rebellion at the age of fourteen against the oppressive climate in his own home. A strict Scotch Presbyterian grandmother raised him under a regime of cold baths, compulsory daily piano practice, and family morning prayers. "Only virtue was prized, virtue at the expense of intellect, health, happiness, and every mundane good." His youthful diary shows a precocious struggle with religious doubts, which he felt compelled to smother rather than allow to upset his grandmother. "During the four following years I rejected, successively, free will, immortality, and belief in God, and believed that I suffered much pain in the process. Yet when it was completed, I found myself far happier than I had been while I remained in doubt."[6]

Using Russell's Humanist credo as a point of departure, it is possible to conjure a loose fellowship, selective and mostly implied, of various people trying to be authentic human beings. The origin of this community lies at the fringe, with outsiders and drop-outs surrounding all the charted world religious systems. I shall name this perennial tradition "Humanist" — the concern to humanize the world, to celebrate, secure, and extend human values. Most Humanists view these basic human values as inherent not in each isolated ego but in communal humanity itself. At the service of such rights, the modern state and its bureaucracy can be conditionally summoned or dismissed. The Humanist label must be broad enough to include heroic social activists but also more contemplative or thoughtful figures like Rilke and Faulkner. It implies a complete human being, not just the sterile intellect parodied in free-thinker and village-atheist stereotypes. Taking a second glance at the capstone statement from Russell's autobiography, notice the passion behind his words and his struggle to combine knowledge, love, and empathy.

For most Humanists, the human condition must never be viewed as separable from the sacred cosmos, within which we are only one evolving component. Responding to a questionnaire once sent him by *Humanist* magazine, Russell hesitated to identify himself with the Humanist tag used by this organization because he had been finding "the nonhuman part of the cosmos much more interesting and satisfactory than the human part."[7] You can expect profound Humanists like Russell or Camus, by the way, to disdain credentials of Humanist orthodoxy. For constitutions, manifestos, hierarchies, journals, rallies, and political lobbies may turn into demonic substitutes for the religious baggage these people have tried to discard.

Though Humanist motifs have surfaced in all the major religions discussed already, the present chapter will treat the Humanist Way as a coherent alternative to these traditions, a distinctive spirituality. Two phases can be identified in the average Humanist credo — first, the human rights and responsibilities endorsed by a Humanist consensus, then an iconoclastic attack against counterfeit Humanisms that undermine these values. In Russell's cited denunciation of Buddhism, Christianity, and other religions, he does not spare Marxist Humanists. "It is possible that humanity," he adds, "is on the threshold of a golden age. But if so, it will be necessary first to slay the dragon that guards the door, and this dragon is religion."[8] Yet Russell could show tougher consistency, I am convinced, by including among his potential dragons any ism, even his own Humanism platform. For as I remarked before, slogans about the

Humanist golden age can also be misused to shut off inquiry and sanction antihuman ignorance and violence. As Kierkegaard aptly concludes, even the truth on the lips of some people can become a lie.

I shall analyze both phases of the Humanist Way — first, its negative critique of the conventional religions and, second, its affirmation of an alternative spirituality. My model calls for a genuinely open Humanist imagination. Tolerant by definition though often anticlerical and antiscriptural by temperament, this Way opens itself to anonymous Humanists anywhere, even people with a traditional religious affiliation.

THE PROJECTION FALLACY

In Attar's *Conference of the Birds,* analyzed at length in chapter 7, the pilgrims after monumental ordeals at last reach the door of heaven. There they discover that the goal of their pilgrimage, the Simurgh, is none other than themselves. Thus, interpreted within a context of Sufi panentheism, their experience points to a God radically immanent, distinct but inseparable from their own human individuality. However, the average monotheist, I think, finishes reading this spiritual classic with some disquiet. The book-long sacred quest, with its stunning demands of time and risk, in retrospect turns into one long, pointless detour. For the alleged treasure beyond the rainbow, as so many fairy tales show, stands buried all the while in your own backyard. It is hard to imagine a spiritual guide so cruel or inept, subjecting pilgrims to this wasteful, circuitous lesson plan. Rather than siphoning off energy on a heavenly search, why not commit yourself to this earthly life and to your own humanity from the start? If the Sacred exists, even Attar insists you will find it only within.

With similar misgivings, Jews, Christians, and Muslims wrestle with the biblical tale of Abraham's sacrifice. He first identifies a voice from God demanding that he kill his son. Interpreting this command as a test of his faith, Abraham prepares for ritual slaughter. However, at the last moment, the voice of an angel stops him from slaying the boy and tells him to offer a ram sacrifice instead. Kierkegaard's interpretation of this story in *Fear and Trembling* has proved no less familiar than the original account in Genesis. Abraham's first impulse to sacrifice his son is commended as a sterling model for the Christian's "teleological suspension of the ethical" — a leap of faith that adheres rigidly to God's word even if it appears to contradict the moral law of conscience and common sense.

Despite all its heated inwardness, Kierkegaard's reading, I believe, sets an irresponsible precedent for violence in the name of religion. Interpreted far differently, Abraham's first impulse to kill the boy could only have been attributed to God by mistake. Perhaps this poor man had been fascinated by some half-understood local fertility rite of firstborn sacrifice. And his second impulse, to offer a ram instead, marks an advance in Abraham's moral perception. The prompting he at last associates with an angel's voice is actually his revived human conscience, a father's love, his moral and religious center. This voice of his humanity should have prevailed from the beginning, no matter how persuasive the summons from rival voices. Read in this way, Abraham's experience represents a conversion from the most irrational religious blindness into a faith integral to his humanity. Recognizing that his loyalty to God has been misdirected, he learns now to distrust any impulse that violates his Humanist conscience. Inverting Kierkegaard's phrase, if you will, the story of Abraham confirms an ethical repudiation of the pseudo-religious.[9]

These two narratives, drawn from the Muslim and Hebrew traditions, lend themselves to a plausible Humanist reinterpretation, which sifts out a recurring pattern. First, I experience a spiritual hope or need. Second, I project or reify it as sacred, imagined as distant and transcendent. Third, recognizing my focus in stage two has been misdirected, I turn back to detect rudiments of the Sacred in my original experience. In other words, imagining the remote Sacred now as spatially near and interior, I try to retroject what has been mistakenly projected. These three stages can be summed up in the following popular Zen koan: when I began Zen, tea was mere tea. As I progressed, tea was no longer tea. Yet now that I am enlightened, tea is indeed tea.

The effort to redirect a religious projection becomes the guiding intent especially for Humanists like Rainer Maria Rilke and Friedrich Nietzsche. Nietzsche deplores the projections that siphon off human energy. "There is a lake which one day refused to drain off. A dam was erected where the water previously flowed away. Ever since, this lake has been rising higher and higher. Maybe that very renunciation will also lend us the strength to bear the renunciation itself. Perhaps humanity will rise ever higher when it once ceases to flow out into a God." And Nietzsche's prophet Zarathustra asserts that "all Gods are the parables and prevarications of poets. We are always lifted higher — specifically to the realm of the clouds. Here we place our motley bastards and call them Gods and supermen."[10]

Rainer Maria Rilke echoes the same motif: "What madness, to distract us to a beyond, when we are surrounded right here by tasks and expectations and futures. What fraud, to steal images of earthly rapture and sell them to heaven behind our backs. It is high time for the impoverished earth to claim back all those loans which have been raised on her bliss to furnish some future-beyond!" Rilke recognized that his earlier poems used to speak with familiarity to and about God. Yet by 1923 he admitted that "now you would hardly ever hear me refer to God.... God's attributes are taken away from God, a name no longer utterable, and returned to the created universe."[11]

The Feuerbach Prelude

The term "projection," a versatile concept in the modern social sciences, was allegedly first imported into English by the novelist George Eliot in her translation of Ludwig Feuerbach. She stretched the word to cover two German concepts, borrowed by Feuerbach from Hegel, and later handed down to Marx — *Vergegenstandlichung* or objectification, and *Entausserung* or alienation. This vital brokerage in concepts stands as an apt metaphor for the role of Feuerbach in the history of modern philosophy. His reputation today has diminished to that of a middleman between Hegel and Marx, an antireligious prelude to Marx, who quickly outgrew his influence.[12] I realize why many critics still find his style too iconoclastic and epigrammatic to sustain a coherent argument. Yet like Thoreau, William James, or Nietzsche, he is the sort of philosopher whose struggles with emerging insights are often more exciting than his completed thought. Writing with an effort to make sense of his own religious ambivalence, his unbelief and half-belief, he acts as a wise Socratic midwife, drawing the reader into a shared process of self-questioning.

In a preface to the first volume of his collected works in 1846, Ludwig Feuerbach presents a clear apologia, designed to soften the misunderstandings long associated with his name: "Whoever says no more of me than that I am an atheist, says and knows nothing of me. The question as to the existence or non-existence of God, the opposition between theism and atheism, belongs to the sixteenth and seventh centuries but not to the nineteenth. I deny God. But that means for me that I deny the negation of humanity. In place of the illusory, fantastic, heavenly position of humanity, which in actual life necessarily leads to the degradation of humanity, I substitute the tangible, actual, and consequently also the political and social position of humanity. The question concerning the existence or non-existence of God is for me nothing but the question concerning the existence or non-existence of humanity."[13] In other words, Feuerbach is a Humanist first and an antitheist second, his antitheism being simply a corollary to his Humanist premise. Presumably if he could be shown that a particular religious tradition supported his Humanist credo, he would not be compelled to oppose that tradition.

Just as Bertrand Russell identified particular factors in his own training to explain his quarrel with conventional religion, so Feuerbach suffered under various abuses of political and religious authority, beginning from his earliest college years. Attracted during adolescence to theology and the ministry, he moved from Heidelberg to Berlin, mostly for study under the theologian Schleiermacher and the philosopher Hegel. At length he had to decide between a career in theology or in philosophy. The choice proved an easy one. By now he recognized that "the theological mishmash of freedom and dependence, reason and faith, was completely repellent to my soul's demand for truth — for unity, decisiveness, absoluteness." Also, as a student he was hounded by Berlin police for his alleged membership in a secret revolutionary cadre and was later denounced by church authorities for writing an anonymous pamphlet that ridiculed conventional beliefs about immortality. This youthful recklessness and its dire censure would damage his academic reputation thereafter and rule out any full-time university appointment.[14]

The single prophetic theme to which Feuerbach devotes his entire life is the emancipation from theology in Feuerbach himself — and by extension, in the entire human condition. The later theologian Karl Barth points out an important irony here: "The attitude of anti-theologian Feuerbach is more theological than that of many theologians." Feuerbach feels the impatience of more combative Humanists like Marx, Nietzsche, and Freud to cut any misguided spiritual impulse down to size. Yet unlike them, he often treats religious experience and symbols with surprising empathy. The purpose of all his writing, he insists, "is far from negative. It is positive. I negate only in order to affirm." He wants "to transform theologians into anthropologists, lovers of God into lovers of humanity, candidates for the next world into students of this world, religious and political flunkeys of heavenly and earthly monarchs and lords into free, self-reliant citizens of the earth."[15]

The abstraction commonly labeled Being, Nature, God, or the Sacred actually can be reinterpreted as a "commonplace book where human beings register their highest feelings and thoughts, the genealogical album into which they enter the names of the things most dear and sacred to them." By turning toward the Sacred, you free yourself from the limitations of life; you throw off whatever oppresses or adversely affects you. The Sacred is your projected "self-awareness, emancipated from all actuality. You feel yourself free, happy, blessed only in your religion, for here you live in your true genius, here you celebrate your Sunday." Even Paul's Letter to the Romans seems to endorse Feuerbach's line of thought — "the Holy Spirit is the sighing creature, the creature's longing for God."[16]

Your God-image or spiritual focus stands for your rejected better half, your unconscious alter ego, and thus only in the process of living your religion do you become again a completed human being. Devout Lutherans, for example, confess their human nature sinful to the lowest degree, yet by the grace of Christ they are saved, restored to an idealized humanity. Like blood rushing back and forth from heart to extremities, so "in the religious systole I propel my own nature from myself, I throw myself outward. In the religious diastole I receive the rejected nature into my heart again. . . . God is the being who acts in me, with me, through me, upon me, for me. God is the principle of my salvation, my good dispositions and actions, consequently my own good principle and nature."[17]

Framing this paradox in the more abstract vocabulary of Hegelian dialectic, Feuerbach explains, "This is the mystery of religion. I project my being into objectivity. And then again I make myself an object in relation to my projected image now converted into a subject. Thus I think of myself as an object to myself, the object of an object, the object of another being than myself." True to the legacy of Fichte and Hegel, Feuerbach views this process of religious projection and reification as a misleading detour, but a necessary stage in one's emerging self-awareness. To transcend itself, the mind must first gauge its scope and limits. It achieves this awareness by differentiating itself, sizing up its projected relationship with nonmind — an external world, a Thou, a God. As Feuerbach explains it, confronting my own unconscious self, which seems alien to me, I ask in wonder: "What am I? Where have I come from? To what end?" And "this feeling that I am nothing without a not-I that is distinct from me yet intimately related to me — something other, which is at the same time my own being — this is the religious feeling."[18]

Religious projection, then, is a necessary *felix culpa* in the process of self-transcendence. Yet if this projection solidifies as final, it can turn into a dangerous form of idolatry. For the earth and my own humanity have been emptied, just in order to funnel all these essential attributes into a heavenly mirage. "The more empty life is, the fuller, the more concrete is God," Feuerbach summarizes. "The impoverishing of the real world and the enriching of God is one act. Only the poor individual has a rich God."[19] And the day this mirage or God-image itself proves too inaccessible or implausible, it will be tossed aside, leaving behind only a dehumanized vacuum. In a reversal of the Prometheus myth, those endowments stolen from humanity, and invested in God, must be restored again to their rightful human origins.

The Marxist Prometheus

The image of a defiant Prometheus, chained to his rock by vengeful Gods, caught the imagination of many Romantics, especially the young Karl Marx. The foreword to his doctoral dissertation on Democritus and Epicurus cites the following verses from Aeschylus' *Prometheus Bound:* "I hate all the Gods. . . . Better to be the servant of this rock than to be faithful boy to Father Zeus." Scoffing at theology as just a mercenary voice for the established Prussian church, Marx sides with the liberal spirit of philosophy against "all heavenly and earthly Gods who do not acknowledge human self-consciousness as the highest divinity."[20] With the same revolutionary enthusiasm, Marx in the early 1840s would support Feuerbach's critique of religion and the split with Hegel. Looking back on this heady era dominated by Bruno Bauer and the Young Hegelians, Frederick Engels observed in 1886, "We all became at once Feuerbachians....Meanwhile the Revolution of 1848 thrust the whole of philosophy aside as ceremoniously as Feuerbach had thrust aside Hegel. And in the process Feuerbach himself was pushed into the background."[21]

The topic of religion, narrowed mostly to its Jewish and Christian forms, takes up surprisingly few pages in Marx's abundant writings. Like Feuerbach, Marx perceives himself living in a postreligious era, a time when God's existence or nonexistence has become an irrelevant question. The few brilliant epigrams about religion associated with his name today date back to young Marx the proto-existentialist of 1844, not to the later social engineer of *Das Kapital,* the Marx canonized by Engels, Lenin, and Soviet orthodoxy. Convinced that Feuerbach had succeeded in killing off religion, Marx piles one vivid metaphor upon another to sum up Feuerbach's critique. Then anxious to get this religious distraction out of his way, he plunges ahead toward the mature task of philosophy, to change the practical world of economics.

Marx thinks of heaven, God, or religion as just a mirror reflecting your own consciousness. This mirror gives an encyclopedic compendium of your values and hopes. It is your moral sanction, your solemn completion as a human being. You are not made in God's image; rather, the God-projection is made in your image. Religion is an illusory projected world, the halo and aroma of something invaluable, the "sigh of the oppressed creature, the heart of a heartless world." Suppose, for instance, you utter a cry for God's help. Marx would translate your prayer as first a cry of actual human distress, and perhaps he might empathize with it. At the same time, he would judge it an ineffectual protest against the oppression causing this distress. Unless you brush aside this distracting imaginary uplift from God, you cannot focus on practical resistance to the actual oppression that gave rise to your original protest. "The abolition of religion as the illusory happiness of people is required for their real happiness," says Marx. "Criticism has plucked imaginary flowers from the chain, not so that human beings will wear the chain without any fantasy or consolation, but so they will shake off the chain and cull the living flower."[22]

Inserted into this Feuerbachian context, Marx's terse description of religion as "opium of the people" deserves a second glance. He probes inside the attitudes, not of the oppressor but of the victim, who yearns for medicine and solace. In contrast, the oppressor's perspective can be detected in Lenin's use of a different preposition: "Opium *for* the people." It is ironical that Lenin himself once cautioned that a declaration of war against religion would be the best means to revive interest in religion and prevent it from dying out.[23] In a similar way, Marx wants to sidestep any direct confrontation with religion. He would treat religious projections as mere symptoms of an unrecognized alienation from the true human condition. The empirical sources of this disease have to be located in specific unjust economic and social conditions. Once you take direct action to humanize these conditions, alienation itself and the grounds for religious protest or escape will vanish.

Though these insights of 1844 lean heavily on Feuerbach, Marx within just a year would clarify a few crucial differences between their two approaches. Feuerbach's concern is the isolated human ego rather than each existential social human being.

Feuerbach deals with the abstract, timeless human species, not the particular social conditions that give rise to a specific religious projection in a given culture and era. Marx denies the premise of Fichte and Hegel that consciousness has to divide, alienate, and objectify itself in order to transcend and become aware of itself. What drives your mind to build religious castles in the air is not the mere internal necessity of psychology or metaphysics. Alienation rises from painful disparities between actual working conditions and prevailing economic custom or from the estrangement between your oppressed working self and your genuine leisure self. Whereas Feuerbach reduces theology to anthropology, Marx intends a further step, to reduce anthropology to practical economics and sociology.[24]

From Marx's viewpoint, just as Feuerbach has deconstructed religion or "the holy form of self-alienation," Marx himself plans to unmask the "unholy" forms of self-alienation in everyday life. Yet paradoxically, once he announces this conscious postreligious agenda, Marx gives a fresh Humanist update of the Hebrew prophets thundering against current idolatries. What are the major unexamined cultural, legal, and moral projections of his own day? In the *Communist Manifesto,* Marx and Engels address the ruling classes: "Your very ideas are but the outgrowth of your bourgeois production and property conditions, just as your jurisprudence is but the will of your class made into a law for all.... The ruling ideas of each age have ever been the ideas of its ruling class."[25] In other words, bourgeois oppressors rationalize their controlling position in society by invoking the right to property and free trade. This rationale is then projected and reified as a moral axiom, imprinted on each individual in the socialization process — and thus initiating a legacy of alienation.

While others were celebrating the midcentury triumph of Eurocentric bourgeois civilization, Marx had an apocalyptic vision that the era was in fact hurtling toward moral suicide. He found naked self-interest poisoning everything in reach. Personal links between people were debased into mere exchange value. The heritage of countless human rights had been reduced to a single inhuman claim, the right to private property. Male laborers had become mere appendages to the machine, worth no more than the cost to feed them. Wives were treated as commodities, as public and private prostitutes, their children a burdensome debt or investment for later security.

Victorian England, of course, provided Marx a showcase of religious rationalizations for this malaise and its cure, both objects well documented in the fiction of Dickens, Trollope, and George Eliot. Marx himself, for instance, once witnessed a Hyde Park demonstration in 1855 by lower classes against the passage of the Beer Bill and Sunday Trading Bill. Both laws were promoted by business lobbies, allegedly to preserve Sabbath rectitude by closing pubs and stores. Their actual economic motive was to instill habits of temperance and thrift among their workers and to discriminate against the small shop, dependent for its survival on weekend local shoppers.[26]

Casting about for a symbol of the worst greed and consumerism imaginable, Marx settled on a repulsive nineteenth-century stereotype, the Yankee peddler bragging of his right to worship and vote as he pleases. Carrying his shop or office in a suitcase or backpack, the restless American entrepreneur roams everywhere, talking of nothing but bargains and shrewd investments. If he grows silent about his own business for an instant, you can presume he wants only to sniff out the business of someone else. "Mammon is the idol to whom he prays, not only with his lips but with all the power of his body and soul. In his eyes, the world is nothing but a stock exchange, and he is convinced that here below he has no other destiny than to become richer than his neighbors."[27]

Mammon is the bourgeois God-image that Marx calls "my Lord Capital." He points out two situations that reinforce each other — the popular Calvinist image of a degraded sinner groveling for mercy before an implacable God and the alienated proletariat bowing before faceless capitalist management. An outrageous interweaving of capitalist and Christian motifs, for example, can be found in the popular Protestant hymn "Rock of Ages Cleft for Me." An avid anti-Methodist, its author, Augustus Toplady, in 1775 explicated his lyrics with a gross analogy from economics. The tab incurred by each sinner before God, computed at the rate of one sin per second, results in a national debt so enormous that all Europe could not pay it off. You can only abase yourself before the Divine Creditor's mercy: "Not the labors of my hands / Can fulfill Thy law's demands. . . . / All my sins could not atone. / Thou must save, and Thou alone."[28]

In *Das Kapital,* Marx lines up parallel mistakes of projection in the realms of both money and religion. From your own human labor and relations you extract a mysterious force and then reify it as a money-fetish, just the way you tend to project your own human endowments upon a God. "Money degrades all the Gods of humanity, and turns them into commodities," he concludes. "Money is the universal self-established value of all things. It has therefore robbed the whole world of its specific value, both the world of humanity and of nature. Money is the estranged essence of human work and human existence. This alien essence dominates us, and we worship it."[29]

To liberate humanity from this enslaving idolatry is the mission of Marx's chosen people, the proletarian class. The idealized proletariat often looks like an unconscious projection of Marx's own self-image — a propertyless and nationless intellectual expelled from one European nation after another, proud yet debt-ridden, forced into grudging dependency on Engels and others to keep his children in a Dickensian atmosphere of threadbare gentility. Yet Marx himself and his proletarian workers, with property and political clout so negligible, have nothing left to renounce except seductive religious distractions. "By heralding the dissolution of a hitherto existing world order," says Marx, "the proletariat merely proclaims the secret of its own existence. For the proletariat is a factual dissolution of that world order."[30]

Marx's lasting significance, in the opinion of theologian Reinhold Niebuhr, has been to express this apocalyptic belief in the proletariat's destiny. Society's brutalized victims, including Marx himself, are now transformed into its moral saviors. To turn deprivation and social defeat of the oppressed into the very forecast of their final victory, to foresee in their loss of all property the fate of a civilization in which no one will have privileges of property — this is to snatch victory out of defeat in the style of the great religious traditions.[31]

The Freudian Reduction

Marx's thought has inspired an astounding range of applications since his death over a century ago. The Soviet Union before its dissolution and China have tried to become rival laboratories testing his social theory. And a range of prominent Buddhist, Muslim, and Christian Marxist theologians still lay claim to the proto-existentialist early Marx of the rediscovered Paris Documents. Yet political regimes invoking the name of Marx have seldom lacked their own prophets denouncing a betrayal of the revolution. Autocratic, provisional five-year plans tend to congeal into fixed policy. If portrayed as too near, the classless millennium proves disillusioning, and if too remote, then beyond imagination. Camus's *The Rebel* recounts the myth of an enthusiastic Prometheus rebelling against human misery and leading his liberated people away to the desert. Yet prone to develop into an authoritarian Caesar, this savior has to be challenged now by yet another Prometheus — thus, a line of successive dissenters, ever rebelling against their own unconscious totalitarian impulses.

Just a decade after the Bolshevist Revolution, Freud wrote a spirited rebuttal to what he called the European Marxist experiment. During this period, his writings and therapy had won a following among many Viennese Russian exiles, and then in the new Soviet regime itself. The Russian translation of Freud sold widely, and the Soviet Republic became the first government to help fund psychoanalysis as a certified science. Also the first psychoanalytic kindergarten was founded there in 1926. Though Freud's critique of bourgeois neuroses at first sounded congenial to the communist leadership, psychoanalysis was outlawed during the Stalinist 1930s as too individualistic and decadent. Today in the former Republic, analysts no longer need to hold sessions underground in doorways and alleys, and Freud has recovered a prestige witnessed almost nowhere else since the Second World War.[32]

Though idealistic in purpose, the Marxist experiment had within a few years proved too impatient and violent for Freud's endorsement. He scorns its promise of a utopian human community, even less plausible than the Judeo-Christian heavenly illusions that Marxists renounced. The movement claims it will alter human nature within a few generations so that people can work freely and live without aggression and hatred. Yet more aggressively still, the new saviors will butcher anyone who cannot change fast enough. Even stripped of their bourgeois property, human beings will never lose the "self-preservative instinct, aggressiveness, the need to be loved," and most of all, their "superego, which represents tradition and past ideals, and would for a time resist the incentives of a new economic situation." Marxist orthodoxy has developed an uncanny likeness to the authoritarian religions from which it claims to liberate a new humanity. Used as a weapon against its own varieties of heresy and doubt, "the writings of Marx have replaced the Bible and the Quran as a source of revelation."[33]

"Why have all revolutions begun as movements of liberation and ended up as tyrannies?" In Ignazio Silone's *Bread and Wine,* this is the pivotal question confronting Spina, the hunted Marxist revolutionary disguised as a Catholic priest in the Italy of Mussolini's Ethiopian War. "You're the best part of us all," his old friend Nunzio assures him. "You don't believe in God anymore, but in the proletariat, with the same absolutism as before." Yet outraged by its inhuman tactics, Spina at length decides to leave the communist party. "I can't sacrifice to the party the reasons that led me to join it," he explains. "It would be like putting the church before Christ."[34] Like ex-communist Silone in actual life, the character of Spina must at last strip away every orthodoxy in order to retain his Humanist integrity.

Sizing up the decay of Eurocentric bourgeois civilization, Freud was paradoxically both more pessimistic and optimistic than Marx about humanity's potential recovery. For example, why did the horrors of the First World War produce so many disillusioned liberals? Because their illusions had been too inflated beforehand, presuming that fellow citizens were living on a higher plane of ethics and culture than had been internalized maturely. That war peeled away a hard-earned civilized veneer to expose the innate human brutality no human being ever outgrows completely. The postwar League of Nations, too, could not be expected to sustain peace without support from a massive police force.

An inhuman war, then, managed to confirm a few momentous Freudian premises about human nature. Despite its brutal child-labor practices, this hypocritical era had sentimentalized childhood innocence. A convinced Hobbesian, Freud views children, on the contrary, as predatory and seductive by nature, competing with siblings for their parents' love. With modest optimism he urges that by sound training, an altruistic morality may awaken from this primary egotism. Another vital Freudian assumption is that illusions, dreams, and wishes express a vital unconscious component and need to be interpreted and reintegrated into the complete human life. However, when illusions contradict reality, they turn into delusions, and thus misleading, must be abandoned. Freud finds that experience has forced upon him the distasteful conviction that human destiny is a tragic conflict between the death-force and life-force or Eros, with no afterlife. "The question is not what belief is more pleasing, comfortable, or advantageous to life," he confides to his friend Pastor Pfister, "but what may approximate more closely to the puzzling reality outside us.... Thus, to me my pessimism seems a conclusion, while the optimism of my opponents seems an a priori assumption."[35]

Treating religion as a delusional projection, both Marx and Freud expect it to wither in the future, once the disorder initiating it is outgrown. Like Feuerbach, Marx, and the later behaviorists, Freud tends to view particular ideas, religious or otherwise, as mere epiphenomena, rationalizations, symptoms rather than causes. Whereas Marx approaches religion as a social construct, shaped by the ideology of a particular ruling class, Freud views it mostly as an individual defense mechanism, a disguised wish-fulfillment for managing insecurity and other unconscious needs. With religion dismissed as just a symptom, Marx will focus all his attention on the particular causes of cultural and economic alienation in a specific society. In a comparable way, Freud sidesteps religious symptoms to track down the particular unresolved neurotic conflict that launched a specific religious projection.

Throughout his work, Freud's analysis of religious experience keeps returning to two principal scenarios. Religion arises from the projected quest, first for forgiveness, or second, for an enlargement of one's ego-boundaries. The setting for the first, more common quest is a typical Jewish or Christian experience of sin and guilt. Hounded by remorse and obsessions, the client projects the God-image of a sovereign judge or eventually at best, a compassionate advocate. Feuerbach's illustrations of religious projection commonly focus on such a pattern — notably the model of Luther's self-destructive remorse healed by a God of mercy and trust.

For the disturbed client, guilt feelings often stem from a superego-imprint of the parents' value system, self-punishing because of a child's unresolved oedipal rebellion and hostility. An image of a provident God, for instance, may represent a reinstatement by adults of their childhood need for parents as a shield against nightly horrors. Belief in a devil may represent the terrifying doppelgänger-half of this same authority, toward whom a child feels ambivalent love-hate, an emotion too threatening for anything other than dualistic expression. Under Freud's scrutiny, what at first looks religious will commonly be reduced to something else. He tends to retroject each immature religious projection back to its origins in the authoritarian bourgeois family structure.

Like many thinkers of the nineteenth century, Freud is intrigued by analogies between ontogenesis and phylogenesis, microcosm and macrocosm. We are asked to imagine each individual and also the entire race evolving from uncontrolled selfish drives to a mature life guided by reason. In his famous Wolfman and Ratman case studies, he notices that both men during early adolescence had passed through a prolonged pseudo-religious phase, dominated by rebellion, doubt, and guilt. Reflecting on this sort of evidence, and borrowing Comte's outline of three progressive phases in history, Freud constructs his own armchair anthropology. From the tendentious perspective of Eurocentric modernism, history seems to begin with primitive societies that are infantile. In its second stage, humanity endures an adolescent or even obsessive-compulsive era of collective religious belief, such as in the Middle Ages. And now the twentieth century approaches an adult millennium centered on the experimental sciences. Each successive phase retains the archeological levels of all preceding stages as an ongoing enticement to regress.

In *Future of an Illusion,* Freud encourages people to speed up the third phase, the reign of Logos or Reason, which he playfully calls his God. Yet he admits that the majority, unwilling to sacrifice their religious addictions, may prove unable to achieve "an education to reality." For renouncing such illusions will mean people "can no longer be the center of the universe, no longer the object of tender care by a loving Providence. They will be in the same position as children who have left their parents' house where they were so warm and comfortable."[36]

Besides this first projected quest, triggered by motifs of religious guilt, fear, and estrangement, Freud recognizes a second type of projected quest, rising instead from the more positive experience of spiritual ecstasy. Its roots can be traced not so much to the oedipal conflict as to a pre-oedipal stage of identification with the mother, the period of primal attachment and gradual separation. The novelist Romain Rolland once wrote Freud about Rolland's spiritual oceanic feeling, as if engulfed in eternity, what William James would call a passionate affirmation of the universe. In *Civilization and Its Discontents,* Freud denies having such an experience himself. Yet conceding its plausibility, he longs to interpret it in his own resourceful way. After all, the oceanic feeling shows an affinity with those puzzling moments of empathy or transference familiar to every analyst. All three experiences give an impression of dissolving ego-boundaries, so that your ego may seem enlarged, cloned, engulfed, or emptied.

Freud tries to explain what he means by the defense mechanism he calls projection. Most of the time your ego seems autonomous, marked off distinctly from the world outside the self. Yet psychotic disorders confront people with occasions when parts of their body or mind appear estranged from the ego. The paranoid individual, for instance, will reify and personify as an outside enemy the internal threat that cannot be faced. At more normal moments, too, the ego's sharp boundaries prove just as permeable. For instance, the lover and beloved, the hypnotist and hypnotized tell of merging their separate identities. Also an infant in the womb or at the breast cannot yet distinguish its ego from the outside world. In the gradual process of separation from the nursing process, of course, you learn that various objects have their own will and identity, resistant at times to your demands.

"Originally the ego includes everything," Freud explains "Later it separates off an external world from itself. Our present ego-feeling is, therefore, only a shrunken residue of a much more inclusive, all-embracing feeling."[37] Thus, the present demarcated ego-margins exist side-by-side with these wider, remembered ego-margins of infancy. Sparked by sudden associations, the broader, regressive ego-boundaries may now erupt into consciousness and be misinterpreted as something projected beyond, and thus uncanny and spiritual. Some years later, carrying this Freudian theme a few steps further, Margaret Mahler in her theory of object-relations would describe the culmination of our human life cycle as "symbiotic fusion with the all-good mother, who was at one time part of the self in a blissful state of well-being." Mahler hopes to explain the powerful smile of motherly recognition, portrayed by centuries of artists in the grace-bearing Christian Madonna or the Buddhist Kuan Yin.[38]

To a disciplined rationalist like Freud, no more disturbing religious projection can be imagined than the ecstatic identification of a mob with its charismatic leader. Today he would have spotted immediate parallels between the suicidal religious obedience shown at Jonestown and Waco, and the wild adulation surrounding popular singers, movie stars, athletes, and political leaders. Devotees seem to act with mindless impetuosity like robots, as if hypnotized or drugged. Caught up in a carnival orgy, they almost yearn to regress in their individual and species history, back to the realm of children and primitives. Yet Freud can understand the widespread secret wish to surrender your hard-won autonomy. It takes heroic effort to maintain boundaries between the coherent ego and the "unconscious and repressed portion left outside it. And we know the stability of this new acquisition is exposed to constant shocks. In dreams and neuroses what is thus excluded knocks for admission at the gates, guarded though they are by resistances." The superego "comprises the sum of all the limitations in which the ego has to acquiesce. For that reason, the abrogation of this ideal would necessarily be a magnificent festival for the ego."[39]

The hardened ego-boundaries that separate one individual in the mob from another, and all of them from their charismatic leader — these margins relax or vanish in an atmosphere of hysterical contagion. According to Freud's book *Group Psychology,* the rationale for such a disorder is regressive identification and projection. Distressed over the death of a kitten, for instance, a small child takes on the lost object's identity and crawls on all fours. A young man in excessive oedipal attachment to his mother, reluctant at puberty to replace her with her sexual rival, may unconsciously transform himself into his mother. Looking about for figures to replace his own lost ego, he wants to give them the love and care shown him by his own mother. Freud describes this process as "identification with an object that is renounced or lost, as a substitute for that object — an introjection of it into the ego."[40]

Perhaps the trauma of loss or anomie explains why those vulnerable to recruitment into religious cults often come from estranged homes or a broken romance. Or they just drift from one codependent family to another, searching for new caregivers. Freud blames churches for preying upon this immature dependency in their converts. Proselytizers play up similarities "between the Christian community and a family, and believers call themselves brothers in Christ." For "Christ stands to individual members of the believing group as a kind elder brother. He is their substitute father."[41]

In Freud's clients and especially in his own personal life, this readiness to merge or lean strikes him as a humiliating weakness. It provides the moist soil for unmanageable transference, religious cults, and totalitarian regimes. Yet according to his biographers, Freud himself ironically gave half-conscious encouragement to a devout inner circle basking in his reflected light. He imagined himself another Hannibal marching against Rome or a new Moses dying just short of the Promised Land. At the height of his career, investing each of his six closest lieutenants with a symbolic ring, he selected, groomed, and banished one disciple after another. In later editions of his books, for instance, you can trace in footnotes the obliterated names of any recent apostate from the psychoanalytic movement. Yet unfortunately, though detailed about the religious distortions to be eliminated, Freud never spells out their spiritual replacement, the Age of the Therapeutic. His utopia of scientific reason would remain as sketchy as Marx's classless society.

After his own turbulent break from Freud, Carl Jung — the disciple whom Freud had once designated his "crown prince" — called attention with mischief to the ghost of religion lurking behind the master's detached professorial style. When Freud in person spoke of Eros or the sexual life-force, his tone became devout, "almost anxious, and all signs of his normally critical and skeptical manner vanished." The antiseptic biological vocabulary could not cover up a hidden daimonic passion. "Freud, who had always made much of his irreligiosity, had now constructed a dogma, . . . scientifically irreproachable and free from all religious taint." In place of "a jealous God whom he had lost, Freud had substituted another competing image, that of sexuality, . . . no less insistent, exacting, domineering, threatening, and morally ambivalent than the original one."[42]

An Iconoclastic Social Psychology

Summing up the history of Freudianism after Freud's death, Erich Fromm calls the psychoanalytic movement a new religion that "shared the fate of most religious movements. . . . Eventually, dogma and ritual and idolization of the leader replace creativity and spontaneity." This tilt toward one-sided orthodoxy has plagued the followers of both Marx and Freud. "Freudians saw the individual unconscious and were blind to the social unconscious. Orthodox Marxists, on the contrary, were keenly aware of the unconscious factors in social behavior, but remarkably blind in their appreciation of individual motivation."[43] Fortunately, after the Second World War, in the process of broadening their respective philosophical foundations, many Marxists and Freudians had begun to discover common ground. The fruition of this dialogue can be traced especially in Jacques Lacan, founder of the Ecole Freudienne de Paris, in the French neo-Marxist Louis Althusser, in scholars of the Frankfort School for Social Research, and in Erich Fromm's many popular books on analytic social psychology.[44]

Lacan's career illustrates how heated such a dialogue can become. Censured for his haphazard practice of therapy, and for his program to update Freud in the light of linguistics, structural anthropology, and social theory, Lacan was expelled from the International Psychoanalytic Association in 1963. An aggressive exile, he then compared himself with the philosopher Spinoza, excommunicated from his synagogue. Lacan's teaching, despite his turgid and quirky style, develops some vital leads in Freud that would otherwise escape notice. For instance, a child's pre-oedipal identification with the mother, Freud's oceanic and symbiotic stage, is reinterpreted by Lacan as presymbolic, precultural — a phase without ego-boundaries, personal identity, unconsciousness, or Marxist alienation. The oedipal moment, represented by the father's intervention, initiates the child into a specific language system, repression, symbolic rules, and taboos of the surrounding culture. At this point a person begins to be socialized and thus alienated, with a unique superego and unconscious. Thus your drives, governed before only by the pleasure principle, are now mediated to you in the context of an incest restriction, for example, or a patriarchal value system. Breaking through this cultural repression, the dreams, jokes, and poetry of adult life can give expression to the deepest presocialized experiences.[45]

As another example of Marxist-Freudian interchange, the Institute for Social Research at Frankfort University from the early 1930s tried to locate barriers to utopia in large-scale social, political, and economic forces, and also in the individual psyche. Why was the average German worker, for example, so susceptible to an authoritarian regime? Figures like Theodor Adorno and Herbert Marcuse felt sufficiently alarmed by their findings to decide on an early emigration. Reacting to government harassment, the institute moved first to Geneva, then to Columbia University in New York. Among those departing for America was Erich Fromm, an influential teacher of psychoanalysis at the institute and founder of the South German Institute for Psychoanalysis. All the principal motifs of the Frankfurt School are present in his social psychology, a distinctive synthesis of Marx and Freud.

For a confirmed Marxist, the ideology behind standard psychoanalytic practice offers a ready target for dialectical critique. Two figures meet in an isolated contractual relationship, a purchased hour of friendship, and center on the trivia of bourgeois existence — an impending career decision, work stress, or a stale love affair. Though clients may gain release from the bondage of personal self-deceptions, they are now left more vulnerable to the larger social evils that once made these unconscious defenses necessary. Treating the mere symptoms of alienation, of course, falls short of healing the social alienation itself. The analyst often smokes out rebellion only to smother it by reinstating the bourgeois father's authority.[46]

At times Freud himself calls into question the unconscious premises of his own era. Who is normal? The people judged most sane in any society are the majority, shaped mostly by the unquestioned values of that culture, whereas the minority often appear deviant. For example, the typical Viennese businessman would seek analysis not for himself but for a depressed wife or unruly children. Yet Freud suspected the man unconsciously wanted his family recycled only to comply with his perverse control, the actual source of their present mental affliction. The analyst was being hired to send them back into a family or social milieu that itself subverted a genuine cure. In his works, Freud conjectures that some epochs, even entire cultures, might be neurotic.[47]

At the point where Freud gives up on this question, Fromm faces it directly. He observes each society projecting its own particular social values as a filter of language, logic, and taboos. In the socialization process, this projected grid then shapes the unaware consciousness of every individual within it. For instance, some complex artistic or spiritual experiences are almost impossible to imagine if a given community never identifies them or coins the words to express them. Unless first helped to reach an awareness of your own lifelong social indoctrination, you cannot expect to liberate yourself from it. Only after achieving such awareness can you begin to reach beyond the unreflective nationalism, xenophobia, and other moral limitations upheld by a particular value system.[48]

Analyzing your own talents and quirks of personality, with some difficulty you can sift out those attributes common to all people, those shared only with some other people, and those unique to yourself. These are respectively the universal, the cultural, and the individual dimensions in any experience. Whereas Freud centers attention on the unique developmental history of each individual in a group, Fromm tries to identify the features that these members have in common, the cultural dimension. By the term "social character" he means the traits shared by most members in a particular group, resulting from a similar mode of life — for instance, the specific kinship you share, in overlapping circles, with anyone of your temperament, gender, race, culture, era, or religious tradition.

A few illustrations will be useful. Like Marx and Max Weber, Fromm explores how the capitalistic spirit or an emphasis on anal, exploitative traits will shape a person's developing consciousness. This bourgeois social character can be distilled in the popular maxims of Benjamin Franklin. Dutiful work, possessiveness, thrift, competitiveness, and privacy become normative ethical values, whether you enjoy your possessions or not. Such features, urgent in shaping a self-made autonomous entrepreneur of the late eighteenth and nineteenth century, prove a liability for the contemporary type of capitalist, attuned to anonymous corporate ownership and consumerism. Directly opposite the Ben Franklin bourgeois stands Marx's idealized proletariat, the social character of a revolutionary. Here the major endowment will be a capacity to disobey, to criticize majority opinion, the marketplace, or those in power, and take action against them. As a revolutionary, you are "identified with humanity, and therefore transcend the narrow limits of your own society. You are able, because of this, to criticize your own society or any others from the standpoint of reason and humanity."[49]

Freud's clients usually approached their analyst as they would a conventional physician, with complaints of easily labeled disorders, such as a hysterical paralysis or a washing compulsion. The cure they sought corresponded to their notion of sickness, the removal of concrete symptoms. Fromm's clients of a later Cold War era, on the contrary, though centered at first on some particular complaint, such as their marriage or job, were more disposed to acknowledge a vast spiritual upheaval underneath. Specific complaints are only the conscious form in which your own society permits you to hint at something inexpressible. You feel outraged that wealth has not brought happiness, that life may give out before you have truly lived, that you have been estranged from nature and others and even your own self.[50]

Freud and Jung tend to treat the Unconscious as a capitalized noun, a projected and reified realm, often with eerie overtones. Fromm reinterprets this noun, however, as just an adjective, the unconscious more a quality of your developing human perception, always more or less conscious. Clients must be helped to free themselves from a relative unawareness about the sources of their alienation or from what Marxists call false consciousness.

Whereas Freud charts out the development of an individual from oral, anal, and phallic stages to maturity, Fromm reconceives these phases as three progressive steps in the socialization process — from the receptive infant, through the cruel, stingy child with a selfish marketing orientation, to the complete creative adult. Any society that generates mutual hateful competitiveness and distrust, depriving a person of self-worth, must be measured by the criterion of human rights transcending any particular culture. Emerging from Fromm's curative therapy, then, clients are sent back into such a dysfunctional society, not merely as receptive or exploitative children to comply but as productive adults to challenge and change it.

Reflecting on Fromm's vignette of the totalitarian social character, one can anticipate his celebrated distinction between two religious character structures, the authoritarian and humanistic. He presupposes that words like "work" or "love" or "God" cannot be abstracted from their emotional matrix and thus show predictable connotations when imported into a particular structure of social character. For the totalitarian or sadomasochistic type of person, love means symbiotic dependence, not mutual affirmation based on equality. Sacrifice means the subordination of individuality to something higher, not assertion of one's mental and moral self. Difference from others means just a difference in power, not the maturity of Jungian individuation. Courage is the readiness to submit and endure suffering, not to assert your human rights against an unjust regime.[51] Illustrations of authoritarian traits center repeatedly on Hitler's Germany, from which Fromm escaped to America in the early 1930s.

In his redefinition of conventional religious language, Fromm describes God as "a symbol of all that is in humanity and yet which humanity is not, the symbol of a spiritual reality you can strive to realize in yourself and yet never describe or define. God is like the horizon which sets the limitations of your sight." Religions are humanistic or authoritarian insofar as they nourish or thwart the model humane society and mature revolutionary individual already defined. "In humanistic religion God is the image of your higher self, a symbol of what you potentially are or ought to become," Fromm explains. "In authoritarian religion God becomes the sole possessor of what was originally your own reason and love. The more perfect God becomes, the more imperfect you become.... Your only access to yourself is through God. In worshipping God you try to get in touch with that part of yourself which you have lost through projection."[52] In this depiction of authoritarian religion, Feuerbach's sweeping critique of all religious experience reappears in its full impact — the tragic error of projecting, reifying, and alienating vital human attributes.

The fallacy of projection helps to explain what the Bible means by sins of idolatry. The central flaw in an authoritarian religious attitude is idolatry, showing absolute loyalty not to God but to something less than God. In Humanist terms, you turn from a God symbolizing your complete humanity and worship a diminished image of yourself — your projected intelligence, for instance, physical strength, or fame. The classical Hebrew prophets denounced idols of stone and wood, symbols of our own deified human creativity, and Fromm extends this iconoclastic attack to the modern idols of both Cold War antagonists, capitalism and communism.

"God as the supreme value and goal," he says, "is not humanity, the state, an institution, ... possessions, sexual powers, or any artifact made by human beings.... The idol is the alienated form of your experience of yourself." By subordinating your complete self to a projected fragment of the self, you limit yourself to this aspect and diminish your totality as a human being. Despite disagreement about how to conceive and name the ultimate mystery, Fromm finds at least a consensus among all spiritual people about what the Sacred is not. The affirmation that I love, follow, or imitate God has to mean, first of all, "I do not love, follow, or imitate idols."[53]

Fromm locates the authoritarian distortion in theists like Calvin or nontheists like Hitler and the humanistic ideal in carefully selected passages from Plato, Lao Tzu, Isaiah, Jesus, and Spinoza — a context that includes theists and nontheists, both the Humanist Way and other major religious traditions. What matters is not the thought system as such but the character traits and values underlying its practice. In other words, the central question for Fromm is not if God exists but if God is a symbol for powers alienated from, or integrated with, the human condition.

Jews and Christians in their Bible trace a gradual disclosure of God's identity. God at first seems just a sort of tribal chief, then a universal Lord of lords with arbitrary power. Later God decides to rule like a constitutional monarch, faithful to covenants. At last this God is revealed as the nameless God of Moses.

Identifying himself as a nontheistic mystic, Fromm prefers the language of apophatic spiritual classics, the Negative Path described at length in chapters 2 and 4. His God is not the separate Supreme Being common to Eurocentric theism, but the Tao, Brahman, Nirvana, or Tillich's Ground of Being — "a God without attributes, who is worshiped in silence."

The moment you accept a God that is nameless, or beyond your projections and anthropomorphisms, "God has ceased to be an authoritarian God," says Fromm. "Humanity must become fully independent, and that means independent even from God."[54]

A SECULAR SPIRITUALITY

The satirical story "Edward and God," published in 1974 by Czech novelist Milan Kundera, explores a situation of existential estrangement, dissent, and questioning — tentative origins of a secular spirituality. A resourceful young teacher, Edward tries to survive with integrity in an authoritarian communist society. His dilemma looks first like a serious conflict of ideologies. He must choose between Christian belief, which his girlfriend Alice expects to share with her potential husband, and official communist atheism, the party orthodoxy Edward must embody if he expects to keep his job.

His hidden psychological conflict, however, is more complex. Playing two games at the same time, he gets involved in sexual affairs with two women, each of whom is drawn to her particular creed by shaky motives. Alice attends church to defy the party atheists who nationalized her father's business, and to legitimize what Edward labels a God-of-no-fornication morality as the safeguard for her virginity. The Directress, in contrast, an ugly older woman attracted to young men, clings to the party out of loneliness and gullible romanticism. Both Alice and the Directress hanker for parallel solace in the church or party — each could not bear hardships in the present if not assured of heaven or a future classless society.

The first gambit of Edward toward Alice is to deceive her by genuflecting and talking theology even more devoutly than she. This deviant behavior in an otherwise reliable teacher, however, is reported to the Directress, quick to abuse her authority by insisting he attend her intimate tutorials in atheism. Prepared to recant his religious sham before school authorities, he learns the orthodoxy committee would judge such a confession implausible. So he feigns an unwilling piety chronic enough to need patient correction from the Directress. Later summoned to her apartment for retraining, he gets drunk in order to spark romantic feelings toward his repulsive hostess. Unable to generate enough libido to play out the seduction the Directress has orchestrated, he chances upon an outlandish sadomasochistic scenario for arousal. To establish macho dominance over this influential party leader, he forces her to grovel at his feet, and renouncing her communist faith, to recite after him, phrase by phrase, the Lord's Prayer.

Meanwhile, Edward's public testimony before the party has canonized him in Alice's eyes as a martyr for their shared Christian faith. Rewarding him for his loyalty, she gives up her strict sexual code and thus her rule-enforcer God. But shocked to find this once impregnable faith so shallow, Edward confronts a woman stripped of her unique spirituality — and her taboo sexual attraction. He now feels Alice no more desirable than he finds the Directress. Since both women have been living a lie, he himself has been induced to lie, first to unmask their lies by ridicule and, further, to outmatch them in the game of lying. By a posture of total cynicism he has managed to survive in a lying society.

Yet on later reflection, Edward drops into church and begins to realize "he himself was only a shadow of all these shadowy people. After all, he had been exhausting his own brain only to adjust to them and imitate them. . . . For even malicious imitation remains imitation, and the shadow that mocks remains a shadow — subordinate, derivative, wretched, and nothing more." Alice had shown herself no more hollow than he. Edward longs to treat people and life seriously. At this point he finds himself entertaining the thought of God, even though convinced regretfully that God does not exist. With nostalgia and happiness, he yearns for someone "who alone is relieved of the distracting obligation of appearing. Someone able merely to be."[55]

This superb story interweaves many themes basic to my preceding analysis of religious projection. As a protest against the government's usurpation of her father's power, Alice's religion seems an act of regressive identification with her father's authority. Examined alongside Alice's belief, the Directress' commitment to the party looks like just another religious projection, susceptible to the same type of distorted rationalizations. Given Fromm's insight into the authoritarian social character sanctioned in this community, it makes sense that sexual arousal between the Directress and Edward would be sparked by a scenario of domination and submission. An effective trickster and prophet, Edward exposes the idolatry in both women's religious loyalty. However, he has not yet discovered a set of universal human values for assessing and replacing what Marx would call the false consciousness in this society. When his brother urges him to tell the truth, Edward answers that truth will not appear truthful in a lying society, nor sanity in what Fromm would call an insane society. He can only long for a moment of self-transcendence, imagined as a distant realm where Being wears no masks at all.

The young man's yearning for truth and truth-telling, of course, might prove just another illusory substitute for action. Yet in the context of Edward's development throughout the story, his final projection matches the bracing humanistic God-image of Fromm — "your higher self, a symbol of what you potentially are or ought to become." This more positive concept of projection has been developed by the American pragmatist and Humanist John Dewey in his book *A Common Faith*. People are urged to distill whatever is genuinely good within the human situation — in art, knowledge, education, growth in mind and body, fellowship and love. These values at present are still embryonic and need creative vision to extend and activate them. "The idealizing imagination seizes upon the most precious things found in the climacteric moments of experience and projects them."[56]

Surely the projection imagined by Dewey will not drain energy and attention away from present action. For that matter, I do not believe that shedding one's illusions about a world beyond or afterward will necessarily lead to more active engagement in this world, as if attention had to be rationed in a zero-sum game. However, to minimize the hazards of projection, Dewey prefers to dissolve that reified compartment of life evoked by the noun "religion" and replace it with the religious adjective or adverb that pervades ordinary experience. The concept of God or the Sacred is a "union of ideal ends with actual conditions" or "ideal possibilities unified through imaginative realization and projection." In other words, to be practically religious is not to leap toward rootless utopias and heaven, nor to settle for the historically actual, but actively to promote the growth of natural forces and ideals already in progress. To be irreligious is to treat people in isolation from physical nature and the human community or to lack what he calls natural piety.[57]

Religious or irreligious attitudes, then, are measured not by acceptance of dogmas, institutions, or a separate Supreme Being but by your moral readiness to transform the actual present into a better future. Dewey has thus broadened the traditional notion of religious experience to include fellow Humanists, those with a spirituality alien to supranaturalism and any institutional religion. Another Humanist spokesman, psychologist Abraham Maslow, regrets his past mistake of allowing sectarians and cranks to usurp the rich language of religion for their own restricted use. "I had let them redefine these words and then accepted their definitions. And now I want to take the words back. I want to demonstrate that spiritual values have naturalistic meaning, that they are not the exclusive possession of organized churches, that they do not need supernatural concepts to validate them." In Maslow's research, a range of people dissociated from any institutional religion report moments intensified by awe, wonder, and cosmic engulfment. He calls these situations peak-experiences and plateau-experiences, or Being-cognition.[58]

Dewey's reconstruction of religion is cited in Jawaharlal Nehru's autobiography, with the comment, "If this is religion, then no one can have the slightest objection to it."[59] Like Dewey, Nehru calls himself a Humanist and passionate advocate of the scientific method, a perspective he picked up during his years of study in England, where he haunted the laboratories of Harrow and Cambridge. The Dalai Lama once remarked that in this prime minister of India he had found not a hint of spiritual fervor. Yet behind the cool handsome facade stood a deeper Nehru, revealed especially in his personal letters and prison journals. It is incredible that Nehru and Gandhi retained their friendship and political alliance, despite huge differences in temperament and spirituality. Whereas Gandhi renounced material wealth, Eurocentric technology, and secularity, Nehru called for industrialism without capitalist exploitation and for a modern Indian secular Constitution, which seemed the only viable foundation for a nation of so many quarrelsome religions.

Nehru often gives voice to the experience of Freud's oceanic feeling or Dewey's natural piety, an organic solidarity with humanity and the natural world. "I have loved life," he writes from his prison cell during a bout of depression. "The mountains and the sea, the sun and rain and storm and snow, and animals, and books and art, and even human beings. And life has been good to me." Elsewhere, he reflects that the main trouble of our era "is a lack of organic connection with nature or life. We have gone off at a tangent from the circle of life, uprooted ourselves and thus lost the sense of fullness and coordination with nature."[60] Though feeling deep wonder and reverence for life, he writes Gandhi about his reluctance to label this a religious experience. "Religion is not a familiar ground for me, and as I have grown older I have definitely drifted away from it. I suppose I have something else in its place, something other than just intellect and reason, which gives me strength and hope." This spiritual source is an "indefinable and indefinite urge, which may have just a tinge of religion in it and yet is wholly different from it."[61]

From his earliest years, Nehru had wanted to sweep India clean of everything connected with the term "religion" — "blind belief and reaction, dogma and bigotry, superstition and exploitation, and the preservation of vested interests." By 1933 he had announced a crucial decision that would affect his public life: "I should like to keep myself away, as far as possible, from all religious rites and ceremonials, all the hallmarks of religion — indeed to be wholly non-religious." To dissociate his own Humanist Way from religious intolerance between Muslims, Hindus, and others, he preferred to name it a philosophy, ethics, metaphysics, or especially a spirituality. "The idea of God, as normally conceived, does not attract me," he explained in 1961. "But the old idea of Hindu philosophy in the Vedanta that everything has some part of the divine essence does appeal to me." Nehru could accept "the deeper essence of religion and, indeed, of all religions which may be called spirituality, but not the rituals and dogmas that have grown up in the name of religion."[62]

The Secular Equivalent

Nehru's moral or spiritual philosophy, Dewey's natural piety, Maslow's cognition of Being — these labels indicate a few Humanist equivalents to fill the niche once reserved for conventional religious language. Though designed to look secular, such terms tackle many of the profound questions associated with traditional religion.[63] Theologian Paul Tillich calls these the great vertical questions: What is the meaning of life? What is my origin and destiny? What should I become in the short stretch between birth and death? Being religious means asking these questions passionately and opening oneself to the answers with courage. The pivotal religious moment, then, embraces the deep unrestricted questioning process itself, no matter what answer one may reach, if any.

I have seen this Tillichian premise contested on each occasion that the philosophy or theology department in a Catholic university must decide about hiring an avowed atheist or agnostic professor. In my opinion, any teacher or scholar worthy of the name, no matter of what religious persuasion, should be capable of inspiring students to track down a serious religious question, without getting in their way. As cited before, Pascal once observed that whoever searches for God has already found God. In his famous letter to a young poet, Rilke advises not to seek the answers now. They "could not be given to you now, because you would not be able to live them.... Live the questions now. Perhaps then, someday far in the future, you will gradually, without even noticing it, live your way into the answer."[64]

Chapter 6 described Karl Rahner's tendency to center his theological inquiry on those situations in which the secular world has come to an end of its resources and confronts mystery. These are moments of genuine self-transcendence and wonder, which most people articulate in the faltering vocabulary of daily life. Adjusted to a climate of secularity, you learn upon reflection that this enclosed world is perishable and finite. You feel surrounded by nothingness, a void where past meanings hide, never to be recovered again. Brushing aside the cynical conclusion that such a world is meaningless and best ignored, at moments you experience astonishment and awe that this fragile life is all you have. Nietzsche knows the terrible cost to live as a rigorously secular human being. "You will never pray again, never adore again, never again rest in endless trust.... There is no avenger for you, no eventual improver. There is no reason any more in events, no love in what will happen to you, no resting place any longer open to your heart."[65]

Proclaiming the death of transcendence, abandoning most of the conventional myths and creeds, there remains for such Humanists only the naked secular instant. In "Dover Beach," Matthew Arnold broods over faith's withdrawing roar. T. S. Eliot's *The Waste Land* ends by trying to shore up a few vital fragments from the cultural past in order to survive great lost patterns of meaning. In contrast, reaching beyond this elegiac backward look, a mood common to the poets of modernism, much of Wallace Stevens' poetry, for example, centers on a beauty inherent in the ever-changing flawed secular world itself. In "Poems of Our Climate" Stevens meditates on a bowl of pink and white carnations in water. Given just these flowers, the never-resting mind wants and needs something more transcendental. Yet since the imperfect is so instinctive with us, our delight consists in flawed words and stubborn sounds. "The imperfect is our paradise." Again, in his poem "Sunday Morning," a woman at worship turns her face away from remote Palestine and the tomb of Jesus, back to marvels of nature nearby. Portrayed as deficient and "mythy" in their cloud abode, the Gods yearn to become incarnate and taste of our perishable world. Heaven is so inhumanly perfect that fruit does not ripen and fall, nor do its trees wear the colors of earth's seasonal changes. "Death is the mother of beauty," the poem asserts. This world's very mortality gives it a unique beauty, which even the Gods must envy.[66]

Freud in his brief essay "On Transience" confirms Stevens' attitude toward the imperfect and perishable. He tells of a summer walk with two friends through a radiant countryside, months before the First World War. All three felt sobered by the inescapable fact that this natural splendor, like human achievements, too, would die someday. How can a person come to terms with this fact? One reaction is an inability to enjoy any beauty so undermined by the threat of mortality. Freud calls this feeling a premature mourning for the loss of beauty. The second reaction might be a rebellious leap beyond the evidence, affirming that anything so beautiful shall never die, but must somehow persist forever. Freud elsewhere rejects such an attitude as greedy, narcissistic, and delusional. At last shaping his own response, Freud uncovers a singular charm in evanescence itself. The aesthetic emotion is intensified precisely because of its precariousness. For even the destruction in war can render temporary what you once took for granted as permanent and spur you to prize your mortal friends and country more than before.[67]

Earlier chapters have explored the apophatic Negative Way to the Sacred. Chapters 5, 6, and 7 have introduced the Jewish exile experience, the Christian participation in Christ's agony and descent into hell, the Muslim identification with Muhammad's night ascension, all as a mystical Dark Night. In a comparable way, you can imagine a secular Dark Night of the human spirit. Keats speaks of it as negative capability, a disposition to remain immersed in doubts and mysteries without any impulsive reaching after fact and reason. Kafka calls himself an attendant upon grace — whether such waiting is grace itself or a foreshadowing of grace, he cannot decide. But most important, he has befriended his ignorance. Vladimir in Beckett's *Waiting for Godot* tries to uncover the barest human meaning in humanity's endless waiting: "We are not saints, but we have kept our appointment."

According to the neo-Marxist Ernst Bloch, a person's God-image is the projected hope for a long-awaited future, a demand from the depths crying out for perfect justice and the Absolute. This hope is something worthy of contemplation and religious awe — a transcendental vacuum always deferred, evolving like humanity itself. What you sometimes picture as an absent God is in fact your humanity itself in the process of being born. Echoing Bloch's approach, Fromm interprets the Humanist God-image as that which humanity is not, the horizon that can never be reached. In Chingiz Aitmatov's novel *The Place of the Skull,* an ex-seminarian imagines his "God of Tomorrow" just this way. Touched deeply by the anthems of a Bulgarian church choir, Kallistratov ponders the centuries of human creativity they represent, destined "to keep alive the God whom they had invented to symbolize the spiritual heights for which humanity reaches out instinctively." The liturgical chants addressed to God are just an epiphany celebrating the indomitable human spirit. Kallistratov's God-image is described as "a shadowy world that consists of all dreams, memories, longings, pangs of remorse, all the joys and sorrows, gain and losses that make up the individual's path through life."[68] Marx spoke more wisely than he knew by calling this realm the heart of a heartless world.

This Humanist reconstruction of the God-image will not satisfy conventional theists, notably those represented by the Russian Orthodox seminary rector in the novel, who expels Kallistratov for defending it. Yet perhaps a Taoist, Hindu Vedantist, Buddhist, or even a Christian panentheist would dispute the rector's sharp boundaries that divide a transcendent God up there from the vital human spirit within. In fact, I must pay close attention to all that might be left unsaid if you speak as a Humanist about accepting or rejecting God. I concede that you may turn out to be the exact atheist your words profess. Yet, on the contrary, the reality of your inner life may prove too massive or subtle to be expressed by any standard labels. For instance, adhering implicitly to an impersonal model of the Sacred, you may be rejecting only a specific personal God-image, such as the old bearded puppeteer or busy-body judge. Maybe your life centers on conscience or the cosmos, much in the way some explicit theists meditate on the transpersonal Dharma or Brahman or Tao.

Fromm has explained how the socialization process itself — a filter of language, logic, and unquestioned assumptions in a particular culture or time — can edit out the very impulse to name a religious experience. As demonstrated before, Nehru had such disdain for religious sectarianism in India that he perceived his Humanist faith not as an alternative religion but as a spiritual philosophy. In a similar manner, Nobel Prize–winning novelist Nadine Gordimer, though describing herself as an atheist, adds a wise proviso. She admits a profoundly religious temperament, and "perhaps, brought up differently in a different milieu, in a different way, I might have been a religious person." On a more superficial level, religious visibility is now flaunted, now disguised, depending on prevailing legal attitudes. In the United States, some groups today actually reject the legitimation that others crave. For example, the Church of Scientology for some years solicited academic support, including my own, to solidify its claim to be a true religion and thus entitled to tax exemption. Yet in New Jersey, Transcendental Meditation advocates lost a case trying to prove themselves not a religion. Members wanted to introduce mind techniques into public school curricula without violating First Amendment cautions against religious favoritism.[69]

My own experience as a volunteer draft counselor during the Vietnam War brought me into contact with many young Humanists, ready to analyze and reformulate their values as an alternative spirituality or Way. Those seeking a Conscientious Objector exemption would be pressed to dredge up every honest religious basis for their dissent. Previous U.S. law had recognized dissent only when tied to actual membership in the Quakers, Jehovah's Witnesses, or some other pacifist church. The 1965 Supreme Court Decision in *U.S. versus Seeger,* however, extended the basis for religious exemption by a quantum leap. As before, dissenters would have to repudiate all war, not just a present war. But the range of religious legitimacy now widened to include the following situations: institutional or private faith, faith in one God or many, and faith that chooses personal or impersonal models of the Sacred.

Furthermore, this well-researched court decision cites specific descriptions of the Sacred — Hindu Brahman, Buddhist Nirvana, the "Hidden Power" mentioned in Catholic teaching from the Second Vatican Council, and even Paul Tillich's "power of Being, which works through those who have no name for it." Most important, the court stated the following functional criterion, which seemed custom-built for my Humanist clients: "Does this claimed belief occupy the same place in the objector's life as an orthodox belief in God holds in the life of one clearly qualified for exemption?"

This counseling work gave me a rare chance to introduce a religious or moral vocabulary to many of the religiously alienated or reticent. As part of a Conscientious Objector network in the Detroit area, I was assigned to interview each applicant, offer help to complete an exemption form and personal essay, and during later sessions, role-play in a tough Socratic coaching style to prepare candidates for their approaching local draft board defense. My most important hours were spent hearing out each value system, trying to grasp what touched a person most about happiness, love, work, the purpose of life. Some of these applicants belonged to readily labeled Christian pacifist churches, but most had a deep religious world of their own, often dense and inarticulate. To be of help to them, I was looking for a coherent ethic, and the faintest intimations of the Sacred, or at least its functional equivalent.

Among dissenter clients, a remarkable number of Humanists adopted the grammar of Taoism, Buddhism, or Tillich's theology to clarify the implicit religious dimension in their otherwise secular moral values. However, with my encouragement, a few undaunted Humanists insisted with integrity on retaining their distinctive secular vocabulary. They studied the three parties represented in the Seeger decision as a model for their own defense. Arno Jacobsen's primary moral value, for instance, was the mystical force of Godness, whereas Daniel Seeger's was a compulsion toward Goodness. The court could not find any functional distinction between these two positions.

"We think it clear," said Justice Clark, "that the beliefs which prompted Seeger's objection occupy the same place in his life as the belief in a traditional deity holds in the lives of his friends, the Quakers."[70]

Human Rights

Prophets of the Humanist Way, alert to every religious distortion, have no doubt eroded the reflex deference once shown leaders of the major religions. Yet the Humanist challenge, I think, has often improved the target of criticism, rendering it more honest. More important, many Humanists have promoted an end to old atrocities between religious rivals, and the search for a wide consensus that can include agnostics, atheists, and all human beings.

The argument in Freud's *Future of an Illusion* illustrates this Humanist contribution. Freud insists that the basis for a common human morality has to be located in the human condition itself, not in its colliding religious myths and visions. Convinced that conventional religions will eventually disappear, he wants morality separated from religious sources and sanctions, or else it will also perish. By pinning the moral consensus against murder to God's revealed commandment, for instance, you invest this human prohibition with a solemn immutability it would otherwise lack. Yet at the same time, you risk making its observance seem to depend exclusively on a belief in God. Freud wants this religious prop left out entirely, so that morality will be based on inherent natural rights or, more clearly, on a consensus enacted into positive law.

A unique moral consensus of this sort emerged as an international groundswell at the end of the Second World War, an impulse which ever since has changed the way almost all modern governments deal with one another, and especially with their own respective citizens. With the overthrow of Hitler's empire and the Axis powers, over fifty nations of the world were confronted with a moment of near unanimity, unprecedented for at least three reasons. First, though too exhilarated to recognize the ironic price of victory, Britain and France had been left so weakened they could no longer police their former colonial empires. A fresh world map could be predicted soon, with many new independent nations. Second, as data on the extent of the Holocaust mounted, world opinion registered a revulsion against the outrages condoned by permitting a national government unhindered control over the lives of its own citizens. In the Nuremberg trials, for instance, the Allied powers were groping for a sense of higher law — common decency, conscience, natural rights, treaty obligations such as the Geneva Convention — that could take moral precedence over arbitrary statutes imposed anywhere by a dictator's plebiscite.

In retrospect, these two factors proved less decisive than a third. Franklin Roosevelt in 1941 had proclaimed the four freedoms — freedom of speech, freedom to worship God in your own way, freedom from economic want, and freedom from fear. "Freedom," he said, "means the supremacy of human rights everywhere." The next year Winston Churchill heralded the era "when this world's struggle ends with the enthronement of human rights."[71] Both leaders had visions of a world congress that would turn human rights into positive law, with an apparatus of interpretation and enforcement. Through uncanny foresight, at least forty-two nongovernmental international human rights organizations were invited to share in framing the UN Charter in 1945 and the pivotal UN Universal Declaration of Human Rights in 1948.

The latter document was prepared by the Commission on Human Rights, chaired by Eleanor Roosevelt. The nongovernmental human rights groups, taxing the patience of seasoned diplomats, lobbied for the insertion of human rights language and pressed diplomats to focus on human persons, not just on treaty obligations between sovereign governments. To monitor rights abuses since then, most later regional and international rights conferences have cooperated with various private agencies flourishing more recently, such as Amnesty International, Helsinki Watch, and the International Commission of Jurists.

In such a climate of revolutionary hope, the human rights movement came into existence — paradoxically late in human history for what claims to be a set of self-evident moral principles. Any attempt to pinpoint where the vocabulary of human rights originated soon becomes mired in the many overlapping philosophical, theological, and legal sources alleged for its pedigree. Phrases in particular lists of human rights are lifted clearly from the preamble to the U.S. Declaration of Independence, from the U.S. Bill of Rights, and from the French Declaration of the Rights of Man and Citizen — a matrix of British common law, the scholastic natural law tradition, social contract theory, and countless Deist and Humanist manifestos.

The current language about rights, however, is more flexible and elusive than those hallowed lists of natural rights from earlier centuries. The term "rights" now reaches beyond the limited overtones of Eurocentric individualism. Marx always insisted that bourgeois talk of rights and freedoms could be reduced mostly to the right of laissez faire and private ownership, a disguised self-justification for the rich and powerful. An authentic Bill of Rights, I am convinced, has to include not just the civil rights of eighteenth-century capitalist democracy but also the social and economic rights of nineteenth-century socialism. The term "human" means the inclusive blend of human life and the nonhuman environment. The appropriate conditions for a life of human dignity are derived not from a fixed concept of natural law or abstract humanity but from an evolving perception of what it means to be truly human.

The growth pains of the United Nations during the last half-century have often been recounted. The early impasse between Western and Soviet blocs of nation members was particularly pronounced. This conflict has now been replaced by an increasing division between the haves of the North and the have-nots of the South. Act 1 opened with fifty-eight nation members under Eurocentric leadership. In act 2, during the next twenty years, power tilted toward the Soviet bloc and nonaligned Third World. Act 3, during the most recent decades, launched the era of Third World prominence, especially in the General Assembly, now increased to more than 150 nation members.

By act 3 in this scenario, the average Malaysian or Nigerian citizen had discovered an enthusiasm for the UN which many U.S. citizens lost after act 1. The dramatic reversal in act 2 can be traced through eighteen years of stormy discussions that followed the surprising approval of the 1948 Universal Declaration of Human Rights. After that approval, a swarm of new members kept insisting on reopening vital measures of the declaration that had already been discussed to death. At the same time, legal experts continued to demand that the rhetoric of aspiration be trimmed down to exacting and viable law.

The Cold War confrontation led to a fatal separation between two lists of human rights, both of which had been interwoven shrewdly in the original version of the

UN declaration. Of primary interest to capitalist democracies, the first document, the Covenant of Civil and Political Rights, centers on individuals' rights against their own national governments. These include rights to life, equal protection under the law, freedom of religion and opinion, and protection against torture, arbitrary arrest, and discrimination because of race, creed, or gender. The second document, the Covenant of Economic, Social, and Cultural Rights, which was of primary interest to the socialist welfare nations, addresses only member states themselves. Governments must protect their people's right to free choice of employment, to security in case of sickness or unemployment, to adequate food, housing, and medical care, and to education and leisure time.[72]

Ratified at last in 1966, both lists of rights, I am convinced, need each other in order to comprise an integral view of a truly human life. It must be conceded that political-civil rights are more easily translated into demonstrable measures fixed by law, and thus monitored. The economic-social rights sound more vague and utopic — rights applauded readily, of course, but harder yet to verify or monitor. Thus, in a familiar recent scenario of politicized human rights, the U.S. State Department, citing the first covenant as a precondition for trade concessions, will document China's crimes of religious persecution and arbitrary imprisonment. In rebuttal, referring to the second covenant, Chinese authorities in self-vindication might point to America's defective medical care and unemployment safeguards or the disproportionate presence of racial minorities in its prisons. World observers yearn that someday both governments, goaded by mutual criticism, will improve their human rights record.

I must acknowledge an impatience with mushrooming lists of rights, churned out each year by various local and international conferences. The rhetoric gets rhapsodic. As opposed to a philosophical treatise, the manifesto genre permits a list of separate dogmatic assertions, with no need to show their logical justification or to define major terms. In such lists, each single right is often declared inalienable and absolute, whereas in fact the rights must be balanced against one another, for the right of the wolf is not the right of the sheep. Rights carry different weight in different cultures. In many moral traditions of the world, the right to abortion or to assisted suicide, for example, is by no means self-evident, but expressly denied.

Some rights sound absurdly broad, such as Roosevelt's "freedom against fear," even though he intended by the phrase to spark a campaign for global disarmament. Heading both UN covenants, the right to self-determination looks too unqualified, for though intended as a claim against colonialism, it could lead to endless compound secessions within each newly constituted nation-state. A crucial right, such as the right to unemployment insurance, may be listed alongside something relatively tenuous, such as the right to an annual paid vacation or to copyright protection. The right to life seems to be a portmanteau concept that includes an endless string of particular rights. The human condition begins to resemble a minefield of easily violated hidden taboos. By making almost anything a right, you cheapen rights talk to the point of bankruptcy.

In this discussion, it is essential to distinguish between four factors — the phenomenon of human rights or human dignity, the recent human rights movement, particular lists of human rights formulated as idealistic guidelines or positive law, and the specific implementation of human rights codes by a particular nation-state or nongovernmental watchdog group. Though the latter two factors deserve constant scrutiny and improvement, the first two have by now earned almost universal approval.

Consider the case of some new nation that refuses to ratify the UN Universal Declaration of Human Rights and the two rights covenants. This country has to coexist alongside a majority of other nations who have borrowed large sections of these documents for their own national constitutions. Though prone to deny charges of human rights violations, an uncooperative nation may still prove responsive indirectly by attempting afterwards to disguise or correct the abuses cited. Once Amnesty International sponsors a particular prisoner of conscience, for instance, you notice that improved treatment or release often follows. Words in treaties and editorials or a barrage of letters in protest should not be underestimated, for they bring hope to victims. Measures of this sort can pressure governments to unexpected self-criticism rather than be shamed under international scrutiny.

The imprecision and inflation that first seem to impair the vocabulary of human rights may, in my opinion, prove an ironic advantage. Andrei Sakharov, creator of the Soviet atom bomb and later a defiant "refusenik," observed in 1983 that "the ideology of human rights is probably the only one which can be combined with such diverse ideologies as communism, social democracy, religion, technocracy, and those ideologies which may be described as national and indigenous. It can also serve as a foothold for those who do not wish to be aligned with theoretical intricacies and dogmas, and who have tired of the abundance of ideologies, none of which have brought humanity a simple happiness. The defense of human rights is a clear path toward the unification of people in our turbulent world and a path toward the relief of suffering."[73]

If the shared task of defending human rights can in fact temper the cultural and ideological differences between nations, it may also tear down idolatrous barriers between differing religious traditions. Perhaps the best common ground for religious dialogue may not be theology but anthropology and ethics, not sacral rights but human rights. A recent effort to build on the enthusiasm for human rights occurs in the Declaration of a Global Ethic, a manifesto approved unanimously by the Chicago Parliament of World Religions in 1993. As explained by its major framer, Catholic theologian Hans Küng, this document was designed to serve a function similar to the 1948 UN Universal Declaration. Its ethic about the individual conscience, family, and environment claims to be only minimal. It does not pretend to offer a new substitute global religion. In other words, it does not try to replace the Christian Sermon on the Mount, the Jewish Torah, or the scriptures of other world traditions.[74]

How have world leaders of religious traditions reacted to this widespread emphasis on human rights, and notably the UN Universal Declaration and subsequent covenants? As might be anticipated, the response has not proved univocal in any particular tradition, but it splits along progressive and traditionalist lines. For instance, during the vote for the UN Universal Declaration in 1948, Saudi Arabia abstained because the document did not acknowledge human rights to be a gift from God. Also the Saudis believed the Quran forbids anyone the freedom to convert from one religion to another. Yet interpreting the Quran more broadly, the Muslim foreign minister of Pakistan approved the declaration. Whereas some Evangelical Protestants blamed the UN for trying to reduce the Gospel to the clichés of secular Humanism, some

Liberal Protestant delegates of the World Council of Churches had been active in framing the original UN Universal Declaration.

As a sample of Catholic opinion, the editor of the official Vatican newspaper *L'Osservatore Romano* at first complained about the declaration's omission of God's name: "The new ethical-juridical edifice in which humanity during the United Nations era is to find the security of a fortress, bears on its threshold the ancient warning — if God be not the builder of the house, its building will be in vain." On the other hand, Pope John XXIII hoped to see the declaration's provisions translated not just into humanitarian assistance but into concrete justice and legislation. The Second Vatican Council and later popes do not hesitate to identify the defense of human rights with the Gospel ministry of liberation. In fact, religious authorities today in almost all world traditions compete with one another to show that their own revealed scriptures long ago anticipated the human rights phenomenon at its most profound.[75]

Since human rights abuses continue as routine policy in many nations today, Humanists of every persuasion face a huge challenge: spotting and reforming the worst crimes on the international scene, while at the same time beginning at home to correct abuses in their own national governments and religious bureaucracies. To render this work effective, the warrant for human rights must draw upon the broadest consensus possible, transcending cultural and religious differences. The rest of humanity may not yet appreciate what seems axiomatic to Eurocentric civilizations, the centrality of such civil rights as freedom of speech, the press, and due process. It must not be forgotten that even this self-confident civil-moral tradition has only within recent memory sensitized itself to the rights of racial minorities or of abused women and children. Meanwhile, even worse crimes than these ought to summon the broadest cross-cultural consensus. The last decade gives uncontested proof of genocide, the systematic use of torture and starvation by foreign invaders and local governments alike, enslavement of populations through forced labor, deliberate separation of children from their parents, and the attempt to wipe out basic religious and ethnic identity.[76]

In this context, the recent Declaration of a Global Ethic by the Parliament of Religions should offer a suitable challenge to international religious leaders. It asserts that every human being without distinction of age, sex, race, skin color, physical or mental ability, language, religion, political view, or national or social origin possesses an inalienable dignity. A human being must always be the subject of rights, an end and never just a means, never the object of commercialization and industrialization in economics, politics, the media, research institutes, and industrial corporations.

The world's religious traditions cannot solve all the problems on earth, but they can offer a basic sense of trust and meaning, ultimate moral standards, and a spiritual home. Humanity needs drastic social and ecological reforms, but it needs spiritual renewal just as urgently. "Of course, religions are credible," the Declaration of a Global Ethic affirms, "only when they eliminate those conflicts that spring from religions themselves — dismantling mutual arrogance, mistrust, prejudice, and even hostile images. They can thus demonstrate respect for the traditions, holy places, feasts, and rituals of people who believe differently."[77]

Such a respect for religious differences — more accurately, cherishing all these kaleidoscopic differences and, whenever possible, attempting to bridge them — has been a major premise in the present study. Yet it is tragic that throughout their history, the major religious traditions have left mostly a record of clumsy incomprehension, even ferocity, toward the *other.* The religious outsider today, wandering by chance into a cozy religious circle, will be treated often as an enemy, someone to be converted forcefully or bracketed out of the group's life, and devalued as a human being.

Christ, on the contrary, throughout his life and especially on the cross, loves and forgives his enemies. In daily meditation, the Dalai Lama keeps reminding himself that particular actions of persons rather than the persons themselves make them your enemy. "Given a change of behavior," he says, "that same person could easily become a good friend." And even in combat, the Taoist and Zen Buddhist martial arts train you to view an adversary as the mirror image of yourself, not as a person to hate or fear.

Gandhi, attacking corrupt systems but not people, insists that you must respect and trust your opponents, giving them credit for the same honest faith as yourself. Also, as mentioned before, the Hindu Vivekananda refuses to endorse a single religious path for everyone. "Your way is very good for you, but not for me," he states repeatedly. "My way is good for me, but not for you.... How can people preach of love who cannot bear another person to follow a different path from their own?"

Moses Mendelssohn, giant of the Jewish Enlightenment, would not support an easy ecumenism that strains to achieve one fold and one shepherd by enlisting everyone under a single formula. His perspective has already been explored in chapter 5. "The unifiers of faith," he concludes, "would simply be collaborating in pinching off a bit from some concept here and there, in enlarging the texture of words elsewhere, until the words become so vague and loose that any ideas, regardless of their inner differences, could if necessary be squeezed in." In contrast to this attitude, Mendelssohn believes that "diversity is obviously the plan and goal of Providence." Not one among us thinks and feels exactly like someone else. "Why should we use masks to make ourselves unrecognizable to each other in the most important concerns of life, when God has given all of us our own distinctive faces for some good reason?"[78]

Among those most appreciative of religious differences is an influential voice within my own Christian tradition — St. Thomas Aquinas, a rare theologian unspoiled by the bitterness of scholastic controversy. I have chosen his words as epigraph to the present book. Dorothy Day, founder of the *Catholic Worker,* was accustomed to cite this balanced ground rule of Aquinas, which animates his best pages: "We must love them both, those whose opinions we share and those whose opinions we reject. For both have labored in the search for Truth, and both have helped us in finding it."[79]

Notes

CHAPTER 1: PRIMAL WAYS

1. Joanne Greenberg, *Rites of Passage* (Holt, Rinehart, Winston, 1972), 94–111.

2. Margaret Mead, *Blackberry Winter: My Earliest Years* (Morrow, 1972), 143.

3. For the sources and implications of this definition, see my *Sacred Lies and Silences: A Psychology of Religious Disguise* (Liturgical Press, 1994), 2–4.

4. See E. E. Evans-Pritchard, "The Nuer Concept of Spirit in Its Relation to the Social Order," in John Middleton, ed., *Myth and Cosmos* (Natural History Press, 1967); and Miguel Leon-Portilla, *Aztec Thought and Culture: A Study of the Ancient Nahuatl Mind* (University of Oklahoma Press, 1963). A development of the African Triangle premise can be found in E. W. Smith, ed., *African Ideas of God,* rev. ed. edited by E. G. Parrinder (Lutterworth, 1962).

5. See Black Elk's retraction in Raymond DeMallie, ed., *The Sixth Grandfather: Black Elk's Teachings Given to John G. Neihardt* (University of Nebraska Press, 1984), 58–61. See also John Lame Deer and Richard Erdoes, *Lame Deer: Seeker of Visions* (Simon and Schuster, 1972), 163.

6. Chinua Achebe, *Girls at War and Other Stories* (Heinemann, 1972), 78–82.

7. See Barbara Myerhoff, *Peyote Hunt: The Sacred Journey of the Huichol Indians* (Cornell University Press, 1974); and Peter Furst, "To Find Our Life: Peyote among the Huichol Indians of Mexico," in Furst, ed., *Flesh of the Gods: The Ritual Use of Hallucinogens* (Praeger, 1972), 136–84. Fernando Benitez's *In the Magic Land of Peyote,* trans. John Upton (University of Texas Press, 1975) gives many Huichol myths but is flawed by intrusive moralizing. Additional essays by Myerhoff, Furst, and other scholars can be sampled in Kathleen Berrin, ed., *Art of the Huichol Indians* (Fine Arts Museums of San Francisco/Abrams, 1978). See also "Matsua," in Joan Halifax, ed., *Shamanic Voices: A Survey of Visionary Narratives* (Dutton, 1979), 249–52, and other case studies collected there.

8. See the superb analysis of selected Native American museum collections in Richard White, "Representing Indians," *New Republic* (April 21, 1997): 28–34.

9. See Terence Turner, "Hunting Magic," in Richard Cavendish, ed., *Man, Myth, and Magic: An Illustrated Encyclopedia of the Supernatural* (Marshall Cavendish, 1970), 10:1370–75.

10. William Faulkner, *Go Down, Moses* (Modern Library, 1942), 351.

11. N. Scott Momaday, *The Way to Rainy Mountain* (University of New Mexico Press, 1969), 4. For a companion volume, see also Momaday, *The Names: A Memoir* (Harper and Row, 1976).

12. See Victor Turner, "The Center Out There: Pilgrim's Goal," *History of Religions* 12 (1973): 191–230.

13. See Mircea Eliade, *Shamanism: Archaic Techniques of Ecstasy,* trans. Willard Trask (Routledge, 1964); and Eliade, "Shaman," in Cavendish, *Man,* 19:2546–9.

14. See Michael Gelfand, *Witch Doctor: Traditional Medicine Man of Rhodesia* (Praeger, 1965); F. John Hitchcock, "A Nepalese Shamanism and the Classic Inner Asian Tradition," *History of Religions* 7 (1967–68): 149–58; Jung Jung Lee, "The Seasonal Rituals of Korean Shamanism," *History of Religions* 12 (1973): 271–87.

15. Leslie Silko, "Coyote Holds a Full House in His Hand," *Pushcart Prize* 6 (Pushcart Press, 1982), 142–50.

16. See Claude Lévi-Strauss, "The Sorcerer and His Magic" and "The Effectiveness of Symbols," in *Structural Anthropology,* trans. Claire Jacobson et al. (Basic Books, 1963), 1:167–85, 186–205.

17. See chapters 5 and 6 of Rollo May, *Love and Will* (Dell, 1969), 121–76.

18. See the photographs of the Hideyuki Oka collection in Michikazu Sakai, *How to Wrap Five Eggs: Japanese Design in Traditional Packaging* (Harper and Row, 1967); and Roland Barthes, *Empire of Signs,* trans. Richard Howard (Hill and Wang, 1982). See also Marcel Mauss, *The Gift: Forms and Functions of Exchange in Archaic Societies,* trans. I. Cunnison (Free Press, 1954); Marcel Mauss and Henri Hubert, *Sacrifice: Its Nature and Function,* trans. W. D. Halls (University of Chicago Press, 1964); and Barry Schwartz, "The Social Psychology of the Gift," in Arnold Birenbaum and Edward Sagarin, eds., *People in Places: Sociology of the Familiar* (Praeger, 1973), 175–90.

19. Linda Hogan, "Making Do," in Paula G. Allen, ed., *Spider Woman's Granddaughters* (Beacon Press, 1989), 162–69.

20. See Ernest Becker, "The Primitive World: Economics as Expiation and Power," in *Escape from Evil* (Free Press, 1975), 26–37; and Rosalie Wax and Murray Wax, "The Magical World View," *Journal for the Scientific Study of Religion* 1 (1961–62): 179–88.

21. See Abraham Maslow, "Synergy in the Society and in the Individual," in *The Farther Reaches of Human Nature* (Penguin, 1978), 191–202; and Claude Lévi-Strauss, "The Principle of Reciprocity," trans. Lewis Coser et al., in Lewis Coser and Bernard Rosenberg, eds., *Sociological Theory,* 3d ed. (Macmillan, 1969), 77–86.

22. Aspirana Taylor, "The Carving," in *He Rau Aroha* (Penguin, 1986), 4–9. For an introduction to masks, see C. Von Furer-Haimendorf, "Masks," in Cavendish, *Man,* 13:1756–65; Ladislaus Segy, *Masks of Black Africa* (Dover, 1976); and Ronald Grimes, "Masking: Toward a Phenomenology of Exteriorization," *Journal of the American Academy of Religion* 43 (1975): 508–16.

23. See the overview and bibliography in Vincent Crapanzano, "Spirit Possession," in Mircea Eliade, ed., *The Encyclopedia of Religions* (Macmillan, 1987), 14:12–19.

24. See Peter Brook, "Lie and Glorious Adjective: An Interview with Peter Brook," *Parabola* 6 (summer 1981): 60–73.

25. Erving Goffman, "Role Distance," in *Encounters* (Bobbs-Merrill, 1961), 85–152.

26. See the sources for this definition cited in my *Sacred Lies,* 2.

CHAPTER 2: CHINESE-JAPANESE WAYS

1. See the discussion in Tetsuo Yamaori, "The Metamorphosis of Ancestors," *Japan Quarterly* 33 (1986): 50–53. What Yamaori says about the role of ancestral spirits in Japanese religions can be applied to many other traditions.

2. Jeremiah 7:4–11; Analects 17:11. Unless otherwise indicated, subsequent references to the Analects will be to the translation by Arthur Waley (Allen-Unwin, 1938).

3. See Analects 3:12, 26; 12:2.

4. See Analects 3:3; 12:11. To trace the development of the Li concept, see Noah Fehl, *Li: Rites and Propriety in Literature and Life* (Hong Kong Chinese University Press, 1971); and the text and introduction of the *Li Ki,* trans. James Legge, in F. Max Muller, ed., *Sacred Books of the East,* 27 and 28 (Oxford University Press, 1885).

5. Maxine Hong Kingston, *China Men* (Knopf, 1980), 179.

6. Catherine Lim, "Or Else, the Lightning God," in *The Best of Catherine Lim* (Heinemann Asia, 1993), 81–101.

7. Analects 11:11.

8. Analects 13:21; 14:26.

9. Analects 1:2.

10. Major sections of this dialogue composed by Kuo Mo Jo are given in Wolfgang Bauer, *China and the Search for Happiness,* trans. Michael Shaw (Seabury, 1976).

11. Chi-tsai Feng, "The Mao Button," in *Chrysanthemums and Other Stories,* trans. Susan Chen (Harcourt Brace, 1985).

12. See Leon Stover, "Games Chinese Play," in *The Cultural Ecology of Chinese Civilization* (Pice, 1974), 242–66. A social psychology based on jen is explored in Wei Ming Tu, "The Confucian Perception of Adulthood," in Erik Erikson, ed., *Adulthood* (Norton, 1978), 113–20; and Yu Wei Hsieh, "The Status of the Individual in Chinese Ethics," in Charles Moore, ed., *The Status of the Individual in East and West* (University of Hawaii Press, 1968), 271–84.

13. See the helpful report by Michael Saso, "Taoism in China, 1993," *China News Analysis* (November 15, 1993): 1–9. This bulletin is published twice monthly in Taiwan.

14. Chuang Tzu, *Complete Works,* trans. Burton Watson (Columbia University Press, 1968), 9:105. This text will be referred to as *C,* followed by the chapter number and then the Watson pagination. The Tao Te Ching will be indicated by *T,* followed by the poem number — Arthur Waley's translation (Allen-Unwin, 1934). For background in Taoist theory and history, see D. Howard Smith, *Chinese Religions* (Holt-Rinehart, 1968); Holmes Welch, *Taoism: The Parting of the Way,* rev. ed. (Beacon Press, 1966); and Michael Saso, *Taoism and the Rite of Cosmic Renewal* (Washington State University Press, 1972).

15. *T* 57; *C* 22:235.

16. Romans 7:7–11.

17. *C* 22:234.

18. *T* 37; 35.

19. *C* 12:134.

20. *C* 29:332.

21. *C* 28:309.

22. *C* 25:287; *T* 78.

23. *C* 26:299; 22:238; 4:58.

24. *C* 23:253.

25. Henry David Thoreau, *Walden* (New American Library, 1980), 215, 118.

26. *C* 25:281; 4:62.

27. See William Prensky, "Tai Chi: Spiritual Martial Art," *Parabola* 4:2 (1979): 68–73.

28. Charles Holcomb, "Theater of Combat: A Critical Look at the Chinese Martial Arts," *Historian* 52 (May 1990): 411–31; and Frank Seitz et al., "The Martial Arts and Mental Health: The Challenge of Managing Energy," *Perceptual and Motor Skills* 70 (April 1990): 459–64.

29. See citations from Chuang Tzu and commentary in S. McFarlane, "Bodily Awareness in the Wing Chun System," *Religion* 19 (July 1989): 241–53.

30. See excerpts from the Yamaga autobiography in Ryusaku Tsunoda et al., eds., *Sources of Japanese Tradition* (Columbia University Press, 1958), 1:397. For further background, see Robert Bellah, *Tokugawa Religion: The Values of Pre-industrial Japan* (Free Press, 1957); and Jean Herbert, *Shinto: At the Fountainhead of Japan* (Stein and Day, 1967).

31. See the overview in Susan Byrne, "Land of the Rising Cults," *World Press Review* (June 1995): 41–42. See also Masaharu Anesaki, *Religious Life of the Japanese People,* 4th rev. ed. (Japanese Cultural Society, 1970).

32. See Yamamoto Tsunetomo, *Hagakure: The Book of the Samurai,* trans. William Wilson (Kodansha International, 1979), 169. Selections in this translation represent about one-fourth of the original text.

33. Cited in Ivan Morris, *The Nobility of Failure: Tragic Heroes in the History of Japan* (Noonday Press, 1988), 320, 322, 326.

34. Lydia Yuriko Minatoya, *Talking to High Monks in the Snow: An Asian-American Odyssey* (HarperCollins, 1992), 33, 102–3, 115.

35. Cited in Winston King, *Zen and the Way of the Sword: Arming the Samurai Psyche* (Oxford University Press, 1993), 229.

36. See extended selections from Fukuda's autobiography, *Half of My Lifetime,* with commentary in Mikiso Hane, ed. and trans., *Reflections on the Way to the Gallows: Rebel Women in Prewar Japan* (University of California Press, 1988), 33, 35–36.

37. See excerpts from Razan Hayashi, *On Mastery of the Arts of Peace and War,* in Tsunoda, *Sources,* 1:347.

38. Besides this quoted document, see the excerpts from contemporary diaries, newspapers, and government manuals collated in Patricia Ebrey, ed., *Chinese Civilization and Society: A Sourcebook* (Free Press, 1981). This evidence shows how recent institutions affect different sectors of the Chinese people.

39. Akio Morita et al., *Made in Japan: Akio Morita and Sony* (Dutton, 1986), 189.

40. Takeo Doi, *The Anatomy of Dependence,* trans. John Bester (Kodansha International, 1973), 63, 57. See also his "Amae: A Key Concept for Understanding Japanese Personality Structure," in Robert Smith and Richard Beardsley, eds., *Japanese Culture: Its Development and Characteristics* (Aldine, 1962), 132–40.

41. Tsunetomo, *Hagakure,* 23, 163.

42. See Sharlie Ushioda, "Man of Two Worlds: An Inquiry into the Value System of Ignazo Nitobe," in F. H. Conroy and T. S. Miyakawa, eds., *East across the Pacific: Historical and Sociological Studies of Japanese Immigration and Assimilation* (Clio, 1972), 187–210.

43. See Hane, *Reflections,* 54, 61.

44. Yukichi Fukuzawa, *The Autobiography of Fukuzawa Yukichi,* trans. Eiichi Kiyooka (Hokuseido Press, 1960), 242, 184–85.

45. Ibid., 220–21, 207.

46. Ibid., 248, 209, 192.

47. See the evidence cited in Hillel Levine, *In Search of Sugihara: The Elusive Japanese Diplomat Who Risked His Life to Rescue 10,000 Jews from the Holocaust* (Free Press, 1996), 14, 201–3.

48. Analects 14:8; 11:23.

49. *C* 6:180.

CHAPTER 3: THE HINDU WAY

1. For further discussion of the Rashtriya Swayamsevak Sangh and Vishva Hindu Parishad parties, see Ainslie Embree, "The Function of the Rashtriya Swayamsevak Sangh: To Define the Hindu Nation," and Peter van der Veer, "Hindu Nationalism and the Discourse of Modernity: The Vishva Hindu Parishad," in Martin Marty and Scott Appleby, eds., *Accounting for Fundamentalisms* (University of Chicago Press, 1994), 617–52, 653–68.

2. For a representative sampling of Gandhi's religious opinions, see "Religion and Truth," in Mohandas Gandhi, *All Men Are Brothers: Life and Thoughts of Mahatma Gandhi,* ed. Krishna Kripalani (Navajivan House, 1960), 73–104.

3. Swami Vivekananda, *Complete Works,* 9th ed. (Advaita Ashrama, 1966), 5:314. Background on the Ramakrishna Movement can be found in Harold French, *The Swan's Wide Waters: Ramakrishna and Western Culture* (Kennikat Press, 1974); Carl Jackson, *Vedanta for the West: The Ramakrishna Movement in the United States* (Indiana University Press, 1994); and the editor's introductions in Robert Ellwood, ed., *Eastern Spirituality in America: Selected Writings* (Paulist Press, 1987).

4. Vivekananda, *Complete Works,* 2:374; 3:131.

5. Ibid., 4:181.

6. Ibid., 3:425.

7. Ibid., 8:523, 237, 129, 505, 134.

8. Ibid., 4:376; 8:135, 140–41.

9. Ibid., 3:279–80.

10. Ibid., 3:424.

11. See the rebuttal to Huston Smith's uncritical enthusiasm for Schuon's terms and premises in Richard Bush, "Frithjof Schuon's *The Transcendent Unity of Religions:* Con," *Journal of the American Academy of Religion* 44 (1976): 715–19. Much of Schuon's approach is supported in Seyyed Nasr, "The Philosophia Perennis and the Study of Religion," in Frank Whaling, ed., *The World's Religious Traditions* (Crossroad, 1986), 181–200.

12. Vivekananda, *Complete Works,* 4:31; 6:52; 8:356. See further evidence in French, *Swan's Wide Waters,* 84.

13. Vivekananda, *Complete Works,* 4:356–57.

14. Ibid., 8:299, 497, 517, 522–23.

15. Ibid., 8:263–64.

16. See the editorial opinion sampled in French, *Swan's Wide Waters,* 82–83, 89.

17. William James, *Varieties of Religious Experience* (New American Library, 1958 [1902]), 115, 395–96.

18. R. K. Narayan, "Such Perfection," in *Malgudi Days* (Viking, 1982), 52–55.

19. Vivekananda, *Complete Works,* 4:180. See the various psychological and spiritual distortions grouped under this threefold typology in my *Sacred Lies and Silences: A Psychology of Religious Disguise* (Liturgical Press, 1994), 60–110.

20. See the sources in French, *Swan's Wide Waters,* 83, 42.

21. Ramakrishna, *The Gospel of Shri Ramakrishna,* trans. and ed. Nikhilananda (Ramakrishna-Vivekananda Center, 1942), 779, 66. Support for my interpretation of Ramakrishna is given in Walter Neevel, Jr., "The Transformation of Shri Ramakrishna," in Bardwell Smith, ed., *Hinduism: New Essays in the History of Religions* (Brill, 1976), 53–97.

22. Vivekananda, *Complete Works,* 4:356.

23. The Bhagavad Gita, trans. Juan Mascaro (Penguin, 1979). After Arjuna's question (3:1), I have based Krishna's fourfold response on the following texts: (A) 12:3–5, 9–10. (B) 3:4. (C) 3:7, 18–19, 30–31; 5:7–14. (D) 12:2, 10–11.

24. See the essays on Caitanya and the medieval bhakti movement by Norvin Hein, Joseph O'Connell, and Eleanor Zellot, in Smith, *Hinduism,* 15–32, 33–52, 143–68. See also "Interview with Shrivatsa Goswami," in Steven Gelberg, ed., *Hare Krishna, Hare Krishna* (Grove Press, 1983), 196–259.

25. A. C. Bhaktivedanta Prabhupada, *Bhagavad Gita as It Is,* 2d ed. (Bhaktivedanta Book Trust, 1989), 745. See especially the Harvey Cox and Thomas Hopkins interviews in Gelberg's anthology. The press accusations against the Krishnas can be sampled in John Hubner and Lindsey Gruson, "Dial Om for Murder," *Rolling Stone,* April 9, 1987, 53–58+.

26. Vivekananda, *Complete Works,* 8:320.

27. Prabhupada, *Bhagavad Gita,* 263, 861. The text is Bhagavad Gita 4:34, 2. See also the Larry Shinn interview in Gelberg, *Hare Krishna,* 79–84.

28. Sri Ramakrishna, *Sayings: An Exhaustive Collection* (Vedanta Press, 1975), 209–10; see also Vivekananda, *Complete Works,* 4:431, and 8:117.

29. R. K. Narayan, *The Vendor of Sweets* (Avon Books, 1967), 220–21.

30. *The Laws of Manu,* trans. G. Buhler, in F. Max Muller, ed., *Sacred Books of the East,* 25 (Motilal Banarsidass, 1886), 2:266, 144, 192.

31. Ibid., 2:200, 238, 218.

32. Ibid., 2:113, 110.

33. See the discussion in Jacques Vigne, "Guru and Psychotherapist: Comparisons from the Hindu Tradition," *Journal of Transpersonal Psychology* 23 (1991): 133.

34. Bhaktivedanta Prabhupada, *Bhagavad Gita as It Is,* 2d ed. (Bhaktivedanta Book Trust, 1989), 34.

35. See the excellent survey of scriptural evidence in Joel Mlecko, "The Guru in Hindu Tradition," *Numen* 29 (July 1982): 33–61.

36. See John Wren-Lewis, "Death Knell of the Guru System?" *Journal of Humanistic Psychology* 34 (spring 1994): 46–61. See his bibliography on the reports of recent guru downfalls.

37. Ruth Prawer Jhabvala, "A Spiritual Call," in *Out of India: Selected Stories* (Morrow, 1986), 69–88.

38. John Burns, "Indian Premier's Swami in Political Crossfire," *New York Times,* September 21, 1995, 1+.

39. For example, see J. S. Neki, "Guru-Chela Relationship: The Possibility of a Therapeutic Paradigm," *American Journal of Orthopsychiatry* 43 (October 1973): 755–66; and Vigne, "Guru," 121–37.

40. See further discussion about the inflated therapist in my *Sacred Lies and Silences,* 116–18.

41. See the interviews with these two gurus in Peter Brent, *Godmen of India* (Quadrangle Books, 1972), 126, 162–65.

42. Mohandas Gandhi, *Collected Works* (Navajivan Press, 1970), 29:76.

43. Ibid., 26:387–88.

CHAPTER 4: THE BUDDHIST WAY

1. See the sources listed in Klaus Klostermaier, "Hindu Views of Buddhism," in Roy Amore, ed., *Developments in Buddhist Thought* (Wilfred Laurier University Press, 1979), 60–82.

2. Anagarika Dharmapala, "Memories of an Interpreter of Buddhism to the Present-Day World," and "The Parliament of Religions, Chicago," in Ananda Guruge, ed., *Return to Righteousness: A Collection of Speeches, Essays, and Letters of the Anagarika Dharmapala* (Sri Lanka Government Press, 1965), 681, 688–89, 655. Dharmapala's exchange with his audience is reported in Guruge's introduction, 44–45.

3. Samyutta Nikaya 3:120.

4. See Manik de Silva, "Righteous Indignation: Buddhist Leaders Boycott Papal Visit," *Far Eastern Economic Review* 158:5 (February 2, 1995): 18–19; and "Pope Tours Asia, Australia," *Facts on File* (January 26, 1995): 43–44.

5. John Paul II, *Crossing the Threshold of Hope,* ed. Vittorio Messori (Knopf, 1994), 84–90.

6. See *L'Express,* March 21, 1997, cited in "News Briefs," *National Catholic Reporter* (April 4, 1997): 8.

7. Dharmapala, *Return to Righteousness,* 807.

8. Majjhima Nikaya 63.

9. Bhikkhu Buddhadasa, *Me and Mine: Selected Essays,* ed. Donald Swearer (State University of New York Press, 1989), 168–69.

10. Dalai Lama (Ngawang Gyatso), *My Land and My People* (McGraw-Hill, 1962), 151.

11. Ibid., 241.

12. For a succinct critique of East-West spiritual clichés, see Aloysius Pieris, S.J., "East in the West: Resolving a Spiritual Crisis," *Horizons* 13:2 (1988): 337–46.

13. See the selections from Shantideva in Lucien Stryk, ed., *World of the Buddha* (Anchor Books, 1969), 300–304.

14. Venerable Sumangalo, *Buddhist Sunday School Lessons,* 2d ed. (Penang Buddhist Association, 1958), 4.

15. Buddhadasa, *Me and Mine,* 148.

16. See the sources in Emanuel Sarkisyanz, *Buddhist Backgrounds of the Burmese Revolution* (Nijhoff, 1965), 71–72.

17. Mahavagga Vinaya I, 5:2–7.

18. See the Pali Text Society edition of the Jataka stories, ed. E. B. Cowell, 3 vols. (Luzac, 1957). Elizabeth Way et al., *Ten Lives of the Buddha: Siamese Temple Paintings and Jataka Tales* (Weatherhill, 1972), gives a popular retelling of the last ten stories, with Thai illustrations.

19. Dalai Lama (Nganang Tenzin Gyatso), *Freedom in Exile: The Autobiography of the Dalai Lama* (HarperCollins, 1990), xiii, 205, 202, 206, 208.

20. Malquinhu, "The Story of a Living Buddha," *Chinese Literature* (February 1981): 91–104.

21. Dalai Lama, *Freedom,* 268.

22. Dalai Lama, *My Land,* 233–34.

23. See Tim Vanderpool, "Buddhists Protest Death Sentence," *Progressive* 58:3 (March 1994): 14.

24. See the Nichiren background in Masaharu Anesaki, *Nichiren: The Buddhist Prophet* (Peter Smith, 1966 [1916]).

25. For the following citations and background, see Stephen Large, "Buddhism, Socialism, and Protest in Prewar Japan: The Career of Seno'o Giro," *Modern Asian Studies* 21:1 (1987): 153–71.

26. U Thant, *View from the U.N.* (Doubleday, 1978), 36–37, 20–28.

27. Cited in Sarkisyanz, *Buddhist Backgrounds,* 211–12. For a summary of Nu's social theory, see 210–28. See also Jerrold Schecter, *The New Face of Buddha: Buddhism and Political Power in Southeast Asia* (Coward-McCann, 1967), 104–30.

28. See the citation and background in Donald Smith, "Religion, Politics, and the Myth of Reconquest," in Tissa Fernando and Robert Kearney, eds., *Modern Sri Lanka: A Society in Transition* (Syracuse University Press, 1979), 83–100, especially 89.

29. See edict no. 12.6.7 in Stryk, *World of the Buddha,* 238–45.

30. See Sarkisyanz, *Buddhist Backgrounds,* 222ff.; and Donald Smith, "The Limits of Religious Resurgence," in Emile Sahliyeh, ed., *Religious Resurgence and Politics in the Contemporary World* (State University of New York Press, 1990), 36–39.

31. See Donald Smith, "Religion, Politics, and the Myth of Reconquest," 94–97; Donald Swearer, "Fundamentalistic Movements in Theravada Buddhism," in Martin Marty and Scott Appleby, eds., *Fundamentalisms Observed* (University of Chicago Press, 1991), 1:639–47.

32. See David Gosling, "Visions of Salvation: A Thai Buddhist Experience of Ecumenism," *Modern Asian Studies* 26:1 (1992): 31–47.

33. Joanna Macy, "Buddhist Approaches to Social Action," *Journal of Humanistic Psychology* 24:3 (summer 1984): 117–29. See also her "Dependent Co-arising: The Distinctiveness of Buddhist Ethics," *Journal of Religious Ethics* 7:1 (spring 1979): 38–51. For further discussion and sources, see George Bond, "A. T. Ariyaratne and the Sarvodaya Shramadana Movement in Sri Lanka," in Christopher Queen and Sallie King, eds., *Engaged Buddhism: Buddhist Liberation Movements in Asia* (State University of New York Press, 1996), 121–46.

34. See the statistics and further illustrations of renewal in the series of articles by Eugenia Yun, James Hwang, and Winnie Chang in *Free China Review* 44:12 (December 1994): 4–35.

35. Buddhadasa, *Me and Mine,* 83.

36. Cited in Roger Corless, "Pure Land Piety," in Takeuchi Yoshinori, ed., *Buddhist Spirituality* (Crossroad, 1993), 266.

37. See Stephen Beyer, "The Doctrine of Meditation in the Hinayana," and "The Doctrine of Meditation in the Mahayana," in Charles Prebish, ed., *Buddhism: A Modern Perspective* (Penn State University Press, 1975), 137–47, 148–60; Klaus Riesenhuber, "Understanding Non-objective Meditation," *Communio* 14 (1988): 451–67; Michael McGhee, "In Praise of Mindfulness," *Religious Studies* 24 (1988): 65–89; and Mark Epstein, "Psychodynamics of Meditation: Pitfalls on the Spiritual Path," *Journal of Transpersonal Psychology* 22 (1990): 17–34.

38. Cited in Buddhadasa, *Me and Mine,* 112.

39. This visualization exercise, called Indra's Net, is attributed to the Kegon Movement in Japan. See Nancy Wilson Ross, *Buddhism: A Way of Life and Thought* (Vintage, 1980), 54. For a development of parallels between this Buddhist concept and Whitehead's process philosophy, see the chapter entitled "The Buddhist Doctrine of Dependent Co-arising," in Joseph Bracken, S.J., *The Divine Matrix* (Orbis Books, 1995), 93–111.

40. See the descriptions of these two methods in Winston King, "Zen as a Vipassana-Type Discipline," in Harry Partin, ed., *Asian Religions — History of Religion: Preprinted Papers* (American Academy of Religion, 1974), 62–79.

41. See William Mahony, "The Artist as Yogi, the Yogi as Artist," *Parabola* 13 (1988): 68–79. For the Mahayanist and Vajrayanist viewpoint, see Lama Govinda, "The Ecstasy of Breaking-through in the Experience of Meditation," in John White, S.J., ed., *The Highest State of Consciousness* (Anchor, 1972), 248–49.

42. Buddhadasa, *Me and Mine,* 168, 106, 83.

43. Shantideva is cited in Paul Griffiths, "Indian Buddhist Meditation," in Takeuchi Yoshinori, *Buddhist Spirituality,* 62. See also Stephen Beyer, "The Doctrine of Meditation in the Mahayana," in Prebish, *Buddhism,* 149.

44. Buddhadasa, *Me and Mine,* 195, 197.

45. Anguttara Nikaya 2:72–73. For a discussion on Buddhist environmentalism, see Kenneth Kraft, "The Greening of Buddhist Practice," *Cross Currents* (summer 1994): 163–79.

46. Buddhadasa, *Me and Mine,* 169.

47. See background and citations in Kenneth Kraft, "Prospects of a Socially Engaged Buddhism," in Kraft, ed., *Inner Peace, World Peace: Essays on Buddhism and Nonviolence* (State

University of New York Press, 1992), 11–30, especially 17ff.; and Sallie King, "Thich Nhat Hanh and the Unified Buddhist Church: Nondualism in Action," in Queen and King, *Engaged Buddhism,* 321–64. See also Daniel Berrigan, S.J., and Thich Nhat Hanh, *The Raft Is Not the Shore: Conversations toward a Buddhist-Christian Awareness* (Beacon Press, 1975), 120.

48. Thich Nhat Hanh, *The Miracle of Mindfulness: A Manual on Meditation,* trans. Mobi Warren (Beacon Press, 1976), 93.

49. Sources cited in King, "Thich Nhat Hanh," 344.

50. Aung San Suu Kyi, *The Voice of Hope: Conversations with Alan Clements* (Seven Stories Press, 1997), 27, 92, 193.

51. Ibid., 27.

52. Dalai Lama, *Freedom,* 207, 271.

CHAPTER 5: THE JEWISH WAY

1. From an October 1990 taped interview, cited in Nathan Katz, "Contacts between Jewish and Indo-Tibetan Civilizations through the Ages," *Judaism* 43 (1994): 58.

2. Golda Meir, *My Life* (Putnam, 1975), 344–45; and David O'Reilly, "Conference to Examine Jewish Ties to Buddhism," *Philadelphia Inquirer,* November 18, 1995, B1+.

3. Golda Meir, *A Land of Our Own: An Oral Autobiography,* ed. Marie Syrkin (Putnam, 1973), 17–19, 177.

4. See Mordecai Kaplan, "The Reconstruction of Judaism," in Paul Mendes-Flohr and Jehuda Reinharz, eds., *The Jew in the Modern World: A Documentary History* (Oxford University Press, 1980), 397.

5. See Gotthold Lessing, *Nathan the Wise,* trans. Bayard Morgan (Ungar, 1955), 3:7, lines 128–38, p. 79.

6. Jean-Paul Sartre, *Anti-Semite and Jew,* trans. George Becker (Schocken, 1948), 55, 57.

7. See Martin Buber, ed., *Tales of the Hasidim: The Early Masters* (Schocken, 1975), 277.

8. See the discussion of Yiddish *mentshlekhkayt* in the introduction to texts of five plays in Joseph Landis, trans. and ed., *The Great Jewish Plays* (Horizon, 1972).

9. Abraham Heschel, *The Insecurity of Freedom: Essay on Human Existence* (Schocken, 1972), 258.

10. Samson Raphael Hirsch, "Religion Allied to Progress," in Mendes-Flohr and Reinharz, *Jew in the Modern World,* 180, 178.

11. See the discussion in Samuel Heilman and Menachem Friedman, "Religious Fundamentalism and Religious Jews: The Case of the Haredim," in Martin Marty and Scott Appleby, eds., *Fundamentalisms Observed* (University of Chicago Press, 1991), 240ff.

12. Isaac Bashevis Singer, "The Little Shoemakers," trans. Isaac Rosenfeld, in *Collected Stories* (Farrar, Straus, 1982), 38–56.

13. See the citations in Harry Zohn, "Franz Kafka," in Morris Adler, ed., *Jewish Heritage Reader* (Taplinger, 1965), 227–34. See also the helpful thematic index in Franz Kafka, *I Am a Memory Come Alive: Autobiographical Writings by Franz Kafka,* ed. Nahum Glatzer (Schocken, 1974).

14. See Zohn, "Franz Kafka," 227–34.

15. See Sigmund Freud and Oskar Pfister, *Psychoanalysis and Faith: The Letters of Sigmund Freud and Oskar Pfister,* ed. Heinrich Meng and Ernst Freud, trans. Eric Mosbacher (Basic Books, 1963), especially Pfister's letter of October 29, 1918. See also the citations in Theodor Reik, "Sigmund Freud," in Adler, *Jewish Heritage,* 221–26.

16. Bernard Malamud, *The Stories of Bernard Malamud* (Farrar, Straus, Giroux, 1983), 144–54.

17. Abraham Mendelssohn, "Why I Have Raised You as a Christian: A Letter to His Daughter," in Mendes-Flohr and Reinharz, *Jew in the Modern World,* 222–23.

18. See Mendes-Flohr and Reinharz, *Jew in the Modern World,* 267–68. See further examples

of Marx's anti-Semitism in Lawrence Stepelevitch, "Marx and the Jews," *Judaism* 23 (1974): 150–60.

19. Rosa Luxemburg, "No Room in My Heart for Jewish Suffering," in Mendes-Flohr and Reinharz, *Jew in the Modern World,* 225.

20. Isaac Deutscher, *The Non-Jewish Jew and Other Essays,* ed. Tamara Deutscher (Oxford University Press, 1968), 58–59.

21. Ibid., 51, 25–26.

22. See letter of July 23, 1882, to Martha in *Letters of Sigmund Freud,* ed. Ernst Freud, trans. Tania and James Stern (Basic Books, 1960), 22.

23. See Pfister's letter of October 29, 1918, in Freud and Pfister, *Psychoanalysis and Faith.*

24. Moses Mendelssohn, *Jerusalem and Other Jewish Writings,* trans. and ed. Alfred Jospe (Schocken, 1969), 104, 106, 109.

25. Heschel, "Israel and Diaspora," in *Insecurity,* 218, 214, 220.

26. Ibid., 233; and Abraham Heschel, *God in Search of Man: A Philosophy of Judaism* (Octagon, 1972), 324–25, 336–37.

27. Heschel, *God in Search,* 336–37.

28. Heschel, *Insecurity,* 217. See also the biographical introduction in Abraham Heschel, *I Asked for Wonder: A Spiritual Anthology,* ed. Samuel Dresner (Crossroad, 1983).

29. See Buber, *Tales,* 313:1 and 2. See also Louis Newman, ed. and trans., *The Hasidic Anthology: Tales and Teachings of the Hasidim* (Schocken, 1972), 417:5, 209:1, 329:1, 470:2.

30. Heschel, *Insecurity,* 213.

31. See Abraham Heschel, *Maimonides: A Biography,* trans. Joachim Neugroschel (Farrar, Straus, Giroux, 1982), 61.

32. Theodor Herzl, *The Diaries,* ed. and trans. Marvin Lowenthal (Dial Press, 1956), 284–85.

33. Meir, *Land of Our Own,* 232–33.

34. Ibid., 158–59.

35. See Nahum Glatzer, *Essay in Jewish Thought* (University of Alabama Press, 1978), 135. My subsequent Zoharic citations are taken from his chapter, "Zion in Medieval Literature: Prose Works," 135–49.

36. This Talmud story is cited in Erich Fromm, *Psychoanalysis and Religion* (Yale University Press, 1978 [1950]), 45–46.

37. For background on Passover, especially the Elijah and *afikomen* rites, see Ruth Fredman, *The Passover Seder: Afikoman in Exile* (University of Pennsylvania Press, 1981); and Monford Harris, "The Passover Seder: On Entering the Order of History," *Judaism* 25 (1976): 473–88.

38. Newman, *Hasidic Anthology,* 416:2, 99:8 and 9.

39. See the Herzl selection in Philip Goodman, ed., *The Passover Anthology* (Jewish Publication of America, 1961), 196.

40. See Ruth Wisse, "Between Passovers," *Commentary* 88 (December 1984): 42–47.

41. Phyllis Berman and Arthur Waskow, "The Seder of Rebirth," *Tikkun* 9 (March 1994): 72–75.

42. Heschel, *God in Search,* 418.

43. Newman, *Hasidic Anthology,* 404–8.

44. Cited in Marc Angel, "Sephardim Shabbat," *Judaism* 31 (winter 1982): 21–25. The entire winter issue focuses on the Sabbath.

45. See the letter of February 22, 1923, in *Letters of Rainer Maria Rilke: 1892–1926,* ed. and trans. Jane Greene and Mary Norton (Norton, 1948).

46. See Erich Fromm, *The Forgotten Language* (Rinehart, 1951), 248. See also a revised version of this interpretation in his *You Shall Be as Gods* (Holt, Rinehart, Winston, 1962), 193–99.

47. See the citations in Elliot Ginsburg, "The Sabbath in the Kabbalah, *Judaism* 31 (winter 1982): 26–36.

48. Newman, *Hasidic Anthology,* 173:3, 4.

49. Ibid., 173:5.

50. Hugh Nissenson, "In the Reign of Peace," in *The Elephant and My Jewish Problem* (Harper and Row, 1988), 159–65.

51. Heschel, *God in Search,* 415–16.

52. Herzl, *Diaries,* 171, 182–83, 426, 100–101.

53. Chaim Potok, *The Chosen* (Fawcett, 1967), 186–87.

54. See Alvin Rosenfeld, "The Americanization of the Holocaust," *Commentary* (June 1995): 35–40. See the excellent sampling of letters, with Rosenfeld's rejoinder, in the September issue, 6–12.

55. See Benny Kraut, "Faith and the Holocaust: A Review-Essay," *Judaism* 31 (1982): 185–201. The two books reviewed are Eliezer Berkovits, *With God in Hell,* and Reeve Brenner, *The Faith and Doubt of Holocaust Survivors.*

56. Potok, *The Chosen,* 180–82.

57. Deutscher, *Non-Jewish Jew,* 40–41, 112–13.

58. See the sources in Joshua Haberman, "The Place of Israel in Reform Jewish Theology," *Judaism* 21 (1972): 437–48.

59. David Ben-Gurion, *Memoirs,* ed. Thomas Bransten (World, 1970), 163–64.

60. Ibid.

61. "A Letter to Gandhi (1939)," reprinted in Martin Buber, *Pointing the Way: Collected Essays,* ed. and trans. Maurice Friedman (Routledge and Kegan Paul, 1957), 141–42.

62. Cited in Maurice Friedman, *Encounter on the Narrow Ridge: A Life of Martin Buber* (Paragon, 1991), 433–34.

63. Ben-Gurion, *Memoirs,* 24.

64. See the exchange with Jacob Blaustein, excerpted in Mendes-Flohr and Reinharz, *Jew in the Modern World,* 414–17.

65. Ben-Gurion, *Memoirs,* 130, 176; and Mendes-Flohr and Reinharz, *Jew in the Modern World,* 479–81.

66. Ben-Gurion, *Memoirs,* 120, 124.

67. Ibid., 178, 124, 131.

68. Ibid., 126.

69. Cited in Friedman, *Encounter,* 422–23.

70. Ibid., 329, 431.

71. Ibid., 422, 348.

72. Ibid., 424.

73. Ibid., 292–93, 339.

74. Saul Bellow, *To Jerusalem and Back: A Personal Account* (Viking, 1976).

75. Meir, *Land of Our Own,* 241.

76. Bellow, *To Jerusalem,* 127.

CHAPTER 6: THE CHRISTIAN WAY

1. Theodor Herzl, *The Diaries,* ed. and trans. Marvin Lowenthal (Dial Press, 1956), 428–29.

2. See the sources in Donald Moore, S.J., *The Human and the Holy: The Spirituality of Abraham Joshua Heschel* (Fordham University Press, 1989), 12–14.

3. Declaration on the Relationship of the Church to Non-Christian Religions, in Walter Abbott, S.J., ed., *The Documents of Vatican II* (Guild Press, 1966), par. 4.

4. See the sources for the Covenant of Omar, Peter the Hermit, and especially the Fourth Lateran Council in Edward Synan, *The Popes and the Jews in the Middle Ages* (Macmillan, 1965), 53–54, 76, 234–36.

5. Martin Luther, *On the Jews and Their Lies,* in *Luther's Works,* ed. Helmut Lehmann (Fortress Press, 1971), 47:268–69.

6. Cited in John O'Malley, S.J., *The First Jesuits* (Harvard University Press, 1993), 278.

7. Karl Rahner and Pinchas Lapide, *Encountering Jesus — Encountering Judaism: A Dialogue,* trans. Davis Perkins (Crossroad, 1987), 79.

8. Cited in Maurice Friedman, *Encounter on the Narrow Ridge: A Life of Martin Buber* (Paragon, 1991), 197, 292–93.

9. See Karl Rahner, *Faith in a Wintry Season: Conversations and Interviews with Karl Rahner in the Last Years of His Life,* ed. Paul Imhof and Hubert Biallowons, trans. Harvey Egan (Crossroad, 1991), 138; and Rahner, "Marxist Utopia and the Christian Future of Man," in *Theological Investigations,* trans. Karl Kruger and Boniface Kruger (Darton, Longman, and Todd, 1969), 6:64.

10. Rahner, "Marxist Utopia," 63, 66. For comments on the Nicaraguan millennium, see Rahner, *Faith in a Wintry Season,* 146. See also Rahner, "On the Presence of Christ in the Diaspora Community," trans. David Bourke, in *Theological Investigations,* 10:97–99.

11. Dietrich Bonhoeffer, *Letters and Papers from Prison,* ed. Eberhard Bethge, trans. Reginald Fuller et al., 2d ed. (Macmillan, 1971), 135, 156–57.

12. John Macquarrie, "The Anthropological Approach to Theology," *Heythrop Journal* 25 (1984): 272–87, especially 277.

13. Cited in Friedman, *Encounter,* 293.

14. Rahner and Lapide, *Encountering Jesus,* 106.

15. Rahner, *Faith in a Wintry Season,* 107.

16. See the 1979 review cited in Leo O'Donovan's obituary on Rahner, "To Lead Us into the Mystery," *America* (June 16, 1984): 453–57.

17. Karl Rahner, *Foundations of Christian Faith,* trans. William Dych (Seabury Press, 1978), 197. See also Pierre Teilhard de Chardin, "Christology and Evolution," in *Christianity and Evolution,* trans. René Hague (Harper, 1971), 76–95. See *Foundations,* 180, where Rahner offers a nimble demurral: "We are trying to avoid theories which Teilhard de Chardin has made current. If we reach the same conclusions, so much the better, and we do not have to avoid that deliberately."

18. Rahner, *Foundations,* 137.

19. Rahner, "Anonymous Christians," in *Theological Investigations,* trans. Karl Kruger and Boniface Kruger (Darton, Longman, and Todd, 1969), 6:394; Karl Rahner and Herbert Vorgrimler, "Jesus Christ," in Cornelius Ernst, O.P., ed., *Theological Dictionary,* trans. Richard Strachan (Herder and Herder, 1965), 241–42.

20. Dogmatic Constitution on the Church, in *Documents of Vatican II,* par. 16.

21. See the two excellent editorials entitled "The Dialectic of Romans 13:1–7 and Revelation 13," in *Journal of Church and State* 18–19 (1976–77): 5–20, 433–43; see also Alan Richardson, *The Political Christ* (Westminster, 1973).

22. See Peter Ackroyd, *T. S. Eliot: A Life* (Simon and Schuster, 1984), 41–42.

23. T. S. Eliot, *The Idea of a Christian Society* (Harcourt, Brace, 1940), 65, 51.

24. Ibid., 60, 49–50.

25. Ibid., appendix, 97, and footnote, 74–75.

26. T. S. Eliot, *After Strange Gods: A Primer of Modern Heresy* (Harcourt, Brace, 1934), 15, 20.

27. Fyodor Dostoyevsky, *The Idiot,* trans. Henry and Olga Carlisle (New American Library, 1969), 560–62.

28. Ronald Berman, ed., *Solzhenitsyn at Harvard: The Address, Twelve Early Responses, and Six Later Reflections* (Ethics and Public Policy Center, 1980), 12–13, 18–19.

29. Cardinal Alfredo Ottaviani, "Church and State: Some Present Problems in the Light of the Teaching of Pope Pius XII," *American Ecclesiastical Review* 128 (May 1953): 321–34, especially 327. To locate sources of various theologians holding this thesis-hypothesis position, all adversaries of Murray, see Thomas Ferguson, *Catholic and American: The Political Theology of John Courtney Murray* (Sheed and Ward, 1993), especially 162–63.

30. Konrad Adenauer, *Memoirs 1945–53,* trans. Beate Ruhm von Oppen (Regnery, 1965), 45, 450.

31. Ibid., 45.

32. Cited in Terence Prittie, *Konrad Adenauer: 1876–1967* (Cowles, 1971), 314.

33. Ibid., 51, 321–22.

34. Leonard Gross, *The Last, Best Hope: Eduardo Frei and Chilean Democracy* (Random House, 1967), 10. See also Richard Bourne, "Eduardo Frei Montalva," in *Political Leaders of Latin America* (Knopf, 1970), 137–74. For the influence of Maritain on Frei, see Bernard Doering, "Jacques Maritain and His Two 'Authentic Revolutionaries,' " in Leonard Kennedy, C.S.B., ed., *Thomistic Papers* (Center for Thomistic Studies, University of St. Thomas, 1987), 3:91–116.

35. See Gross, *The Last, Best Hope,* 10; Caro is cited on 87.

36. See the theories summarized in Gustavo Benavides, "Religion and the Modernization of Tradition in Latin America," in Charles Fu and Gerhard Spiegler, eds., *Religious Issues and Inter-religious Dialogues: An Analysis and Sourcebook of Developments since 1945* (Greenwood Press, 1989), 177–96, esp. 178–82.

37. Gross, *The Last, Best Hope,* 89–91.

38. Ibid.

39. For evidence of change in church-state relations after Frei, see Brian Smith, "Christians and Marxists in Allende's Chile: Lessons for Western Europe," in Suzanne Berger, ed., *Religion in West European Politics* (Frank Cass, 1982), 108–26.

40. Søren Kierkegaard, *Attack upon Christendom: 1854–1855,* trans. Walter Lowrie (Princeton University Press, 1944), 140, 192.

41. Ibid., 284.

42. Graham Greene, *The Honorary Consul* (Bodley Head, 1973), 143–44, 242–43.

43. Camilo Torres, *Revolutionary Priest: The Complete Writings and Messages of Camilo Torres,* ed. John Gerassi, trans. June Alcantara et al. (Random House, 1971), 29.

44. Ibid., 325, 368–69. Matthew 5:23–24.

45. Torres, *Revolutionary Priest,* 371, 313.

46. See Juan Luis Segundo, "Capitalism-Socialism: A Theological Crux," in Claude Geffre and Gustavo Gutiérrez, eds., *The Mystical and Political Dimension of the Christian Faith* (Concilium/ Herder and Herder, 1974), 118.

47. Reinhold Niebuhr, *Faith and Politics,* ed. Ronald Stone (Braziller, 1968), 56, 61.

48. Harry Davis and Robert Good, eds., *Reinhold Niebuhr on Politics* (Scribner, 1960), 197.

49. Kenneth Kaunda, *A Humanist in Africa,* ed. Colin Morris (Abingdon, 1966), 39.

50. Kenneth Kaunda, *Letter to My Children* (Longman, 1975), 22–23.

51. Kaunda, *Humanist,* 21, 36.

52. Ibid., 38.

53. Cited in Fergus MacPherson, *Kenneth Kaunda of Zambia: The Times and the Man* (Oxford University Press, 1974), 134; and see Kaunda *Humanist,* 38.

54. Kaunda, *Humanist,* 22.

55. Ibid., 41, 27.

56. Ibid., 43.

57. Ibid., 45; and see citations in MacPherson, *Kenneth Kaunda,* 460.

58. See the pictures and sample reviews of the more celebrated Jesus films in Roy Kinnard and Tim Davis, *Divine Images: A History of Jesus on the Screen* (Citadel, 1992).

59. See Ignatius Loyola, *The Spiritual Exercises of St. Ignatius,* trans. Louis Puhl, S.J. (Newman, 1951), 52–53.

60. Carl Jung, *Memories, Dreams, Reflections,* ed. Aniela Jaffe, trans. Richard and Clara Winston (Vintage, 1965), 280.

61. See the sources in John Willis, S.J., ed., *The Teachings of the Church Fathers* (Herder and Herder, 1966), nos. 570 and 581.

62. Cited in Gordon Rupp, "Protestant Spirituality in the First Age of the Reformation," in G. J. Cuming and Derek Baker, eds., *Popular Belief and Practice* (Cambridge University Press, 1972), 155–70, esp. 159.

63. See the methodology in Alexander Malik, "Confessing Christ in the Islamic Context," in R. S. Sugirtharajah, ed., *Asian Faces of Jesus* (Orbis, 1993), 75.

64. 1 Corinthians 9:20, 22–23.

65. See Carol Collins, "Desire to Stay On: Interview with Peter Henriot, S.J.," *National Catholic Reporter* 32 (July 12, 1996): 10–11.

66. See Epistle to the Hebrews 2:5–18. See the development of the initiation analogy in Anselm Sanon, "Jesus, Master of Initiation," in Robert Schreiter, ed., *Faces of Jesus in Africa* (Orbis, 1991), 85–102.

67. See Leonard Prince, "Indigenous Yoruba Psychiatry," in Ari Kiev, ed., *Magic, Faith, and Healing* (Free Press, 1964), 84–121; and Cece Kolie, "Jesus as Healer?" in Schreiter, *Faces,* 128–50.

68. See Stephen Barton, "Jesus and Health," *Theology* 87 (July 1984): 266–72; John Carroll, "Sickness and Healing in the New Testament Gospels," *Interpretation* 49 (April 1995): 130–42; and Peder Borgen, "Miracles of Healing in the New Testament," *Studia Theologica* 35 (1981): 91–105.

69. See the introductory notes to Clement of Alexandria, *Christ the Educator,* trans. Simon Wood, C.P. (Fathers of the Church, 1954).

70. See Roland Murphy, O. Carm., "The Theological Contributions of Israel's Wisdom Literature," *Listening* (winter 1984): 30–40; and Kathleen O'Connor, *The Wisdom Literature* (Michael Glazier, 1988), 13–34, 185–92. For a development of the wisdom banquet theme, in the light of intertestamental literature, see Vernon Ruland, "Sign and Sacrament: John's Bread of Life Discourse (Chapter 6)," *Interpretation* (October 1964): 450–62.

71. See Bhagavad Gita, trans. Juan Mascaro (Penguin, 1979), 12:8, 20; 14:1.

72. Ibid., 11:4, 13.

73. See L. W. Barnard, "Early Christian Art as Apologetic," *Journal of Religious History* 10 (June 1978): 20–31; and Jaroslav Pelikan, *Imago Dei: The Byzantine Apologia for Icons* (Princeton University Press, 1990). See also Albert Moore, "Christianity," in *Iconography of Religions* (Fortress, 1977), 228–77.

74. Bhagavad Gita 9:23; 4:6–7.

75. Cited in Francis D'Sa, S.J., "Christian Incarnation and Hindu Avatara," in Leonardo Boff and Virgil Elizondo, eds., *Any Room for Christ in Asia?* (Concilium/Orbis, 1993), 79–80.

76. Irenaeus, *Adversus Hereses* 3.18, cited in John Lawson, *The Biblical Theology of St. Irenaeus* (Epworth, 1948), 153.

77. Ibid., 3.7; 2.22.4; cited in Lawson, *Biblical Theology,* 153.

78. See Gregory of Nyssa, cited in Teilhard de Chardin, *The Divine Milieu: An Essay on the Interior Life* (Harper and Row, 1957), 110. See the quotations from "Le Christique" and "Le Coeur de la Matiere," in Claude Tresmontant, *Pierre Teilhard de Chardin: His Thought* (Helicon Press, 1959), 76.

79. Fyodor Dostoyevsky, *The Brothers Karamazov,* trans. Constance Garnett (Modern Library, 1950), 351.

80. For a discussion of the descent into hell motif, see Ralph Turner, "Descendit ad Inferos: Medieval Views on Christ's Descent into Hell and the Salvation of the Ancient Just," *Journal of the History of Ideas* 27 (April–June 1966): 173–93.

81. Albert Schweitzer in 1906 found such a source in Karl Heinrich Venturini (1768–1849). For an application of this pattern to a number of works in the twentieth century, see Gerald O'Collins, S.J., and Daniel Kendall, S.J., "On Reissuing Venturini," *Gregorianum* 75 (1994): 241–65.

82. See D. H. Lawrence, *The Man Who Died* (Knopf, 1931); Nikos Kazantzakis, *The Last Temptation of Christ,* trans. P. A. Bien (Bantam, 1960); and John Updike, "Jesus on Honshu," in *Museums and Women* (Knopf, 1972), 213–17.

83. Nicolas Notovitch, *The Unknown Life of Jesus Christ,* trans. J. H. Connelly and L. Landsberg (Dillingham, 1894).

84. *The Gospel of Barnabas,* translation of the Italian text by Lonsdale Ragg and Laura Ragg (Oxford University Press, 1907). See especially the Raggs' introduction and also David Sox, *The Gospel of Barnabas* (Allen and Unwin, 1984). The author of *Barnabas* is commonly believed to have been a genuine Muslim convert or a mischievous sixteenth-century Catholic monk, prone to embarrass church authorities. See William Watt, *Muslim-Christian Encounters: Perceptions and Misperceptions* (Routledge, 1991), 117–18.

85. See Chung Hyun Kyung, "Who Is Jesus for Asian Women?" in Sugirtharajah, *Asian Faces,* 223–46; and Aloysius Pieris, S.J., "Does Christ Have a Place in Asia? A Panoramic View," in Boff and Elizondo, *Any Room?* 33–47.

86. Kwok Pui-lan, "Chinese Non-Christian Perceptions of Christ," in Boff and Elizondo, *Any Room?* 24–32.

87. See Barton, "Jesus and Health," 267–69.

88. See Martin Luther King Jr., *A Testament of Hope: Essential Writings of Martin Luther King, Jr.,* ed. James Washington (Harper and Row, 1986), 259–67.

89. Dostoyevsky, *The Idiot,* 427–28.

90. See St. John of the Cross, *Dark Night of the Soul,* trans. Allison Peers (Image Books, 1959), 54–55, 68. See also Hans Urs Von Balthasar, "Some Points of Eschatology," in *Word and Redemption: Essays in Theology,* trans. A. Littledale and Alexander Dru (Herder and Herder, 1965), 2:158–59.

CHAPTER 7: THE MUSLIM WAY

1. Quran 2:177. I have used the N. J. Dawood translation-interpretation, *The Koran* (Penguin, 1974).

2. Farid ud-Din Attar, *The Conference of the Birds,* trans. Garcin de Tassy and C. S. Nott (Shambhala, 1971), 34, 87–88.

3. See Muhammed Talbi, "Possibilities and Conditions for a Better Understanding between Islam and the West," *Journal of Ecumenical Studies* 15 (spring 1988): 161–93.

4. See John Raines, "The Politics of Religious Correctness: Islam and the West," *Cross Currents* (spring 1996): 39–49.

5. See Roger Johnson, "Inter-religious Conflict and the Voyages of Columbus," *Muslim World* 83 (January 1993): 1–19.

6. For further Jewish-Muslim parallels, see Trude Weiss-Rosmarin, "The Islamic Connection," *Judaism* 29 (1980): 272–78.

7. See Annemarie Schimmel, "The Prophet Muhammad as a Center of Muslim Life and Thought," in Schimmel and Abdoldjavad Falaturi, eds., *We Believe in One God: The Experience of God in Christianity and Islam* (Crossroad, 1979), 37.

8. See Quran 5:68–69.

9. Quran 3:85. On the dilemmas of supersession or abrogation, see Abdulaziz Sachedina, "Is Islamic Revelation an Abrogation of Judaeo-Christian Revelation? Islamic Self-identification in the Classical and Modern Age," in Hans Küng and Jürgen Moltmann, eds., *Islam: A Challenge for Christianity* (Concilium/Orbis Books, 1994), 94–102.

10. Quran 2:125–30.

11. Genesis 21:14–21.

12. See Sheik Nur Al Jerrahi, "The Dream," in Steven Barboza, ed., *American Jihad: Islam after Malcolm X* (Doubleday, 1993), 199.

13. Idries Shah, "Pilgrimage to Mecca," in *Caravan of Dreams* (Octagon, 1971), 58.

14. Malcolm X, *The Autobiography of Malcolm X,* ed. Alex Haley (Grove Press, 1965), 340.

15. Cited in Ismail Raji al-Faruqi, "The Islamic Critique of the Status Quo of Muslim Society," in Barbara Stowasser, ed. *The Islamic Impulse* (Croom Helm, 1987), 234.

16. See Idris Diaz, "Just Take Me!" in Barboza, *American Jihad,* 314.

17. Sayyed Nasr, *Ideals and Realities of Islam* (Praeger, 1967), 116.

18. Some of the rival pilgrimage shrines are discussed in Erich Isaac, "The Pilgrimage to Mecca," *Geographical Review* 63 (July 1973): 405–9. For criticisms of hajj abuses, see Narifumi Maeda, "The Aftereffects of Hajj and Kaan Buat," *Journal of Southeast Asian Studies* 6 (September 1975): 178–85; and Raymond Scupin, "The Social Significance of the Hajj for Thai Muslims," *Muslim World* 72 (January 1982): 25–33.

19. See Simon Coleman and John Elsner, "The Center in the Desert: Muslim Pilgrimage to Mecca," in *Pilgrimage: Past and Present in the World Religions* (Harvard University Press, 1995), 52–73, especially 57–58; see also Ezzedine Guellouz, *Mecca: The Muslim Pilgrimage* (Paddington, 1979).

20. Hamid Enayat, *Modern Islamic Political Thought* (University of Texas Press, 1982), 19.

21. See Vernon Schubel, "The Muharram Majlis: The Role of a Ritual in the Preservation of Shi'a Identity," in Earle Waugh et al., eds., *Muslim Families in North America* (University of Alberta Press, 1991), 118–31.

22. For discussion of the Muharram rites sketched here and below, see Earle Waugh, "Muharram Rites: Community Death and Rebirth," in Frank Reynolds and Earle Waugh, eds., *Religious*

Encounters with Death (Penn State University Press, 1977), 200–213; and Gustav Thaiss, "Religious Symbolism and Social Change: The Drama of Husain," in Nikki Keddie, ed., *Scholars, Saints, and Sufis* (University of California Press, 1972), 349–66. See a popular account of the passion play tradition in Royston Pike, *The Strange Ways of Man* (Hart, 1967), 180–89.

23. This Sufi tale is attributed to Bektash, fourteenth-century founder of the Bektashi order of dervishes. See Shah, *Caravan,* 112–13.

24. Cited in Annemarie Schimmel, *Gabriel's Wing: A Study into the Religious Ideas of Sir Muhammad Iqbal* (E. J. Brill, 1963), 195.

25. Cited in ibid., 196.

26. Gamal Abdul Nasser, *Egypt's Liberation: The Philosophy of the Revolution* (Public Affairs Press, 1955), 111–12. See also Yvonne Haddad, "The Arab-Israeli Wars, Nasserism, and the Affirmation of Islamic Identity," in John Esposito, ed., *Islam and Development: Religion and Sociopolitical Change* (Syracuse University Press, 1980), 107–21.

27. See Albert Hourani, conclusion to James Piscatori, ed., *Islam in the Political Process* (Cambridge University Press, 1983), 229.

28. See Eric Davis, "The Concept of Revival and the Study of Islam and Politics," and Richard Mitchell, "The Islamic Movement: Its Current Condition and Future Prospects," in Stowasser, *Islamic Impulse,* 37–58, 75–86.

29. Alan Makovsky, "Responding to Turkey's Eastward Drift," *New York Times,* August 17, 1996, 17.

30. Imam Ruhollah Khomeini, "Islamic Government (1970)," in *Islam and Revolution,* trans. Hamid Algar (Mizan Press, 1981), 38–39.

31. Ibid., 141–43.

32. See the development of this comparison in Edward Mortimer, *Faith and Power: The Politics of Islam* (Random House, 1982), 136ff. For further historical background, see Ergun Ozbudun, "Islam and Politics in Modern Turkey: The Case of the National Salvation Party," in Stowasser, *Islamic Impulse,* 141–56.

33. Cited in John Kinross, *Ataturk: A Biography of Mustafa Kemal, Father of Modern Turkey* (William Morrow, 1965), 396.

34. See the summary of legislation in T. B. Millar, "Turkey," in Mohammed Ayoob, ed., *The Politics of Islamic Reassertion* (St. Martin's Press, 1981), 79–89.

35. Kinross, *Ataturk,* 16.

36. Ibid., 437, 29–30.

37. Cited in Enver Karal, "The Principles of Kemalism," in Ali Kazancigil and Ergun Ozbudun, eds., *Ataturk: Founder of a Modern State* (Archon Books, 1981), 23, 15. Karal gives special attention to Comte's influence.

38. See the sources and discussion in Nikki Keddie, *Sayyid Jamal ad-Din "al-Afghani": A Political Biography* (University of California Press, 1972), 189–99, especially 191–92.

39. Cited in Kinross, *Ataturk,* 468, 472.

40. Ibid., 437; and Mortimer, *Faith and Power,* 147.

41. Cited in Millar, "Turkey," 83–84.

42. Cited in Bernard Lewis, "The Return of Islam," in Michael Curtis, ed., *Religion and Politics in the Middle East* (Westview Press, 1981), 24–25.

43. See James Piscatori, "The Nature of the Islamic Revival," in Andrew Kimmens, ed., *Islamic Politics and the Modern World* (H. W. Wildon, 1991), 105–6; and Mortimer, *Faith and Power,* 272–77.

44. Cited in Kimmens, *Islamic Politics,* 106.

45. From an interview published in a Tehran daily newspaper, 1980, "The Religious Scholars Led the Revolt," reprinted in Kimmens, *Islamic Politics,* 114–27, esp. 119.

46. See William Beeman, "Images of the Great Satan: Representations of the United States in the Iranian Revolution," in Nikki Keddie, ed., *Religion and Politics in Iran* (Yale University Press, 1983), 191–218.

47. See the interview in Kimmens, *Islamic Politics,* 119–21.

48. See the history of Pahlavi dynasty-ulama conflicts in Shahrough Akhavi, *Religion and*

Politics in Contemporary Iran: Clergy-State Relations in the Pahlavi Period (State University of New York Press, 1980).

49. Cited in Beeman, "Images," 215–16.

50. Cited in Hamid Dabashi, *Theology of Discontent: The Ideological Foundations of the Islamic Revolution in Iran* (New York University Press, 1993), 448.

51. See the cover articles, "Man of the Year: The Mystic Who Lit the Fires of Hatred," in *Time* 115 (January 7, 1980): 9–33.

52. See a resourceful analysis of the Khomeini legend in Michael Fischer, "Imam Khomeini: Four Levels of Understanding," in John Esposito, ed., *Voices of Resurgent Islam* (Oxford University Press, 1983), 150–74.

53. See the discussion of these calendars in Dabashi, *Theology of Discontent,* 487ff.

54. Cited in Mary Hegland, "Two Images of Husayn: Accommodation and Revolution in an Iranian Village," in Keddie, *Religion and Politics,* 228–29.

55. See Fischer, "Imam Khomeini," 164, and especially 173n.21. I cannot support Hamid Algar's unqualified claim that "the word *imam* applied to Khomeini has its general and original sense of leader, and not the particular and technical sense it has acquired when applied to the Twelve Imams." See Algar's introduction in Khomeini, *Islam and Revolution,* 10.

56. "Man of the Year," 28.

57. See the sources cited in Dabashi, *Theology of Discontent,* 440–45.

58. Ibid., 445, 443, 476–77. See also Khomeini's *Islamic Government* treatise in Khomeini, *Islam and Revolution,* 30, 43.

59. Khomeini's repeated phrase is "Islami-Insani," cited in Dabashi, *Theology of Discontent,* 449.

60. For a discussion of factors affecting the spread of Iran's revolution, see Elaine Sciolino, "Iran's Durable Revolution," *Foreign Affairs* 61 (spring 1983): 893–920; and Fouad Ajami, "Iran: The Impossible Revolution," *Foreign Affairs* 67 (1988–89): 135–55. For a summary of the conflict between Shiism and Arabism, see three essays in Martin Kramer, ed., *Shiism, Resistance, and Revolution* (Westview Press, 1987), 135–89.

61. Quran 73:1.

62. Besides this experience, see further examples of meetings with Muslims in my *Sacred Lies and Silences: A Psychology of Religious Disguise* (Liturgical Press, 1994), 19–20.

63. Cited in Annemarie Schimmel, *Mystical Dimensions of Islam* (University of North Carolina Press, 1975), 171. My Sufi quotations will be drawn mostly from Schimmel's extracts in this book, along with her interpretations. See also R. Caspar's survey of current approaches to Sufism in "Muslim Mysticism: Tendencies in Recent Research," in Merlin Swartz, ed., *Studies on Islam* (Oxford University Press, 1981), 164–84; and David Brewster, "The Study of Sufism: Towards a Methodology," *Religion* 6:1 (spring 1976): 31–47.

64. Nasr, *Ideals,* 177.

65. See Schimmel, *Mystical Dimensions,* 17, 99.

66. Ibid., 157ff., and Annemarie Schimmel, *Islam: An Introduction* (State University of New York Press, 1992), 45–50.

67. To grasp the Quran's place as an icon in an otherwise iconoclastic situation, see Leonard Librande, "The Calligraphy of the Quran: How It Functions for Muslims," *Religion* 9 (spring 1979): 36–58; and Marshall Hodgson, "Islam and Image," *History of Religions* 3:2 (winter 1964): 220–60.

68. Attar, *Conference of the Birds,* 131.

69. Ibid., 31–32. See the discussion of divine concealment and revelation in Belden Lane, "In Quest of the King," *Horizons* 14 (1987): 39–48.

70. Attar, *Conference of the Birds,* 132, 3, 31.

71. Compare ibid., 117 and 92, with Jalaluddin Rumi, *Mathnawii* 1:3056–64, cited in Schimmel, *Mystical Dimensions,* 314.

72. Attar, *Conference of the Birds,* 30, 115–16.

73. See Schimmel, *Mystical Dimensions,* 5, 9.

74. For example, see Schimmel's warning that the many Sufi anthologies by Idries Shah ought

to be avoided by all serious students, in ibid., 9n.5. See also R. C. Zaehner, "Why Not Islam?" *Religious Studies* 11 (1975): 167–79, where Shah is treated as an "egregious popularizer."

75. Cited in Schimmel, *Mystical Dimensions,* 267. Notice the difficulties mentioned here in translating the term *wujud.* Because the Arabic lacks an explicit verb "to be," the infinitive is rendered "to be found." Thus, "to be" already implies "to be perceived" or at least the potential to be perceived. See also the distinction between modes of philosophy, theology, and mysticism in William Chittick, "Mysticism versus Philosophy in Earlier Islamic History," *Religious Studies* 17 (March 1981): 87–104.

76. D. H. Lawrence, *Studies in Classic American Literature* (Viking, 1961 [1924]), 165.

77. Cited in Perry Miller, *Jonathan Edwards* (Meridian, 1965), 292.

78. Attar, *Conference of the Birds,* 4.

79. Rumi, *Mathnawii* 3:801, cited in Schimmel, *Mystical Dimensions,* 214.

80. Quran 33:21.

81. See sources in "Offending Book Recalled," *National Catholic Reporter* (May 16, 1997): 10.

82. See James Royster, "Muhammad as Teacher and Exemplar," *Muslim World* 68:4 (October 1978): 235–58, especially the al-Ghazali citation on 244. For a comparison between the lives of al-Ghazali, Ibn Khaldun, and Muhammad, see Ira Lapidus, "Adulthood in Islam: Religious Maturity in the Islamic Tradition," *Daedalus* (spring 1976): 93–101.

83. Cited in Royster, "Muhammad as Teacher," 244.

84. Hadith and other sources cited in Schimmel, *Mystical Dimensions,* 215.

85. Quran 17:1; 53:7ff.

86. For sources and discussion of the *miraj,* see Earle Waugh, "Following the Beloved: Muhammad as Model in the Sufi Tradition," in Frank Reynolds and Donald Capps, eds., *The Biographical Process* (Mouton, 1976), 63–86; J. R. Porter, "Muhammad's Journey to Heaven," *Numen* 20 (1974): 64–80; and Nazeer El-Azma, "Some Notes on the Impact of the Story of the Miraj on Sufi Literature," *Muslim World* 63:2 (April 1973): 93–104. The last article includes a valuable translation of al-Bistami's vision.

87. See sources in Schimmel, *Mystical Dimensions,* 219–20.

88. Ibn Arabi names the three stages *fana fish-shaykh, fana fir-Rasul,* and *fana fi-Allah.* Also see Attar, *Tadhkirat al-auliya,* 2:41, cited among other sources in Schimmel, *Mystical Dimensions,* 267, 214.

CHAPTER 8: THE HUMANIST WAY

1. Mark Twain, "Bible Teaching and Religious Practice," in *What Is Man? And Other Philosophical Writings,* ed. Paul Baender (University of California Press, 1973), 71–75. For the impact of modern secularity on the churches, see also Langdon Gilkey, *Naming the Whirlwind: The Renewal of God-Language* (Bobbs-Merrill, 1969), 63ff.

2. Albert Camus, *The Plague,* trans. Stuart Gilbert (Knopf, 1948), 230–31.

3. Bertrand Russell, *The Autobiography* (Little, Brown, 1967), 1:3–4.

4. Ibid., 221.

5. Bertrand Russell, *Why I Am Not a Christian,* ed. Paul Edwards (Allen and Unwin, 1961), xi, 180.

6. Bertrand Russell, *The Basic Writings of Bertrand Russell: 1903–1959,* ed. Robert Egner and Lester Denonn (Simon and Schuster, 1961), 52, 31.

7. See Warren Smith, "Are You a Humanist? Some Authors Answer," *Humanist* 41 (1981): 15–26, a reprint of the 1951 article. It gives endless qualifications of the label, as people like Bertrand Russell, George Santayana, Thomas Mann, Norman Mailer, and Arthur Koestler apply it to their situations.

8. Russell, *Why I Am Not a Christian,* 37.

9. See the critique of Kierkegaard's interpretation in Sidney Hook, *The Quest for Being* (St. Martin's, 1961), 136–42.

10. See the sources selected in Erich Heller, "Rilke and Nietzsche, with a Discussion on Thought, Belief, and Poetry," in *The Importance of Nietzsche* (University of Chicago Press, 1988), 87–126; and Walter Kaufman, "Nietzsche and Rilke," in *The Owl and the Nightingale* (Faber and Faber, 1959), 200–218, especially 209 and 213. See also aphorism no. 285 from *The Joyous Cosmology,* in Friedrich Nietzsche, *The Portable Nietzsche,* ed. and trans. Walter Kaufman (Viking Press, 1966), 98.

11. See the Rilke sources cited in Kaufman, "Nietzsche and Rilke," 209.

12. For an assessment of Feuerbach's later influence, see Marx Wartofsky, *Feuerbach* (Cambridge University Press, 1977), 1–27; Van Harvey, *Feuerbach and the Interpretation of Religion* (Cambridge University Press, 1995), 1–24; and Eugene Kamenka, *The Philosophy of Ludwig Feuerbach* (Praeger, 1969), 15–32, especially 167n.43. Within the context of an insightful discussion of projection, Harvey argues for crucial differences between Feuerbach's two major works, whereas I see mostly continuity and recapitulation.

13. Cited in Kamenka, *Philosophy,* 17.

14. See the sources in ibid., 23.

15. Ludwig Feuerbach, *Lectures on the Essence of Religion,* trans. Ralph Manheim (Harper and Row, 1967), 23. See the introductory essay by Karl Barth in Feuerbach's *The Essence of Christianity,* trans. George Eliot (Harper, 1957), x.

16. See the sources noted in Barth's introduction to Feuerbach, *Essence of Christianity,* xvi–xviii.

17. Feuerbach, *Essence of Christianity,* 195, 31.

18. Ibid., 29–30, 311. For a discussion of the Fichtean concept of alienation as a necessary error, see Kamenka, *Philosophy,* 7–11.

19. Feuerbach, *Essence of Christianity,* 73.

20. Karl Marx and Frederick Engels, *Works* (International Publishers, 1975), 1:30–31. For background on Marx, see David McLellan, *Karl Marx: His Life and Thought* (Harper and Row, 1973); Frank Manuel, *A Requiem for Karl Marx* (Harvard University Press, 1993); and Terrell Carver, ed., *The Cambridge Companion to Marx* (Cambridge University Press, 1991).

21. See selections from Frederick Engels, *Ludwig Feuerbach and the End of Classical German Philosophy,* in *Karl Marx and Frederick Engels on Religion,* trans. anon. (Schocken, 1964), 224–25.

22. Karl Marx, introduction to *Contribution to the Critique of Hegel's Philosophy of Right,* in ibid., 41–42.

23. Cited in Owen Chadwick, *The Secularization of the European Mind in the Nineteenth Century* (Cambridge University Press, 1975), 130, 122.

24. Karl Marx, *Theses on Feuerbach,* in *Karl Marx and Frederick Engels On Religion,* 69–72. For an explication of all eight theses, phrase by phrase, see Sidney Hook, *From Hegel to Marx: Studies in the Intellectual Development of Karl Marx* (Humanities Press, 1958), 272–307.

25. Marx and Engels, *The Communist Manifesto,* in *Works,* 6:501, 503.

26. See Karl Marx, "Anti-church Movement: Demonstration in Hyde Park," in *Karl Marx and Frederick Engels on Religion,* 127–34.

27. See Marx's quote from Hamilton's study in *On the Jewish Question,* in *Works,* 3:170–71.

28. Cited in Chadwick, *Secularization,* 128–29.

29. Marx, *On the Jewish Question,* in *Works,* 3:172. See also *Das Kapital,* bk. 1, chap. 1, and the notes to chapters 13 and 23, in *Works,* 35.

30. Marx, introduction to *Contribution,* 57.

31. Reinhold Niebuhr, *Moral Man and Immoral Society* (Scribner, 1960 [1932]), 154.

32. See Alessandra Stanley, "Freud in Russia: Return of the Repressed," *New York Times,* December 11, 1996, 1A, 8A.

33. Sigmund Freud, *New Introductory Lecture on Psychoanalysis,* in *Standard Edition of the Complete Psychological Works,* ed. and trans. James Strachey (Hogarth Press, 1953–74), 22:176–81.

34. Ignazio Silone, *Bread and Wine,* rev. ed., trans. Harvey Fergusson (New American Library, 1962), 43, 41, 183.

35. Freud, "Thoughts for the Times on War and Death," in *Standard Edition,* 14:273–302;

"Why War?" in *Standard Edition,* 22:197–215; and Freud's letter of July 2, 1930, in Sigmund Freud and Oskar Pfister, *Psychoanalysis and Faith: The Letters of Sigmund Freud and Oskar Pfister,* ed. Heinrich Meng and Ernst Freud, trans. Eric Mosbacher (Basic Books, 1963).

36. Freud, *Future of an Illusion,* in *Standard Edition,* 11:49.

37. Freud, *Civilization and Its Discontents,* in *Standard Edition,* 11:64–68, 72.

38. See the Mahler citation in Jarl Dyrud, "The Contemporary Debate on 'Narcissism' as a Dominant Cultural Type," in Steven Kepnes and David Tracy, eds., *The Challenge of Psychology to Faith* (Seabury, 1982), 71. See the review of recent attachment theory in Robert Karen, "Becoming Attached," *Atlantic Monthly* (February 1990): 35–50, 63–82.

39. Freud, *Group Psychology and the Analysis of the Ego,* in *Standard Edition,* 18:131.

40. Ibid., 18:109.

41. Ibid., 18:94. See Max Weber and H. Kohut citations on religious charisma, cited in Charles Lindholm, "Lovers and Leaders: Comparison of Social and Psychological Models of Romance and Charisma," *Social Science Information* 27 (1988): 3–45.

42. Carl Jung, *Memories, Dreams, Reflections,* ed. Aniela Jaffe, trans. Richard and Clara Winston (Vintage, 1965), 150–51.

43. Erich Fromm, *Sigmund Freud's Mission: An Analysis of His Personality and Influence* (Harper and Row, 1972), 106, 110.

44. For an overview of these thinkers, see the special issue of *Political Psychology* 14:2 (1993), *Political Theory and Political Psychology,* ed. Fred Alford. See also Perry Meisel, "The Unanalyzable" (Review of Elisabeth Roudinesco's *Jacques Lacan*), *New York Times Book Review,* April 13, 1997, 12.

45. See Jacques Lacan, "Excommunication," in Jacques-Alain Miller, ed., *The Four Fundamental Concepts of Psychoanalysis,* trans. Alan Sheridan (Norton, 1978), 1–13; and Jacques Lacan, "The Mirror Stage as Formative of the Function of the I," in Jacques Lacan, *Ecrits: A Selection,* trans. Alan Sheridan (Norton, 1977), 1–7.

46. See the Marxist critiques surveyed in Richard Lichtman, *The Production of Desire: The Integration of Psychoanalysis into Marxist Theory* (Free Press, 1982).

47. Freud, *Civilization and Its Discontents,* 11:144. See also his assessment of the father's role in "The Psychogenesis of a Case of Homosexuality in a Woman," in *Standard Edition,* 18:150.

48. This grid theory is summarized in Erich Fromm, "Psychoanalysis and Zen Buddhism," in D. T. Suzuki et al., *Zen Buddhism and Psychoanalysis* (Harper, 1960), 95–113.

49. Fromm, "Psychoanalytic Characterology and Its Relevance for Social Psychology," in *The Crisis of Psychoanalysis* (Jonathan Cape, 1970), 163–89; and idem, "The Revolutionary Character," in *The Dogma of Christ and Other Essays* (Holt, Rinehart, Winston, 1963), 162.

50. Fromm, "Psychoanalysis and Zen Buddhism," 85–86.

51. Erich Fromm, *Escape from Freedom* (Rinehart, 1959 [1941]), 279.

52. Erich Fromm, *Psychoanalysis and Religion* (Yale University Press, 1978 [1950]), 115, 49–50.

53. Erich Fromm, *You Shall Be as Gods* (Holt, Rinehart, Winston, 1966), 43–44.

54. Ibid., 62.

55. Milan Kundera, "Edward and God," in *Laughable Loves,* trans. Suzanne Rappaport (Knopf, 1974), 205–42.

56. John Dewey, *A Common Faith* (Yale University Press, 1934), 48.

57. Ibid., 50–51, 53.

58. Abraham Maslow, *Religions, Values, and Peak-Experiences,* rev. ed. (Viking, 1970), 4.

59. Jawaharlal Nehru, *An Autobiography,* 2d ed. (Bodley Head, 1958 [1942]), 380.

60. Jawaharlal Nehru, *An Anthology,* ed. Sarvepalli Gopal (Oxford University Press, 1980), 160, 193.

61. Ibid., 160.

62. Nehru, *Autobiography,* 374, 378; and Nehru, *Anthology,* 163, 575.

63. See the discussion in Wayne Booth, "Systematic Wonder: The Rhetoric of Secular Religions," *Journal of the American Academy of Religion* 50:3 (1985): 677–702.

64. Rainer Maria Rilke, *Letters to a Young Poet,* trans. Stephen Mitchell (Random House, 1984), 34–35.

65. Nietzsche, aphorism no. 285 from *The Joyous Cosmology,* in *The Portable Nietzsche,* 98. See the discussion in Charles Scott, "Wonder and Worship: An Exploration into Non-theistic Religious Experience," *Soundings* 53 (fall 1970): 310–22.

66. Wallace Stevens, *The Palm at the End of the Mind: Selected Poems and a Play,* ed. Holly Stevens (Vintage, 1972), 158, 5–8.

67. Freud, "On Transience," in *Standard Edition* 14:304–6.

68. Chingiz Aitmatov, *The Place of the Skull,* trans. Natasha Ward (Grove Press, 1989), 53.

69. "Nadine Gordimer," in George Plimpton, ed., *Writers at Work: The Paris Review Interviews* (Viking Press, 1984), 6:269–70.

70. For text of the Supreme Court Decision, see *U.S. versus Seeger,* in *United States Reports* 380 (1965): 163–93. See sources and further discussion of conscientious objector situations in my *Sacred Lies and Silences: A Psychology of Religious Disguise* (Liturgical Press, 1994), 7–12.

71. Cited in Robert Traer, *Faith in Human Rights: Support in Religious Traditions for a Global Struggle* (Georgetown University Press, 1991), 6–7. For background to the human rights movement, see Louis Henkin, ed., *The International Bill of Rights: The Covenant on Civil and Political Rights* (Columbia University Press, 1981); Walter Laqueur and Barry Rubin, eds., *The Human Rights Reader,* rev. ed. (Meridian, 1989); Robert Drinan, S.J., *Cry of the Oppressed: The History and Hope of the Human Rights Revolution* (Harper and Row, 1987); Hugo Bedau, "International Human Rights," in Tom Regan and Donald Van de Veer, eds., *And Justice for All* (Rowman and Littlefield, 1982), 287–308.

72. See Louis Henkin, introduction to Henkin, *International Bill of Rights,* 10–13.

73. Cited in Osnos, "Review," *Manchester Guardian Weekly,* January 30, 1983, cited in Traer, *Faith,* 210.

74. Hans Küng, "The History, Significance, and Method of the Declaration toward a Global Ethic," in Hans Küng and Karl-Josef Kuschel, eds., *A Global Ethic: The Declaration of the Parliament of the World Religions* (Continuum, 1993), 55, 73. This work also contains a text of the declaration.

75. See the Muslim, Protestant, and Catholic range of opinion summarized in Traer, *Faith,* especially 111, 56–58, 173–76.

76. See the discussion in Peter Berger, "Are Human Rights Universal?" *Commentary* (September 1977): 60–63.

77. See Declaration of a Global Ethic, sec. 2, pars. 4 and 2, in Küng and Kuschel, *Global Ethic,* 22–23.

78. See Moses Mendelssohn, *Jerusalem and Other Jewish Writings,* trans. and ed. Alfred Jospe (Schocken, 1969), 109.

79. Cited in Margaret Quigley and Michael Garvey, eds., *The Dorothy Day Book* (Templegate, 1982), 99.

Bibliography

Abbott, Walter, S.J., ed. *Documents of Vatican II.* Guild Press, 1966.

Achebe, Chinua. *Girls at War and Other Stories.* Heinemann, 1972.

Ackroyd, Peter. *T. S. Eliot: A Life.* Simon and Schuster, 1984.

Adenauer, Konrad. *Memoirs 1945–53.* Trans. Beate Ruhm von Oppen. Regnery, 1965.

Adler, Morris, ed. *Jewish Heritage Reader.* Taplinger, 1965.

Aitmatov, Chingiz. *The Place of the Skull.* Trans. Natasha Ward. Grove Press, 1989.

Ajami, Fouad. "Iran: The Impossible Revolution." *Foreign Affairs* 67 (1988–89): 135–55.

Akhavi, Shahrough. *Religion and Politics in Contemporary Iran: Clergy-State Relations in the Pahlavi Period.* State University of New York Press, 1980.

Alford, Fred, ed. *Political Theory and Political Psychology.* Special issue of *Political Psychology* 14:2 (1993).

Allen, Paula G., ed. *Spider Woman's Granddaughters.* Beacon Press, 1989.

Amore, Roy, ed. *Developments in Buddhist Thought.* Wilfred Laurier University Press, 1979.

Anesaki, Masaharu. *Nichiren: The Buddhist Prophet.* Peter Smith, 1966 (1916).

———. *Religious Life of the Japanese People.* 4th rev. ed. Japanese Cultural Society, 1970.

Angel, Marc. "Sephardim Shabbat." *Judaism* 31 (winter 1982): 21–25.

Attar, Farid ud-Din. *The Conference of the Birds.* Trans. Garcin de Tassy and C. S. Nott. Shambhala, 1971.

Aung San Suu Kyi. *The Voice of Hope: Conversations with Alan Clements.* Seven Stories Press, 1997.

Ayoob, Mohammed, ed. *The Politics of Islamic Reassertion.* St. Martin's Press, 1981.

Barboza, Steven, ed. *American Jihad: Islam after Malcolm X.* Doubleday, 1993.

Barnard, L. W. "Early Christian Art as Apologetic." *Journal of Religious History* 10 (June 1978): 20–31.

Barthes, Roland. *Empire of Signs.* Trans. Richard Howard. Hill and Wang, 1982.

Barton, Stephen. "Jesus and Health." *Theology* 87 (July 1984): 266–72.

Bauer, Wolfgang. *China and the Search for Happiness.* Trans. Michael Shaw. Seabury, 1976.

Becker, Ernest. *Escape from Evil.* Free Press, 1975.

Bellah, Robert. *Tokugawa Religion: The Values of Pre-industrial Japan.* Free Press, 1957.

Bellow, Saul. *To Jerusalem and Back: A Personal Account.* Viking, 1976.

Ben-Gurion, David. *Memoirs.* Ed. Thomas Bransten. World, 1970.

Benitez, Fernando. *In the Magic Land of Peyote.* Trans. John Upton. University of Texas Press, 1975.

Berger, Peter. "Are Human Rights Universal?" *Commentary* (September 1977): 60–63.

Berger, Suzanne, ed. *Religion in West European Politics.* Frank Cass, 1982.

Berman, Phyllis, and Arthur Waskow. "The Seder of Rebirth." *Tikkun* 9 (March 1994): 72–75.

Berman, Ronald, ed. *Solzhenitsyn at Harvard: The Address, Twelve Early Responses, and Six Later Reflections.* Ethics and Public Policy Center, 1980.

Berrin, Kathleen, ed. *Art of the Huichol Indians.* Fine Arts Museums of San Francisco/Abrams, 1978.

The Bhagavad Gita. Trans. Juan Mascaro. Penguin, 1979.

Birenbaum, Arnold, and Edward Sagarin, eds. *People in Places: Sociology of the Familiar.* Praeger, 1973.

Boff, Leonardo, and Virgil Elizondo, eds. *Any Room for Christ in Asia?* Concilium/Orbis Books, 1993.

Bonhoeffer, Dietrich. *Letters and Papers from Prison.* Ed. Eberhard Bethge, trans. Reginald Fuller et al. 2d ed. Macmillan, 1971.

Booth, Wayne. "Systematic Wonder: The Rhetoric of Secular Religions." *Journal of the American Academy of Religion* 50:3 (1985): 677–702.

Borgen, Peder. "Miracles of Healing in the New Testament." *Studia Theologica* 35 (1981): 91–105.

Bourne, Richard. *Political Leaders of Latin America.* Knopf, 1970.

Bracken, Joseph, S.J. *The Divine Matrix.* Orbis Books, 1995.

Brent, Peter. *Godmen of India.* Quadrangle Books, 1972.

Brewster, David. "The Study of Sufism: Towards a Methodology." *Religion* 6:1 (spring 1976): 31–47.

Brook, Peter. "Lie and Glorious Adjective: An Interview with Peter Brook." *Parabola* 6 (summer 1981): 60–73.

Buber, Martin. *Pointing the Way: Collected Essays.* Ed. and trans. Maurice Friedman. Routledge and Kegan Paul, 1957.

———, ed. *Tales of the Hasidim: The Early Masters.* Schocken, 1975.

Buddhadasa, Bhikkhu. *Me and Mine: Selected Essays.* Ed. Donald Swearer. State University of New York Press, 1989.

Burns, John. "Indian Premier's Swami in Political Crossfire." *New York Times,* September 21, 1995, 1.

Bush, Richard. "Frithjof Schuon's *The Transcendent Unity of Religions:* Con." *Journal of the American Academy of Religion* 44 (1976): 715–19.

Byrne, Susan. "Land of the Rising Cults." *World Press Review* (June 1995): 41–42.

Camus, Albert. *The Plague.* Trans. Stuart Gilbert. Knopf, 1948.

Carroll, John. "Sickness and Healing in the New Testament Gospels." *Interpretation* 49 (April 1995): 130–42.

Carver, Terrell, ed. *The Cambridge Companion to Marx.* Cambridge University Press, 1991.

Cavendish, Richard, ed. *Man, Myth, and Magic: An Illustrated Encyclopedia of the Supernatural.* 24 vols. Marshall Cavendish Corporation, 1970.

Chadwick, Owen. *The Secularization of the European Mind in the Nineteenth Century.* Cambridge University Press, 1975.

Chittick, William. "Mysticism versus Philosophy in Earlier Islamic History." *Religious Studies* 17 (March 1981): 87–104.

Chuang Tzu. *Complete Works.* Trans. Burton Watson. Columbia University Press, 1968.

Clement of Alexandria. *Christ the Educator.* Trans. Simon Wood, C. P. Fathers of the Church, 1954.

Coleman, Simon, and John Elsner. *Pilgrimage: Past and Present in the World Religions.* Harvard University Press, 1995.

Collins, Carol. "Desire to Stay On: Interview with Peter Henriot, S.J." *National Catholic Reporter* 32 (July 12, 1996): 10–11.

Confucius. *Analects.* Trans. Arthur Waley. Allen-Unwin, 1938.

Conroy, F. H., and T. S. Miyakawa, eds. *East across the Pacific: Historical and Sociological Studies of Japanese Immigration and Assimilation.* Clio, 1972.

Coser, Lewis, and Bernard Rosenberg, eds. *Sociological Theory.* 3d ed. Macmillan, 1969.

Cuming, G. J., and Derek Baker, eds. *Popular Belief and Practice.* Cambridge University Press, 1972.

Curtis, Michael, ed. *Religion and Politics in the Middle East.* Westview Press, 1981.

Dabashi, Hamid. *Theology of Discontent: The Ideological Foundations of the Islamic Revolution in Iran.* New York University Press, 1993.

Dalai Lama (Tenzin Gyatso). *Freedom in Exile: The Autobiography of the Dalai Lama.* HarperCollins, 1990.

———. *My Land and My People.* McGraw-Hill, 1962.

Davis, Harry, and Robert Good, eds. *Reinhold Niebuhr on Politics.* Scribner, 1960.

Day, Dorothy. *The Dorothy Day Book.* Ed. Margaret Quigley and Michael Garvey. Templegate, 1982.

DeMallie, Raymond, ed. *The Sixth Grandfather: Black Elk's Teachings Given to John G. Neihardt.* University of Nebraska Press, 1984.

Deutscher, Isaac. *The Non-Jewish Jew and Other Essays.* Ed. Tamara Deutscher. Oxford University Press, 1968.

Dewey, John. *A Common Faith.* Yale University Press, 1934.

Dharmapala, Anagarika. *Return to Righteousness: A Collection of Speeches, Essays, and Letters of the Anagarika Dharmapala.* Ed. Ananda Guruge. Sri Lanka Government Press, 1965.

"Dialectic of Romans 13:1–7 and Revelation 13." *Journal of Church and State* 18 (1976): 433–43, and 19 (1977): 5–20.

Doi, Takeo. *The Anatomy of Dependence.* Trans. John Bester. Kodansha International, 1973.

Dostoyevsky, Fyodor. *The Brothers Karamazov.* Trans. Constance Garnett. Modern Library, 1950.

———. *The Idiot.* Trans. Henry and Olga Carlisle. New American Library, 1969.

Drinan, Robert, S.J. *Cry of the Oppressed: The History and Hope of the Human Rights Revolution.* Harper and Row, 1987.

Ebrey, Patricia, ed. *Chinese Civilization and Society: A Sourcebook.* Free Press, 1981.

El-Azma, Nazeer. "Some Notes on the Impact of the Story of the Miraj on Sufi Literature." *Muslim World* 63:2 (April 1973): 93–104.

Eliade, Mircea. *Shamanism: Archaic Techniques of Ecstasy.* Trans. Willard Trask. Routledge, 1964.

———, ed. *Encyclopedia of Religions.* 16 vols. Macmillan, 1987.

Eliot, T. S. *The Idea of a Christian Society.* Harcourt, Brace, 1940.

———. *After Strange Gods: A Primer of Modern Heresy.* Harcourt, Brace, 1934.

Ellwood, Robert, ed. *Eastern Spirituality in America: Selected Writings.* Paulist Press, 1987.

Enayat, Hamid. *Modern Islamic Political Thought.* University of Texas Press, 1982.

Epstein, Mark. "Psychodynamics of Meditation: Pitfalls on the Spiritual Path." *Journal of Transpersonal Psychology* 22 (1990): 17–34.

Erikson, Erik, ed. *Adulthood.* Norton, 1978.

Esposito, John, ed. *Islam and Development: Religion and Sociopolitical Change.* Syracuse University Press, 1980.

———, ed. *Voices of Resurgent Islam.* Oxford University Press, 1983.

Faulkner, William. *Go Down, Moses.* Modern Library, 1942.

Fehl, Noah. *Li: Rites and Propriety in Literature and Life.* Hong Kong Chinese University Press, 1971.

Feng, Chi-tsai. *Chrysanthemums and Other Stories.* Trans. Susan Chen. Harcourt Brace, 1985.

Ferguson, Thomas. *Catholic and American: The Political Theology of John Courtney Murray.* Sheed and Ward, 1993.

Fernando, Tissa, and Robert Kearney, eds. *Modern Sri Lanka: A Society in Transition.* Syracuse University Press, 1979.

Feuerbach, Ludwig. *The Essence of Christianity.* Trans. George Eliot. Harper, 1957.

———. *Lectures on the Essence of Religion.* Trans. Ralph Manheim. Harper and Row, 1967.

Fredman, Ruth. *The Passover Seder: Afikoman in Exile.* University of Pennsylvania Press, 1981.

French, Harold. *The Swan's Wide Waters: Ramakrishna and Western Culture.* Kennikat Press, 1974.

Freud, Sigmund. *Letters.* Ed. Ernst Freud. Trans. Tania and James Stern. Basic Books, 1960.

———. *Standard Edition of the Complete Psychological Works.* 46 vols. Ed. and trans. James Strachey. Hogarth Press, 1953–74.

———, and Oskar Pfister. *Psychoanalysis and Faith: The Letters of Sigmund Freud and Oskar Pfister.* Ed. Heinrich Meng and Ernst Freud. Trans. Eric Mosbacher. Basic Books, 1963.

Friedman, Maurice. *Encounter on the Narrow Ridge: A Life of Martin Buber.* Paragon, 1991.

Fromm, Erich. *Crisis of Psychoanalysis.* Jonathan Cape, 1970.

———. *The Dogma of Christ and Other Essays.* Holt, Rinehart, Winston, 1963.

———. *Escape from Freedom.* Rinehart, 1959 (1941).

———. *The Forgotten Language.* Rinehart, 1951.

———. *Psychoanalysis and Religion.* Yale University Press, 1978 (1950).

————. *Sigmund Freud's Mission: An Analysis of His Personality and Influence.* Harper and Row, 1972.

————. *You Shall Be as Gods.* Holt, Rinehart, Winston, 1966.

Fu, Charles, and Gerhard Spiegler, eds. *Religious Issues and Interreligious Dialogues: An Analysis and Sourcebook of Developments since 1945.* Greenwood Press, 1989.

Fukuzawa, Yukichi. *Autobiography of Fukuzawa Yukichi.* Trans. Eiichi Kiyooka. Hokuseido Press, 1960.

Furst, Peter, ed. *Flesh of the Gods: The Ritual Use of Hallucinogens.* Praeger, 1972.

Gandhi, Mohandas. *All Men Are Brothers: Life and Thoughts of Mahatma Gandhi.* Ed. Krishna Kripalani. Navajivan House, 1960.

————. *Collected Works.* 96 vols. Navajivan Press, 1970.

Geffre, Claude, and Gustavo Gutiérrez, eds. *The Mystical and Political Dimension of the Christian Faith.* Concilium/Herder and Herder, 1974.

Gelberg, Steven, ed. *Hare Krishna, Hare Krishna.* Grove Press, 1983.

Gelfand, Michael. *Witch Doctor: Traditional Medicine Man of Rhodesia.* Praeger, 1965.

Gilkey, Langdon. *Naming the Whirlwind: The Renewal of God-Language.* Bobbs-Merrill, 1969.

Ginsburg, Elliot. "The Sabbath in the Kabbalah." *Judaism* 31 (winter 1982): 26–36.

Glatzer, Nahum. *Essay in Jewish Thought.* University of Alabama Press, 1978.

Goffman, Erving. *Encounters.* Bobbs-Merrill, 1961.

Goodman, Philip, ed. *The Passover Anthology.* Jewish Publication of America, 1961.

Gosling, David. "Visions of Salvation: A Thai Buddhist Experience of Ecumenism." *Modern Asian Studies* 26:1 (1992): 31–47.

The Gospel of Barnabas. Trans. Lonsdale Ragg and Laura Ragg. Oxford University Press, 1907.

Greenberg, Joanne. *Rites of Passage.* Holt, Rinehart, Winston, 1972.

Greene, Graham. *The Honorary Consul.* Bodley Head, 1973.

Grimes, Ronald. "Masking: Toward a Phenomenology of Exteriorization." *Journal of the American Academy of Religion* 43 (1975): 508–16.

Gross, Leonard. *The Last, Best Hope: Eduardo Frei and Chilean Democracy.* Random House, 1967.

Guellouz, Ezzedine. *Mecca: The Muslim Pilgrimage.* Paddington, 1979.

Haberman, Joshua. "The Place of Israel in Reform Jewish Theology." *Judaism* 21 (1972): 437–48.

Halifax, Joan, ed. *Shamanic Voices: A Survey of Visionary Narratives.* Dutton, 1979.

Hane, Mikiso, ed. and trans. *Reflections on the Way to the Gallows: Rebel Women in Prewar Japan.* University of California Press, 1988.

Harris, Monford. "The Passover Seder: On Entering the Order of History." *Judaism* 25 (1976): 473–88.

Harvey, Van. *Feuerbach and the Interpretation of Religion.* Cambridge University Press, 1995.

Heller, Erich. *The Importance of Nietzsche.* University of Chicago Press, 1988.

Henkin, Louis, ed. *The International Bill of Rights: The Covenant on Civil and Political Rights.* Columbia University Press, 1981.

Herbert, Jean. *Shinto: At the Fountainhead of Japan.* Stein and Day, 1967.

Herzl, Theodor. *The Diaries.* Ed. and trans. Marvin Lowenthal. Dial Press, 1956.

Heschel, Abraham. *God in Search of Man: A Philosophy of Judaism.* Octagon, 1972 (1955).

————. *I Asked for Wonder: A Spiritual Anthology.* Ed. Samuel Dresner. Crossroad, 1983.

————. *The Insecurity of Freedom: Essay on Human Existence.* Schocken, 1972.

————. *Maimonides: A Biography.* Trans. Joachim Neugroschel. Farrar, Straus, Giroux, 1982.

Hitchcock, F. John. "A Nepalese Shamanism and the Classic Inner Asian Tradition." *History of Religions* 7 (1967–68): 149–58.

Hodgson, Marshall. "Islam and Image." *History of Religions* 3:2 (winter 1964): 220–60.

Holcomb, Charles. "Theater of Combat: A Critical Look at the Chinese Martial Arts." *Historian* 52 (May 1990): 411–31.

Hook, Sidney. *From Hegel to Marx: Studies in the Intellectual Development of Karl Marx.* Humanities Press, 1958.

————. *The Quest for Being.* St. Martin's Press, 1961.

Hubner, John, and Lindsey Gruson. "Dial Om for Murder." *Rolling Stone,* April 9, 1987, 53–58.

Ignatius Loyola, St. *Spiritual Exercises.* Trans. Louis Puhl, S.J. Newman, 1951.

Isaac, Erich. "The Pilgrimage to Mecca." *Geographical Review* 63 (July 1973): 405–09.

Jackson, Carl. *Vedanta for the West: The Ramakrishna Movement in the United States.* Indiana University Press, 1994.

James, William. *Varieties of Religious Experience.* New American Library, 1958 (1902).

Jataka Tales. Ed. E. B. Cowell. Various translators. 3 vols. Pali Text Society: Luzac, 1957.

Jhabvala, Ruth Prawer. *Out of India: Selected Stories.* Morrow, 1986.

John of the Cross, St. *Dark Night of the Soul.* Trans. Allison Peers. Image Books, 1959.

John Paul II, Pope. *Crossing the Threshold of Hope.* Ed. Vittorio Messori. Knopf, 1994.

Johnson, Roger. "Inter-religious Conflict and the Voyages of Columbus." *Muslim World* 83 (January 1993): 1–19.

Jung, Carl. *Memories, Dreams, Reflections.* Ed. Aniela Jaffe. Trans. Richard and Clara Winston. Vintage, 1965.

Kafka, Franz. *I Am a Memory Come Alive: Autobiographical Writings by Franz Kafka.* Ed. Nahum Glatzer. Schocken, 1974.

Kamenka, Eugene. *The Philosophy of Ludwig Feuerbach.* Praeger, 1969.

Karen, Robert. "Becoming Attached." *Atlantic Monthly* (February 1990): 35–50, 63–82.

Katz, Nathan. "Contacts between Jewish and Indo-Tibetan Civilizations through the Ages." *Judaism* 43 (1994): 46–60.

Kaufman, Walter. *The Owl and the Nightingale.* Faber and Faber, 1959.

Kaunda, Kenneth. *A Humanist in Africa.* Ed. Colin Morris. Abingdon, 1966.

———. *Letter to My Children.* Longman, 1975.

Kazancigil, Ali, and Ergun Ozbudun, eds. *Ataturk: Founder of a Modern State.* Archon Books, 1981.

Kazantzakis, Nikos. *The Last Temptation of Christ.* Trans. P. A. Bien. Bantam, 1960.

Keddie, Nikki. *Sayyid Jamal ad-Din "al-Afghani": A Political Biography.* University of California Press, 1972.

———, ed. *Religion and Politics in Iran.* Yale University Press, 1983.

———, ed. *Scholars, Saints, and Sufis.* University of California Press, 1972.

Kennedy, Leonard, C. S. B., ed. *Thomistic Papers.* Vol. 3. Center for Thomistic Studies, University of St. Thomas, 1987.

Kepnes, Steven, and David Tracy, eds. *The Challenge of Psychology to Faith.* Seabury, 1982.

Khomeini, Imam Ruhollah. *Islam and Revolution.* Trans. Hamid Algar. Mizan Press, 1981.

Kierkegaard, Søren. *Attack upon Christendom: 1854–1855.* Trans. Walter Lowrie. Princeton University Press, 1944.

Kiev, Ari, ed. *Magic, Faith, and Healing.* Free Press, 1964.

Kimmens, Andrew, ed. *Islamic Politics and the Modern World.* H. W. Wildon, 1991.

King, Martin Luther, Jr. *A Testament of Hope: The Essential Writings of Martin Luther King, Jr.* Ed. James Washington. Harper and Row, 1986.

King, Winston. *Zen and the Way of the Sword: Arming the Samurai Psyche.* Oxford University Press, 1993.

Kingston, Maxine Hong. *China Men.* Knopf, 1980.

Kinnard, Roy, and Tim Davis. *Divine Images: A History of Jesus on the Screen.* Citadel, 1992.

Kinross, John. *Ataturk: A Biography of Mustafa Kemal, Father of Modern Turkey.* William Morrow, 1965.

The Koran. Trans. N. J. Dawood. Penguin, 1974.

Kraft, Kenneth. "The Greening of Buddhist Practice." *Cross Currents* (summer 1994): 163–79.

———, ed. *Inner Peace, World Peace: Essays on Buddhism and Nonviolence.* State University of New York Press, 1992.

Kramer, Martin, ed. *Shiism, Resistance, and Revolution.* Westview, 1987.

Kraut, Benny. "Faith and the Holocaust: A Review-Essay." *Judaism* 31 (1982): 185–201.

Kundera, Milan. *Laughable Loves.* Trans. Suzanne Rappaport. Knopf, 1974.

Küng, Hans, and Jürgen Moltmann, eds. *Islam: A Challenge for Christianity.* Concilium/Orbis Books, 1994.

Küng, Hans, and Karl-Josef Kuschel, eds. *A Global Ethic: The Declaration of the Parliament of the World Religions.* Continuum, 1993.

Lacan, Jacques. *Ecrits: A Selection.* Trans. Alan Sheridan. Norton, 1977.

———. *The Four Fundamental Concepts of Psychoanalysis.* Ed. Jacques-Alain Miller. Trans. Alan Sheridan. Norton, 1978.

Lame Deer, John, and Richard Erdoes. *Lame Deer: Seeker of Visions.* Simon and Schuster, 1972.

Landis, Joseph, trans. and ed. *The Great Jewish Plays.* Horizon, 1972.

Lane, Belden. "In Quest of the King." *Horizons* 14 (1987): 39–48.

Lao Tzu. *Tao Te Ching.* Trans. Arthur Waley. Allen-Unwin, 1934.

Lapidus, Ira. "Adulthood in Islam: Religious Maturity in the Islamic Tradition." *Daedalus* (spring 1976): 93–101.

Laqueur, Walter, and Barry Rubin, eds. *The Human Rights Reader.* Rev. ed. Meridian, 1989.

Large, Stephen. "Buddhism, Socialism, and Protest in Prewar Japan: The Career of Seno'o Giro." *Modern Asian Studies* 21:1 (1987): 153–71.

Lawrence, D. H. *The Man Who Died.* Knopf, 1931.

———. *Studies in Classic American Literature.* Viking, 1961 (1924).

Laws of Manu. Trans. G. Buhler. In F. Max Muller, ed., *Sacred Books of the East,* 25. Motilal Banarsidass, 1886.

Lawson, John. *The Biblical Theology of St. Irenaeus.* Epworth, 1948.

Lee, Jung Jung. "The Seasonal Rituals of Korean Shamanism." *History of Religions* 12 (1973): 271–87.

Leon-Portilla, Miguel. *Aztec Thought and Culture: A Study of the Ancient Nahuatl Mind.* University of Oklahoma Press, 1963.

Lessing, Gotthold. *Nathan the Wise.* Trans. Bayard Morgan. Ungar, 1955.

Levine, Hillel. *In Search of Sugihara: The Elusive Japanese Diplomat Who Risked His Life to Rescue 10,000 Jews from the Holocaust.* Free Press, 1996.

Lévi-Strauss, Claude. *Structural Anthropology.* Trans. Claire Jacobson et al. Basic Books, 1963.

Librande, Leonard. "The Calligraphy of the Quran: How It Functions for Muslims." *Religion* 9 (spring 1979): 36–58.

Lichtman, Richard. *The Production of Desire: The Integration of Psychoanalysis into Marxist Theory.* Free Press, 1982.

Li Ki. Ed. F. Max Muller. Trans. James Legge. *Sacred Books of the East,* 27, 28. Oxford University Press, 1885.

Lim, Catherine. *The Best of Catherine Lim.* Heinemann Asia, 1993.

Lindholm, Charles. "Lovers and Leaders: Comparison of Social and Psychological Models of Romance and Charisma." *Social Science Information* 27 (1988): 3–45.

Luther, Martin. *Luther's Works.* Ed. Helmut Lehmann. Fortress Press, 1971.

MacPherson, Fergus. *Kenneth Kaunda of Zambia: The Times and the Man.* Oxford University Press, 1974.

Macquarrie, John. "The Anthropological Approach to Theology." *Heythrop Journal* 25 (1984): 272–87.

Macy, Joanna. "Buddhist Approaches to Social Action." *Journal of Humanistic Psychology* 24:3 (summer 1984): 117–29.

———. "Dependent Co-arising: The Distinctiveness of Buddhist Ethics." *Journal of Religious Ethics* 7:1 (spring 1979): 38–51.

Maeda, Narifumi. "The Aftereffects of Hajj and Kaan Buat." *Journal of Southeast Asian Studies* 6 (September 1975): 178–85.

Mahony, William. "The Artist as Yogi, the Yogi as Artist." *Parabola* 13 (1988): 68–79.

Makovsky, Alan. "Responding to Turkey's Eastward Drift." *New York Times,* August 17, 1996, 17.

Malamud, Bernard. *The Stories of Bernard Malamud.* Farrar, Straus, Giroux, 1983.

Malquinhu. "The Story of a Living Buddha." *Chinese Literature* (February 1981): 91–104.

"Man of the Year: The Mystic Who Lit the Fires of Hatred." *Time* 115 (January 7, 1980): 9–33.

Manuel, Frank. *A Requiem for Karl Marx.* Harvard University Press, 1993.

Marty, Martin, and Scott Appleby, eds. *Accounting for Fundamentalisms.* University of Chicago Press, 1994.

————, eds. *Fundamentalisms Observed.* University of Chicago Press, 1991.

Marx, Karl, and Frederick Engels. *Karl Marx and Frederick Engels on Religion.* Trans. anon. Schocken, 1964.

————. *Works.* 46 vols. International Publishers, 1975.

Maslow, Abraham. *The Farther Reaches of Human Nature.* Penguin, 1978.

————. *Religions, Values, and Peak-Experiences.* Rev. ed. Viking, 1970.

Mauss, Marcel. *The Gift: Forms and Functions of Exchange in Archaic Societies.* Trans. I. Cunnison. Free Press, 1954.

————, and Henri Hubert. *Sacrifice: Its Nature and Function.* Trans. W. D. Halls. University of Chicago Press, 1964.

May, Rollo. *Love and Will.* Dell, 1969.

McFarlane, S. "Bodily Awareness in the Wing Chun System." *Religion* 19 (July 1989): 241–53.

McGhee, Michael. "In Praise of Mindfulness." *Religious Studies* 24 (1988): 65–89.

McLellan, David. *Karl Marx: His Life and Thought.* Harper and Row, 1973.

Mead, Margaret. *Blackberry Winter: My Earliest Years.* Morrow, 1972.

Meir, Golda. *A Land of Our Own: An Oral Autobiography.* Ed. Marie Syrkin. Putnam, 1973.

————. *My Life.* Putnam, 1975.

Meisel, Perry. "The Unanalyzable." *New York Times Book Review,* April 13, 1997, 12.

Mendelssohn, Moses. *Jerusalem and Other Jewish Writings.* Trans. and ed. Alfred Jospe. Schocken, 1969.

Mendes-Flohr, Paul, and Jehuda Reinharz, eds. *The Jew in the Modern World: A Documentary History.* Oxford University Press, 1980.

Middleton, John, ed. *Myth and Cosmos.* Natural History Press, 1967.

Miller, Perry. *Jonathan Edwards.* Meridian, 1965.

Minatoya, Lydia Yuriko. *Talking to High Monks in the Snow: An Asian-American Odyssey.* HarperCollins, 1992.

Mlecko, Joel. "The Guru in Hindu Tradition." *Numen* 29 (July 1982): 33–61.

Momaday, N. Scott. *The Names: A Memoir.* Harper and Row, 1976.

————. *The Way to Rainy Mountain.* University of New Mexico Press, 1969.

Moore, Albert. *Iconography of Religions.* Fortress, 1977.

Moore, Charles, ed. *The Status of the Individual in East and West.* University of Hawaii Press, 1968.

Moore, Donald, S.J. *The Human and the Holy: The Spirituality of Abraham Joshua Heschel.* Fordham University Press, 1989.

Morita, Akio, et al. *Made in Japan: Akio Morita and Sony.* E. P. Dutton, 1986.

Morris, Ivan. *The Nobility of Failure: Tragic Heroes in the History of Japan.* Noonday Press, 1988.

Mortimer, Edward. *Faith and Power: The Politics of Islam.* Random House, 1982.

Muller, F. Max, ed. *Sacred Books of the East.* 50 vols. Oxford University Press, 1879–1910.

Murphy, Roland, O. Carm. "The Theological Contributions of Israel's Wisdom Literature." *Listening* (winter 1984): 30–40.

Myerhoff, Barbara. *Peyote Hunt: The Sacred Journey of the Huichol Indians.* Cornell University Press, 1974.

Narayan, R. K. *Malgudi Days.* Viking, 1982.

————. *The Vendor of Sweets* (Avon Books, 1967).

Nasr, Sayyed. *Ideals and Realities of Islam.* Praeger, 1967.

Nasser, Gamal Abdul. *Egypt's Liberation: The Philosophy of the Revolution.* Public Affairs Press, 1955.

Nehru, Jawaharlal. *An Anthology.* Ed. Sarvepalli Gopal. Oxford University Press, 1980.

————. *An Autobiography.* 2d ed. Bodley Head, 1958 [1942].

Neki, J. S. "Guru-Chela Relationship: The Possibility of a Therapeutic Paradigm." *American Journal of Orthopsychiatry* 43 (October 1973): 755–66.

Newman, Louis, ed. and trans. *The Hasidic Anthology: Tales and Teachings of the Hasidim.* Schocken, 1972.

"News Briefs." *National Catholic Reporter* (April 4, 1997): 8.

Nhat, Thich Hanh. *The Miracle of Mindfulness: A Manual on Meditation.* Trans. Mobi Warren. Beacon Press, 1976.

———, and Daniel Berrigan, S.J. *The Raft Is Not the Shore: Conversations toward a Buddhist-Christian Awareness.* Beacon Press, 1975.

Niebuhr, Reinhold. *Faith and Politics.* Ed. Ronald Stone. Braziller, 1968.

———. *Moral Man and Immoral Society.* Scribner, 1960 (1932).

Nietzsche, Friedrich. *The Portable Nietzsche.* Ed. Walter Kaufman. Viking Press, 1966.

Nissenson, Hugh. *The Elephant and My Jewish Problem.* Harper and Row, 1988.

Notovitch, Nicolas. *The Unknown Life of Jesus Christ.* Trans. J. H. Connelly and L. Landsberg. Dillingham, 1894.

O'Collins, Gerald, S.J., and Daniel Kendall, S.J. "On Reissuing Venturini." *Gregorianum* 75 (1994): 241–65.

O'Connor, Kathleen. *The Wisdom Literature.* Michael Glazier, 1988.

O'Donovan, Leo, S.J. "To Lead Us into the Mystery." *America* (June 16, 1984): 453–57.

"Offending Book Recalled." *National Catholic Reporter* (May 16, 1997): 10.

O'Malley, John, S.J. *The First Jesuits.* Harvard University Press, 1993.

O'Reilly, David. "Conference to Examine Jewish Ties to Buddhism." *Philadelphia Inquirer,* November 18, 1995, B1+.

Ottaviani, Cardinal Alfredo. "Church and State: Some Present Problems in the Light of the Teaching of Pope Pius XII." *American Ecclesiastical Review* 128 (May 1953): 321–34.

Partin, Harry, ed. *Asian Religions — History of Religion: Preprinted Papers.* American Academy of Religion, 1974.

Pelikan, Jaroslav. *Imago Dei: The Byzantine Apologia for Icons.* Princeton University Press, 1990.

Pieris, Aloysius, S.J. "East in the West: Resolving a Spiritual Crisis." *Horizons* 13:2 (1988): 337–46.

Pike, Royston. *The Strange Ways of Man.* Hart, 1967.

Piscatori, James, ed. *Islam in the Political Process.* Cambridge University Press, 1983.

Plimpton, George, ed. *Writers at Work: The Paris Review Interviews.* 9 vols. Viking, 1958–92.

"Pope Tours Asia, Australia." *Facts on File* (January 26, 1995): 43–44.

Porter, J. R. "Muhammad's Journey to Heaven." *Numen* 20 (1974): 64–80.

Potok, Chaim. *The Chosen.* Fawcett, 1967.

Prabhupada, Bhaktivedanta. *Bhagavad Gita as It Is.* 2d ed. Bhaktivedanta Book Trust, 1989.

Prebish, Charles, ed. *Buddhism: A Modern Perspective.* Penn State University Press, 1975.

Prensky, William. "Tai Chi: Spiritual Martial Art." *Parabola* 4:2 (1979): 68–73.

Prittie, Terence. *Konrad Adenauer: 1876–1967.* Cowles, 1971.

Queen, Christopher, and Sallie King, eds. *Engaged Buddhism: Buddhist Liberation Movements in Asia.* State University of New York Press, 1996.

Rahner, Karl, S.J. *Faith in a Wintry Season: Conversations and Interviews with Karl Rahner in the Last Years of His Life.* Ed. Paul Imhof and Hubert Biallowons. Trans. Harvey Egan. Crossroad, 1991.

———. *Foundations of Christian Faith.* Trans. William Dych. Seabury, 1978.

———. *Theological Investigations.* 23 vols. Darton, Longman, and Todd; Herder and Herder; Helicon; Seabury, 1961–79.

———, and Herbert Vorgrimler, S.J. *Theological Dictionary.* Ed. Cornelius Ernst, O.P., trans. Richard Strachan. Herder and Herder, 1965.

———, Karl, and Pinchas Lapide. *Encountering Jesus — Encountering Judaism: A Dialogue.* Trans. Davis Perkins. Crossroad, 1987.

Raines, John. "The Politics of Religious Correctness: Islam and the West." *Cross Currents* (spring 1996): 39–49.

Ramakrishna. *The Gospel of Shri Ramakrishna.* Trans. and ed. Nikhilananda. Ramakrishna-Vivekananda Center, 1942.

———. *Sayings: An Exhaustive Collection.* Vedanta Press, 1975.

Regan, Tom, and Donald Van de Veer, eds. *And Justice for All.* Rowman and Littlefield, 1982.

Reynolds, Frank, and Donald Capps, eds. *The Biographical Process.* Mouton, 1976.

————, and Earle Waugh, eds. *Religious Encounters with Death.* Penn State University Press, 1977.

Richardson, Alan. *The Political Christ.* Westminster, 1973.

Riesenhuber, Klaus. "Understanding Non-objective Meditation." *Communio* 14 (1988): 451–67.

Rilke, Rainer Maria. *Letters: 1892–1926.* 2 vols. Ed. and trans. Jane Greene and Mary Norton. Norton, 1948.

————. *Letters to a Young Poet.* Trans. Stephen Mitchell. Random House, 1984.

Rosenfeld, Alvin. "The Americanization of the Holocaust." *Commentary* (June 1995): 35–40; (September 1995): 6–12.

Ross, Nancy W. *Buddhism: A Way of Life and Thought.* Vintage, 1980.

Royster, James. "Muhammad as Teacher and Exemplar." *Muslim World* 68:4 (October 1978): 235–58.

Ruland, Vernon, S.J. *Sacred Lies and Silences: A Psychology of Religious Disguise.* Liturgical Press, 1994.

————. "Sign and Sacrament: John's Bread of Life Discourse (Chapter 6)." *Interpretation* (October 1964): 450–62.

Russell, Bertrand. *The Autobiography.* 2 vols. Little, Brown, 1967.

————. *The Basic Writings of Bertrand Russell: 1903–1959.* Ed. Robert Egner and Lester Denonn. Simon and Schuster, 1961.

————. *Why I Am Not a Christian.* Ed. Paul Edwards. Allen and Unwin, 1961.

Sahliyeh, Emile, ed. *Religious Resurgence and Politics in the Contemporary World.* State University of New York Press, 1990.

Sakai, Michikazu. *How to Wrap Five Eggs: Japanese Design in Traditional Packaging.* Harper and Row, 1967.

Sarkisyanz, Emanuel. *Buddhist Backgrounds of the Burmese Revolution.* Nijhoff, 1965.

Sartre, Jean-Paul. *Anti-Semite and Jew.* Trans. George Becker. Schocken, 1948.

Saso, Michael. *Taoism and the Rite of Cosmic Renewal.* Washington State University Press, 1972.

————. "Taoism in China, 1993." *China News Analysis* (November 15, 1993): 1–9.

Schecter, Jerrold. *The New Face of Buddha: Buddhism and Political Power in Southeast Asia.* Coward-McCann, 1967.

Schimmel, Annemarie. *Gabriel's Wing: A Study into the Religious Ideas of Sir Muhammad Iqbal.* E. J. Brill, 1963.

————. *Islam: An Introduction.* State University of New York Press, 1992.

————. *Mystical Dimensions of Islam.* University of North Carolina Press, 1975.

————, and Abdoldjavad Falaturi, eds. *We Believe in One God: The Experience of God in Christianity and Islam.* Crossroad, 1979.

Schreiter, Robert, ed. *Faces of Jesus in Africa.* Orbis Books, 1991.

Sciolino, Elaine. "Iran's Durable Revolution." *Foreign Affairs* 61 (spring 1983): 893–920.

Scott, Charles. "Wonder and Worship: An Exploration into Non-theistic Religious Experience." *Soundings* 53 (fall 1970): 310–22.

Scupin, Raymond. "The Social Significance of the Hajj for Thai Muslims." *Muslim World* 72 (January 1982): 25–33.

Segy, Ladislaus. *Masks of Black Africa.* Dover, 1976.

Seitz, Frank, et al. "The Martial Arts and Mental Health: The Challenge of Managing Energy." *Perceptual and Motor Skills* 70 (April 1990): 459–64.

Shah, Idries. *Caravan of Dreams.* Octagon, 1971.

Silko, Leslie. "Coyote Holds a Full House in His Hand." *Pushcart Prize* 6 (Pushcart Press, 1982), 142–50.

Silone, Ignazio. *Bread and Wine.* Rev. ed. Trans. Harvey Fergusson. New American Library, 1962.

Silva, Manik de. "Righteous Indignation: Buddhist Leaders Boycott Papal Visit." *Far Eastern Economic Review* 158:5 (February 2, 1995): 18–19.

Singer, Isaac Bashevis. *Collected Stories.* Trans. Isaac Rosenfeld. Farrar, Straus, 1982.

Smith, Bardwell, ed. *Hinduism: New Essays in the History of Religions.* Brill, 1976.

Smith, D. Howard. *Chinese Religions.* Holt-Rinehart, 1968.

Smith, E. W. *African Ideas of God.* Rev. ed. edited by E. G. Parrinder. Lutterworth, 1962.

Smith, Robert, and Richard Beardsley, eds. *Japanese Culture: Its Development and Characteristics.* Aldine, 1962.

Smith, Warren. "Are You a Humanist? Some Authors Answer." *Humanist* 41 (1981): 15–26.

Sox, David. *The Gospel of Barnabas.* Allen and Unwin, 1984.

Stanley, Alessandra. "Freud in Russia: Return of the Repressed." *New York Times,* December 11, 1996, 1A, 8A.

Stepelevitch, Lawrence. "Marx and the Jews." *Judaism* 23 (1974): 150–60.

Stevens, Wallace. *The Palm at the End of the Mind: Selected Poems and a Play.* Ed. Holly Stevens. Vintage, 1972.

Stover, Leon. *The Cultural Ecology of Chinese Civilization.* Pice, 1974.

Stowasser, Barbara, ed. *The Islamic Impulse.* Croom Helm, 1987.

Stryk, Lucien, ed. *World of the Buddha.* Anchor Books, 1969.

Sugirtharajah, R. S., ed. *Asian Faces of Jesus.* Orbis Books, 1993.

Sumangalo, Venerable. *Buddhist Sunday School Lessons.* 2d ed. Penang Buddhist Association, 1958.

Suzuki, D. T., et al. *Zen Buddhism and Psychoanalysis.* Harper, 1960.

Swartz, Merlin, ed. *Studies on Islam.* Oxford University Press, 1981.

Synan, Edward. *The Popes and the Jews in the Middle Ages.* Macmillan, 1965.

Takeuchi Yoshinori, ed. *Buddhist Spirituality.* Crossroad, 1993.

Talbi, Muhammed. "Possibilities and Conditions for a Better Understanding between Islam and the West." *Journal of Ecumenical Studies* 15 (spring 1988): 161–93.

Taylor, Aspirana. *He Rau Aroha.* Penguin, 1986.

Teilhard de Chardin, Pierre, S.J. *Christianity and Evolution.* Trans. René Hague. Harper, 1971.

———. *The Divine Milieu: An Essay on the Interior Life.* Harper and Row, 1957.

Thant, U. *View from the U.N.* Doubleday, 1978.

Thoreau, Henry David. *Walden.* New American Library, 1980.

Torres, Camilo. *Revolutionary Priest: The Complete Writings and Messages of Camilo Torres.* Ed. John Gerassi. Trans. June Alcantara et al. Random House, 1971.

Traer, Robert. *Faith in Human Rights: Support in Religious Traditions for a Global Struggle.* Georgetown University Press, 1991.

Tresmontant, Claude. *Pierre Teilhard de Chardin: His Thought.* Helicon, 1959.

Tsunoda, Ryusaku, et al., eds. *Sources of Japanese Tradition.* 2 vols. Columbia University Press, 1958.

Turner, Ralph. "Descendit ad Inferos: Medieval Views on Christ's Descent into Hell and the Salvation of the Ancient Just." *Journal of the History of Ideas* 27 (April–June 1966): 173–93.

Turner, Victor. "The Center Out There: Pilgrim's Goal." *History of Religions* 12 (1973): 191–230.

Twain, Mark. *What Is Man? And Other Philosophical Writings.* Ed. Paul Baender. University of California Press, 1973.

Updike, John. *Museums and Women.* Knopf, 1972.

Urs Von Balthasar, Hans. *Word and Redemption: Essays in Theology.* Vol. 2. Trans. A. Littledale and Alexander Dru. Herder and Herder, 1965.

U.S. Versus Seeger. In *United States Reports* 380 (1965): 163–93.

Vanderpool, Tim. "Buddhists Protest Death Sentence." *Progressive* 58:3 (March 1994): 14.

Vigne, Jacques. "Guru and Psychotherapist: Comparisons from the Hindu Tradition." *Journal of Transpersonal Psychology* 23 (1991): 121–37.

Vivekananda, Swami. *Complete Works.* 9th ed. Advaita Ashrama, 1966.

Wartofsky, Marx. *Feuerbach.* Cambridge University Press, 1977.

Watt, William. *Muslim-Christian Encounters: Perceptions and Misperceptions.* Routledge, 1991.

Waugh, Earle, et al., eds. *Muslim Families in North America.* University of Alberta Press, 1991.

Wax, Rosalie, and Murray Wax. "The Magical World View." *Journal for the Scientific Study of Religion* 1 (1961–62): 179–88.

Way, Elizabeth, et al. *Ten Lives of the Buddha: Siamese Temple Paintings and Jataka Tales.* Weatherhill, 1972.

Weiss-Rosmarin, Trude. "The Islamic Connection." *Judaism* 29 (1980): 272–80.

Welch, Holmes. *Taoism: The Parting of the Way.* Rev. ed. Beacon Press, 1966.

Whaling, Frank, ed. *The World's Religious Traditions.* Crossroad, 1986.

White, John, S.J., ed. *The Highest State of Consciousness.* Anchor, 1972.

White, Richard. "Representing Indians." *New Republic* (April 21, 1997): 28–34.

Willis, John, S.J., ed. *The Teachings of the Church Fathers.* Herder and Herder, 1966.

Wisse, Ruth. "Between Passovers." *Commentary* 88 (December 1984): 42–47.

Wren-Lewis, John. "Death Knell of the Guru System?" *Journal of Humanistic Psychology* 34 (spring 1994): 46–61.

X, Malcolm. *The Autobiography of Malcolm X.* Ed. Alex Haley. Grove Press, 1965.

Yamamoto, Tsunetomo. *Hagakure: The Book of the Samurai.* Trans. William Wilson. Kodansha International, 1979.

Yamaori, Tetsuo. "The Metamorphosis of Ancestors." *Japan Quarterly* 33 (1986): 50–53.

Yun, Eugenia, et al. *Buddhist Revival in Taiwan.* Special issue of *Free China Review* 44:12 (December 1994): 4–35.

Zaehner, R. C. "Why Not Islam?" *Religious Studies* 11 (1975): 167–79.

Index

The first number in each entry locates the definition or first significant use of a term. Boldface entries indicate chapter titles, with subheads serving as a precis guide to that chapter. Many key rites and concepts display subheads referring to more than one religious Way. By exploring these implied comparisons between Ways, it is possible to track down motifs developed throughout the book.

Society, the ideal just (*continued*): (Humanist) in Freud's future era of mature scientific rationality, 245, 247, or in Marx's future classless society, 242, or in a transcendental vacuum, what humanity has not yet become, 256; (Jewish) in Ben-Gurion's final Israeli "return of the exiles," 143–44, 148–51, 158, and in Kabbalist recovery of the Shekhinah's scattered sparks, 140; (Muslim) in the restored reign of the first four caliphs or Imam Husayn, 208, 218, or in a righteous millennium ruled by the Mahdi or Hidden Imam, 204, 208; (Taoist) in return to an idealized past of natural beauty, without laws or hypocrisy, 42–43.

   See also Sacred, representative notions of the

Solzhenitsyn, Aleksandr, 167

Spirituality. *See* Religious Way; and particular Ways in chapter titles

Stein, Joseph, 123

Stevens, Wallace, 255

Suffering, religious interpretations of: African Primal, 180–81; Buddhist, 94–95, 102, 103, 114–15; Christian, 171, 177, 180–81, 188–91; Humanist, 255–56; Jewish, 134–35, 136, 141, 144–47; Muslim, 206–7, 216–17

Sufi mystics: defined, 221; pantheistic misreadings of unitive experiences in, 223–26; rooted in the Quran and sharia, 220–21; representative teaching of, 194–95, 206, 220, 222–23, 225–26, 229.

   See also Muslim Way

Sugihara, Chinune, 56

Sunnite (Sunna) and Shiite (Shia) Muslims, 204, 206–7, 219

Tai chi rituals, 47, 48

Tanha (selfish craving), 94, 103, 108

Tantric spirituality, 71–72, 82

Taoist religious motifs in art: of acrobatics, dance, and the martial arts, 47–48; of fiction and film illustrated in Andersen, "The Nightingale," 46, Kosinski, *Being There*, 46–47; of painting and photography, 46;of Tai chi, 47–48

Taoist Way, the: defined, 40–41, 33–34, 41–42; centrality of *Tao Te Ching* and *Chuang Tzu* classics in, 40–48; Confucian-Taoist polarities (yang-yin) in, 33–34, 42, 44; myths of the ideal Taoist leader and society in, 42–44; and parallels with Primal and Shinto Ways, 14, 32, 47, 48–49; and the Sacred conceived as the cosmic Tao emanating in yin-yang dialectic, 32–33, 43, or as the apophatic Void, 43, or the immanent Tao-Te (chi) force, 34, 43, or the Eight Immortals or Jade Emperor at the apex of a pantheon, 32, 41; tao chia-tao chiao polarities in, 41, 62; wu-wei as basis for a spirituality in, 43–48; and the Zhengyi Taoist Movement in contemporary China, 41–42.

   See also Chinese-Japanese Ways; Taoist religious motifs in art

Taylor, Aspirana, 26

Teilhard de Chardin, Pierre, 104, 160–62, 176, 185, 275 n.17

Thaipusan Rite, 28

Theravada-Mahayana Buddhist polarities, 91–92

Theological Method, premises of a comparative: centered on the moment of self-transcendence, 159, 161, 255; committed to equity in treatment of differing traditions, 5; dialectic of particularist-universalist in, 3, 8, 59–62, 64–65, 156–57; empathy as a precondition for, 2–4; hermeneutics of suspicion and second naivete in, 4, 8, 181; integrated with an activism self-critical of class, gender, cultural bias, 173–74; warnings against utopianism and scriptural literalism in, 158, 173.

   See also Imagination, the religious

Tholuck, F. D., 224

Thoreau, Henry David, 45

Tillich, Paul, 254–55, 257

Toplady, Augustus, 242

Torres, Camilo, 172–73, 232

Transcendental Meditation Movement, 59, 257

Trimurti, the (three-faceted), 68–69

Turner, Victor, 15–16

Other Titles in the Faith Meets Faith Series

291
R9351

LINCOLN CHRISTIAN COLLEGE AND SEMINARY

98626

3 4711 00151 9810